THE MISREPRESENTED MINORITY

THE MISREPRESENTED MINORITY

New Insights on Asian Americans and Pacific Islanders, and the Implications for Higher Education

EDITED BY

Samuel D. Museus, Dina C. Maramba,
and Robert T. Teranishi

STERLING, VIRGINIA

COPYRIGHT © 2013 BY
STYLUS PUBLISHING, LLC.

Published by Stylus Publishing, LLC
22883 Quicksilver Drive
Sterling, Virginia 20166-2102

Library of Congress Cataloging-in-Publication Data
The misrepresented minority : new insights on Asian Americans and Pacific Islanders, and the implications for higher education / edited by Samuel D. Museus, Dina C. Maramba, and Robert T. Teranishi.—First edition.
    pages cm
Includes bibliographical references and index.
ISBN 978-1-57922-351-9 (cloth : alk. paper)
ISBN 978-1-57922-469-1 (pbk. : alk. paper)
ISBN 978-1-57922-907-8 (library networkable e-edition)
ISBN 978-1-57922-908-5 (consumer e-edition)   1. Asian
Americans—Education (Higher)   2. Pacific Islander
Americans—Education (Higher)   3. Academic
achievement—United States.   4. Minorities in higher
education—United States.   5. Asian Americans—Ethnic
identity.   6. Pacific Islanders—United States—Ethnic
identity.   I. Museus, Samuel D.
LC2633.6.M57   2013
378.008—dc23   2013006033

13-digit ISBN: 978-1-57922-351-9 (cloth)
13-digit ISBN: 978-1-57922-469-1 (paper)
13-digit ISBN: 978-1-57922-907-8 (library networkable
    e-edition)
13-digit ISBN: 978-1-57922-908-5 (consumer e-edition)

Printed in the United States of America
All first editions printed on acid-free paper
that meets the American National Standards Institute
Z39-48 Standard.

Bulk Purchases

Quantity discounts are available for use in workshops and for staff development.
Call 1-800-232-0223

First Edition, 2013

10 9 8 7 6 5 4 3 2 1

To Daniello Balón,
who dedicated his life to advocating for
diversity, equity, and social justice,
and who strove to make the world
a better place than he found it.
Rest in peace and power.

CONTENTS

vii

INTRODUCTION

Samuel D. Museus, Dina C. Maramba, and Robert T. Teranishi

I n 1952, Ralph Ellison first published *The Invisible Man*, a book that addressed many social and political issues faced by African Americans at that time. In the prologue to the novel, Ellison writes the following:

> I am an invisible man. I am a man of substance, of flesh and bone, fiber and liquids—and I might even be said to possess a mind. I am invisible, understand, simply because people refuse to see me.

Although this quotation is now 60 years old and was first invoked in literature around Black experiences and issues in America, there may be no quote that better captures the historical and contemporary realities of Asian Americans and Pacific Islanders (AAPIs) in both society in general and higher education in particular. For example, in higher education, scholars have thoroughly discussed how AAPIs have often found themselves invisible in research and policy—an invisibility that has resulted from normally being marginalized and, in many cases, completely excluded on the basis of race (Museus, 2009a, 2009b; Museus, & Chang, 2009; Museus & Kiang, 2009; Museus & Vue, in press; Osajima, 1995; Suzuki, 2002; Teranishi, Ceja, Antonio, Allen, & McDonough, 2004).

Chapter 1 of this volume emphasizes that this aforementioned racial exclusion is no longer acceptable. It underscores the fact that census figures indicate that the number of AAPIs is increasing faster than any other racial group. Yet, owing to the invisibility of AAPIs in postsecondary education research and discourse (Museus & Kiang, 2009), they arguably remain the most misunderstood population in higher education (Chang, 2008). Thus, higher education researchers, policy makers, and practitioners are ill equipped to serve a rapidly growing segment of their student populations.

Moving forward, those engaged in higher education research, policy, and practice can either negligently continue to ignore AAPI students, or prudently join in efforts to generate more authentic understandings of this population.

Just as invisibility characterizes the lives of AAPIs in society and higher education, for many within this population, fighting for visibility is also a reality that permeates their existence. Although such efforts have led to minimal progress and AAPIs continue to struggle for visibility in higher education, a handful of noteworthy achievements have been made. In this introduction, we briefly discuss some of those achievements, which we hope are symbolic of positive shifts in public discourse and a growing recognition of the importance of acknowledging the need to understand and serve this population. Finally, we conclude this introductory piece with a clarification of the multiple purposes of this volume.

Emerging Visibility in Higher Education Policy and Practice

AAPIs have historically and consistently been excluded and misrepresented in higher education policy and practice. In 1999, for example, the College Board, a leading policy research organization in education, published a report on minority student achievement in which it lumped Whites and Asian Americans into the same category in an examination of educational attainment. The College Board's analysis is symbolic of the persisting misconception that Asian Americans are not really racial minorities (Museus & Kiang, 2009). Shortly after the release of the College Board report, scholars criticized the board for its treatment of Asian Americans and noted that it led to misleading conclusions about this population (Gándara, 1999; Kiang, 2002). Yet, 13 years later, in June 2012, the highly respected Pew Research Center repeated history when it released a report with the headline "Asians Take Over Hispanics," reinforcing model minority myths and yellow peril stereotypes that characterize Asian Americans as foreigners taking over American education and society (Museus, Antonio, & Kiang, forthcoming). These examples are not isolated incidents, but common misrepresentations of AAPIs across the field of higher education.

There is evidence that society is making incremental progress toward developing greater interest in, and more authentic views of, AAPIs. For instance, in the last decade, several national policy reports have underscored the need for more complex analyses of AAPI populations and reinforced the fact that these groups are racial and ethnic minorities who face unique challenges that require the attention of higher education policy makers and practitioners (e.g., Chang, Park, Lin, Poon, & Nakanishi, 2007; National Commission on Asian American and Pacific Islander Research in Education [CARE], 2008, 2010, 2011; U.S. General Accounting Office, 2007).

Another example of how national discourse around AAPIs has shifted in a positive direction is the establishment of the Asian American Native American and Pacific Islander Serving Institutions (AANAPISI) designation. Historically, discourse around Minority Serving Institutions (MSIs) excluded AAPIs (Park & Teranishi, 2008). In 2002, however, Congressman Robert Underwood (Guam) proposed an amendment to Title III of the Higher Education Act of 1965. Prior to 2002, Title III provided federal funds to MSIs, which included historically Black colleges and universities (HBCUs), tribal colleges and universities (TCUs), Alaskan Native–serving institutions, and Native Hawaiian–serving institutions. Underwood's amendment was aimed at expanding the ability of the federal government to provide funding to institutions that served significant numbers of AAPIs. Three years later, in 2005, Senators Barbara Boxer (CA) and Daniel Akaka (HI) introduced a second bill, which was titled the Asian American and Pacific Islander–Serving Institutions Act, and also aimed at amending the Higher Education Act of 1965 to authorize the distribution of grants to institutions serving large numbers of AAPIs. And, in 2007, Congress enacted the AANAPISI program into law. Today, there are a total of 78 two- and four-year institutions that are designated as AANAPISIs and are eligible to acquire federal funds to develop programs to serve these AAPI college student populations, and 21 of these campuses have received such resources.

Perhaps incremental progress can also be seen in the restoration of the Advisory Commission and White House Initiative on Asian Americans and Pacific Islanders (WHIAAPI). In 2009, approximately 10 years after President Bill Clinton established the WHIAAPI, it has been reestablished. The WHIAAPI is aimed at enhancing opportunities and quality of life among AAPIs and also works to bring attention to the unmet needs of various AAPI communities. The WHIAAPI has been instrumental in providing national visibility for AAPI voices and issues in society in general and in higher education in particular. Also indicative of the growing recognition that AAPIs have needs that deserve attention is the Department of Education's (DOE) most recent efforts to gather information about effective practices in data disaggregation of AAPI populations. The DOE has acknowledged that aggregated data on AAPIs can mask important academic achievement and other disparities within the population and therefore lead to concealed problems within AAPI communities, and the department has finally initiated efforts to address this critical issue. Indeed, given that most national data sets do not collect data in a way that allows researchers to analyze AAPI populations in meaningful ways (Museus, 2009b), the Department of Education's efforts could have a profound impact on the quality of research conducted on AAPI populations and help address common misconceptions about, and current challenges faced by, these groups.

Most recently, signs of increased self-determination among Asian Americans in particular have surfaced in the debates around affirmative action (Chang, 2012). In October 2012, the U.S. Supreme Court heard arguments in *Fisher v. University of Texas at Austin*. The plaintiff in this case has sued the University of Texas at Austin, claiming that its race-conscious admissions policy violates the Equal Protection Clause of the 14th Amendment. Earlier in 2012, multiple Asian American advocacy groups mobilized to construct and submit pro– and anti–affirmative action amicus briefs to the court. Chang (2012) has underscored the reality that although Asian Americans were historically excluded from affirmative action debates they moved from the position of bystander to a potentially pivotal role in this most recent Supreme Court case.

Emerging Visibility in Scholarly Research and Discourse

Historically, just as AAPIs have often been excluded in higher education policy and practice, they have also often been relatively invisible in higher education scholarly research and discourse (Museus, 2009b; Museus & Kiang, 2009). For example, one recent analysis of five of the most widely read peer-reviewed journals in the field of higher education revealed that fewer than 1% of the articles published in these venues over the last decade had given specific attention to AAPI populations (Museus, 2009b).[1] This invisibility is likely due to several factors, including the paucity of AAPI professors in the field of higher education; racial bias in the publishing process; the prevalence of data that are not sufficient for disaggregating AAPIs and analyzing them in complex ways; and the pervasive model minority myth, which incorrectly suggests that all AAPIs achieve universal and unparalleled academic and occupational success (Museus, 2009b; Museus & Chang, 2009; Museus & Kiang, 2009; Teranishi et al., 2004).

Parallel to the recent events that signal progress in higher education policy and practice arenas are several recent developments that also indicate that there is an increased recognition of the importance of paying attention to AAPIs and understanding their needs in the scholarly community. For instance, in response to the invisibility of AAPIs in scholarly research and discourse, over the last decade, AAPI scholars and their allies have collectively mobilized to address this invisibility and produced books that have helped fill the existing gap in knowledge of AAPIs in higher education (see Ching & Agbayani, 2012; McEwen, Kodama, Alvarez, Lee, & Liang, 2002; Museus, 2009a, forthcoming; Teranishi, 2010). In 2002, *Working with Asian American College Students* provided what may be the first high-profile volume that specifically focused on Asian Americans in higher education and highlighted some key issues related to the model minority myth, diversity of the Asian American population, and Asian American identity (McEwen et al., 2002). In 2009, *Conducting Research on Asian Americans in Higher Education* was published, shedding light on many of the issues that higher education researchers face when studying Asian Americans and offering frameworks for methods useful in conducting empirical inquiries on Asian Americans in postsecondary education (Museus, 2009a). In 2010, *Asians in the Ivory Tower: Dilemmas of Racial Inequality in American Higher Education* debunked stereotypes and offered new insights, critical issues relevant to Asian Americans in postsecondary education (Teranishi, 2010). In 2012, *Asian Americans and Pacific Islanders in Higher Education: Research and Perspectives on Identity, Leadership, and Success* was published, offering the most comprehensive collection of analyses of AAPI experiences and issues in postsecondary education to date (Ching & Agbayani, 2012). Finally, later this year, *Asian American Students in Higher Education* will be published and provide a critical synthesis and analysis of existing and emerging contexts, theories, research, and insights relevant to understanding the Asian American undergraduate student population (Museus, forthcoming).

AAPI scholars have also called on the higher education scholarly community to make efforts to generate more authentic understandings of these populations in postsecondary education (Museus & Chang, 2009; Museus & Kiang, 2009). Museus and Chang, for example, note that the exclusion of an entire racial group from higher education scholarship is unacceptable, and higher education researchers have a social and ethical responsibility to address this racial exclusion and the invisibility of AAPIs. They also explain that the inclusion of AAPI voices in scholarly research and discourse can add unique and diverse perspectives that improve understanding of critical issues related to diversity, equity, and students of color in postsecondary education. Therefore, scholars who care about such issues should find value and importance in generating more authentic understandings of AAPIs' experiences and perspectives, which can ultimately lead to achieving more holistic understandings of diversity and equity issues and how to best serve students of color in postsecondary education.

Finally, multiple leading AAPI educational research organizations have emerged over the last decade. For example, the CARE Project has conducted research that has increased awareness about AAPI presence in community colleges, access to and use of financial aid, and the collection and reporting of data. The project has released three highly visible reports that examine these and other critical issues in AAPI education (CARE, 2008, 2010, 2011). In addition, in a historic development in October 2012, more than a dozen AAPI scholars from a wide range of ethnic backgrounds, geographic regions, institutional affiliations, and scholarly perspectives from across the continental United States and the Pacific converged on Honolulu, Hawaii, and organized to construct a collective national voice among AAPI researchers in education. During the summit, the national team of scholars reviewed more than 300 pieces of existing literature on AAPIs in education to identify areas of paucity and density in the knowledge base on AAPIs (for a comprehensive review, see Museus et al., forthcoming), established a national collective research-focused organization called the AAPI Research Coalition (ARC), and constructed a national research agenda on AAPIs in the education system. There is potential for the ARC to provide a much-needed collective voice among AAPI scholars, a common vision and important directions for future research on AAPIs in higher education, a collaboration that can respond to the research needs of diverse AAPI communities, and an organization that can facilitate the development of a new generation of AAPI researchers.

These recent advances and current efforts to make the AAPI population in higher education more visible are promising, but much more work needs to be done to address the exclusion that has historically characterized and continues to plague the AAPI community. The chapters within this volume, in part, are a continuation of these past accomplishments and a part of current efforts to move AAPIs toward greater visibility in higher education research, policy, and practice. It is in this spirit that we turn to the purpose of this book.

Multiple Purposes of This Volume

The purpose of this volume is twofold. First, the volume was intended to create a space for seasoned and young scholars to share their work on AAPIs in higher education. We editors have had the importance of our work on AAPIs challenged by other researchers and journal reviewers in our field, we have heard stories of AAPI graduate students being advised to study other populations because research on AAPIs is not marketable and will not help them get a professional position when they finish school, and we have observed consistent messages of the importance of AAPI scholarship being dismissed. Thus, at its inception, our hope was that this book would serve as a vehicle of voice for everyone, from senior scholars, who have struggled to have their work on AAPIs acknowledged in the past, to graduate students, who might face challenges framing themselves as AAPI scholars in our field.

Second, this volume is intended to offer new perspectives, conceptual frameworks, and empirical research that contribute to the emerging knowledge base on AAPIs in higher education and offer new directions for future scholarship on this population. As mentioned, although the field of higher education has witnessed recent advances, it is far from seeing a solid foundation of knowledge on AAPIs in higher education materialize. Indeed, much more research is needed to establish such a knowledge base, and this book is intended to constitute one small step toward building such a foundation in the areas of AAPI identity, the experiences of specific subgroups within the AAPI population, and the AAPI leadership pipeline in higher education.

Therefore, we hope that this volume contributes to the ongoing discussion about AAPIs by enhancing current levels of understanding of this population and stimulating readers to think in more complex ways about AAPIs. On a related note, to avoid the misperception that we have approached this project with simplistic thinking and adoption of the AAPI category, it is important to clarify the context and rationale for our use of this classification. Thus, we conclude this chapter with such a clarification in the following section.

Use of the Asian American and Pacific Islander Category

In the current volume, we use the term *Asian American and Pacific Islander* to refer to individuals with ethnic origins in Asia and the Pacific. Consistent with the U.S. Census Bureau (2011) definition, *Asian American* refers to people with origins in Asia, including Cambodia, China, India, Japan, Korea, Malaysia, Pakistan, the Philippines, Thailand, and Vietnam. The *Pacific Islander* category includes those with origins in the Pacific, such as Hawaii, Fiji, Guam, Samoa, Tahiti, Tonga, and other Pacific Islands. The authors use this umbrella term where necessary, but refer to specific AAPI subpopulations (e.g., lesbian, gay, and bisexual Asian Americans) and ethnic groups where appropriate.

We understand that the AAPI classification is problematic for numerous reasons. In constructing the AAPI racial category, forcing a wide range of ethnic groups into it, and attaching misleading overgeneralizations and misconceptions of its members as universally successful, dominant political and social forces have helped render the diversity and unique realities of communities and individuals within this population invisible. These are realities that negatively affect all AAPI communities, but arguably disadvantage smaller and underserved ethnic groups more than others. For example, one of the many negative consequences that have resulted from the use of the AAPI category is the marginalization of the voices of Southeast Asian American and Pacific Islander populations within AAPI circles, which has resulted in their voices and needs being masked or ignored.

In determining the scope of this volume, we struggled with the question of whether to include Pacific Islanders in the book. This project was initially conceived to be a volume focused on Asian Americans, and we do not wish to contribute to the aforementioned racialization of AAPIs or engage in the tokenism of Pacific Islanders in any way. Yet, in the end, we decided to include Pacific Islanders in the volume because we believe strongly that their voices should be included in scholarly discourse in higher education, they have much valuable knowledge and insights to offer this discourse, and ultimately we choose not to contribute to the same racial marginalization and exclusion that the field of higher education has used to render both Asian Americans and Pacific Islanders invisible in postsecondary education for centuries. In addition, moving forward, we acknowledge that greater engagement of Pacific Islander voices in higher education research is warranted, and we underscore that there is a vital need for the increased inclusion of Pacific Islander communities in future postsecondary education scholarship.

In this volume, authors use the term *AAPI*, rather than other similar labels that have been associated with the same group, such as Asian and Pacific American, Asian Pacific Islander, and Asian and Pacific Islander American. However, as in previous volumes (e.g., Ching & Agbayani, 2012), the authors in this book vary in their focus, with some writing about AAPI trends and characteristics, others examining Asian Americans or focusing on Pacific Islander populations, and still others focusing on specific identity groups (e.g., lesbian, gay, and bisexual) within these larger racial categories. We believe that all of these efforts are necessary to develop a more holistic understanding of AAPIs in higher education, and the authors herein have made valuable contributions to such understandings by advancing knowledge on this rapidly growing, yet still invisible, population in postsecondary education.

Note

1. The five journals reviewed were *Journal of College Student Development, The Journal of Higher Education, NASPA Journal, Research in Higher Education,* and *The Review of Higher Education.*

References

Chang, M. J. (2008). Asian evasion: A recipe for flawed solutions. *Diverse Issues in Higher Education, 25*(7), 26.

Chang, M. J. (2012). *Multiple representations but shared aspirations: Asian American organizations weigh-in on Affirmative Action.* Paper presented at the Asian American and Pacific Islander Research Coalition Summit, Honolulu, HI.

Chang, M. J., Park, J. J., Lin, M. H., Poon, O. A., & Nakanishi, D. T. (2007). *Beyond myths: The growth and diversity of Asian American college freshmen, 1971–2005.* Los Angeles, CA: Higher Education Research Institute.

Ching, D., & Agbayani, A. (2012). *Asian Americans and Pacific Islanders in higher education: Research and perspectives on identity, leadership, and success.* Washington, DC: NASPA Foundation.

Ellison, R. (1952). *The invisible man.* New York: Random House.

Gándara, P. (1999). *Priming the pump: Strategies for increasing the achievement of underrepresented minority undergraduates.* Washington, DC: College Board.

Kiang, P. N. (2002). Stories and structures of persistence: Ethnographic learning through research and practice in Asian American studies. In Y. Zou & H. T. Trueba (Eds.), *Advances in ethnographic research: From our theoretical and methodological roots to post-modern critical ethnography* (pp. 223–255). Lanham, MD: Rowman & Littlefield.

McEwen, M. K., Kodama, C. M., Alvarez, A. N., Lee, S., & Liang, C. T. H. (2002). *Working with Asian American college students: New directions for student services.* San Francisco, CA: Jossey-Bass.

Museus, S. D. (Ed.). (2009a). *Conducting research on Asian Americans in higher education: New directions for institutional research* (No. 142). San Francisco, CA: Jossey-Bass.

Museus, S. D. (2009b). A critical analysis of the exclusion of Asian Americans from higher education research and discourse. In L. Zhan (Ed.), *Asian American voices: Engaging, empowering, enabling* (pp. 59–76). New York: NLN Press.

Museus, S. D. (forthcoming). *Asian American students in higher education: Toward a more authentic understanding.* New York: Routledge.

Museus, S. D., Antonio, A. L., & Kiang, P. N. (forthcoming). *The state of scholarship on Asian Americans and Pacific Islanders in education: Anti-essentialism, inequality, context, and relevance.* Honolulu, HI: Asian American and Pacific Islander Research Coalition.

Museus, S. D., & Chang, M. J. (2009). Rising to the challenge of conducting research on Asian Americans in higher education. In S. D. Museus (Ed.), *Conducting research on Asian Americans in higher education: New directions for institutional research* (No. 142, pp. 95–105). San Francisco, CA: Jossey-Bass.

Museus, S. D., & Kiang, P. N. (2009). The model minority myth and how it contributes to the invisible minority reality in higher education research. In S. D. Museus (Ed.), *Conducting research on Asian Americans in higher education: New directions for institutional research* (No. 142, pp. 5–15). San Francisco, CA: Jossey-Bass.

Museus, S. D., & Vue, R. (in press). A structural equation modeling analysis of the role of socioeconomic status in Asian American and Pacific Islander students' transition to college. *The Review of Higher Education.*

National Commission on Asian American and Pacific Islander Research in Education (CARE). (2008). *Facts, not fiction: Setting the record straight.* New York: Author.

National Commission on Asian American and Pacific Islander Research in Education (CARE). (2010). *Federal higher education policy priorities and the Asian American and Pacific Islander community.* New York: Author.

National Commission on Asian American and Pacific Islander Research in Education (CARE). (2011). *The relevance of Asian Americans and Pacific Islanders in the college completion agenda.* New York: Author.

Osajima, K. (1995). Racial politics and the invisibility of Asian Americans in higher education. *Educational Foundations, 9*(1), 35–53.

Park, J. J., & Teranishi, R. T. (2008). Asian American and Pacific Islander Serving Institutions: Historical perspectives and future prospects. In M. Gasman, B. Baez, & C. S. V. Turner (Eds.), *Understanding minority serving institutions* (pp. 111–126). Albany: SUNY Press.

Suzuki, B. H. (2002). Revisiting the model minority stereotype: Implications for student affairs practice and higher education. In M. K. McEwan, C. M. Kodama, A. N. Alvarez, S. Lee, and C. H. T. Liang (Eds.), *Working with Asian American college students: New directions for student services* (No. 97, pp. 21–32). San Francisco: Jossey-Bass.

Teranishi, R. T. (2010). *Asians in the ivory tower: Dilemmas of racial inequality in American higher education.* New York: Teachers College Press.

Teranishi, R. T., Ceja, M., Antonio, A. L., Allen, W. R., & McDonough, P. M. (2004). The college-choice process for Asian Pacific Americans: Ethnicity and socioeconomic class in context. *The Review of Higher Education, 27*(4), 527–551.

U.S. Census Bureau. (2011). *Overview of race and Hispanic origin: 2010.* Washington, DC: Author.

U.S. General Accounting Office. (2007). *Asian Americans and Pacific Islanders' educational attainment: A report to congressional requesters.* Washington, DC: Author.

I

ASIAN AMERICANS AND PACIFIC ISLANDERS

A National Portrait of Growth,
Diversity, and Inequality

Samuel D. Museus

In 1859, Charles Dickens first wrote, "It was the best of times, it was the worst of times . . . it was the spring of hope, it was the winter of despair" (Dickens, 2008, p. 1). When Dickens constructed this quote, it is unlikely that he was thinking about Asian Americans and Pacific Islanders (AAPIs)[1] in the twenty-first century. Yet, in many ways, this paradoxical quotation accurately explains the context in which scholars, policy makers, and practitioners who are concerned about AAPIs in higher education find themselves today. On one hand, recent publications that underscore the need to pay attention to AAPIs in postsecondary education and new advances in policy that signify a growing interest in understanding and serving this community have reinvigorated many of us and engendered new hopes of greater AAPI visibility and voice in higher education arenas (see the introduction of this volume for discussion of these advances). On the other hand, racial stereotypes of AAPIs as model minorities who achieve universal and unparalleled academic and occupational success continue to lead to widespread misconceptions about an unprecedented and increasing number of AAPI students entering college, as well as the common dismissal of their needs and interests (Museus, 2009a, 2009b; Museus, Antonio, & Kiang, 2012; Museus & Kiang, 2009; Osajima, 1995; Pendakur & Pendakur, 2012; Suzuki, 2002).

When people dismiss the needs and interests of AAPIs in higher education research and discourse on the basis of race, it is symbolic of larger systemic racial exclusion. My colleagues and I have underscored that several factors have contributed to the historical exclusion of AAPIs from postsecondary education, including the model minority myth; absence of sufficient data for developing more complex and authentic understandings of this population; and overemphasis on degree completion as the primary, and sometimes only, measure of success by researchers and policy makers (Museus, 2009b; Museus & Kiang, 2009).

It is important to note at least two other factors that have contributed to the exclusion of AAPIs from higher education research and discourse: (1) the disciplinary expectation to justify higher education research, policy, and practice efforts with well-founded educational problems and (2) the overreliance on one-dimensional analyses of race to understand equity issues. As for the first point, whereas the assumption that AAPIs are model minorities who do not encounter salient challenges has, at least in part, prevented the exploration necessary to substantiate problems within the AAPI community, the problem-based orientation of higher education requires a developed understanding of validated problems to justify work on this population. These interconnected realities create a cycle of exclusion, whereby there is a limited number of empirically validated problems to justify important work on AAPIs, even though such problems do exist (Museus & Kiang, 2009), and there is also an insufficient foundation of scholarship on AAPIs in the field to thoroughly elucidate the range of problems that exist within the AAPI community.

Regarding the second point, the overreliance on one-dimensional analyses of race to understand equity issues is problematic for those aiming to do work with AAPIs in higher education because, as the following discussion demonstrates, such one-dimensional analyses of racial inequalities mask the ethnic and socioeconomic diversity within racial groups. Such analyses typically suggest that AAPI populations do better than other racial groups and, therefore, do not face challenges or need attention and support (Museus & Kiang, 2009). Moreover, when these race-based analyses do not consider the ethnic, socioeconomic, and other forms of diversity that exist within the AAPI population, higher education scholars, policy makers, and practitioners often incorrectly and negligently conclude that they have a right to render the millions of AAPIs in higher education irrelevant.

Indeed, despite previous advances in diversity in higher education research, policy, and practice, work that focuses on the general population or the White racial majority remains the norm (see Pascarella & Terenzini, 1991, 2005). When college students of color are the primary focus of analyses, scholars and policy makers underscore one-dimensional racial inequalities to contextualize and problematize their work (e.g., Museus, 2011). The underlying rationale is that if Black, Latino, and Native American students are achieving at rates lower than White students then they are worthy of empirical inquiry or advocacy. Unfortunately, this rationale also suggests that if AAPIs are attaining college degrees at rates higher than other racial groups they can easily be dismissed and forgotten. Yet, as Mitchell Chang and I have pointed out, if anyone was to suggest that White students were not worthy of attention or energy because they attain college degrees at higher rates than Black, Latino, and Native American students, it would be considered offensive by many (Museus & Chang, 2009). However, such racial comparisons are commonly used to justify such racist dismissals of AAPI realities and experiences.

Owing to the aforementioned racial realities, those of us who are concerned about AAPIs must be equipped to justify the need for research, policies, and programs that are aimed at better understanding and serving the AAPI population in compelling ways. The primary purpose of this chapter is to use multidimensional analyses of some of the most current national data available on AAPI communities to offer up-to-date empirical support for the importance of work on this population. A secondary purpose of the chapter is to provide the context for the following chapters of this volume. Yet another purpose of this chapter is to take stock of the current social conditions within the AAPI community and use this information as a foundation for envisioning future directions for research on AAPIs in higher education.

In the following sections, I use census, American Community Survey, and Integrated Postsecondary Education Data Systems (IPEDS) data to examine the growth, diversity, and inequality that characterize AAPI communities today and clarify the need to study and advocate for these communities. In the next section, I discuss the recent and rapid growth of AAPI populations. The subsequent section provides a brief overview of the ethnic diversity that exists within the AAPI community. The third section focuses on an examination of the intersections among ethnicity, socioeconomic status, educational achievement, and occupational attainment. The chapter concludes with some implications for higher education research.

Asian American and Pacific Islander Populations Are Rapidly Growing

Asian Americans are the fastest growing racial group in the nation, and Pacific Islanders are the second most rapidly expanding racial population. In fact, between 2000 and 2010, the Asian American community grew at a rate that was four times faster than the national population, and Pacific Islander communities expanded at a rate three times faster than the overall national populace (U.S. Census Bureau, 2011, 2012a, 2012b). Specifically, between 2000 and 2010, Asian Americans grew at a rate of 43% and Pacific Islanders expanded at a rate of more than one-third. In regard to raw numbers, between 2000 and 2010, the Asian American alone population grew from 10.2 million to 14.7 million people, and the Asian American alone or in combination with other racial groups population increased in size from 11.9 million in 2000 to 17.3 million in 2010.[2] During that same period, the Pacific Islander alone population expanded from 398,835 to 540,013 people, and the Pacific Islander alone or in combination with other racial groups population increased from 874,414 in 2000 to 1,225,195 in 2010. And, in terms of their share of the national population, AAPIs alone or in combination with other racial groups represented approximately 4.5% of the nation in 2000 and 6% of the national population in 2010. Not surprisingly, the number of AAPIs enrolling in institutions of higher education has also increased. Figure 1.1 shows the actual (1999–2009) and projected (2010–2019) enrollments of AAPI undergraduate and graduate students. Between 1999 and 2009, the number of AAPI undergraduate and graduate students enrolled in higher education increased from approximately 0.91 million to about 1.34 million—an increase of approximately 430,000 students.

Moving forward, it is also important to note that the AAPI population will likely continue to grow rapidly. Indeed, although the Census Bureau has not released growth projections for Pacific Islanders, population projections for Asian Americans show rapid expected growth. Figure 1.2 displays the projected growth of the Asian American alone population in millions and suggests that the Asian American community will more than double in size over the next 40 years, increasing from 14.7 million in 2010 to approximately 33 million in 2050. Figure 1.3 shows population projections in the form of the percentage of the total U.S. population composed of Asian Americans and indicates that about 1 out of every 10 U.S. citizens will be of Asian descent by the year 2050 (U.S. Census Bureau, 2004). In addition, reflecting the growth of the general AAPI population is the fact that, between the years 2008 and 2019, AAPI undergraduate and graduate enrollments are projected to grow by 30%, which is an estimated increase of about 395,000 students, bringing expected AAPI enrollments in 2019 to 1.7 million (figure 1.1).

Asian Americans Are Concentrated in the West and Growing Fastest in the South

Most Asian Americans reside in the West.[3] Indeed, figure 1.4 shows the percentage of the Asian American population that was located in the four major geographic regions of the country in 2000 and 2010, and these figures indicate that they are heavily concentrated in the Western states. In fact, almost half of the Asian American alone or in combination with other racial groups population was located in the West (46.2%). These statistics also suggest that the proportion of the Asian American alone or in combination with other races population that was located in the West (49.3% to 46.2%) and Northeast (19.9% to 19.8%) regions of the nation declined between 2000 and 2010, whereas the proportion of the Asian American alone or in combination with other racial groups population living in the Midwest (11.7%

FIGURE 1.1

Actual and Projected Asian American and Pacific Islander Undergraduate and Graduate Enrollment in Postsecondary Institutions

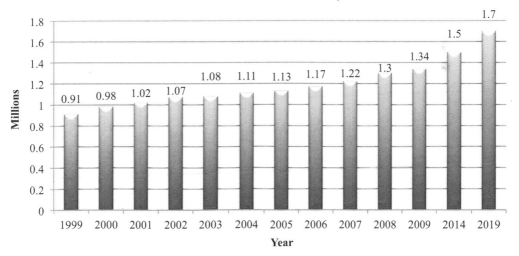

Note: Integrated Postsecondary Education Data System (IPEDS), 1999–2000. Figures are expressed in millions.

FIGURE 1.5
Representation of Asian Americans in Raw Numbers by State

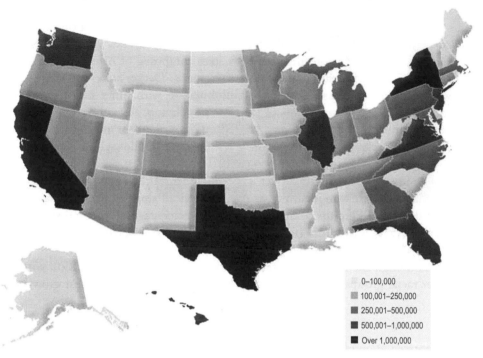

	0–100,000
■	100,001–250,000
■	250,001–500,000
■	500,001–1,000,000
■	Over 1,000,000

Note: Data Source: U.S. Census Bureau (2012a).

is occurring in the Southern states. The Asian American alone or in combination with other racial groups population grew by 69% in the South, 48%
in the Midwest, 45% in the Northeast, and 36% in the West. Figure 1.7
shows the rates of growth of the Asian American alone or in combination
with other races population by state. Darker states signify faster growth.
Between 2000 and 2010, the share of the population composed of Asian
Americans alone or in combination with other racial groups grew in every
state in the country. In fact, Hawaii was the only state in which the Asian
American alone or in combination with other racial groups population did
not grow by at least 25%. However, as mentioned, the fastest growth occurred in the South. In fact, 5 of the 10 states with the fastest growing Asian
American alone or in combination with other racial groups populations were
in the South (i.e., North Carolina, Delaware, Arkansas, Florida, and Texas),

FIGURE 1.6
Representation of Asian Americans in Percentages by State

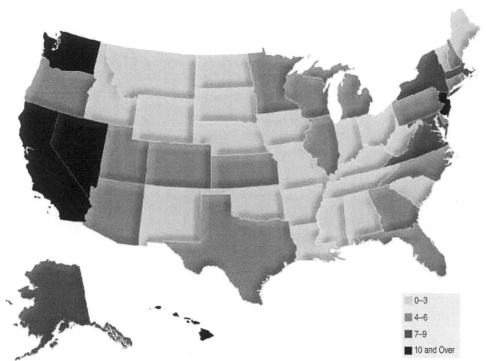

Note: Data Source: U.S. Census Bureau (2012a).

2 were in the West (Nevada and Arizona), 2 were in the Midwest (North Dakota and Indiana), and 1 was in the Northeast (New Hampshire). The fastest growth occurred in Nevada (116%), Arizona (95%), North Carolina (85%), North Dakota (85%), New Hampshire (80%), Delaware (78%), Arkansas (77%), Indiana (74%), Florida (72%), and Texas (72%).

Pacific Islanders Are Concentrated in the West and Growing Fastest in the South

Pacific Islanders are also largely concentrated in the West. Figure 1.8 shows the proportion of the Pacific Islander alone or in combination with other racial groups population located in the four major geographic regions of the country in 2000 and 2010. These figures illustrate that more than two-thirds of the Pacific Islander alone or in combination with other racial groups'

FIGURE 1.7
Rate of Growth of Asian Americans in Percentages by State, 2000–2010

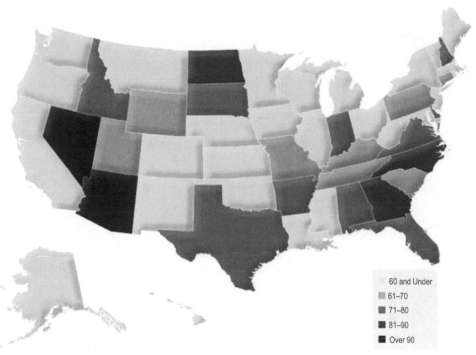

60 and Under
61–70
71–80
81–90
Over 90

Note: Data Source: U.S. Census Bureau (2012a).

population reside in Western states. Because Pacific Islanders make up such a small proportion of the national population, their share of each state's population is not presented here. However, figure 1.9 shows the representation of Pacific Islanders alone or in combination with other racial groups in raw numbers by state. Four of the eight states with the largest Pacific Islander populations are located in the West. Specifically, the states with the largest Pacific Islander alone or in combination with other racial groups populations were Hawaii (more than 280,000), California (more than 220,000), Washington (more than 42,000), Texas (more than 29,000), New York (more than 28,000), Florida (just under 24,000), and Utah (more than 21,000).

Although the number of individuals identifying as Pacific Islanders alone or in combination with other races grew at the second fastest rate of all racial groups, similar to Asian Americans, much of this growth took place in the

FIGURE 1.8
Representation of Pacific Islanders by Geographic Region, 2000 and 2010

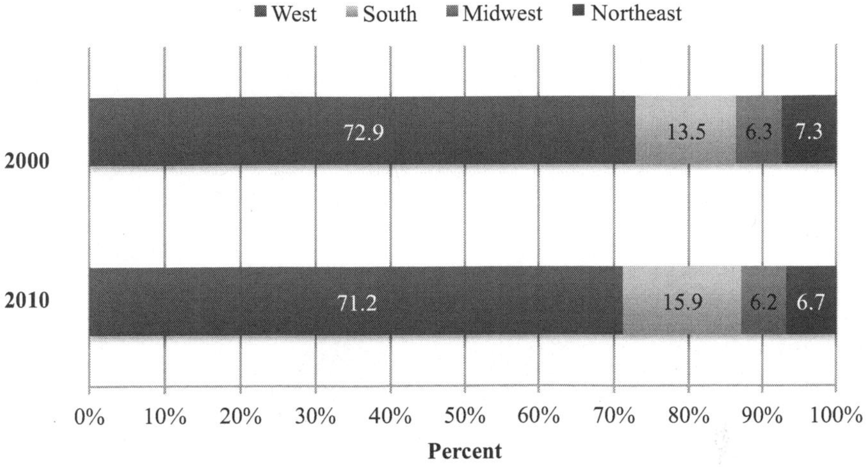

■ West   ■ South   ■ Midwest   ■ Northeast

2000	72.9	13.5	6.3	7.3
2010	71.2	15.9	6.2	6.7

0%   10%   20%   30%   40%   50%   60%   70%   80%   90%   100%

Percent

Note: Data Source: U.S. Census Bureau (2012b).

South. The proportion of Pacific Islanders alone or in combination with other racial groups who lived in the South increased from 2000 to 2010 (13.5 to 15.9), whereas the proportion residing in the other three regions declined in that same time frame. Between 2000 and 2010, the Pacific Islander alone or in combination with other racial groups population grew by 66% in the South, 37% in the West and Midwest, and 29% in the Northeast. Figure 1.10 shows the rate of growth in percentages by state, between 2000 and 2010, and indicates that 4 of the 10 states with the fastest growth were located in the South (Arkansas, Alabama, Delaware, and North Carolina), and 5 were in the West (Nevada, Alaska, Arizona, Idaho, and Wyoming), and 1 was located in the Midwest (Iowa). The 10 states with the fastest growth rates among Pacific Islanders were Arkansas (150%), Nevada (102%), Alaska (102%), Alabama (87%), Arizona (87%), Delaware (81%), Idaho (79%), Iowa (75%), Wyoming (73%), and North Carolina (72%).

Diversity of the Asian American and Pacific Islander Population

Before moving forward to discuss the inequalities that exist within the Asian American and Pacific Islander populations, it is important to include a word

FIGURE 1.9
Representation of Pacific Islanders in Raw Numbers by State

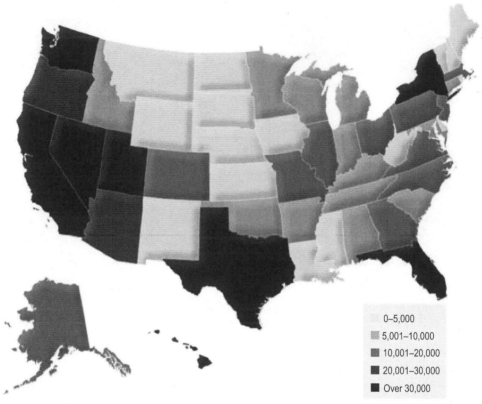

0–5,000
5,001–10,000
10,001–20,000
20,001–30,000
Over 30,000

Note: Data Source: U.S. Census Bureau (2012b).

about the vast diversity that exists within the AAPI population.[4] The 2010 census identified 25 distinct Asian American ethnic groups and 24 distinct Pacific Islander ethnic categories. The 10 largest Asian American groups composed the vast majority of the total Asian American population in 2010 and are displayed in figure 1.11. Specifically, Chinese Americans were the largest population, and they made up 22% of the Asian American population, followed by Filipino (20%), Asian Indian (18%), Vietnamese (10%), Korean (10%), Japanese (8%), Pakistani (2%), Cambodian (2%), Hmong (2%), and Thai (1%) Americans. In addition, the six largest Pacific Islander groups in 2010 are shown in figure 1.12. Native Hawaiians (43%) were the

FIGURE 1.10
Rate of Growth of Pacific Islanders in Percentages by State, 2000–2010

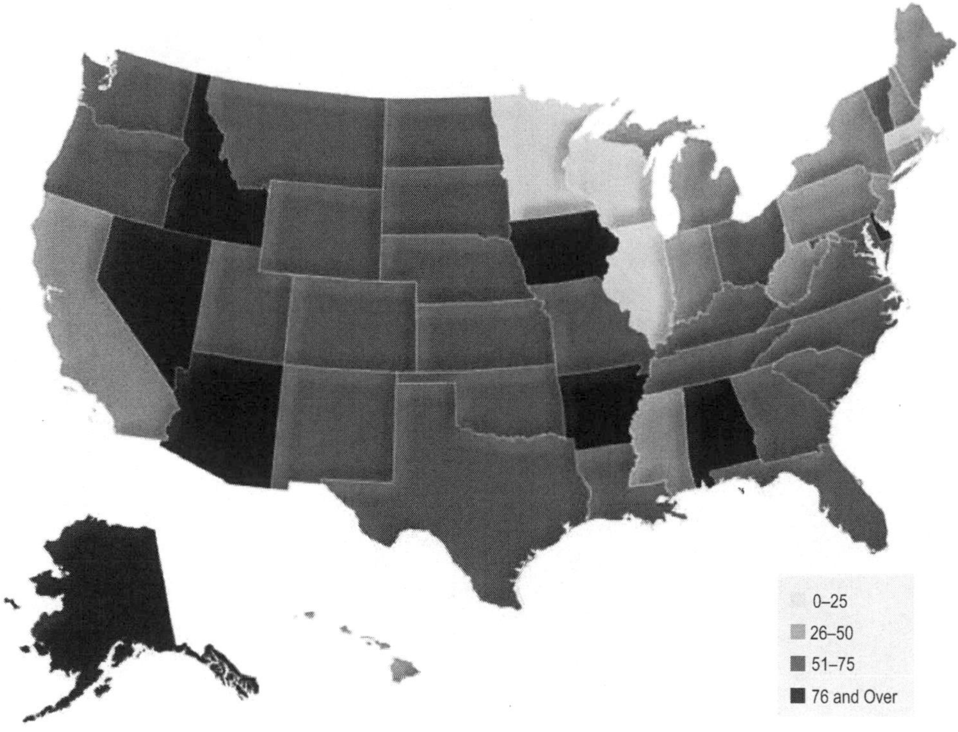

0–25
26–50
51–75
76 and Over

Note: Data Source: U.S. Census Bureau (2012b).

largest Pacific Islander group, followed by Samoans (15%), Guamanians or Chamorros (12%), Tongans (5%), Fijians (3%), and Other Micronesians (2%).[5]

As is shown in the following section, when this diversity is taken into account, some of the most recent and comprehensive national statistics on ethnicity, socioeconomic status, and educational attainment reveal drastic inequalities. It is to these inequalities that I now turn.

Inequalities in the Asian American and Pacific Islander Population

The many different ethnic groups mentioned in the previous section live within unique social contexts and exhibit varying rates of degree attainment

FIGURE 1.11
Ten Largest Asian American Ethnic Groups and Their Share of the Total Asian American Population

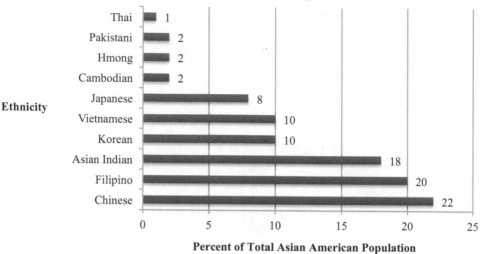

Percent of Total Asian American Population

Note: Data Source: U.S. Census Bureau (2011).

FIGURE 1.12
Six Largest Pacific Islander Ethnic Groups and Their Share of the Total Pacific Islander Population

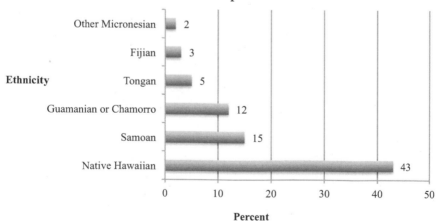

Percent

Note: Data Source: U.S. Census Bureau (2012b).

and wealth. Data from the American Community Survey were used to estimate and analyze these disparities. In this section, I provide an overview of
ethnic disparities in educational attainment, occupational attainment, and
socioeconomic status, as well as socioeconomic disparities in educational
attainment.[6]

Ethnic Inequalities in Educational Attainment

Recent national data on educational attainment rates indicate that several
Asian American groups lag behind the national population. Figures 1.13 and
1.14 include data by ethnicity on the percentage of Asian Americans (25 years
old and over) who have not earned a high school diploma and who have
earned a bachelor's degree, respectively. Of the 16 Asian American ethnic
groups in figure 1.13, 6 are more likely to have dropped out of school before
earning a high school diploma than the overall national population. In contrast, Hmong (39%), Cambodian (38%), Laotian (33%), and Vietnamese
(29%) Americans are about or more than twice as likely than the national
population (15%) and as much as five times more likely than other Asian
American ethnic groups (e.g., Taiwanese at 5%) to have dropped out of
school before earning a high school diploma. When Asian American bachelor's degree completion rates are disaggregated, they also reveal drastic ethnic
disparities (see figure 1.14). Whereas Asian Indian (76%) and Taiwanese
(72%) Americans hold baccalaureate degrees at more than twice the rate of
the national population, Hmong (14%), Cambodian (13%), and Laotian
(12%) Americans hold bachelor's degrees at less than half the rate of the
overall population (28%).

Figures 1.15 and 1.16 display the percentages of Pacific Islanders (25 years
of age or older) who have not earned a high school diploma and who have
attained a bachelor's degree, respectively. When national data on Pacific
Islanders are disaggregated, they reveal ethnic disparities in educational
attainment as well. Indeed, some Pacific Islander groups suffer from both
racial and ethnic disparities when compared with the overall national population and from ethnic disparities within the Pacific Islander category. Other
Micronesians (20%), Tongans (21%), and Fijians (24%) are all more likely
than the overall national population and more than twice as likely as some
other Pacific Islanders to have dropped out before earning a high school
diploma (figure 1.15). When examining college completion, all seven of the
largest Pacific Islander groups are less likely to hold a bachelor's degree than
the overall national population (figure 1.16). In fact, Guamanians (13%),

FIGURE 1.13
Percent of Asian Americans Without High School Diploma by Ethnicity

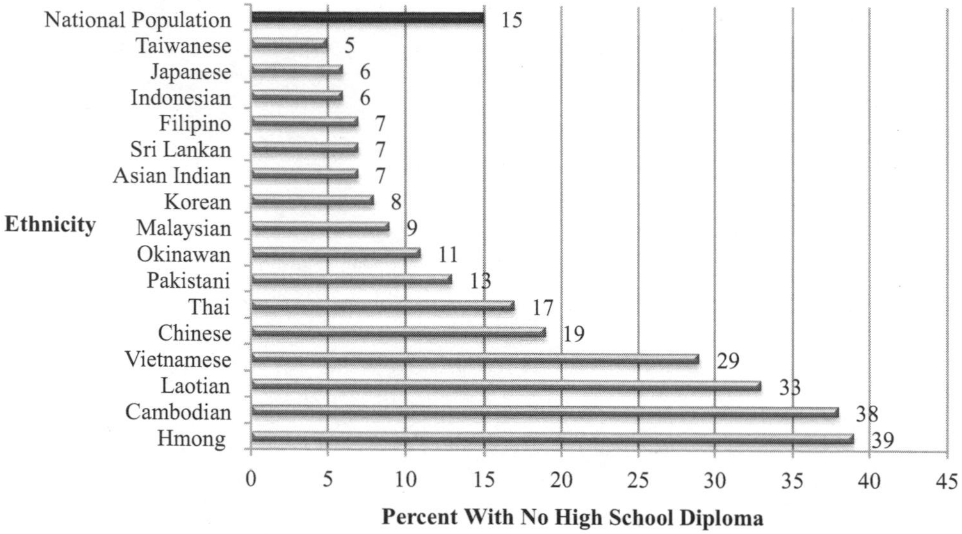

Ethnicity (vertical axis): National Population 15, Taiwanese 5, Japanese 6, Indonesian 6, Filipino 7, Sri Lankan 7, Asian Indian 7, Korean 8, Malaysian 9, Okinawan 11, Pakistani 13, Thai 17, Chinese 19, Vietnamese 29, Laotian 33, Cambodian 38, Hmong 39

Percent With No High School Diploma (horizontal axis: 0, 5, 10, 15, 20, 25, 30, 35, 40, 45)

Note: Data Source: Public Use Microdata Sample (PUMS): 2006–2010, 5-year estimates. Appropriate sample weights were applied, and individuals 25 and over were included in the analysis.

Tongans (11%), Fijians (11%), Samoans (10%), and Other Micronesians (4%) all hold bachelor's degrees at less than half the rate of the national population (28%).

Ethnic Inequalities in Occupational Attainment

Just as the disaggregation of national data reveals that ethnic disparities exist in educational attainment, such disaggregated analyses illuminate inequalities in the attainment of jobs and disparities in the acquisition of jobs in various professions. Regarding the former, figures 1.17 and 1.18 show the average unemployment rate for Asian Americans and Pacific Islanders (25 years old or over). Among Asian Americans, there are significant disparities in unemployment, with some groups (e.g., Cambodian, Hmong, and Laotian Americans) having higher unemployment rates than the total national average (7.9%) and others being well under the national rate. Moreover, Laotian and Hmong (9%) Americans are three times as likely and Cambodian Americans (8%) are more than twice as likely to be unemployed than

FIGURE 1.14
Percent of Asian Americans With Bachelor's Degree by Ethnicity

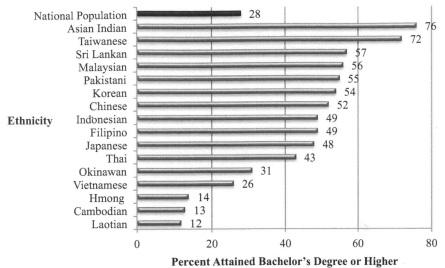

Percent Attained Bachelor's Degree or Higher

Note: Data Source: Public Use Microdata Sample (PUMS): 2006–2010, 5-year estimates. Appropriate sample weights were applied, and individuals 25 and over were included in the analysis.

Japanese and Okinawan persons (3%). Pacific Islanders exhibit relatively high unemployment rates, with four out of the seven Pacific Islander ethnic groups included in figure 1.18 exhibiting rates above the overall national average: Tongans (12.3), Samoans (11.2), Fijians (8.7), and Chamorros (8.3). Moreover, there are differences across ethnic groups in this population as well, with Tongans (12%) and Samoans (11%) significantly more likely to be unemployed than Guamanians and Other Micronesians (7%).

Regarding career types, there are significant disparities across professions among Asian Americans 25 years of age or older (figure 1.19). Specifically, several East and South Asian American groups are highly represented in business and management, as well as health and science fields, compared with Southeast Asian Americans. For example, approximately 23% of Taiwanese and 22% of Japanese Americans have careers in business and management, and fewer than 8% of Cambodian, Hmong, and Laotian populations have careers in this area. Similarly, more than 20% of Asian Indian and Filipino Americans have careers in the health and science fields, compared with fewer than 7% of Cambodian, Laotian, and Hmong populations. In

FIGURE 1.15
Percent of Pacific Islanders Without High School Diploma by Ethnicity

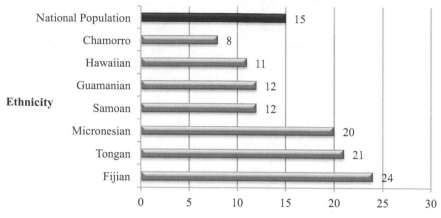

Percent With No High School Diploma

Note: Data Source: Public Use Microdata Sample (PUMS): 2006–2010, 5-year estimates. Appropriate sample weights were applied, and individuals 25 years of age and over were included in the analysis.

FIGURE 1.16
Percent of Pacific Islanders With Bachelor's Degree by Ethnicity

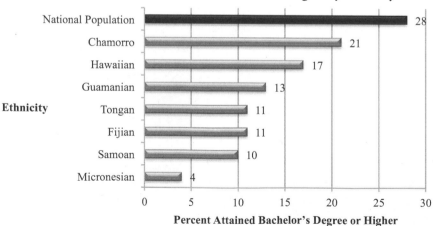

Percent Attained Bachelor's Degree or Higher

Note: Data Source: Public Use Microdata Sample (PUMS): 2006–2010, 5-year estimates. Appropriate sample weights were applied, and individuals 25 years of age and over were included in the analysis.

FIGURE 1.17
Unemployment Among Asian Americans by Ethnicity

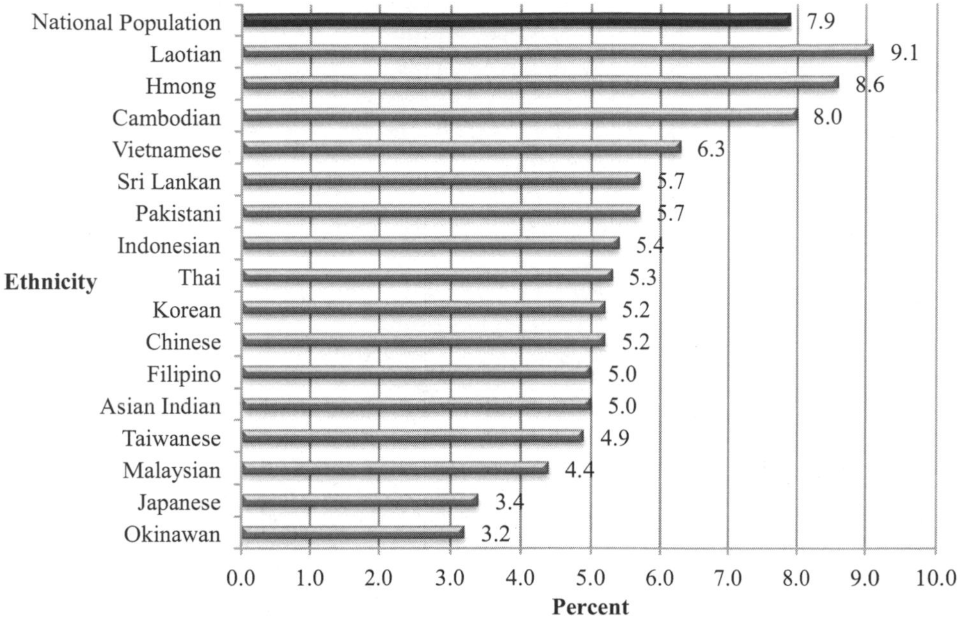

Ethnicity	Percent
National Population	7.9
Laotian	9.1
Hmong	8.6
Cambodian	8.0
Vietnamese	6.3
Sri Lankan	5.7
Pakistani	5.7
Indonesian	5.4
Thai	5.3
Korean	5.2
Chinese	5.2
Filipino	5.0
Asian Indian	5.0
Taiwanese	4.9
Malaysian	4.4
Japanese	3.4
Okinawan	3.2

Note: Data Source: Public Use Microdata Sample (PUMS): 2006–2010, 5-year estimates. Appropriate sample weights were applied, and individuals 25 years of age and over were included in the analysis.

contrast, 46% of Laotian, 43% of Hmong, and 38% of Cambodian Americans have careers in production and transportation. Data on Pacific Islanders show that all ethnic groups within this category are more likely to be in the production and transportation industry than in business and management or health and science (figure 1.20). However, again, ethnic disparities exist within the Pacific Islander population, with Chamorro (14%) and Guamanian (13%) groups more likely than Hawaiians (9%), Fijians (8%), Samoans (7%), Tongans (7%), and Other Micronesians (3%) to be in business and management. In addition, Fijians (11%) and Tongans (10%) are more likely to be in health and science fields than Samoans (7%), Hawaiians (7%), Guamanians (6%), Chamorro Islanders (6%), or Other Micronesians (4%). Other Micronesians are the most likely to be in production and transportation positions (24%), followed by Fijians and Samoans (23%), Guamanians

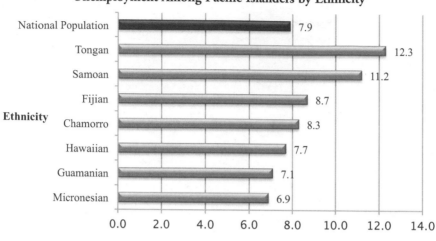

FIGURE 1.18
Unemployment Among Pacific Islanders by Ethnicity

Note: Data Source: Public Use Microdata Sample (PUMS): 2006–2010, 5-year estimates. Appropriate sample weights were applied, and individuals 25 years of age and over were included in the analysis.

and Tongans (17%), and Chamorro Islanders and Hawaiians (16%). Of course, the significance of these disparities in part lies in the fact that East and South Asian American groups are more likely to be in professions that are much more lucrative and associated with higher levels of socioeconomic status, which is the focus of the next section.

Ethnic Inequalities in Socioeconomic Status

Just as ethnic disparities in educational and occupational attainment exist within the AAPI population, a critical examination of this group also reveals that ethnic inequalities in socioeconomic status are also evident. Indeed, different ethnic populations also vary drastically in socioeconomic status, with some reporting annual individual earnings that are far above the national average and others facing significant economic disparities. Figures 1.21 and 1.22 show the mean earnings of Asian Americans and Pacific Islanders (25 years of age or over) by ethnic group, between 2006 and 2010, when adjusted for inflation. On average, Asian Indians ($50,988) and Sri Lankans ($43,283) report earnings that are approximately $22,000 and $15,000 above

FIGURE 1.19
Concentration of Asian Americans in Professional Fields by Ethnicity

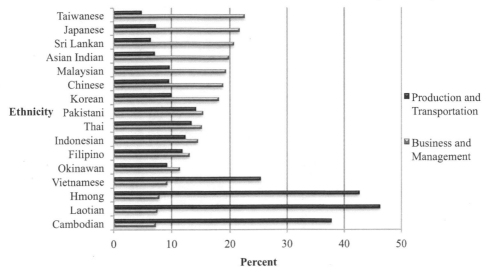

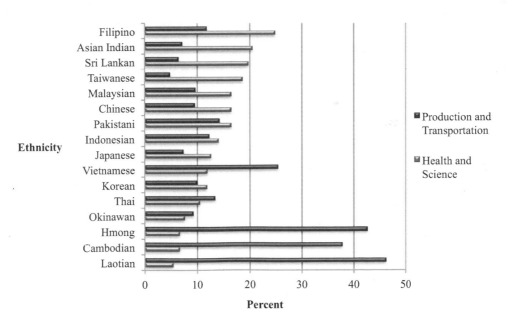

Note: Data Source: Public Use Microdata Sample (PUMS): 2006–2010, 5-year estimates. Appropriate sample weights were applied, and individuals 25 years of age and over were included in the analysis.

FIGURE 1.20
Concentration of Pacific Islanders in Professional Fields by Ethnicity

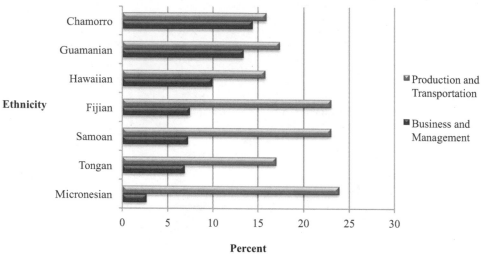

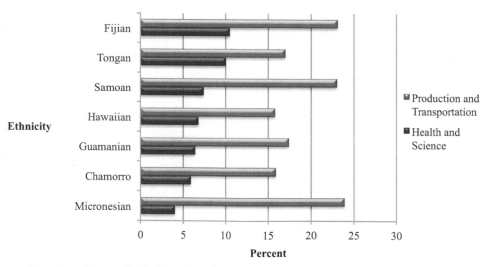

Note: Data Source: Public Use Microdata Sample (PUMS): 2006–2010, 5-year estimates. Appropriate sample weights were applied, and individuals 25 years of age and over were included in the analysis.

the national average ($28,452), respectively. In contrast, Hmong ($19,053), Cambodian ($20,737), Laotian ($22,111), Thai ($24,509), Vietnamese ($26,352), Okinawan ($27,162), and Indonesian ($28,251) Americans all have average annual earnings that are below the national average. Moreover, these disparities are quite substantial for some groups. For example, Hmong and Cambodian Americans report average annual earnings of approximately $19,000 (67% of the national average) and $21,000 (73% of the national average), respectively.

Some Pacific Islanders have average earnings higher than the national average as well, although those differences are minimal (figure 1.22). Guamanians ($28,995) and Chamorro Islanders ($29,919) have earnings slightly higher than the national average. In contrast, Native Hawaiians ($26,826), Samoans ($23,402), Fijians ($23,383), Tongans ($18,392), and Other Micronesians ($15,492) have average annual earnings that are well below the national average. Other Micronesians exhibit the lowest average annual earnings of all Asian American or Pacific Islander populations—amounting to just 54% of the average earnings reported by all populations across the nation.

Educational Inequalities in Socioeconomic Status

It is relatively common knowledge that those who have higher levels of educational attainment have higher earning potential in the job market. Nevertheless, examining economic earnings by varying levels of educational attainment can help us understand the extent of the impact that education has on future earnings. Moreover, such analyses among AAPIs can further demystify the belief that they are all economically successful and highlight the importance of considering the needs of individuals within these communities.

An analysis of average annual earnings by education level among those who are at or above the age of 25 also reveals drastic disparities within both Asian American and Pacific Islander populations (figure 1.23). On average, Asian Americans with a professional degree ($92,188) earn more than twice as much annually as those with a bachelor's degree ($40,622), more than five times as much as those with a high school diploma ($16,486), and more than nine times more than those with no high school diploma ($8,935). On average, Asian Americans with a bachelor's degree earn approximately 2.5 times as much as those with a high school diploma and 4.5 times as much as those with no high school diploma. Among Pacific Islanders, those with a doctoral

FIGURE 1.21

Asian Americans' Average Annual Earnings by Ethnicity

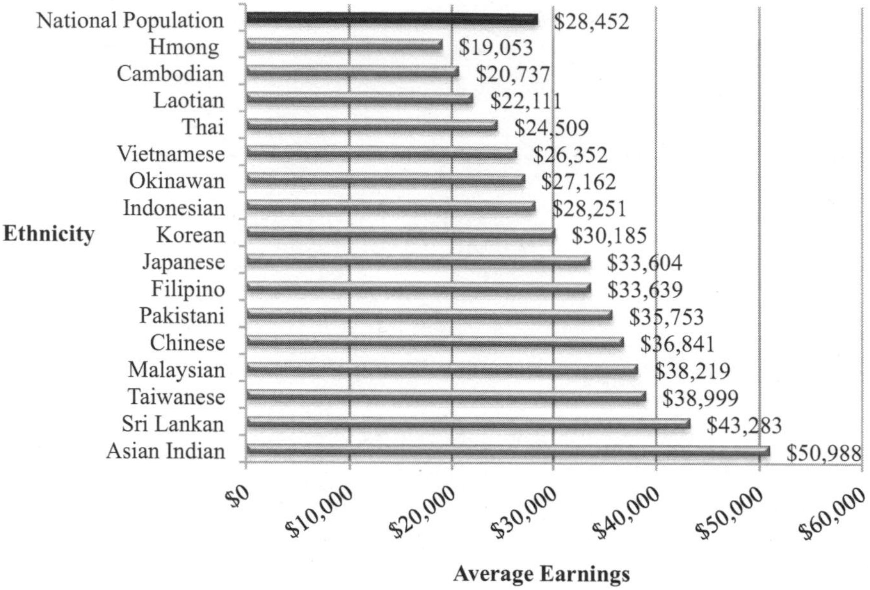

Note: Data Source: Public Use Microdata Sample (PUMS): 2006–2010, 5-year estimates. Appropriate sample weights were applied, and individuals 25 and over were included in the analysis. Earnings were adjusted for inflation and are expressed in 2010 dollars.

degree ($64,688) have average annual earnings that are 61% more than those with a bachelor's degree ($39,748), more than three times as much as those with a high school diploma ($20,513), and more than five times as much as those without a high school diploma ($12,383). In addition, on average, Pacific Islanders who have attained a bachelor's degree report earnings that are almost twice as much as those reported by Pacific Islanders with a high school diploma and more than three times as much as those with no high school diploma.

It is important to note that ethnic and socioeconomic inequalities within the AAPI population are geographically context-specific. That is, although the preceding statistics illuminate disparities nationally, the nature of these inequalities might vary across specific geographic regions within the United States. We can examine disparities in Hawaii, for example, to demonstrate this geographic region-specificity. Among Southeast Asian Americans in Hawaii, disaggregated data show that Cambodian (27%), Laotian (14%),

FIGURE 1.22
Pacific Islanders' Average Annual Earnings by Ethnicity

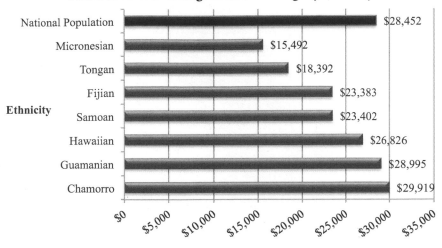

Note: Data Source: Public Use Microdata Sample (PUMS): 2006–2010, 5-year estimates. Appropriate sample weights were applied, and individuals 25 and over were included in the analysis. Earnings were adjusted for inflation and are expressed in 2010 dollars.

and Vietnamese (12%) Americans earn baccalaureate degrees at rates below the national average. These inequalities are congruent with the national figures just discussed, although the rate of bachelor's degree attainment among Cambodians is much higher in Hawaii than across the nation. Among Pacific Islanders in Hawaii, Fijians (18%), Guamanians (15%), Native Hawaiians (14%), Chamorro Islanders (11%), Samoans (8%), Tongans (8%), and Other Micronesians (5%) also exhibit bachelor's degree attainment rates below the national average. These inequalities are slightly different from, but consistent with, national statistics as well. However, inconsistent with the national figures previously discussed is the fact that in Hawaii, Filipino (18%) and Sri Lankan (17%) Americans also attain degrees at rates well below the national average.

Conclusion

The preceding analysis makes one reality clear: It is no longer acceptable to racially exclude AAPIs from higher education research, policy, and practice.

FIGURE 1.23
Asian American and Pacific Islanders' Average Annual Earnings by Degree

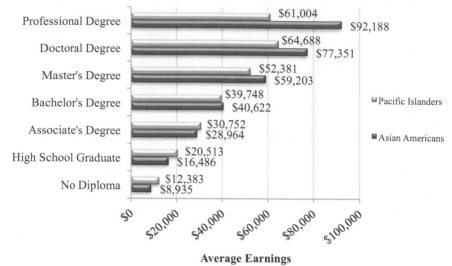

Average Earnings

Note: Data Source: Public Use Microdata Sample (PUMS): 2006–2010, 5-year estimates. Appropriate sample weights were applied, and individuals 25 and over were included in the analysis. Earnings were adjusted for inflation and are expressed in 2010 dollars.

Asian Americans and Pacific Islanders are the fastest growing racial groups in the nation and, as such, will be enrolling in colleges and universities in increasing numbers in the years to come. Moreover, many AAPI subgroups suffer from disparities in educational attainment and wealth. Thus, it is the social and moral obligation of higher education scholars to advance knowledge on these populations and the responsibility of postsecondary education policy makers and practitioners to help better understand and serve these communities. Accordingly, I conclude this chapter with a few implications for advancing research to inform policy and practice focused on AAPIs.

Foster and Pursue a National Research Agenda

It is imperative that higher education scholars, policy makers, and practitioners clarify the research needs of the AAPI education community and establish and organize around an agenda to meet these needs. Although the AAPI research community has historically lacked a collective agenda, in October 2012, more than a dozen AAPI scholars participated in an AAPI educational research summit in Honolulu, Hawaii, that was aimed at establishing a national research-focused coalition of AAPIs in education called the Asian American and Pacific Islander Research Coalition (ARC) and crafting a national research agenda that is designed to reflect and respond to the voices and needs of geographically and ethnically diverse AAPI communities (Museus et al., forthcoming). This national agenda is the first step in the collective mobilization of the AAPI research community in education and the collaborative declaration of future critical directions for advancing knowledge on these communities. However, although ARC's national agenda can provide an important initial direction for future work on the AAPI population, it is important to continue such conversations about the research needs of AAPIs in education to maintain a clear and evolving vision for how scholars can pursue work that informs the larger knowledge base on AAPIs in education, as well as policy and practice that are aimed at serving this population.

Collect Large-Scale and High-Quality Disaggregated Data

Although the U.S. Census Bureau now collects data that can be disaggregated and analyzed in the preceding ways, the utility of such analyses in understanding a wide array of educational experiences and outcomes is limited. Most large-scale national education data sets that can be used to understand such experiences and outcomes currently are inadequate for disaggregating and analyzing AAPIs in complex ways. However, in a very positive development, the U.S. Department of Education has recently requested information on challenges and promising practices related to collecting data on AAPIs. If the department is able to craft an effective plan to disaggregate and analyze large-scale data on AAPIs, such efforts could have an enormously positive impact on advancing knowledge of AAPI needs and experiences. And, if other research institutions that collect national data in postsecondary education, such as the University of California–Los Angeles's Higher Education Research Institute and the National Survey of Student Engagement, can eventually engage in similar efforts, many opportunities for advancing knowledge on AAPIs could be realized.

Indeed, there is a need for large-scale data that permits the analysis of specific ethnic populations. Similarly, there is a desperate need for data that allow researchers to disaggregate by nativity and citizenship (i.e., foreign-born) and socioeconomic status. Until higher education researchers are able to conduct such disaggregated analyses, we will only have a partial picture of

AAPI students' access to college, experiences in higher education, or actual rates of success.

Conduct Research on Underserved Populations

It is critical for higher education scholars to advance knowledge of the most underserved AAPI populations in postsecondary education. Despite the fact that the preceding analyses show that Southeast Asian Americans and Pacific Islanders suffer from drastic inequalities—disparities greater than those faced by other ethnic groups—there is scant literature for higher education policy makers and practitioners to use as resources to help them understand how they can better serve these populations. Similarly, the large numbers of low-income AAPIs that seek to enroll in and graduate from higher education are not represented in higher education research and discourse, and knowledge of these groups is also critical to educators' ability to meet their needs. Indeed, college educators who might be working with Pacific Islander under-graduates in Washington, Hmong college students in Minnesota, or low-income Chinese Americans in Boston have few resources to which they can turn to help them better understand the needs of these diverse communities. Therefore, it is critical that higher education researchers generate a knowledge base that can help advance current levels of understanding regarding how to serve these populations effectively.

Broaden Focus to Examine Diverse Outcomes

One of the many factors that have contributed to the dismissal of AAPIs from higher education research and discourse is the disproportionate emphasis on college degree completion as the primary, and sometimes the only, worthy measure of success (Museus, 2009b; Museus & Kiang, 2009). In my own work, AAPI students have clarified that the attainment of a degree is only one of many measures of success. Among other measures that they note as being important are health and well-being, learning and development, the acquisition of leadership skills, the ability to graduate and find a job in a professional field that will make them happy, and the ability to acquire the tools to accomplish goals that have a positive impact on their communities. There are few available data that can help us measure these diverse educational outcomes. Yet, if we are to truly and authentically understand whether higher education is serving AAPI populations effectively, then research that refocuses college success discourse on these varied measures of achievement and examines these outcomes is absolutely essential.

As increasing numbers of AAPIs enter institutions of higher education, it is indeed the best of times and the worst of times. Given recent developments and growing interest in understanding AAPIs, it is a time full of promise. However, given the lack of authentic understandings of AAPIs and the fact that college educators are ill equipped to serve these communities, it is a time full of uncertainty. Higher education scholars, policy makers, and practitioners must strategically develop an agenda for addressing these significant problems and engage in an endeavor to generate a substantial and informative knowledge base on this population.

Notes

1. The term *Asian American* refers to people with origins in Asia, including Cambodia, China, India, Japan, Korea, Malaysia, Pakistan, the Philippines, Thailand, and Vietnam. The *Pacific Islander* category includes individuals with origins in the Pacific, including Hawaii, Fiji, Guam, Samoa, Tahiti, Tonga, and other Pacific Islands (U.S. Census Bureau, 2011, 2012a, 2012b).

2. Two types of census racial categorization are used in this analysis. The (1) "Asian American alone" and "Pacific Islander alone" categories encompass those who only identify with the focal racial group, and (2) the "Asian alone or in combination" and "Pacific Islander alone or in combination" labels are used to refer to both individuals who only identified with the focal racial group and those who identified with the focal racial group and one or more additional racial groups.

3. The Northeast census region encompasses Connecticut, Maine, Massachusetts, New Hampshire, New Jersey, New York, Pennsylvania, Rhode Island, and Vermont. The Midwest region encompasses Illinois, Indiana, Iowa, Kansas, Michigan, Minnesota, Missouri, Nebraska, North Dakota, Ohio, South Dakota, and Wisconsin. The South region refers to Alabama, Arkansas, Delaware, the District of Columbia, Florida, Georgia, Kentucky, Louisiana, Maryland, Mississippi, North Carolina, Oklahoma, South Carolina, Tennessee, Texas, Virginia, and West Virginia. The West census region encompasses Alaska, Arizona, California, Colorado, Hawaii, Idaho, Montana, Nevada, New Mexico, Oregon, Utah, Washington, and Wyoming (U.S. Census Bureau, 2011, 2012a, 2012b).

4. When interpreting statistics in the "Diversity of the Asian American and Pacific Islander Population" section, it is important to note that these figures include those who selected the focal ethnicity "alone or in combination" with another racial or ethnic group. If researchers analyze those who identified only as the focal ethnicity, then they could generate different results from those presented herein.

5. For purposes of this chapter, the categories "Other Micronesian" and "Micronesian" are used interchangeably, to refer to those who identified as "Micronesian," but did not specify a major ethnic subgroup within that category (e.g., Chamorro, Marshallese, Palauan, Chuukese).

6. When interpreting statistics in the "Inequalities in the Asian American and Pacific Islander Population" section, it is important to note that these figures include

those who selected only the focal ethnicity. If researchers analyze those who identified as the focal ethnicity "alone or in combination" with another racial or ethnic
group, then they could generate different results from those presented herein.

References

Dickens, C. (2008). *A tale of two cities*. Oxford, UK: Oxford University Press.

Museus, S. D. (Ed.). (2009a). *Conducting research on Asian Americans in higher
education: New directions for institutional research* (No. 142). San Francisco, CA:
Jossey-Bass.

Museus, S. D. (2009b). A critical analysis of the invisibility of Southeast Asian
American students in higher education research and discourse. In L. Zhan (Ed.),
Asian voices: Engaging, empowering, and enabling (pp. 59–76). New York: NLN
Press.

Museus, S. D. (2011). Mixing quantitative national survey data and qualitative interview data to understand college access and equity: An examination of first-
generation Asian Americans and Pacific Islanders. In K. A. Griffin & S. D.
Museus (Eds.), *Using mixed-methods approaches to study intersectionality in higher
education: New directions for institutional research* (No. 151, pp. 63–75). San Francisco, CA: Jossey-Bass.

Museus, S. D., Antonio, A. L., & Kiang, P. N. (forthcoming). *The state of scholarship
on Asian Americans and Pacific Islanders in education: Anti-essentialism, inequality,
context, and relevance*. Honolulu, HI: Asian American and Pacific Islander
Research Coalition.

Museus, S. D., & Chang, M. J. (2009). Rising to the challenge of conducting
research on Asian Americans in higher education. In S. D. Museus (Ed.), *Conducting research on Asian Americans in higher education: New directions for institutional research* (No. 142, pp. 95–105). San Francisco, CA: Jossey-Bass.

Museus, S. D., & Kiang, P. N. (2009). The model minority myth and how it
contributes to the invisible minority reality in higher education research. In S. D.
Museus (Ed.), *Conducting research on Asian Americans in higher education: New
directions for institutional research* (No. 142, pp. 5–15). San Francisco, CA: Jossey-
Bass.

Osajima, K. (1995). Racial politics and the invisibility of Asian Americans in higher
education. *Educational Foundations, 9*(1), 35–53.

Pascarella, E. T., & Terenzini, P. T. (1991). *How college affects students: Findings and
insights from twenty years of research* (Vol. 1). San Francisco, CA: Jossey-Bass.

Pascarella, E. T., & Terenzini, P. T. (2005). *How college affects students: A third
decade of research* (Vol. 2). San Francisco, CA: Jossey-Bass.

Pendakur, S., & Pendakur, V. (2012). Let's get radical: Being a practitioner-ally for
Asian Pacific Islander American college students. In D. Ching & A. Agbayani
(Eds.), *Asian Americans and Pacific Islanders in higher education: Research and*

perspectives on identity, leadership, and success (pp. 31–56). Washington, DC: National Association of Student Personnel Administrators.

Suzuki, B. H. (2002). Revisiting the model minority stereotype: Implications for student affairs practice and higher education. In M. K. McEwan, C. M. Kodama, A. N. Alvarez, S. Lee, and C. H. T. Liang (Eds.), *Working with Asian American college students: New directions for student services* (N. 97, pp. 21–32). San Francisco: Jossey-Bass.

U.S. Census Bureau. (2004). *U.S. interim projections by age, sex, race, and Hispanic origin.* Washington, DC: Author.

U.S. Census Bureau. (2011). *Overview of race and Hispanic origin: 2010.* Washington, DC: Author.

U.S. Census Bureau. (2012a). *The Asian population: 2010.* Washington, DC: Author.

U.S. Census Bureau. (2012b). *The Native Hawaiian and Other Pacific Islander population: 2010.* Washington, DC: Author.

PART ONE

ASIAN AMERICAN AND
PACIFIC ISLANDER IDENTITY

Mitchell J. Chang

Before University of California–Berkeley professor Ronald Takaki passed away at the age of 70 in June 2009, he had created a reputation as one of the most influential scholars on race and ethnicity in the nation. Professor Takaki not only helped redefine the notions of race and ethnicity through careful historical analyses, but he also helped launch the field of ethnic studies across the nation. He wrote one of my favorite historical accounts of U.S. society, *Iron Cages: Race and Culture in 19th-Century America*. For this book, Takaki (1990) borrowed the term *iron cages* from the eminent German sociologist and political economist Max Weber to use as a graphic metaphor to describe how the complex blend of ideology and culture came to create an oppressive hegemonic superstructure that constrained the ways men and women viewed the world, and thereby imprisoned them in unique ways during different periods in U.S. history. In *Iron Cages*, Takaki focused squarely on racial domination and documented how race imprisoned us and limited possibilities toward reaching what he called "a new world of respect and unconditional opportunity for all who toiled and suffered from oppression" (p. 310).

When we apply Takaki's insights to the collection of chapters in this part, "Asian American and Pacific Islander Identity," it can be said that, through a widely held and resilient stereotype, Asian Americans and Pacific Islanders (AAPIs) have been "imprisoned" in an iron cage. According to Guofang Li and Lihshing Wang (2008), the image of AAPIs as the "model minority," which characterizes us as hardworking, problem-free overachievers, has endured for more than 40 years. They maintain that, although this image might suggest a more positive than negative mainstream view to some, this stereotype has ironically "worked against Asian American students because such labeling not only impedes access to educational opportunities but also results in anti-Asian sentiment between the majority and other minority groups" (p. 2).

In exploring identity development and construction, the chapters in this part not only demystify the model minority image by highlighting the complexity and diversity of the experiences of AAPI students, but also document the varied ways in which undergraduates grapple with their individual identities in spite of this pervasive stereotype. Taken together, these chapters suggest that there is a unique racial dimension associated with how students arrive at their individual identities or their sense of campus belonging, and these undergraduates' narratives can be understood as paths or patterns that can be framed through different theoretical lenses. What is also interesting is that despite the authors' careful consideration of identity, they can only give us a snapshot of how individual students identify themselves, because identity itself appears to be quite fluid and the act of identifying oneself can also be unpredictable. In other words, when it comes to studying students' identities and the varied ways that they identify themselves, we are dealing with a moving target that is evolving in complex ways over time.

The exploration of identity through these chapters also makes clear that individuals who are categorized broadly as "AAPIs" or other versions of such labels do not necessarily share a common culture, language, heritage, socioeconomic status, political persuasion, immigration experience, religious or philosophical orientation, worldview, and so on. Given this population's extraordinary diversity, as well as the fact that identities are quite fluid and their related developmental processes and patterns vary widely, it would seem that the core essence of "Asian Americanness" is more fake than real, as might be suggested by the Tripmaster Monkey—the saint of Chinese legend in Maxine Hong Kingston's novel (1989) of the same title. After all, what is really at the core of an identity associated with these labels?

Indeed, specifying the core essence of being AAPI is perhaps one of the most difficult challenges for research concerning identity development among this group of students. Without some deeper understanding of the common bond among AAPIs guiding this body of work, the exploration of identity can devolve into an exercise of self-indulgence rather than remain as one that addresses the circumstances of those who Takaki referred to as having suffered from oppression. Thus, the challenge of specifying the core essence of being AAPI not only concerns the processes by which AAPI students develop during college, but also concerns the larger sociopolitical contexts associated with identity.

In considering this challenge, it may be helpful to keep Takaki's notion of iron cages in mind and what he called the "hegemonic superstructure" that constrains the ways AAPIs are viewed in society. By doing this, it reminds us that one of our common bonds as AAPIs may well be a shared experience as prisoners of a set of iron cages. Perhaps, as AAPIs, there is little that we collectively share besides a distinct vulnerability to certain stereotypes and their ensuing discriminatory effects. For example, not only are we at high risk of being stereotyped as model minorities, we are also vulnerable to being regularly stereotyped as foreigners and subsequently disqualified or held under suspicion. Likewise, we are also vulnerable to being stereotyped as spies, mass killers, or terrorists.

If vulnerability to certain forces (e.g., stereotyping, prejudice, discrimination) that are shaped by a larger hegemonic superstructure serves to bond AAPIs, then how students identify themselves does indeed have implications that extend beyond those individuals' own sense of self and personal development. That is, there may be a larger collective purpose associated with identity formation, and perhaps the identity one assumes and the intensity of that identification contribute to larger sociopolitical purposes that can either shorten or prolong our imprisonment in these iron cages. If so, researchers need to look beyond personal lives and also consider how those lives and developmental pathways collectively respond to what sociologists Michael Omi and Howard Winant (1986) refer to as a larger racial project. Although identity research is seemingly more psychological than sociological, this body of scholarship must also possess a sociological imagination that considers the broader set of social forces that either further oppress or liberate the lives of those imprisoned in Takaki's iron cages. If not, this line of research risks overemphasizing private lives and concerns, which might lead to more narrowly oriented individualistic solutions or, worse, fuel narcissistic tendencies.

As the chapters in this part begin to do, the next level of scholarship focused on identity development and formation among AAPIs in higher education will need to point us toward a larger racial project. Asking and answering several fundamental questions may help us move toward this end, including the following: What are the differences between racial identity development and other forms of identity development among AAPI students? How do the different paths of development and assumed identities either empower or disempower AAPI students to take part in collective action, especially as they relate to larger hegemonic structures? How might various paths of racial identity development among AAPI students subsequently serve different personal or sociopolitical purposes?

According to Li and Wang (2008), "Mainstream American society's perceptions of Asian Americans" seem to swing "back and forth on the pendulum, indicating a conflicted 'love and hate' relationship" (p. 5). Certainly, the research that is conducted on identity can help us better understand how we might collectively dictate this relationship, rather than individually suffer at the mercy of a temperamental pendulum. The chapters in this part begin to provide us with a better sense of how AAPIs' lives are negotiated within an "iron cage," or the ideological and cultural hegemony that constrains our society's worldviews, experiences, and spheres of association. In reading Part One, readers are urged to also keep in mind that the complexities of the lives and insights documented in these chapters play out in an equally complex world of power relationships that dictate the assembling and disassembling of racial categories and stereotypes. Unchallenged, these power relationships can perpetually imprison us in a *Takakian cage*, which subsequently limits our capacity to identify ourselves, either individually or collectively, in more authentic ways. Identity research that understands the complex interplay between personal lives and the hegemonic superstructure stands to enhance the potential of developing more sustained collective action that will move us a step closer to what Takaki described as a "new world of respect and unconditional opportunity."

References

Kingston, M. H. (1989). *Tripmaster Monkey: His fake book*. New York: Alfred A. Knopf.

Li, G., & Wang, L. (Eds.). (2008). *Model minority myth revisited: An interdisciplinary approach to demystifying Asian American educational experiences*. Charlotte, NC: Information Age Publishing.

Omi, M., & Winant, H. (1986). *Racial formation in the United States*. New York: Routledge.

Takaki, R. (1990). *Iron cages: Race and culture in 19th-century America*. New York: Oxford University Press.

2

A SOUTHEAST ASIAN AMERICAN IDENTITY MODEL

Merging Theoretical Perspectives
and Considering Intersecting Identities

Samuel D. Museus, Rican Vue,
Tu-Lien Kim Nguyen, and Fanny PF Yeung

Major differences exist across various ethnic groups within the Asian American and Pacific Islander (AAPI) population (Hune, 2002; Museus, 2009; Museus & Kiang, 2009). The aggregation of data on AAPIs in higher education research, policy, and practice conceals the tremendous diversity that is present within the larger AAPI category (Hune, 2002; Hune & Chan, 1997; Museus, 2009; Museus & Kiang, 2009). In reality, the AAPI category consists of more than 40 ethnic groups that differ greatly in cultural heritages, historical experiences, socioeconomic backgrounds, and educational circumstances (Hune, 2002; Kiang, 2002; Museus, 2009).

In this chapter, we focus on one subpopulation within the AAPI category—Southeast Asian Americans (SEAAs). For the purposes of this chapter, SEAAs include Cambodian, Hmong, Laotian, Mien, and Vietnamese Americans. We focus on SEAAs for several reasons. First, given the vast differences between SEAAs and other Asian American populations, scholars have underscored the need to generate knowledge of authentic SEAA experiences in higher education (e.g., Museus, 2009; Museus & Kiang, 2009). Yet, although a few scholars have made invaluable contributions to research on SEAAs in college (e.g., Chhuon & Hudley, 2008; Kiang, 1996, 2002, 2003,

2009; Lin & Suyemoto, 2009; Lin, Suyemoto, & Kiang, 2009; Museus, Maramba, Palmer, Reyes, & Bresonis, in press), SEAA students are still largely underrepresented in higher education research and discourse. Thus, it is time to move beyond arguing for the inclusion of SEAAs in higher education scholarship to generating a knowledge base that can help provide a better understanding of their experiences.

The Historical, Social, and Cultural Contexts of Southeast Asian American Experiences

Southeast Asian American identities develop within unique historical, social, and cultural contexts. Those contexts include (1) the nature of the refugee experience, (2) inequalities in socioeconomic conditions, (3) racial and ethnic disparities in education, (4) cultural adjustment issues, and (5) racial and ethnic prejudice and discrimination. We review these contextual influences in this section.

Unlike the majority of other Asian Americans—who arrived as voluntary immigrants seeking to improve their social, cultural, or economic situations—the bulk of Southeast Asians entered the United States as refugees (Portes & Rumbaut, 1996; Zhou & Bankston, 1998). The fact that SEAAs arrived as refugees means they came to the United States because of "a well-founded fear of being persecuted in their homeland, for reasons of their race, religion, nationality, social group or political opinion" (Refugee Act of 1980). Indeed, many Southeast Asians who fought with the United States against the communist regime during the Vietnam War fled their home countries to escape political persecution after the end of the war in 1975 (Barringer, Gardner, & Levin, 1995; Portes & Rumbaut, 1996). Thus, the majority of Southeast Asian refugees immigrated out of necessity and, because they are not voluntary immigrants, many of them might face challenging circumstances and not view their migration through an opportunistic lens. Moreover, although staying in or returning to their countries of origin is rarely an option, SEAAs may face many negative consequences associated with their migration to the United States, such as a losses of economic security, social status, and self-esteem, which are often observed among refugee groups (Kibria, 1993).

As a result of the Vietnam War and refugee experiences, many SEAAs have experienced a range of traumas that continue to affect their physical and psychological well-being (Chan, 2003). For example, many SEAAs experienced war-related trauma from persecution, loss of loved ones, widespread violence, refugee camps with unsanitary conditions, and uncertainty about their future (Abueg & Chun, 1996; Koltyk, 1998). As a result, SEAAs are at relatively high risk for mental health issues. They also exhibit disproportionately low health care and mental health service use rates (Hsu, Davies, & Hansen, 2004).

Regarding socioeconomic status, many SEAAs came from economically underdeveloped countries (e.g., Cambodia, Laos, and Vietnam) and arrived in the United States from socioeconomically disadvantaged backgrounds (Hsu et al., 2004). Thus, a majority of SEAAs were displaced and came to the United States under poor economic conditions and with less capital (e.g., education and income), and poverty rates in SEAA communities are estimated to be two to three times greater than the national average (Hune, 2002). In addition, in regard to occupational attainment, SEAAs are also concentrated in lower level occupations, such as manufacturing and service sectors (Pfeifer, 2008).

With respect to education, SEAAs also exhibit drastically lower levels of attainment than their East and South Asian American counterparts (Gloria & Ho, 2003; Hune, 2002; Kiang, 2002; Museus, 2009; Museus & Kiang, 2009). For example, the percentage of the adult Asian Indian population (75%) holding a bachelor's degree is over five times that of their Hmong (14%), Cambodian (13%), and Laotian (12%) counterparts (Chapter 1, this volume). One likely reason for these disparities in educational attainment could be that SEAAs tend to have less pre-migratory education than other Asian immigrants who voluntarily came to the United States in large numbers (Ima & Rumbaut, 1995; Portes & Rumbaut, 2001). For instance, Hmong refugees come from a cultural background with no written language prior to the 1950s. Another cause of these disparities could be that Asian American refugee students place less priority on education because there are more important issues and stressors with which they have to deal (Yeh, 2002).

Resettlement in the United States also poses numerous cultural challenges for Southeast Asian Americans. First, like other immigrants, SEAAs have had to adjust to a new language and culture (Hsu et al., 2004). Second, many SEAAs face substantial challenges associated with the changing gender role expectations, altered family expectations, and large differences in generational perspectives that have resulted from adaptation to the culture of the United States (Kinzie, Boehnlein, & Sack, 1998). Specifically, SEAA student–parent relationships can be complicated and strained by accelerated rates of acculturation that students experience via schooling, where they are exposed to the American value system. These relationships are further complicated by the student–parent role reversal that occurs when students acquire English and must serve as linguistic and cultural brokers for their parents, who overwhelmingly remain linguistically isolated (Pfeifer & Lee, 2004). Even while expected to serve these roles, however, many SEAA students continue to struggle with language acquisition (Ima & Rumbaut, 1995). Third, coming from cultural backgrounds that emphasize family interdependence may force SEAAs to choose between continuing education and caring for their family.

Racial and ethnic prejudice and discrimination are salient aspects of the experiences of SEAAs and other Asian Americans as well (Chou & Feagin, 2008; Cress & Ikeda, 2003; Lewis, Chesler, & Forman, 2000; Museus, 2008; Museus & Truong, 2009; Sue, Bucceri, Annie, Nadal, & Torino, 2007). Asian Americans, for example, face considerable pressure to conform to the model minority stereotype and also face overt acts of racial discrimination that range from being targeted by racial slurs to being the victims of hate crimes (Chou & Feagin, 2008; Lewis et al., 2000; Museus, 2008; Museus & Truong, 2009). Compounding their experiences with racism, SEAA ethnic groups are perceived as culturally deficient and unwilling or unable to assimilate (Adler, 2004). This could be one reason why they also experience marginalization and discrimination from other groups within the Asian American community (Lee, 1996). Ongoing experiences with such racial and ethnic prejudice and discrimination are realities that can enhance distress, suicidal behaviors, and identity confusion among SEAAs (Cress & Ikeda, 2003; Lau, Jernewall, Zane, & Myers, 2002; Sue et al., 2007).

Defining Key Terms in the Discussion of Southeast Asian American Identity

Before discussing existing identity models and presenting our emergent model, it is necessary to define some key terms related to an individual's sense of membership in various groups within society. For the purposes of this chapter, we build on the important work of Kiang (2002) and other scholars (Helms, 1994; Yinger, 1994) to designate and employ the following definitions:

- *Racial Minority Identity*: a sense of collective identity that is based on an individual's perceived shared experiences with other non-White members of society, which include racial prejudice and discrimination, racial exclusion and isolation, and race-related disenfranchisement;
- *Racial Identity*: a sense of collective identity that is based on the notion that the individual shares a common heritage or experience with members of a specific racial group, which, in the case of SEAAs, would be Asian Americans and Pacific Islanders;
- *Ethnic Identity*: a sense of collective identity that is based on an individual's understanding that he or she shares a common origin, history, culture, and language with a specific cultural group;
- *Immigrant Identity*: a sense of collective identity with other individuals who entered the United States after birth and must adjust to a new culture, climate, living conditions, and status;
- *Refugee Identity*: a sense of collective identity with other individuals who were forced out of their home countries and came to the United States, and consequently experienced trauma resulting from escape from persecution in their homeland, loss of loved ones, widespread violence, refugee camps with poor health conditions, and uncertainty about their future.

In the following section, we provide an overview of existing models relevant to Asian American identity development.

Existing Identity Models Relevant to Asian Americans

Most existing identity models relevant to Asian Americans can be separated into four categories: (1) racial identity stage models, (2) racial and ethnic identity stage models, (3) multiracial and multiethnic identity typologies, and (4) monoracial and multiracial identity factor models that focus on environmental influences. Each type of model has both strengths and weaknesses. We review these four sets of existing models as we attempt to incorporate their strengths and weaknesses into our SEAA identity model.

Racial Identity Stage Models

The earliest Asian American identity models were presented as stagelike, or sequential, processes (Kim, J. 1981; Sue & Sue, 1971). For example, Kim's Asian American identity model includes five progressive stages: In the first stage of *Ethnic Awareness*, the individual's attitudes toward being Asian are generally positive or neutral. *White Identification* is the second stage and is defined by the individual's recognition of differences from White people and the possible internalization of White values. The adoption of White values can result in alienation from other Asian Americans. This stage can be experienced in two different ways: actively and passively. When individuals experience White identification actively, they consider themselves to be very similar to their White peers and do not acknowledge any differences between them and their White counterparts; in essence, they attempt to eliminate their Asian selves. If individuals passively experience White identification, they do not consider themselves to be White or distance themselves from Asians, but they do accept White values, beliefs, and standards. Stage three consists of an *Awakening to Social Political Consciousness*, in which individuals recognize themselves as a minority and adopt a more positive political consciousness and Asian American self-concept. In stage four, *Redirection to Asian American Consciousness*, individuals embrace their Asian American identity and heritage. And, finally, the fifth stage of *Incorporation* consists of the individual learning how to balance his or her own identity with an appreciation of others.

These racial identity stage models provided a foundation for understanding Asian American identity. They also provided practitioners with a framework for comprehending how to facilitate that development among members of this population. The limitations of these early stagelike racial identity models, however, are inherent in the fact that they focus on one specific dimension of identity and ignore others mentioned previously (e.g., identification with an ethnic group or immigrant populations). In addition, these models tend to be presented in a way that clearly distinguishes various forms of identification that are not as easily separated in Asian Americans' actual lives. That is, hypothetically, it could be argued that an Asian American can be at the stage of Incorporation, experience a very racist incident, and shift to a redirection to Asian American consciousness within a matter of seconds and transfer back to incorporation when he or she has left the space in which the incident occurred. Thus, actual identification could be more flexible and fluid than these models suggest.

Racial and Ethnic Identity Stage Models

Over the past decade, alternative progressive stagelike models have been developed to account for both racial and ethnic identity (Ibrahim, Ohnishi, &

Sandhu, 1997; Nadal, 2004). For example, in response to the unique historical and social context of the lives of Pilipino Americans, Nadal proposed a model of Pilipino American identity. Adapting previous literature on Asian American identity (Kim, J., 1981; Kitano & Daniels, 1995; Suinn, Ahuna, & Khoo, 1992), Nadal (2004) contested that social, cultural, economic, and psychological differences between Pilipino Americans and the rest of the Asian American population warranted a model to explain the unique identity development of Pilipino Americans. Nadal's model consists of six stages. The first three stages are similar to those in Kim's model. Stage four is labeled *Panethnic Asian American Consciousness*, in which individuals may seek power in numbers vis-à-vis membership in the larger Asian community to find coalitions based on similarity. *Ethnocentric Realization* is the fifth stage, and it is characterized by a realization that the Asian American community has marginalized Pilipino Americans and an increased awareness of the social injustices that are specific to this group. The final stage of *Incorporation* is characterized by an ethnocentric consciousness that is defined as "a sense of one's personal collective identity, centered on a specific concern for the issues and situations of one's specific ethnic group" (p. 59).

These racial and ethnic identity stage models contribute to existing understandings of Asian American identity in several ways. First, they highlight the role of ethnicity, which plays a significant role in the ways that Asian Americans self-identify in relation to other racial and ethnic groups. Second, they underscore the fact that the process might be different for various ethnic groups within the Asian American population and the factors (e.g., historical and social) influencing identity might vary across those subpopulations. Finally, they illuminate the ways in which racial and ethnic identity can be equally salient and interacting components of the identity development process for Asian Americans. Like the racial identity stage models, however, it could be argued that their stages suggest that forms of identification are more distinguishable than might be the case in the actual Asian American experience.

Nadal (2004), for example, asserts that Pilipino Americans are socialized to accept their role as Asian American and argues that Pilipino Americans "will accept the Asian American identity as a means of coalition, not as a term of identity," but in subsequent stages those individuals realize that they are unjustly classified as Asian Americans and develop a greater ethnocentric identity (p. 57). This model, therefore, suggests that Pilipino Americans only espouse an Asian American identity because they are not yet aware of the injustices committed toward Pilipino Americans and relinquish that racial identity to adopt a Pilipino American identity as a result of a newfound awareness of the marginalization of Pilipino Americans in society. In doing so, the model does not make room for the possibility of individuals authentically espousing an Asian American identity any time after they become aware of those injustices. In contrast, in the following discussion, we assume that SEAAs who have been racialized as Asian American can authentically espouse both a racial and ethnic identity as a means of coalition and power and to embrace multiple aspects of their identity that is co-constructed between themselves and society. Moreover, in contrast to the Pilipino model, we assume that SEAAs can embrace their Asian Americanness even after they become aware of injustices faced by their specific ethnic groups.

Multiracial and Multiethnic Identity Typologies

Other scholars have conceptualized different forms of identification in more fluid and nonprogressive ways (Chaudhari & Pizzolato, 2008; Renn, 2004; Root, 1996). These researchers have noted that mixed-race Asian Americans and other multiracial individuals can identify in several different ways and shift from one identity to another, depending on the context. Building on the work of Root, Renn identified the following five identity patterns among multiracial college students: *monoracial identity* (one racial identity), *multiple monoracial identities* (two or more distinct identities), *multiracial identity* (identification with mixed-race individuals), *extraracial identity* (refusal to identify with racial categories), and *situational identity* (shifting among these options based on the situation). This typology has been modified and applied to multiethnic college students as well (Chaudhari & Pizzolato, 2008).

    These typologies also have both strengths and weaknesses. They have challenged previous positivist conceptualizations of racial and ethnic identity and underscored the flexibility and fluidity with which identity can operate. Specifically, these typologies suggest that individuals' identities can constantly shift, depending on the time or space within which those persons are self-identifying. However, because the typologies suggest that individuals can validly identify any of several ways and are nonlinear, nonsequential, and nonprogressive, it could be argued that they also suggest that one form of identification is not more desirable than another. This might not be a popular perspective, particularly for some educators who find it important for individuals to be conscious of how society perceives them and subjects them to various forms of oppression. For example, educators who hope that their monoracial or multiracial Asian American students understand that they are racial minorities who are disadvantaged by, and suffer from, racism might argue that it is not equally valuable for a multiracial Asian/White person to (1) identify as White and not believe in systems of racism and identify as Asian or Asian/White and (2) recognize that he or she is a member of a disadvantaged and oppressed racial or ethnic group.

Monoracial and Multiracial Identity Factor Models

Instead of focusing on various patterns of development and the various levels of awareness or multiple identities, identity factor models are nonhierarchical models that focus on the various factors that may influence one's or multiracial identity (Accapadi, 2012; Kodama, McEwen, Liang, & Lee, 2002; Wijeyesinghe, 2001). Kodama et al., for example, situate monoracial Asian American identity within the external influences that exist in the individuals' environment. Specifically, they assert that Asian American identity is shaped by racism from dominant culture in society and traditional Asian family values, such as the values of collectivism, interdependence, placement of primary importance on the needs of the family, interpersonal harmony, and deference to authority (Kim, Atkinson, & Yang, 1999). These models contribute to the discussion on Asian American identity because they highlight the multiplicity of ways in which environmental factors can play a significant role in identity determination. These models are limited, however, in the extent to which they explain the process by which Asian Americans develop their sense of ethnic consciousness and identify in different ways (e.g., ethnically and racially).

A Model of Southeast Asian American Identity

Our SEAA identity model consists of five processes. We prefer using "process" over "phase," "stage," or "status" because we view the factors that shape SEAA identity development as distinct but interconnected and interactive processes, as opposed to separate levels within the same process. In addition, it will become apparent that some of these processes consist of multiple interacting dimensions.

A few points are worth making before we present our model. First, we recognize that some may balk at our aggregation of SEAAs in this discussion. We recognize that different ethnic groups within the SEAA category have distinct histories, languages, cultures, and communities. However, as discussed, they also share important historical and social contexts. Thus, we aggregate SEAAs to begin a dialogue about identity formation among this population, but we are aware that identity development processes may differ among various SEAA ethnic groups, just as they might vary across SEAAs with different generational statuses. Second, although we focus on SEAAs, we acknowledge that this discussion and model might apply to other racial and ethnic minority groups as well. Third, in constructing our model, we borrow strengths from the various identity theories discussed previously. For example, like racial and ethnic identity stage models (Ibrahim et al., 1997; Nadal, 2004), we highlight the importance of both race and ethnicity. We also emphasize the situational nature of identity and fluidity of the identity development process, similar to multiracial and multiethnic identity typologies (Chaudhari & Pizzolato, 2008; Renn, 2004; Root, 1996). And, we borrow from factor models (Kodama et al., 2002; Wijeyesinghe, 2001) to underscore the importance of context and the simultaneous influence of multiple cultures on one's identity. Finally, we recognize that everyone will not agree with the model that we propose, and we hope those dissident voices will help facilitate future discussion of SEAA identity development beyond this chapter.

Process I: Enculturation to Ethnic Cultures

The first process in our model is enculturation to one's ethnic culture. *Enculturation* can be defined as the socialization into and maintenance of various elements of one's traditional culture, which includes cultural values, ideas, and norms (Herskovits, 1948). This process is aligned with the ethnic awareness stages found within previous identity stage models (Kim, J., 1981; Nadal, 2004). Ethnic awareness stages in those earlier models suggest that individuals usually learn about their own cultures at a very young age, prior to schooling, during the period in which they are taught about their family's and community's cultural values, customs, norms, food, and language. Enculturation, however, can occur later in life—especially among those who are born and grow up in the United States (Kim, B., 2009). Thus, unlike previous models, we underscore the fact that older SEAAs can also engage in a process of enculturation and learn about their own traditional cultural heritages at any time throughout their lives. Indeed, SEAAs do not have to cease learning about their own families' and communities' histories and cultures in college. For example, Asian American studies classes, other courses, and extracurricular experiences can all contribute to SEAAs' increased knowledge of their own heritage and how it shapes their identity and experience.

Process II: Acculturation to the Dominant Culture

The second process in our model is acculturation to the dominant culture. The term *acculturation* has been used to describe the changes in attitudes, beliefs, and identity that an individual experiences as a result of being in contact with other cultures (Graves, 1967). In regard to racial and ethnic minorities in the United States, this term is often used to refer to the process of adapting to dominant, White American cultural values, customs, norms, and food. Although the term *acculturation* might not be explicitly discussed in previous racial and ethnic identity stage models, it is related to the stages of White identification or assimilation (Kim, J., 1981; Nadal, 2004), in which individuals change so much as a result of their contact with dominant White American culture that they reject their own racial or ethnic group's cultural heritage, internalize White values and standards, and prefer the dominant culture (e.g., European American values, customs, norms, and food). Whereas earlier stage models imply that individuals are either in a stage of assimilation or not, because individuals can begin learning about the dominant culture at a very early age and can continue to do so into adulthood, this vector suggests that adaptation to the dominant culture is an ongoing process that influences SEAA identity construction and SEAAs are acculturated to varying degrees at any given point throughout their lives.

Process III: Awareness of Oppression

Our third process is awareness of oppression. This is congruent with the social and political awakening stages in earlier models. This process is characterized by individuals gaining increased social and political consciousness, resulting from their learning about racial and ethnic inequalities and injustices. Unlike earlier models (Kim, J., 1981; Nadal, 2004), however, our awakening process is multidimensional and highlights the fact that SEAAs can gain an increased awareness of inequities among the various groups to which they belong, including (1) racial minorities in general, (2) Asian Americans, (3) their ethnic group within the Asian American category (e.g., ethnic discrimination from East Asian Americans toward Southeast Asian Americans), and (4) immigrant/refugee populations (e.g., discrimination experienced by refugees who might not be fluent in English because of their linguistic abilities). SEAAs can become increasingly aware of injustices faced by any one of these groups, while continuing to be unaware of the injustices faced by others, or they can become aware of injustices faced by multiple groups simultaneously. Finally, awakening to the oppression of one group can be accompanied by an increased desire and agency to combat the injustices or inequalities experienced by that specific group, or an interest in advocating against oppression in general.

Process IV: Redirection of Salience

We label our fourth process the redirection of salience, and it refers to an individual's situational redirection of salience to various identities (e.g., from his or her identity as a person of color to an Asian American) in a given time or space. That is, at any given time or place, an SEAA can consciously or subconsciously underscore the salience of his or her identity as (1) a racial minority, (2) an Asian American, (3) a member of an ethnic group, or (4) a refugee or immigrant—all of which have been recognized as important identities among SEAA college students (Kiang, 1991, 1995, 2002). We assume that all four identities are continually present to some degree for SEAAs, with the exception of the immigrant and refugee identities that likely progressively change or diminish among second or subsequent generations.

Whereas earlier racial and racial/ethnic identity stage models highlight an increased ownership of being Asian American or the embracement of an Asian American and subsequent shift to ownership of an ethnic identity (Ibrahim et al., 1997; Kim, J., 1981; Nadal, 2004), our redirection of salience complicates this picture and indicates that the process of enacting one identity over another is more fluid. First, the redirection of salience suggests that SEAAs can consciously or subconsciously highlight the salience of various identities. Second, the emphasis on a particular identity can constantly shift across time and space. For example, within a matter of hours, Cambodian Americans can fully embrace or enact their Khmer identity and not really think about themselves as having anything in common with Blacks, Latinos, or Native Americans (i.e., other people of color) when they are at home, then drive to a conference on race and racism and increasingly embrace their ownership of being a racial minority with experiences similar to those of other racial minority groups in the latter context. This flexibility is inherent in multiracial and multiethnic typology models that suggest that individuals can shift back and forth to enact various identities, depending on the situation (Chaudhari & Pizzolato, 2008; Renn, 2004).

Process V: Integration of Dispositions

Our final process is the integration of dispositions, and it refers to the process by which SEAAs integrate their (1) identification with various groups, (2) attitudes about the dominant majority, and (3) sense of activism and agency to address oppression and inequities among those populations. Whereas other theorists have identified this as the pinnacle of identity development (Ibrahim et al., 1997; Kim, J., 1981; Nadal, 2004), we argue that this is an ongoing process that begins at a very young age. SEAAs can begin integrating their sense of membership in various groups and attitudes about the dominant majority when they first begin to navigate multiple cultures as a child. This sense of group membership and attitudes about the majority culture are both influenced by processes of enculturation (which is related to more positive attitudes about one's minority group) and acculturation (which is related to more positive attitudes about the dominant culture in society). The more SEAAs learn about their own and the majority culture, the more they must learn to balance their membership in marginalized groups with their attitudes about the majority and membership in the larger American community. When SEAAs become more aware of injustices and inequities faced by the marginalized groups to which they belong, they may increasingly integrate their sense of membership in these groups, sense of belonging to larger American society, and views around activism and agency related to addressing those injustices and inequities. In doing so, they must determine their level of desire and commitment to advocate for the ethnic, Asian American, minority, immigrant, and refugee communities to which they belong.

Implications for Higher Education Research and Practice

Our model outlines the processes that shape SEAA identity, which includes multiple dimensions: identification with one's ethnic group, Asian Americans, racial minorities, and immigrants and refugees. The model has several implications for research and practice. Future research should examine this model with empirical data on the lived experiences of SEAAs in college. The voices of SEAA college students can illuminate whether, as well as how well, the model explains the experiences of various individuals and groups within the SEAA category. Because distinct groups that vary in language, religion, and culture are included under the term *SEAA*, it can be hypothesized that the influence of these processes on an individual SEAA's identity might vary across ethnic groups. Additionally, research indicates that gender plays an important role in the negotiation of racial and ethnic identity (Kurien, 1999; Lee, 1997). Thus, there is a need to understand how gender shapes these processes. Other variables that may influence the process discussed herein include family, generational status, socioeconomic status, and contextual factors—all of which need to be examined and better understood.

The earliest Asian American identity models focus on race (e.g., Kim, J., 1981), and more recent models underscore the role of both race and ethnicity (Ibrahim et al., 1997; Nadal, 2004). Our model expands on these by incorporating additional and important interconnected elements of SEAA identity, which have been identified by other researchers (Kiang, 2002), into the discussion. We believe that the multidimensional and fluid nature of this model can be an especially useful tool for understanding the complexity of individual identity among SEAAs, but we also think that it could potentially help better understand the identity of other Asian Americans as well. Indeed, recent research suggests that racial and ethnic identities are very different constructs for some Asian American ethnic groups (Philip, 2007), and our model suggests that there are other distinct aspects of identity that should be considered, including one's sense of membership to communities of color in general or immigrant and refugee communities. All of these elements of identity should be taken into account when understanding and analyzing the identity of SEAA college students.

Another important implication for research is the potential application of this model to comprehend the experiences of other Asian American ethnic groups. We focus on SEAAs in this chapter, but we acknowledge that many of the ideas we discuss herein are applicable to other populations. Indeed, Chinese Americans or Puerto Rican Americans can also identify along multiple dimensions. Thus, researchers should try to understand the process of other populations developing an awareness of the struggles faced by the different groups to which they belong, as well as how such understanding can contribute to the construction of more complex identities among these other groups.

In regard to implications for practice, educators can use this model to develop and provide culturally appropriate and sensitive programs and practices. For example, counselors and advisors should understand the struggles and issues faced by the many different groups to which SEAAs belong. This could mean expanding their knowledge of the trauma that can result from refugee experiences or existing interracial tensions that are a consequence of a lack of understanding of the common struggles among Asian American and other racial minority groups. Student affairs educators can also use this model to develop and plan extracurricular activities that incorporate information that is relevant to Asian Americans, as well as those other dimensions of SEAA identity.

The concepts of learning and growth are central to the identity development process. Alvarez (2002) argued that "there is an assumption that change, from racial naiveté to racial awareness, is not only desirable but also possible" (p. 41). In regard to learning and growth, this model underscores the fact that naïveté and awareness are multidimensional, and it suggests that it is imperative that higher education institutions foster the holistic development of SEAA students along the various dimensions of ethnicity, Asian Americanness, minority status, and immigrant and refugee status. Because Asian Americans can fail to develop ownership of their racial minority status because of a lack of knowledge regarding their groups' role in history and society (Inkelas, 2003), nurturing SEAA students' awareness of their groups' role within the larger systems of historical and societal racism is critical. Fostering such growth can result in both greater development among the individual student and opportunities for learning and community-building across various racial and ethnic minority groups on campus. For example, learning about common struggles and issues across racial and ethnic minority groups could potentially serve to create a more inclusive campus environment for all students.

Finally, this model provides a very different framework for those who want to understand and foster SEAA identity. It suggests that processes of enculturation, acculturation, awareness, redirection, and integration are continuous and interacting. Thus, rather than suggesting the application of stage models to assess where individuals are in their identity development and how they can move students from one phase to the next, our model indicates that educators should consider all of these processes when developing programs and practices to ensure that they are considering how they can contribute to overall identity growth by (1) teaching students about their SEAA cultural heritage; (2) fostering awareness of injustices faced by various racial, ethnic, immigrant, and refugee populations; and (3) cultivating a sense of membership in all four of the aforementioned groups with which SEAA students might identify.

References

Abueg, F. R., & Chun, K. M. (1996). Traumatization stress among Asians and Asian Americans. In A. J. Marsella, M. J. Friedman, E. T. Gerrity, & R. M. Scurfield (Eds.), *Ethnocultural aspects of posttraumatic stress disorder: Issues, research, and clinical applications* (pp. 285–299). Washington, DC: American Psychological Association.

Accapadi, M. M. (2012). Asian American identity consciousness: A polycultural model. In D. Ching & A. Agbayani (Eds.), *Asian Americans and Pacific Islanders in higher education: Research and perspectives on identity, leadership, and success* (pp. 57–94). Washington, DC: National Association of Student Personnel Administrators.

Adler, S. M. (2004). Home-school relations and the construction of racial and ethnic identity of Hmong elementary students. *The School Community Journal, 14*(2), 57–75.

Alvarez, N. (2002). Racial identity and Asian Americans: Support and challenges. In M. K. McEwen, C. M. Kodama, A. N. Alvarez, S. Lee, & C. T. H. Liang (Eds.), *Working with Asian American college students: New directions for student services* (No. 97, pp. 33–44). San Francisco, CA: Jossey-Bass.

Barringer, H., Gardner, R. W., & Levin, M. J. (1995). *Asian and Pacific Islanders in the United States.* New York: Russell Sage Foundation.

Chan, S. (2003). Scarred, yet undefeated: Hmong and Cambodian women and girls in the United States. In S. Hune & G. M. Nomura (Eds.), *Asian/Pacific Islander American women: A historical anthology* (pp. 253–267). New York: New York University Press.

Chaudhari, P., & Pizzolato, J. E. (2008). Understanding the epistemology of ethnic identity development in multiethnic college students. *Journal of College Student Development, 49*(5), 443–458.

Chhuon, V., & Hudley, C. (2008). Factors supporting Cambodian American students' successful adjustment into the university. *Journal of College Student Development, 49*(1), 15–30.

Chou, R. S., & Feagin, J. R. (2008). *The myth of the model minority: Asian Americans facing racism.* Boulder, CO: Paradigm.

Cress, C. M., & Ikeda, E. K. (2003). Distress under duress: The relationship between campus climate and depression in Asian American college students. *NASPA Journal, 40*(2), 74–97.

Gloria, A. M., & Ho, T. A. (2003). Environmental, social, and psychological experiences of Asian American undergraduates: Examining issues of academic persistence. *Journal of Counseling and Development, 81*, 93–105.

Graves, T. D. (1967). Psychological acculturation in a tri-ethnic community. *Southwestern Journal of Anthropology, 23*, 337–350.

Helms, J. E. (1994). The conceptualization of racial identity and other racial constructs. In E. J. Trickett, R. J. Watts, & D. Birman (Eds.), *Human diversity: Perspectives on people in context* (pp. 285–311). San Francisco, CA: Jossey-Bass.

Herskovits, M. J. (1948). *Man and his works: The science of cultural anthropology.* New York: Knopf.

Hsu, E., Davies, C. A., & Hansen, D. J. (2004). Understanding mental health needs of Southeast Asian refugees: Historical, cultural, and contextual challenges. *Clinical Psychology Review, 24*, 193–213.

Hune, S. (2002). Demographics and diversity of Asian American college students. In M. K. McEwen, C. M. Kodama, A. N. Alvarez, S. Lee, & C. T. H. Liang (Eds.), *Working with Asian American college students: New directions for student services* (No. 97, pp. 11–20). San Francisco, CA: Jossey-Bass.

Hune, S., & Chan, K. S. (1997). Special focus: Asian Pacific American demographic and educational trends. In D. J. Carter & R. Wilson (Eds.), *Fifteenth annual status report on minorities in higher education* (pp. 39–67). Washington, DC: American Council on Education.

Ibrahim, F., Ohnishi, H., and Sandhu, D. S. (1997). Asian American identity development: A culture specific model for South Asian Americans. *Journal of Multicultural Counseling and Development, 25,* 34–50.

Ima, K., & Rumbaut, R. G. (1995). Southeast Asian refugees in American schools: A comparison of fluent-English-proficient and limited-English-proficient students. In D. T. Nakanishi & T. Y. Nishida (Eds.), *The Asian American educational experience: A source book for teachers and students* (pp. 54–75). New York: Routledge.

Inkelas, K. K. (2003). Caught in the middle: Understanding Asian Pacific American perspectives on affirmative action through Blumer's group position theory. *Journal of College Student Development, 44*(5), 625–643.

Kiang, P. N. (1991). About face: Recognizing Asian and Pacific American Vietnam veterans in Asian American Studies. *Amerasia Journal, 17*(3), 22–40.

Kiang, P. N. (1995). Bicultural strengths and struggles of Southeast Asian American students. *Journal of Narrative and Life History, 6*(1), 39–64.

Kiang, P. N. (1996). Persistence stories and survival strategies of Cambodian Americans in college. *Journal of Narrative and Life History, 6*(1), 39–64.

Kiang, P. N. (2002). Stories and structures of persistence: Ethnographic learning through research and practice in Asian American Studies. In Y. Zou & H. T. Trueba (Eds.), *Ethnography and schools: Qualitative approaches to the study of education* (pp. 223–255). Lanham, MD: Rowman & Littlefield.

Kiang, P. N. (2003). Pedagogies of PTSD: Circles of healing with refugees and veterans in Asian American Studies. In L. Zhan (Ed.), *Asian Americans: Vulnerable populations, model interventions, clarifying agendas* (pp. 197–222). Sudbury, MA: Jones & Bartlett.

Kiang, P. N. (2009). A thematic analysis of persistence and long-term educational engagement with Southeast Asian American college students. In L. Zhan (Ed.), *Asian voices: Engaging, empowering, enabling.* New York: NLN Press.

Kibria, N. (1993). *Family tightrope: The changing lives of Vietnamese Americans.* Princeton, NJ: Princeton University Press.

Kim, B. (2009). Acculturation and enculturation of Asian Americans: A primer. In N. Tewari & A. N. Alvarez (Eds.), *Asian American psychology: Current perspectives* (pp. 97–112). New York: Taylor & Francis Group.

Kim, B. S. K., Atkinson, D. R., & Yang, P. H. (1999). The Asian values scale: Development, factor analysis, validation, and reliability. *Journal of Counseling Psychology, 46*, 342–352.

Kim, J. (1981). *Processes of Asian American identity development: A study of Japanese American women's perceptions of their struggle to achieve positive identities as Americans of Asian ancestry* (Unpublished doctoral dissertation). University of Massachusetts–Amherst.

Kinzie, J. D., Boehnlein, J., & Sack, W. I.-I. (1998). The effects of massive trauma on Cambodian parents and children. In Y. Danieli (Ed.), *International handbook of multigenerational legacies of trauma* (pp. 211–221). New York: Plenum.

Kitano, H. H., & Daniels, R. (1995). *Asian Americans: Emerging minorities.* Englewood Cliffs, NJ: Prentice Hall.

Kodama, C. M., McEwen, M., Liang, C. T. H., & Lee, S. (2002). An Asian American perspective on psychosocial student development theory. In M. K. McEwen, C. M. Kodama, A. N. Alvarez, S. Lee, & C. T. H. Liang (Eds.), *Working with Asian American college students: New directions for student services* (No. 97, 45–60). San Francisco, CA: Jossey-Bass.

Koltyk, J. (1998). *New pioneers in the heartland: Hmong life in Wisconsin.* Boston, MA: Allyn & Bacon.

Kurien, P. (1999). Gendered ethnicity: Creating a Hindu Indian identity in the United States. *American Behavioral Scientist, 42*(4), 648–670.

Lau, A. S., Jernewall, N. M., Zane, N., & Myers, H. F. (2002). Correlates of suicidal behaviors among Asian American outpatient youths. *Cultural Diversity and Ethnic Minority Psychology, 8*(3), 199–213.

Lee, S. J. (1996). *Unraveling the model minority stereotype: Listening to Asian American youth.* New York: Teachers College Press.

Lee, S. J. (1997). The road to college: Hmong American women's pursuit of higher education. *Harvard Educational Review, 67*(4), 803–827.

Lewis, A. E., Chesler, M., & Forman, T. A. (2000). The impact of "colorblind" ideologies on students of color: Intergroup relations at a predominantly White university. *The Journal of Negro Education, 69*(1/2), 74–91.

Lin, N. J., & Suyemoto, K. L. (2009). Bridging the broken narrative: How student-centered teaching contributes to healing the wounds of trauma. In L. Zhan (Ed.), *Asian American voices: Engaging, empowering, and enabling* (pp. 123–146). New York: NLN Press.

Lin, N., Suyemoto, K. L., & Kiang, P. N. (2009). Education as catalyst for intergenerational refugee family communication about war and trauma. *Communication Disorders Quarterly, 30*(4), 195–207.

Museus, S. D. (2008). The model minority and the inferior minority myths: Inside stereotypes and their implications for student involvement. *About Campus, 13*(3), 2–8.

Museus, S. D. (2009). A critical analysis of the exclusion of Asian Americans from higher education research and discourse. In L. Zhan (Ed.), *Asian American voices: Engaging, empowering, enabling* (pp. 59–76). New York: NLN Press.

Museus, S. D., & Kiang, P. N. (2009). The model minority myth and how it contributes to the invisible minority reality in higher education research. In S. D. Museus (Ed.), *Conducting research on Asian Americans in higher education: New directions for institutional research* (No. 142, pp. 5–15). San Francisco, CA: Jossey-Bass.

Museus, S. D., Maramba, D. C., Palmer, R. T., Reyes, A., & Bresonis, K. (in press). An explanatory model of Southeast Asian American college student success: A grounded theory analysis. In R. Endo & Xue Lan Rong (Eds.), *Asian American educational achievement, schooling, and identities.* Charlotte, NC: Information Age Publishers.

Museus, S. D., & Truong, K. A. (2009). Disaggregating qualitative data on Asian Americans in campus climate research and assessment. In S. D. Museus (Ed.), *Conducting research on Asian Americans in higher education: New directions for institutional research* (No. 142, pp. 17–26). San Francisco, CA: Jossey-Bass.

Nadal, K. L. (2004). Pilipino American identity development model. *Journal of Multicultural Counseling and Development, 32,* 45–62.

Pfeifer, M. (2008). Cambodian, Hmong, Lao and Vietnamese-Americans in the 2005 American Community Survey. *Journal of Southeast Asian American Education & Advancement, 3,* 1–21.

Pfeifer, M. E., & Lee, S. (2004). Hmong population, demographic, socioeconomic, and educational trends in the 2000 census. In H. Hmong National Development Inc. and the Hmong Cultural and Resource Center (Eds.), *Hmong census publication: Data and analysis* (pp. 3–11). Washington, DC: Hmong National Development & Hmong Cultural and Resource Center.

Philip, C. (2007). *Asian American identities: Racial and ethnic identity issues in the twenty-first century.* Youngstown, NY: Cambria Press.

Portes, A., & Rumbaut, R. G. (1996). *Immigrant America: A portrait* (2nd ed.). Berkeley: University of California Press.

Portes, A., & Rumbaut, R. G. (2001). *Legacies: The story of the immigrant second generation.* Berkeley: University of California Press.

Refugee Act of 1980, Pub. L. No. 96-212, sec. 412, 94 Stat. 111 (1980).

Renn, K. A. (2004). *Mixed race students in college: The ecology of race, identity, and community on campus.* Albany: State University of New York Press.

Root, M. P. P. (1996). *The multiracial experience: Racial borders as the new frontier.* Thousand Oaks, CA: Sage.

Sue, D. W., Bucceri, J. M., Annie, I. L., Nadal, K. L., & Torino, G. C. (2007). Racial microaggressions and the Asian American experience. *Cultural Diversity and Ethnic Minority Psychology, 13*(1), 72–81.

Sue, S., & Sue, D. W. (1971). Chinese-American personality and mental health. *Amerasia Journal, 1,* 36–49.

Suinn, R. M., Ahuna, C., & Khoo, G. (1992). The Suinn-Lew Asian Self-Identity Acculturation Scale: Concurrent and factorial validation. *Educational and Psychological Measurement, 52*(4), 1041–1046.

Wijeyesinghe, C. L. (2001). Racial identity in multiracial people: An alternative paradigm. In C. L. Wijeyesinghe & B. W. Jackson III (Eds.), *New perspectives on racial identity development: A theoretical and practical anthology* (pp. 129–152). New York: New York University Press.

Yeh, T. L. (2002). Asian American college students who are educationally at risk. In M. K. McEwen, C. M. Kodama, A. N. Alvarez, S. Lee, & C. T. H. Liang (Eds.), *Working with Asian American college students: New directions for student services* (No. 97, pp. 61–71). San Francisco, CA: Jossey-Bass.

Yinger, J. M. (1994). *Ethnicity: Source of strength? Source of conflict?* Albany: State University of New York Press.

Zhou, M., & Bankston, C. L., III. (1998). *Growing up American: How Vietnamese children adapt to life in the United States.* New York: Russell Sage Foundation.

3

TO BE MICE OR MEN

Gender Identity and the Development of Masculinity Through Participation in Asian American Interest Fraternities

Minh C. Tran and Mitchell J. Chang

I f good humor reflects social realities in society, consider one of Asian
American comedian Esther Ku's jokes. Ku was a 2008 finalist on a popular television show called *Last Comic Standing* and one of her jokes
broadcasted nationally takes aim at Asian American men:

> I don't want to marry an Asian guy, I want to marry regular people. . . .
> Seriously, Asian girls are going out with White guys, Black guys, you know,
> everybody but Asian guys. You know, like what's going to happen with
> Asian guys, they're going to go extinct or something? As they sit at home
> playing video games. I feel bad that they're all single, but, like, not bad
> enough to date them. Like last week this Asian guy asked me out, and I
> was just like, when are they going to realize that Asian girls are just way
> out of their league?

The consistently negative racial stereotyping of Asian American men seems
to be ingrained deeply in our culture and has led to distorted, yet wildly
popular, misperceptions about their masculinity. This stereotyping is fueled
by negative media images and demeans Asian American men. Not only are
their low social standing and lack of sexual prowess fodder for comedians,
but even their physical attributes are points of derogatory remarks on the
Internet. If one types the words *Asian men* in the Google search engine, the
results will invariably include discussions that raise questions about their

sexuality, attractiveness, and physical attributes. This negative racial stereo-typing strikes at the very core of Asian American men's sense of masculinity.

The stereotypes that shape Asian American men's sense of masculinity take on even greater significance in college, where undergraduate students are developing their social identities and coming to terms with their "man-hood." During this critical period of their development, the emasculating effects of these stereotypes can more forcefully impact their sense of mascu-linity and, therefore, negatively affect their overall self-image, confidence, and mental health. This chapter examines how heterosexual Asian American men negotiate those negative stereotypes and the norms that shape their sense of masculinity. Specifically, this study analyzes how an Asian American fraternity enables undergraduate students to develop their sense of masculin-ity in more collective and structured ways in college.

The Role of Asian American Greek Organizations in College

Asian American Greek-letter organizations emerged nearly a century ago, with the establishment of Rho Psi Fraternity at Cornell University in 1916 (National APIA Panhellenic Association, 2007). The Chinese American men who founded this fraternity were inspired by the establishment of the first Black fraternity, Alpha Phi Alpha, which was also founded at Cornell Uni-versity only 10 years earlier (National APIA Panhellenic Association). Many of the early Asian American fraternities and sororities were established in response to racial and ethnic exclusion on college campuses and provided similar opportunities previously available only to their White counterparts. In 2007, there were more than 65 Asian American fraternities and sororities in existence with more than 420 total chapters (National APIA Panhellenic Association).

Despite the long-term and growing presence of Asian American fraterni-ties, few college administrators, including those who work extensively with Greek life, know much about their history and mission. Walter Kimbrough, a higher education scholar and president of Philander Smith College, aptly stated, "I do presentations where I show photos of Asian fraternities, and people are completely shocked that they exist" (Rivenburg, 2005, p. B3). One contributing factor to why these student organizations are widely ignored is the lack of research on the experiences of Asian American students. Relatively higher college enrollment, persistence, and graduation rates for some Asian American ethnic groups (but not others) have led many educators to wrongly conclude that all Asian American students have few problems and do not suffer from social disadvantages (Kawaguchi, 2003; Yeh, 2002).

Moreover, previous research on fraternity members has overwhelmingly focused on mainstream, predominantly White Greek-letter organizations (e.g., Chang & DeAngelo, 2002; Maisel, 1990; Pascarella et al., 1996; Pike, 2000; Rhoads, 1995). The majority of this literature suggests that few positive learning outcomes can be associated with predominantly White fraternity membership, which tends to promote substantial abuse of alcohol, disruptive behavior, and negative effects on students' cognitive development.

In contrast, research on Black fraternities shows that these organizations exist within larger unwelcoming campus racial climates and provide valuable venues for ethnic identity development, peer support, and leadership development (Harper & Quaye, 2007; Kimbrough, 1995; Sutton & Terrell, 1997). Similarly, Asian American fraternities provide their members with comparable opportunities within the context of student alienation from the dominant culture and estrangement from the mainstream Greek system (Jones, 2004; Lee, 1955). Indeed, although Asian American students still experience campus alienation and have limited options for social engagement (Kawaguchi, 2003; Kumashiro, 1999; Liu, 2002), Asian American fraternities can offer safe havens from that unwelcoming environment. For example, in one of the few studies of Asian American fraternities, Chan (1999) studied Lambda Phi Epsilon at the University of California–Santa Barbara, and found that this fraternity provided a context of safety and nonjudgment, where a member was "no longer a minority, and he does not have to deal with the stereotypes associated with Asian American men" (p. 70).

Asian American fraternities seem to share other attributes commonly found among Black fraternities. It is widely known that Black fraternities practice hazing rituals that tend to be physically severe and sometimes violent. Between the years 1987 and 1990, nearly 94% of hazing cases in Black fraternities involved physical abuse, compared with only 5% of cases in predominantly White fraternities (Nuwer, 1990 in Jones, 2004). Physical abuse was also the cause of all Black fraternity deaths, whereas no deaths were caused by physical abuse in White fraternities, where pledges commonly died from alcohol poisoning, choking on raw food, or accidental falls from rooftops or cliffs (Jones, 2004). According to Haley (2009), Asian American fraternities exhibit a similar penchant for physical hazing.

When Asian American fraternities do get noticed, it is usually negative attention driven by highly publicized incidents of substance abuse violations, hazing, and physical abuse. Most disconcerting were the incidents of student deaths between 2003 and 2005 at San Jose State University, the University of California–Irvine, and the University of Texas at Austin, all of which were attributed to hazing, substance abuse, or violence (Rivenburg, 2005; "Three Indicted," 2006). Even members have begun to voice public criticism of this dangerous trend within their own organizations. On March 23, 2009, several members of Pi Alpha Phi, an Asian American fraternity, appeared on National Public Radio (NPR) for a news broadcast titled "Asian-American Frat Life Marred by Hazing" (Martin, 2009). During the program, an alumnus of the fraternity openly described "physical injury" and "heavy exercise to the point of exhaustion" becoming commonplace rituals in the pledging process. Brian Gee, president of Pi Alpha Phi's alumni board, also shared the following observations:

> Since I have been in a fraternity, I have seen a lot of changes. It seems there is a much more brutal mentality, where you really have to prove your masculinity by either how much you can take physically or mentally.

Gee's remarks are very telling and suggest that severe hazing rituals are closely linked to members' collective sense of masculinity. To better understand the unique context that shapes how Asian American fraternities address masculinity, the next section briefly reviews the status of Asian men in U.S. society.

Asian American Masculinities

According to the late historian Ronald Takaki (1989), the first significant wave of Asian immigrants was brought to the United States as cheap labor to fill the void after African Americans had been freed from slavery. Since their arrival, at various times in history, exclusionary immigration policies and antimiscegenation laws have prohibited Asian men from gaining citizenship, marrying, or even bringing their wives to the United States—an injustice to which even Black slaves had not been subjected (Cheng, 1999). According to Takaki (1989), a sense of masculinity was stripped from these men because they could no longer reproduce or form nuclear families.

Scholars have also argued that the media further emasculated Asian American men on a broader normative scale through recurrent portrayals of them as being cheap, misogynistic, effeminate, or asexual (Mok, 1998; Shek, 2006). Films as early as the 1920s began promoting the stereotype of the

"Yellow Peril," which portrayed Asian men as devious and sinister (Mok, 1998). Widely viewed images, such as the bucktoothed Asian man from the movie *Breakfast at Tiffany's* (Mr. Yunioshi, played by Mickey Rooney), tend to characterize Asian men as nerds who are both physically and socially inferior to their White counterparts. According to Cheng (1999), such portrayals of Asian men through American cinema, fashion, and advertising are essentially powerful and sophisticated forms of modern-day racism. Over time, American film and television roles for Asian men have become more varied, but Mok (1998) claims that, far too often, they are still portrayed one-dimensionally in paradoxical ways as being either sexless or sexually deviant creatures.

The negative stereotypes of Asian American men yield harmful effects. In one study, for example, Cheng (1996) found that, in spite of having higher qualifications than their college classmates, Asian American men were the least likely to be chosen for leadership positions across all racial and gender groups. Asian American men also report a significantly higher awareness of racism than their female counterparts, and some attribute this to a form of racism toward Asian Americans that has historically targeted men (Kohatsu as cited in Shek, 2006). Although stereotypes of Asian women as exotic and hypersexual, for example, are contemptible, Mok (1998) maintains that those images have not increased social distance among Asian American women and other groups or obstructed their opportunities to rise to prominent or desirable positions in the public eye. In contrast, some studies have found that the pervasive negative stereotypes of Asian American men contribute to a preference for White male partners even among some Asian American women (Chua & Fujino, 1999; Mok, 1998).

These pervasive and negative stereotypes, in part, shape the context within which members of Asian American fraternities develop a collective sense of masculinity. Liu (2002) maintains that Asian American men may reluctantly adopt aggressive behavior as a strategy to negotiate and endure racism in order to gain patriarchal privilege, and Jones (2004) claims that marginalized men seek out alternative means to prove their manhood, because they have been denied political and social means for achieving masculinity. Indeed, drawing from the findings of his 1998 quantitative study, Chan concluded that Asian American men tend to have an extremely conflicted sense of their masculinity, because they must simultaneously accept and reject the dominant White masculine norm in search of alternative definitions of masculinity.

A Gender Social Representation Framework

To guide our study, we draw from theories of gender social representation, which illuminate how power and privilege can affect the ways that Asian American men choose to negotiate and construct their own sense of masculinity. In this framework, gender is believed to be socially constructed through stereotypes or characteristics widely agreed upon by society as typical of either men or women (Courtenay, 2000). Although men are often privileged in society, according to Kumashiro (1999), the intersection between racial and gender identities can supersede any one representation. These intersected racial and gender stereotypes can lead to new and unique forms of oppression, as in the case for Asian American men. At the same time, Gerson and Peiss (1985) state that gender is "a set of socially constructed relationships," and it can be "produced and reproduced through people's actions" (p. 327). Thus, gender "is better understood as a verb than as a noun" (Courtenay, 2000, p. 1387), because, unlike biological sex differences, gender is not intrinsic within oneself, but instead is demonstrated or achieved through social interactions and relationships (Bohan, 1993) and can function to create and uphold unequal power relations.

The basic premise of social representation theory implies that, despite emasculating racial stereotypes, Asian American men can actively shape their own sense of masculinity. Chua and Fujino (1999) claim that Asian American men possess some agency in negotiating and reproducing dominant masculine norms, which "refers not only to the power men have over women, but also the way some men have power over other men" (p. 393). This agency, however, may be somewhat limited. In his study, Kumashiro (1999) found that "feminine" stereotypes of Asian American men often forced them to reject their Asian racial identity in order to conform to dominant male norms. Alternatively, Chua and Fujino (1999) suggest that some Asian American men in college have been able to negotiate new and expanded notions of nondominant masculinity that are not viewed in opposition to femininity or racial identity. They also found that masculinity was considered a more important component of self-concept for White men than for Asian American men, as White men had much more negative perceptions of reverse gender roles, such as doing domestic work.

Guided by this social representation framework, we examined the unique challenges faced by heterosexual Asian American male undergraduates as they develop their sense of masculinity. Specifically, this study investigates if and how membership in an Asian American fraternity mediates an undergraduate's sense of masculinity.

Methods

In this study, we employed a phenomenological approach, which focuses on understanding the "lived experiences" of the participants involved in the study (Denzin & Lincoln, 2000) and provides full, detailed descriptions of the phenomenon under study (Miles & Huberman, 1994). We sought to add to the scarce knowledge concerning how Asian American men negotiate their own sense of masculinity. In doing this, we focused on the unique context of Asian American fraternities. Because of page restrictions, we will only briefly overview our methods here, but can provide a more detailed explanation upon request.

We interviewed 31 undergraduate Asian American fraternity members in 6 focus groups consisting of 4–6 participants each. We screened prospective participants in order to select a sample of students with variability in terms of years of fraternity involvement and ethnic background. The resulting sample included 4 freshmen (13%), 9 sophomores (29%), 7 juniors (22%), 7 seniors (22%), and 4 students in their fifth or greater year of college (13%). The ethnic makeup of the sample was somewhat skewed, with 21 participants identifying as Chinese (68%). The rest of the sample consisted of 5 Vietnamese (16%), 2 Koreans (6.5%), 2 Filipinos (6.5%), and 1 Japanese student (3%). Four of these students, or 13% of the sample, identified as multiethnic or multiracial. Individual participants were recruited from four chapters of two distinct long-standing Asian American fraternal organizations, which were located at three different public universities in California. The focus group interviews were guided by a semi-structured interview protocol, which addressed the following broad thematic areas: (1) The extent to which fraternity members recognize stereotypes about Asian American men, and (2) whether and how participation in a fraternity mediates members' sense of masculinity and other forms of development, both social and academic. This semi-structured technique allowed us to respond to the situation at hand, while also increasing our understanding of the phenomenon in question (Maxwell, 2005; Merriam, 1998).

Findings

Through systematic analyses of the interview data, several themes emerged related to the general purpose of the study. Although it was difficult to separate the overlapping effects of race and gender, given the purposes of this study, we focused the analyses only on the themes that related broadly to masculinity.

Recognition of Stereotypes

All of the participants in our study demonstrated an acute awareness of the demeaning stereotypes of Asian American men as being nerdy, socially awkward, and physically inadequate. As one fraternity member articulated, some of the most common stereotypes of Asian American men are that they are "good at math, smart, someone to cheat off of, or plays computer games and video games all the time." Another participant referenced the expression *F.O.B.*, or "fresh off the boat," as a term that is often used to characterize Asian men. He added that this stereotype contributes to Asian American men's lack of social acceptance, because they are widely held as being "foreign" or "un-American." Others also recognized that these stereotypes have had a negative impact by compelling people to treat Asian men with "disrespect." As one participant put it, "Like, I've met racist people, and I've seen White people walk all over other Asian people, but I definitely think that's part of the Asian male image, I guess."

Participants also commonly recognized stereotype differences between Asian American men and women. As one member noted:

> I think, like, Asian males get more of a negative connotation than Asian females. 'Cause, I mean, if you refer to Asian girls, usually the stereotype is they're intelligent or attractive or something, but if you talk about an Asian guy, he's just like some F.O.B. or he's just some nerd.

According to some participants, stereotypes that promote the "exotification" of Asian American women were highly problematic, but they also added that these stereotypes tended to present more attractive and socially acceptable images than the often unappealing or threatening images of Asian American men. Similarly, Chua and Fujino (1999) found that women in general, including Asian Americans, tend to think of Asian American men as generally less attractive than White men. Previous research by Mok (1998) on the effects of stereotypical media images also shows that Asian women are generally viewed as being more desirable and are subsequently more likely than Asian men to be accepted into American society. In effect, study participants appear to recognize that when stereotypes intersect both gender and race they advance unique forms of oppression, as suggested by Kumashiro (1999).

Whereas negative stereotypes appear to affect the ways that others uniquely perceive Asian American men, stereotypes also shaped Asian American men's sense of belonging and the ways they viewed themselves. As one student explained:

When I was younger, there were a lot of stereotypes of Asian people. You feel the perception, like you can feel it right away when you're there. You feel like you don't belong. You don't fit in.

Many participants spoke about having internalized the negative stereotypes about Asian American men while growing up, which they believe adversely affected their self-confidence. For example, several participants described themselves as having been shy, unconfident, and somewhat socially awkward before they joined their fraternity. These men noted that, before finding their current peer support structure, they lacked opportunities to address their low self-image and to improve upon their leadership and social skills. Some also acknowledged now being viewed by peers in a slightly different way, as a result of their fraternity membership: "As a fraternity we're all Asians, so they think groups of Asians are all like gang members, but then, like, I guess when society looks at one Asian person, I guess we're geeky."

Few Alternatives for Meaningful Engagement

The study participants cited a multitude of reasons for joining an Asian American fraternity, but one common thread was a feeling of isolation or neglect. Several participants described feeling disengaged when they first entered college. As one study participant explained, "I wanted to be more involved, and I lived off campus for my first year, so it was kind of hard." Another participant reported feeling severe isolation after he first arrived on campus:

I was pretty depressed. I hated this place. I'm pretty sure if I didn't do it, like if I didn't meet them, I probably would have moved back home. They just kinda gave us something, like a family away from home, you know. Like you get a sense of belonging.

Even those who did not feel as isolated and were relatively satisfied with college complained that except for members of Asian American fraternities no other students or staff on campus actively reached out to them. One participant noted that fraternity members had made a strong positive impression on him when they assisted new students and their parents on "move-in day," whereas another participant claimed that "every day during the fall, they called us up."

Not only did members of Asian American fraternities actively recruit students, but many who eventually joined noted few other options for campus engagement. Some indicated that many of their Asian American male friends and roommates outside of the fraternity were disengaged from campus life because there were so few social options for them. For example, one fraternity member shared:

> I decided to commit myself to something, and honestly, like one of the reasons I decided to do [fraternity name] was because my roommates don't do anything. They have their own group of friends. They're actually really close, but all they do is just play video games and just smoke pot all day.

Many participants admitted that if it had not been for their fraternity involvement, they probably would have ended up much like their friends, who spent the bulk of their time hanging out in their room, doing "nothing" worthwhile. Perhaps those friends were not taking the initiative to identify extramural pursuits. However, nearly all participants described feeling overlooked and unsupported when they did take an initiative, which likely contributed to their strong sense of disengagement from campus life prior to joining their fraternity. One participant aptly stated, "I don't think the campus even knows or cares about us," and another confirmed, "Yeah. We pretty much get ignored." The consensus among participants was that their universities frequently ignored the unique struggles of Asian American men, and this conclusion subsequently led to the perception that their campuses did not care about their existence.

Why not join the many other student clubs, athletic teams, or even mainstream Greek-letter organizations that exist on campus? Many did not do so because those options did not adequately address their multiple needs. As one member said:

> I feel like a lot of times sports teams can kinda be the same. They get you to all work together. If you don't have a sense of belonging, you can join a sports team. It's a group of people trying to strive for a common goal. The difference between a sports team and a fraternity is a sports team a lot of times is determined on your ability to do that specific sport . . . versus an Asian fraternity is not based on, like, a physical performance. It's not dependent on your size and stuff. It's more on your will to do something. Anyone can join.

Likewise, other campus clubs were not structured to provide the deeper friendships and higher levels of commitment sought by many of these men. As for the mainstream Greek-letter system, participants discussed how it remained relatively exclusive by race on their campuses, whereas the Asian

American fraternities devoted countless hours toward recruiting Asian American men. Their approach to membership was distinctively different from the mainstream Greek organizations', because those fraternities, being well established and drawing from a larger pool of White students, could simply attract new members with little if any effort. Because Asian American men had few satisfactory alternatives for addressing their needs, Asian American fraternities came to hold a very unique role in developing both their gender and racial identities.

Addressing the Unmet Needs of Asian American Men

Another major theme that emerged from the data concerns the broad purpose of Asian American fraternities, which many participants stated is first and foremost to provide a service to Asian American men by helping them cultivate friendships, philanthropy, and the awareness of Asian American issues. For instance, when selecting new members, several fraternity members said they purposefully sought out unassuming and socially awkward individuals, who stood to benefit most from the leadership opportunities and social networks that their fraternities had to offer. One fraternity member explained it this way:

> I know about what this fraternity provides. Which one of these guys can we actually really help? Which one of these guys can we make a difference to? No offense to them, but you see a square kinda kid walking around. Talking to him, you're like, this guy has the potential to be something more and better, and those are the kinda people I look for.

Thus, although it was not the official purpose of the organizations to serve Asian American men who could benefit from the unique social structure of their fraternity, this was widely understood as one of the objectives of the fraternity. One member discussed this unspoken rule:

> It's just, like, unwritten, you know. I don't think anyone ever said it, but it's in everyone's mind. Members of the fraternity know what it represents, how it helped us. No one ever said this to me. I just understood that that's what it is, you know, how we can utilize this fraternity to help people.

Unlike the perception of mainstream fraternities as elite and exclusive, Asian American fraternities aim to provide an accessible and supportive environment for men with particular needs that are unmet by other campus activities. This function clearly speaks to the significance of Asian American fraternal organizations in the lives of these men.

Participants described how membership has had a positive effect on their level of self-confidence and their capacity to navigate their social and academic environments. As one participant declared, "I'm more able to find what I need, because I used to be a pretty shy person, but I'm more able to approach professors and stuff now." The participants attributed this positive change in their social and academic self-confidence to long-term membership in the fraternity, as well as to the pledging process. One member described a healthy change in his sense of well-being resulting from the initiation activities: "You finally achieve, like, that sense of, like, peace, like you can't explain it, but you just have to go through it yourself." Other members reported that the pledging process helped them "become a better man," "gives you this confidence," and enabled them to realize their hidden potential after overcoming some of their own physical and psychological limitations. As one participant said:

> I know for me, part of the reason I did it was to prove to myself I could. Like, I don't know if it's masculinity, but I mean, like, it's like getting past that stereotype, to be more than just the stereotypical nerdy Asian.

Indeed, many participants pointed to the restrictive nature of Asian male stereotypes in limiting their potential prior to joining the fraternity. Those stereotypes discussed earlier appear to have severely affected how these men chose and performed social representations of gender and race. For example, one fraternity member provided his personal reasons for engaging in such an emotionally and physically demanding pledging process:

> If you're known to be good at academics, and you prove yourself in another way, either physically, emotionally, or mentally, of course it feels better than doing what everybody else expects you to do. I feel good doing good on a test, but I feel great by accomplishing so much physically and emotionally on top of that.

In addition to gains in overall self-confidence and well-being, participants reported that fraternity involvement also enhanced their leadership and their social networking skills. They discussed how the responsibilities of managing an organization provided them with meaningful opportunities to practice and develop leadership capacity. They also indicated vast improvements in their social skills, attributed to the sheer numbers of people they came in contact with through various fraternity events. Opportunities to develop their leadership capacity and social competence were especially salient for these men, because those experiences provided them with alternative forms of expression that extended beyond the negative stereotypes that diminished their sense of masculinity. In short, membership has its privileges, and in this case, it enabled these young men to embrace both their racial and gender identities. This unique context for developing their sense of masculinity, however, has its share of shortcomings.

Overcompensation Through Hypermasculinity

The pervasive stereotypes also appear to have another distinct impact on masculinity within the context of fraternity membership. Although the participants refrained from disclosing details about their new-member initiation process, many described the process in general terms as being physically demanding and at times violently abusive. That hazing occurs during the pledging process for Asian American fraternities is widely known within university circles. Several members admitted to having knowingly engaged in the hazing process, despite having some initial reservations. One member related the following:

> Yeah, I did hear about hazing. Like, I heard it was pretty much the hardest hazing fraternity on campus. So, like, I heard about it, so you have to, like, think about it, but it didn't stop me.

Participants acknowledged that reports of hazing and physical abuse had negative consequences in terms of their organization's reputation within the university community and also among their friends and family back home. Many participants also noted that the severe hazing contributed to them being viewed as gangsters by their friends outside the fraternity. As one member described:

> I'm pretty sure, like, everything I got out of them was all negative. They all were pretty much, like, scared for me. Almost like, "Don't do it, man." You know, all they hear about are bad rumors, so then they're like, "Oh yeah, so you guys are like a gang and stuff, huh?"

Another fraternity member explained why Asian American fraternities adopt such severe physically oriented rituals and processes:

> I think for White people, I think it's more about the name and a sense of fun. I feel like we're tougher because of pride. We're proud to be in this Asian fraternity. We're also kind of representing the Asian community, so

seeing it racially that's why there's so much more hazing, because when we cross, what we want to represent is, like, "We are Asians, and we are tough." You know, we're able to do this because we feel like we are representing more than just, like, our specific house, but, like, the Asian community of men.

Although participants offered competing explanations for the severe physical and sometimes violent nature of the pledging process, Asian male stereotypes were regularly cited as motivating factors for engaging in hazing:

I live with a lot of White people back in my dorm, and there's definitely that "You're Asian. You're weak," whatever crap you get. Like, definitely being in a fraternity, it kind of goes to show a point. Like, they kind of respect you more. Like, they don't think less of you as a man.

Although members might suffer from a negative public perception for participating in an organization that is physically abusive, this perception ironically enhances their sense of masculinity. That is, these men may well be resisting effeminate and emasculating stereotypes by engaging in hypermasculine behaviors. The previous comment suggests that the severe physical abuse endured by fraternity members enables them to challenge long-standing negative representations of Asian males as socially and physically inferior. However, the irony is that by engaging in abuse, they effectively reinforce another set of equally problematic stereotypes of Asian American males as violent and threatening.

Likewise, in expressing their masculinity, many of the participants admitted to spending a considerable amount of time and energy throwing parties, smoking, binge drinking, and objectifying women. As expressed by one participant, "Of course there is the stereotype of all fraternity people in general of being perhaps cocky or, like, always trying to get with girls." However, by engaging in such behaviors, they not only expand their opportunities to interact more frequently with women, but also perceive themselves as being more fun-loving and attractive than the stereotypical Asian man. As one fraternity member put it:

A lot of times, like, girls are just kind of like, "He knows how to have fun. He's able to have humor. He's able to have a lot of friends. He's just a very likeable person." At the same time, some people say, "Oh, he's going to be a player 'cause I'm sure he meets a lot of women."

Some participants seemed to recognize the shortcomings of having their organization viewed as being hypermasculine, admitting that their reputation for drinking and hazing made it much "harder to attract, like, the right type of people."

Discussion

To appreciate what Asian American interest fraternities mean to members and their development, one must recognize the unique impact demeaning stereotypes popularized through the media have had on Asian American men's sense of masculinity. We found that Asian American fraternity members were acutely aware of, and sensitive to, those popular social representations of Asian men. For many, their lives prior to joining a fraternity had been constrained by the norms that shaped those stereotypes. Participants in the study reported on how those norms and expectations negatively affected their sense of masculinity and limited their range of social expression. However, consistent with social representation theory, participants adopted a different set of norms through fraternity membership, which provided them with a stronger sense of agency to resist the negative stereotypes and to expand their potential. Accordingly, participation in these organizations enables Asian American undergraduates to develop in ways that embrace both their racial and gender identities, rather than having to minimize one identity in order to embrace the other. In this way, these organizations fulfilled unmet needs of participants by providing one of the few platforms and support structures for them to resist the dominant norms that confined their sense of self and range of social expression, especially with respect to masculinity.

However, the results of this study also indicate that Asian American fraternity members collectively resist emasculating stereotypes through hypermasculinity, evidenced by extreme social behaviors, such as participation in hazing, binge drinking, and the objectification of women. These findings are consistent with previous research (Jones, 2004; Liu, 2002) that suggests that the marginalized status of Asian American men may lead some to overcompensate and seek out more extreme ways to express their masculinity. Because of this, fraternity members often participated and consented to being hazed as a rite of passage to validate their masculinity in light of the long-standing demeaning social representations. However, it would be somewhat misleading to say that these Asian American men are complicit with all hegemonic forms of masculinity. Contrary to Chan's (1999) argument that fraternity members "[strive] to be as mainstream as possible," we found evidence of extreme physical, sometimes violent, behavior, which is relatively uncharacteristic of mainstream predominantly White fraternities (Haley, 2009; Jones, 2004). These opposing strategies of acquiescence and defiance of dominant norms embodied the dual and conflicting identities of Asian American men shaped by the contradictory stereotypical position of these men in society (Chua & Fujino, 1999).

Conclusion and Implications

Although joining an Asian American fraternity has mixed effects on developing undergraduates' sense of masculinity, study participants were unable to find other alternatives on campus that supported and assisted Asian male students in navigating the unique challenges related to their development. Their options will not likely improve if educators continue to ignore Asian American students and create policies, programs, and services based on the myth that they are successful and do not suffer from social disadvantages (Kawaguchi, 2003; Yeh, 2002). This study raises not only concerns about social representation in the lives of students, but also awareness about the unmet needs of Asian American students. Our hope is that educators and counselors will use the overall pattern of findings from this study to develop policies and programs that effectively support Asian American men. For instance, fraternity members commonly benefit from certain aspects of the pledging process, but this process need not include hazing. Were it not for the social pressures linked to stereotypes, these Asian men would have fewer reasons to engage in severe physical hazing. If Asian American undergraduates had more options to address those stereotypes in constructive and educationally appropriate ways, physically abusive practices would more likely give way to a healthier process of developing their sense of masculinity.

Among the four fraternity chapters in this study, two had been operating "underground" after being suspended many years prior for policy violations, in which the participants had no direct involvement. We included such chapters, who were no longer under formal university oversight, because they revealed unique patterns concerning masculinity. Without having supportive structures in place, suspending or cutting ties with minority fraternities and causing them to go "underground" is a poor solution. By doing this, the colleges effectively eliminated key guidance and support systems for those students. As it stands, Asian American interest fraternities are already relatively self-regulated and only loosely governed by undergraduates and inexperienced alumni rather than a paid staff of full-time professionals and trained educators (Haley, 2009). We agree with Walter Kimbrough, who, after conducting extensive research on ethnic fraternities, has reached the conclusion that "the institution has to play a much bigger role in those organizations than in predominantly White organizations" (Haley, 2009, para. 12). For instance, a few institutions have provided venues for students to explore and discuss issues of masculinity through mentoring programs, support groups, workshops, and courses addressing Asian American issues. By working with these fraternities rather than eliminating them, colleges stand to better support these undergraduates in the long run.

Fraternity members must also recognize that continued violence and physical abuse not only jeopardizes the existence of Asian American fraternities but also presents a real and imminent threat to the lives of young men. Despite the existence of a true headquarters, the students and alumni charged with leading these organizations must begin to use the wealth of training and resources available to them through universities and professional associations. Accordingly, Greek-affairs advisors should improve their outreach efforts and become more responsive to the unique needs of the Asian Greek-letter community, which has experienced unprecedented expansion in recent years (National APIA Panhellenic Association, 2007).

References

Bohan, J. S. (1993). Regarding gender: Essentialism, constructionism and feminist psychology. *Psychology of Women Quarterly, 17*(1), 5–21.

Chan, J. W. (1998). Contemporary Asian American men's issues. In L. R. Hiraayashi (Ed.), *Teaching Asian America: Diversity and the problem of community* (pp. 93–102). Lanham, MD: Rowman & Littlefield.

Chan, J. W. (1999). Asian American interest fraternities: Competing masculinities at play. In T. K. Nakayama (Ed.), *Asian Pacific American genders and sexualities* (pp. 65–73). Tempe: Arizona State University Press.

Chang, M. J., & DeAngelo, L. (2002). Going Greek: The effects of racial composition on White students' participation patterns. *Journal of College Student Development, 43*(6), 809–823.

Cheng, C. (1996). We choose not to compete: The merit discourse in the selection process, and Asian and Asian American men and their masculinity. In C. Cheng (Ed.), *Masculinities in organizations* (pp. 177–200). Thousand Oaks, CA: Sage.

Cheng, C. (1999). Marginalized masculinities and hegemonic masculinity: An introduction. *Journal of Men's Studies, 7*(3), 295–315.

Chua, P., & Fujino, D. C. (1999). Negotiating new Asian-American masculinities: Attitudes and gender expectations. *Journal of Men's Studies, 7*(3), 391–413.

Courtenay, W. H. (2000). Constructions of masculinity and their influence on men's well-being: A theory of gender and health. *Social Science and Medicine, 50*(10), 1385–1401.

Denzin, N., & Lincoln, Y. (2000). Introduction: The discipline and practice of qualitative research. In N. Denzin & Y. Lincoln (Eds.), *Handbook of qualitative research* (2nd ed., pp. 1–28). Thousand Oaks, CA: Sage.

Gerson, J. M., & Peiss, K. (1985). Boundaries, negotiation, consciousness: Reconceptualizing gender relations. *Social Problems, 32*(4), 317–331.

Haley, D. (2009, March 22). The new animal houses: Asian fraternities have created their own brutal hazing rituals based on physical punishment rather than alcohol abuse—with some tragic consequences. *Daily Beast.* Retrieved June 1, 2009, from http://www.thedailybeast.com/blogs-and-stories/2009-03-22/the-new-animal-house/

Harper, S. R., & Quaye, S. J. (2007). Student organizations as venues for Black identity expression and development among African American male student leaders. *Journal of College Student Development, 48*(2), 127–144.

Jones, R. L. (2004). *Black haze: Violence, sacrifice, and manhood in Black Greek-letter fraternities.* Albany: State University of New York Press.

Kawaguchi, S. (2003). Ethnic identity development and collegiate experience of Asian Pacific American students: Implications for practice. *NASPA Journal, 40*(3), 13–29.

Kimbrough, W. M. (1995). Self-assessment, participation, and value of leadership skills, activities, and experiences for Black students relative to their membership in historically Black fraternities and sororities. *The Journal of Negro Education, 64*(1), 63–67.

Kumashiro, K. K. (1999). Supplementing normalcy and otherness: Queer Asian American men reflect on stereotypes, identity, and oppression. *Qualitative Studies in Education, 5,* 491–508.

Lee, A. M. (1955). *Fraternities without brotherhood: A campus report on racial and religious prejudice.* Boston, MA: Beacon.

Liu, W. M. (2002). Exploring the lives of Asian American men: Racial identity, male role norms, gender role conflict, and prejudicial attitudes. *Psychology of Men and Masculinity, 3*(2), 107–118.

Maisel, J. M. (1990). Social fraternities and sororities are not conducive to the educational process. *NASPA Journal, 28*(1), 8–12.

Martin, M. (Host). (2009, March 23). *Asian-American frat life marred by hazing* [Radio broadcast]. Washington, DC: National Public Radio.

Maxwell, J. A. (2005). *Qualitative research design: An interactive approach* (2nd ed.). Thousand Oaks, CA: Sage.

Merriam, S. B. (1998). *Qualitative research and case study applications in edu*
San Francisco, CA: Jossey-Bass.

Miles, M. B., & Huberman, A. M. (1994). *Qualitative data analysis: An expand*
sourcebook (2nd ed.). Thousand Oaks, CA: Sage.

Mok, T. A. (1998). Getting the message: Media images and stereotypes and their
effect on Asian Americans. *Cultural Diversity and Mental Health, 4*(3), 185–202.

National APIA Panhellenic Association. (2007). *Asian Greek History.* Retrieved
November 10, 2008, from http://www.napa-online.org/Site/Pages/About/Asian
GreekHistory.php

Nuwer, H. (2004). *The hazing reader.* Bloomington: University of Indiana Press.

Nuwer, H. (1990). *Broken pledges: The deadly rite of hazing.* Atlanta, GA: Longstreet.

Pascarella, E. T., Whitt, E. J., Nora, A., Edison, M., Hagedorn, L. S., & Terenzini,
P. T. (1996). What have we learned from the first year of the national study of
student learning? *Journal of College Student Development, 37*(2), 182–192.

Pike, G. (2000). The influence of fraternity and sorority membership on students'
college experiences and cognitive development. *Research in Higher Education,
41*(1), 117–139.

Rhoads, R. (1995). Whales tales, dog piles, and beer goggles: An ethnographic case
study of fraternity life. *Anthropology & Education Quarterly, 26*(3), 306–323.

Rivenburg, R. (2005, September 6). Asian frat in spotlight after death: Police are
investigating whether a pledge's death after a football game in Irvine was due to
hazing—Lambda Phi Epsilon's latest brush with the law. *Los Angeles Times*, p. B3.

Shek, Y. L. (2006). Asian American masculinity: A review of literature. *The Journal
of Men's Studies, 14*(3), 379–391.

Sutton, E. M., & Terrell, M. C. (1997). Identifying and developing leadership
opportunities for African American men. *New Directions for Student Services, 80*,
55–64.

Takaki, R. (1989). *Strangers from a different shore: A history of Asian Americans* (Rev.
ed.). Boston, MA: Little, Brown and Company.

Three indicted in hazing death of fraternity pledge at U. of Texas at Austin (2006,
December 13). *The Chronicle of Higher Education.* Retrieved June 1, 2009, from
http://chronicle.com/article/3-Indicted-in-Hazing-Death-of/37978

Yeh, T. L. (2002). Asian American college students who are educationally at risk.
New Directions for Student Services, 97, 61–71.

4

RACIAL IDENTITY CONSTRUCTION AMONG CHINESE AMERICAN AND FILIPINO AMERICAN UNDERGRADUATES

Alina Wong

Asian American student communities are diverse, and Asian American constructions of identity are influenced by personal markers and experiences, as well as by contextual factors. As in most communities, Asian American students perform, reify, and (re)create identities for themselves. As a result of these constructions of Asian American identities, similarities and differences emerge, providing insight into the myriad ways of being Asian American. In this chapter, I discuss a qualitative study of Chinese American and Filipino American college students at two universities that examined how Chinese and Filipino American students construct, understand, and live their racial, ethnic, and cultural identities. Their experiences also provide new insight into the ways that race and racial identities are constructed.

Because Asian American students are frequently perceived as academically successful, they are understudied and underserved in higher education (Museus, 2009; Museus & Chang, 2009). Moreover, little is known about their racial and ethnic identities and experiences with racism during college. This oversight has led to cultural assumptions that *all* Asian American students share similar perspectives, experience the same levels of academic success, and share one racial identity (Chan & Wang, 1991; Chang & Kiang,

2002; Kim & Yeh, 2002; McEwen, Kodama, Alvarez, Lee, & Liang, 2002; Osajima, 1991). Furthermore, a lack of understanding of Asian American racial and ethnic identities often leaves Asian American students without adequate support or resources (Osajima, 1991, 1995). Indeed, without more knowledge of how students construct and express their racial and ethnic identities, educators may be unprepared to give students the support and attention they need—or worse, make assumptions about students' needs that could affect them negatively. This study not only illuminates how racial and ethnic identities are constructed and actualized, but also how colleges and universities can provide supportive spaces for Asian Americans as they develop confidence in their sense of self.

Only recently has more attention been given to Asian American students' racial identities, and that attention is still rather limited. Broadly, research related to Asian American racial and ethnic identities has been studied primarily through identity development models. Another approach is racial formation theory, although this has not been applied widely in education research. Very few studies have looked specifically at the impact of college experiences on students' identities. Each category represents a broad area of literature, and a detailed discussion of each approach is not possible here. I limit this discussion to those studies directly relevant to understanding the experiences of Asian American undergraduate students.

Racial Identity Development Models

Three models dominate the literature on monoracial Asian Americans: the Multi-Ethnic Identity Development Model (MEIM) (Phinney, 1992, 1996; Phinney & Alpuria, 1997), the Racial Identity Schema (Alvarez, 2002; Alvarez & Helms, 2001), and the Asian American Identity Development model (AAID) (Kim, 1981, 2001). The MEIM is a three-stage model with a progression from not thinking about racial identity, to developing a growing recognition of race, to developing confident, independent identities. Lee and Yoo (2004) and Kawaguchi (2003) found that Phinney's three-stage model accurately described the identities of their samples of Asian American college students. However, Yeh and Huang (1996) critiqued the MEIM for conceptualizing identity as a "fixed outcome" (p. 648), resulting from a unidirectional, linear process. They argued that these models were inadequate to study Asian American students, because Asian American identities were more collective and externally influenced than the psychologically grounded model allowed.

Similar to the MEIM, the racial identity schema views racial identity development as linear, although this model categorizes the progression through "statuses" (Alvarez, 2002, p. 36). Those statuses include conformity, dissonance, immersion, emersion, internalization, and integrative awareness. Students moved through a process of not thinking about their identities, feeling pressured to assimilate to dominant norms, becoming aware of racism and discrimination, developing community with Asian American peers and hostility toward others, and finally to understanding broader racial dynamics and having meaningful relationships across social and cultural groups. Racial climate played an important part in students' experiences.

Kim (2001) developed the AAID specifically to address Asian American experiences. Kim (1981, 2001) was primarily concerned with how Asian Americans developed a positive sense of self and negotiated identity conflict between their Asian heritage and American contexts. Although it has been applied to all Asian Americans, the AAID was based on Kim's (1981) dissertation, which included third-generation Japanese American women, ages 20 to 40. The AAID model outlined five sequential stages: ethnic awareness, White identification, awakening to social political consciousness, redirection to Asian American consciousness, and incorporation (see Chapter 2 of this text for a more in-depth discussion of the AAID model). These stages are similar to the progression of both the MEIM and the racial identity schema. A primary assumption of the AAID model was that Asian Americans experience identity conflict because of the prevalence of racism in the United States. Kim (2001) argued that Asian Americans internalize negative images and become hindered by racial barriers, believing in their own inferiority. She also contended that because of Asian Americans' collectivist orientation, they were unduly affected by external images and surroundings.

Racial Formation Theory

Identity development models are grounded in psychology and emphasize the internal and individual processes through which racial and ethnic identities are formed. In contrast, racial formation theory conceptualized race as a social construct dependent upon immediate social and historical contexts (Espiritu, 1992; Kibria, 1998; Lewis, 2003; Omi & Winant, 1994). Racial formation theory emphasizes the effects of dominant racial discourses on constructions of race as power shifts and struggles position groups differently.

The underlying foundation of racial formation is an understanding of race as a social construct, rather than a biological or genealogical one. Omi and Winant (1994) point to the importance of sociocultural and sociohistorical contexts, noting that constructions of race must include how members of a group understand their own racial identifications, as well as how racial identities are understood and ascribed by others. Moreover, understandings and meanings of race may change over time and between contexts. The racial category of "Asian [Pacific] American" came out of federally and state imposed homogeneity upon Asian American bodies, but was later (re)-claimed by Asian American activists who sought collective power and action. Kibria (1998) and Espiritu (1992) traced the social, cultural, political, and historical genealogy of an "Asian American" pan-ethnic identity as a uniquely "American" construction.

Historically, stereotypes of Asian Americans as "model minorities" influenced students' experiences, academically and socially. Some Asian American students consider the model minority stereotype to be a positive portrayal of Asian Americans and even felt pride in being identified as academically gifted (Lee, 1996; Teranishi, 2002). Other students felt pressured to assimilate, expressing a desire to fit in with their non-Asian peers, distancing themselves from other Asian Americans and adopting White or dominant norms (Asher, 2000; Kuo, 2001; Osajima, 1991). Still others recognized the racism behind stereotypes, resisted dominant norms, and attempted to carve a space in their schools for their racial identities as they understood and expressed them (Asher, 2000; Kuo, 2001; Lee, 1996). Finally, some students, primarily Southeast Asian American, had to contend with both the model minority stereotype and assumptions of delinquency and gang membership (Lee, 1996; Lei, 2003).

Role of College in Asian American Students' Racial Identity

Although many of the previously discussed studies included Asian American college students as participants, there are only a few studies that examined directly how college experiences impacted students' racial identities (Inkelas, 2004; Kibria, 2002; Sears, Fu, Henry, & Bui, 2003). Sears et al. (2003) found that students' identities did not change during college and that, for the most part, college did not affect students' attitudes, awareness, and self-definitions. However, Sears et al. also noted that, at the end of college, eth were linked to political attitudes, suggesting that some occurred in students of color during college.

Kibria (2002) and Inkelas (2004) examined the role of student organizations in students' racial identities and awareness. In both studies, the presence of other Asian American students and organizations prompted students to explore their racial and ethnic identities. However, many students resisted the expectation that Asian American students should interact exclusively with other Asian American peers or that not participating in ethnic organizations was indicative of a lack of cultural awareness (Kibria, 2002). Inkelas found that almost half of students felt they developed strong Asian American awareness and understanding through participation in ethnic clubs, and participation was strongly correlated with ethnic community commitment.

Limitations of Identity and Racial Formation Perspectives

Existing identity development models do not adequately capture the complex and dynamic nature of Asian American identities. The MEIM, racial identity schema, and AAID models treated identity as a product, achieved at the end of a linear progression of individual exploration. Although such models may offer some insight into how Asian American students develop a positive sense of self, they do not explore what their racial and ethnic identities mean to the students. That is, there is no in-depth discussion of how undergraduates understood, expressed, or constructed their identities.

Although racial formation theory allows for greater consideration of social contexts, its focus on group identities and historical processes limits the agency for creating one's own identities—both individually and collectively. Omi and Winant (1994) discussed how race has been constructed, challenged, and changed over time, particularly in regard to social movements and governmental policies. Although these are important considerations, so, too, are how students develop and hold on to their own identities, despite how they are defined by others. The current study considers both social contexts and individual processes in identity formation.

Methods

Qualitative research is inquiry that is "exploratory or descriptive" and "assumes the value of context and setting, and that searches for a deeper understanding of the participants' lived experiences of the phenomenon" (Marshall & Rossman, 1999, p. 60). Further, decolonizing methodologies (Smith, 1999) suggest that the voices and lived experiences of colonized subjects (as well as subjugated, oppressed, or marginalized peoples) need to be centered in and valued by social research. As Denzin and Lincoln (2003) note, however, researchers cannot "directly capture lived experience," and all experiences must be considered "in the social text written by the researcher" (p. 28). Thus, participants' narratives are cast through my interpretations.

Site Selection

I chose two public predominantly White universities, with important similarities and differences. California has one of the largest populations of Asian Americans in the United States and outside of Asia and is thus a critical and unique location to examine the experiences of Asian American students in the state, as well as in California state institutions. California University is located in the southern part of the state, and at the time of the interviews, its student body included 44% Asian Americans. I chose Michigan University because it has similar institutional characteristics, but is dissimilar in student racial diversity, state demographics, and geographic location. Michigan University's student body was 12% Asian American at the time the interviews were conducted. Although this is not a comparative study, I included two institutions so as to include social and geographic context in my study.

Participants

I used a purposeful sampling to select third- and fourth-year Chinese American and Filipino American students (Patton, 1990), because senior students have had more experiences with the institutional climate and culture and also have a more mature sense of self. Because the assumption that students of different Asian ethnic backgrounds have the same or similar experiences in higher education is problematic, and it is important to recognize how ethnic differences may affect students' experiences, I focused on two ethnic groups to allow for comparison of the different experiences of those groups, as well as deeper analysis of experiences within each specific ethnic group.

I chose Chinese and Filipino American students, because they are the two largest Asian American communities in the United States. According to the 2000 census, 22.6% of Asian Americans in the United States were Chinese, and 18.3% were Filipino (U.S. Census Bureau, 2002). I also wanted to capture the experiences of a Northeastern Asian ethnic group (e.g., Chinese, Japanese, Korean) and Southeast Asian ethnic group (e.g., Filipino, Hmong, Laotian). In addition, China and the Philippines have and have had different relationships with the United States. The colonial and (neo)colonial stat of the Philippines to the United States needs to be considered in understanding how Filipino Americans situate themselves and are situated in the contemporary United States.

Students were identified and contacted through ethnically affiliated student organizations (e.g., Chinese American Student Associations, Asian American Student Associations, Filipino Cultural Clubs), student affairs personnel (e.g., director of multicultural affairs, advisor to Asian American student groups), and ethnic studies and Asian American studies academic departments. I limited participants to students who self-identified as Chinese and Filipino American. Of the 20 participants included in the study, there were 8 male students (5 Filipino American and 3 Chinese American). All male students were included for gender balance. I randomly selected from female participants to complete the sample (5 Filipina American and 7 Chinese American). Interviews ranged from 40 to 120 minutes and were audio recorded and professionally transcribed. Participants were all U.S. citizens, and 5 were first-generation and 15 second-generation. Only two students at Michigan University were nonresidents, and all California University students had grown up in the state. Twenty-four majors and minors are represented, and 1 student had transferred from a community college during her second year. Of the Filipino Americans, 5 were fluent in Tagalog, 1 in Ilokano, and 2 in Spanish. Of the Chinese American students, 7 spoke Cantonese, 6 Mandarin, 1 Shanghainese, and 1 Toishan.

Data Collection: Individual Interviews

At the beginning of the interview, I asked students to complete a short demographic survey that inquires about their birthplace, generational status, language fluency, parental education and occupation, academic majors, and potential career goals. I started with questions about their families, immigration and generation status, birthplace, ethnicity, family background, and geographic context. I then transitioned to talk about their understandings of race, ethnicity, and culture, as well as their own identities. As much as possible, I attempted not to impose my own definitions and encouraged participants to speak from their own experiences and perspectives. I constructed
___ is that explored how they understood and talked about
___ ic identities, as well as the meanings they give to these
___ ed students to reflect on interactions with Asian Ameri-
___ American peers, faculty, administrators, and staff. The

* Interracial Interactions

focus of the interviews was on salient college experiences and relationships that influenced their sense of self and racial identities. I wrote a participant memo after each interview and research memos at various stages of the research process.

Data Analysis: Coding and Grounded Theory

Audio files were transcribed professionally and checked for accuracy. I then used an emic approach, following an iterative, grounded theory process in developing the research questions and emergent themes (Strauss & Corbin, 1998; Weiss, 1994). This iterative process involved reading each interview for salient themes and then working across interviews. I used thematic coding schemes to perform cross-case analysis. I used a grounded theory approach to look for how racial and ethnic identities were constructed both within and between Chinese and Filipino American ethnic groups. I chose a grounded theory approach to move away from identity development models and racial identity schemas and permit the identity construction process to independently emerge from the participants' experiences (Strauss & Corbin, 1998).

After the initial coding across cases, I used AtlasTI (a qualitative analysis software program) to organize and deepen my analysis. Specifically, I used a phenomenological approach that focuses on the "lived experiences and the ways we understand those experiences to develop a worldview" (Marshall & Rossman, 1999, p. 112). My focus was on process, examining how students recognize and talk about their racial and ethnic identities, as well as how they perceive institutional climate and culture, and interact with peers, professors, and other professionals.

Toward a Multifaceted Understanding of Racial Identity

The participants discussed their identities with sophistication. Generally, participants who were more involved with Asian American and Pacific Islander (AAPI) organizations or AAPI studies classes had more complex understandings of their identities, but they all had thought about what being Asian American, Chinese American, or Filipino American meant.

Students illuminated the ways they developed and were developing their sense of self. In some ways, identities were being constructed in the very process of the interview itself, because the opportunity to consciously think and talk about their racial identities allowed them to draw connections among their identities, experiences, and college activities. I learned that identities are not only dynamic, but are also in flux. It is a constant process of negotiation and choice, while still holding on to some core sense of self. Students' self-conceptions were constantly changing—often depending on immediate context, assumptions, comfort level, relationships, and interactions—even when they had a strong sense of their identities. What it meant, collectively and individually, to be Asian American (or Chinese and Filipino American) was a dynamic process of (re)negotiation and (re)definition.

As I expected, myriad meanings of "Asian American" emerged, particularly with the ways that students had consciously, and sometimes strategically, considered who they were as Asian Americans and how they were perceived by others. I discovered three distinct, though interrelated, understandings of being Asian American: as a political coalition, as an identity informed by shared experiences with racism, and as familial heritage and personal experiences.

Strength in Numbers: AAPI Coalition

As students described it, the AAPI political coalition included people of multiple ethnicities, cultures, generations, and locations because of U.S. immigration policy and social practices that often grouped all people of Asian descent together. Participants noted that, in other contexts, the many nationalities, ethnicities, and cultures that compose Asia are not grouped together in the same way. Interestingly, all participants recognized "Asian American" as a category and coalition, but many did not identify as Asian American or hold it as a strong identity. Being Asian American was how others saw them, and, as a result, students had to negotiate this identity that had been imposed upon them.

Both Chinese and Filipino American participants understood a pan-Asian identity as a uniquely American construction and struggled to take ownership of an imposed identity that is often used to discriminate against peoples of Asian descent. The lack of awareness of the many nationalities, ethnicities, and cultures that compose Asian America, and the resulting stereotypes, assumptions, and racism, were often cited as the basis for AAPI coalitions, communities, and, ultimately, an inclusive and broad AAPI identity. Finding agency in claiming an Asian American identity, rather than simply having one placed onto their bodies, was important for students. Mary, a senior Filipina American student at CU and anthropology major, with a minor in AAPI studies, summarized this by saying the following:

I would describe it as a category . . . imposed on a group of people by an entity in power . . . the United States government. I see it as an imposed identity, but then I'm beginning to see it as something that's empowering.

As a senior Filipino American student at MU, majoring in political science and biology, Marc felt that, although the grouping of all Asian ethnicities together was artificial, Asian Americans had forged a unique identity that grew out of a political coalition:

> [W]e've had to create sort of this hodgepodge because society here in America has kind of forced us to. [I]t takes all of us, Chinese American, Korean American, Japanese American, Filipino Americans . . . all in our collective, to own any sort of issue that would affect our communities even in some way. [I]f we're to do that only by ourselves, we wouldn't be able to really get so much of a voice out there.   ** strength in numbers*

Sam, a junior Chinese American student from MU, shared Marc's perspective and emphasized the importance of an AAPI community as a means to create a stronger coalition against racism, but also to support Pacific Islanders:

> I think it's really important to include Pacific Islanders, because we as Asian, Asian Americans, have, you know, considerable amount of power in our society, but Pacific Islanders alone, you know what I mean? Like they're already a very invisible community. . . . I think it's important that they're a part of a community that we can move forward. So that we can both benefit from . . . that shared struggle.

Sherry, also Chinese American, was a senior at CU, majoring in international development, with a minor in AAPI studies. Sherry noted the diversity of experiences within Asian America, and that Asian Americans were not simply grouped together but, rather, came together with purpose:

> It's just, like, you have to have the distinction that each, like, Korean American or Chinese American, is, like, totally different from each other, but as an Asian American community it's, like, you're uniting under a cause, but you're uniting under to fight for something.

For most students, being part of this AAPI coalition was important and part of being Asian American. This sense of a pan-AAPI identity initially emerged as a strategy for political power and protection, rather than as a shared identity. And, because AAPIs had been grouped together by others into a racial category, students found it empowering to claim ownership of that identity and use it toward productive means. However, not all students felt confident in claiming a pan-AAPI identity. Christopher, a senior at CU, majoring in international development and French and linguistics, was born in the Philippines and immigrated to the United States when he was one year old. Christopher had an intellectual understanding of the importance of coalition and being included in a broader community, but did not necessarily identify with or feel part of an AAPI or Asian American identity:

> I've learned that there's been solidarity movements. I feel that our struggles are similar, but I characterize Asian American more by its diversity than its unity. I think that our experience in discrimination in terms of being discriminated against has been very similar in the States. But then again, this is only an intellectual argument, because it's not something that I personally feel or have known.

Misery Loves Company: Shared Experiences of Racism

All students talked at length about the diversity of ethnicities, cultures, experiences, and perspectives, and the importance of recognizing that, despite being grouped together, Asian American was not a monolithic identity. One of their shared experiences, and frustrations, was with racialization and racism. Because students often felt racialized as Asian American without regard to their specific ethnic, cultural, or familial backgrounds, they experienced the same stereotypes and discrimination. Sam made the following remarks:

> Because, when I'm walking down the street, people don't care whether or not I'm Chinese, Cantonese, Mandarin speaking, Japanese, Korean. They're gonna look at me and think I'm Asian. [AAPIs] have a shared history of discrimination, and, you know, like lots of folks, a lot of White people [are] going to look at you and think you're Asian.

Similarly, Marc thought that, although Asian Americans first came together because they were grouped together, it was important to "create" an Asian American identity that they could own. Marc also felt that, rather than letting ethnic and cultural differences divide Asian Americans, those differences should be embraced:

> [I]t's just like we've had to create an Asian American identity. . . . I feel like what needs to be done is to . . . embrace the differences between our

cultures . . . but at the same time realize we still, because of, because of the White man, we've been put together in this group, and we have to stick this [out] together.

Daniel, a Chinese American senior at MU, furthered this by suggesting that struggle was a marker of Asian American culture. Daniel's family had a Chinese restaurant in a predominantly Black neighborhood, and he felt that racism connected all communities of color:

> Asian American culture struggles in the USA. I mean, every Asian, you know, ethnicity in the USA, in the past they, they screwed it [up for] someone coming in because, if they, like you came in and took all of our jobs. And then some Chinese came in, Japanese came in, it just goes on. So struggles . . . I mean, that's a culture.   Hmm

Another common element in participants' narratives was immigrant experiences and the related pressures to assimilate to dominant cultural norms, while maintaining connections to familial traditions and cultural practices. Angela, a junior at MU, who was born in Taiwan, and a political science and creative writing major, with a minor in AAPI studies, talked about this struggle as a common experience among Asian Americans: "Well, the way we grew up. The way we felt like we had to assimilate. The way we felt like, the struggles that we had to go through to construct our own identity."

Many students discussed their desire to preserve and practice their family and cultural traditions despite being marginalized for doing so, and food was particularly important. Eddie, a Chinese American junior at CU, who majored in political science and wanted to pursue a law career, had grown up in a predominantly Chinese American community and went to CU because it had a large Asian American student population. He thoroughly discussed his fears of leaving the campus, because he was fearful of more diverse and integrated settings, in which he would be pressured to forgo values, foods, and practices that were important to him and his family.

Interestingly, students at both MU and CU talked about feeling marginalized at their respective institutions, despite CU having a large AAPI student population. This reality suggests that numbers alone do not mitigate the prevalence and negative impact of racism. With a few exceptions, students looked for and found support in AAPI student organizations and AAPI studies courses to navigate their college campuses. These spaces became critical for students to not only explore their identities and histories, but also to develop strategies and support networks to counter both the institutional and individual forms of racism they experienced. For Dedric, a senior Filipino American student at MU, with an English major and AAPI studies minor, taking a Filipino American studies class that had a community engagement component was the first time he had really explored his heritage, despite living in a strong Filipino community in Michigan. He volunteered at a Filipino cultural center near the university and continued to do so after the class ended. Dedric felt empowered by talking with Filipino American youth about not letting stereotypes limit their identities and experiences. Dedric had not had a strong Filipino American identity prior to this course, because he had not wanted to be "lumped together" with other Asian American students because of the model minority myth. Through this class and his volunteering, he realized that there were multiple ways of being Filipino and Asian American, one of which was to work against racist stereotypes and empower youth in the community.

Tamara, a senior Chinese American student at MU, majoring in biology and international health, had also stayed away from AAPI and Chinese American student organizations, choosing to work with the Community Engagement Center instead. Tamara talked about not feeling a need to be active with the AAPI student community, yet all of her roommates were AAPI students. They had been good friends during their four years at MU, and, although they had not sought each other out because they were Asian Americans, she admitted that she did feel more comfortable with them because they shared experiences and perspectives similar to those of Asian American women.

It is important to note that, although all students grew up with an awareness of their cultural heritage, it was not until they confronted racist behavior or racial marginalization that they began to question or explore their identities. For some, this happened in elementary school, and others experienced it in college. For example, Angela had not thought about her racial identity until, while writing for the school newspaper, a hate incident occurred. She talked about how much this affected her personally and that she had had several arguments with her peers on the newspaper staff who did not see it as an act of racism. It was this experience that caused her to join the Asian American student group and become more involved with Asian American social issues.

I Am, We Are: Holding Simultaneous Identities

What surprised me about students' identities were the sophisticated ways that they held simultaneous identities, as well as multiple understandings of

race, ethnicity, and culture. They understood that *Asian America*
were used as broad racial categories and as political coalitions. *A*
time, they also considered the ways that *Asian American* was being constructed as a unique identity in the United States. As discussed, dealing with
racism and discrimination was part of that cultural experience, as well as
food, relationships with parents and extended family, and a collective worldview. However, most Filipino American students did not identify as Asian
American, although they did recognize the ways that Asian American and
AAPI coalitions were constructed to be inclusive of all ethnic and cultural
groups.

All Chinese American participants claimed both Asian American and
Chinese American identities, understanding *Asian American* as a broader
racial identity and *Chinese American* as a more specific and personal identity.
Sherry, Tanya (a junior biochemistry major at CU), and Eddie noted that,
most of the time, they identified themselves as Chinese American when
asked, but it also depended on who was asking. Tamara also identified as
both Asian American and Taiwanese American, conceiving of the latter as a
more specific descriptor of the former:

> I guess I identify with both communities, so it's not like an either-or.
> Like, I do define myself as Asian American. But I'm usually a little more,
> specifically, like, I consider myself Taiwanese American. So, I mean, I guess
> I identify with both communities.

Molly, a senior Chinese American student at CU, who majored in political
science and grew up in San Francisco, noted that it was often an unconscious
choice or reflex that led to her identifying as Asian American or Chinese
American. For Molly, group dynamics or the specificity of the question
impacted her answer:

> Yeah, yeah, it just rolls off the tongue easier, so I just say Asian American.
> But it's not like I consciously, like, think; like I don't want them to know
> I'm Chinese or anything. If I'm writing something down like on ethnicity,
> I write Chinese American. If we're in a group, and I'll say, like, if I'm
> conscious, I'll just say, like, "oh, I'm Asian American." Like, I won't say,
> like, "I'm Chinese American," because it's kind of exclusive. But I don't
> consciously think about it. It just comes out.

Leslie was a junior, majoring in psychology, with minors in education
studies and Southeast Asian studies. She had a strong Filipina American

identity, and more specifically Ilokano, where her family is from, and Pinay American, in recognition of the dominance of Tagalog in the Philippines and "Filipino" as an imposed colonial identity itself. Although she did understand the importance of coalition, she felt the experiences of Filipino Americans were distinct from those of other ethnic groups because of the colonization of the Philippines as well as differential immigration patterns, racial, ethnic, and class hierarchies. She stated the following:

> [*Asian American*] is more like an overarching, like, umbrella term, but for me, I know it doesn't apply to me. [W]hen I was growing up, like, I was, like, I'm not Asian, I'm Pacific Islander. Like, for me, it's like, 'cause like, for me, I felt like *Asian American* had this own identity. And for me, I didn't feel like I really was a part of it.

Mary asserted, "Somewhere in there I want to fit in, like, that I do have an Asian American identity, as well, but I think at the forefront of my identity is me being Filipino American."

For Rosa, a senior Asian American studies major and education minor, recognizing the colonial history of the Philippines, as well as the internal oppression of Filipinos and Filipino Americans within Asian America, was very important. Although Rosa understood the construction of Asian American as an identity, she struggled to reconcile the unique experiences of Filipino Americans within such a generalized group:

> For me, to kind of put Filipinos under there would kind of disregard what has happened in the past. And, so that's why I always advocate on Filipinos first, rather than the entire Asian American community, 'cause like, working with other APIs in this, that coalition . . . the understanding of, like, privilege and oppression is totally different. Like for me, like no, this whole thing especially of oppression that has stemmed from colonization of people, and that kind of thing, whereas other people within the Asian American category have not necessarily experienced that. . . . I do categorize Filipinos under Asian American when I see Asian American Pacific Islander, but . . . I guess to me anyways, [East Asians] fit more of the mold of an Asian American.

Many Filipino American students, mostly from CU, were also aware of a hierarchy within Asian America, which generally placed Filipino Americans and Southeast Asian Americans at the bottom of the social strata. Students often felt marginalized or excluded from Asian America because of this prejudice; indeed, Leslie and Rosa identified themselves as "brown," while

Brown vs. Yellow

describing Asian Americans as "yellow." Both Leslie and Rosa grew up in one of the oldest Filipino American communities in California and were also very involved in leadership roles in the Filipino American Students Association on campus.

Interestingly, students at MU were more likely to use Asian American and Chinese and Filipino American more interchangeably. It is possible that this finding was related to California having one of the largest and most diverse Asian American communities in the United States, particularly in Southern California, where CU is located. Students from California had more ethnically centered experiences, whereas in Michigan, pan-AAPI communities were more common because there were fewer and smaller ethnic groups. In the 2000 census, California's population included 12.3% Asian residents, whereas Michigan had 2.1% Asian residents (U.S. Census Bureau, 2002). The California city where CU is located has the second highest Asian population in the United States (10.9%), and the city where MU is located ranked tenth (1.3%).

Moreover, Chinese American students were more likely than Filipino American students to identify as Asian American or with a pan-AAPI community. The Filipino American students in this study were all actively engaged on campus and also expressed political consciousness around racism in the United States, as well as internal prejudices within Asian American communities and between Asian countries. Rosa, Christopher, Leslie, Henry, and Ruby all talked about the hiring of Filipino domestic workers in Asian countries, as well as the disparate socioeconomic statuses of Filipino Americans as compared to those of Northeast Asian American communities.

Strengthening Asian American Identities and Institutional Practices

This study sheds light on the multiple constructions of Asian American identities and communities, challenging the homogenizing discourse of racial identity politics, as well as the conceptualization of identity as a product of linear stage models. All participants had a strong sense of self, citing family practices, peer groups, cocurricular activities, and academic coursework as influential catalysts for exploring their identities. At the same time, social interactions and experiences with racism challenged how they saw themselves. Their sense of belonging in and identification as a pan-ethnic AAPI changed, often depending on how they were positioned in local, regional, and international contexts. Their dynamic and multilayered constructions of Asian American identities and communities created space for the myriad ways of being Asian American. Their narratives demonstrated the ways that identities are constantly in flux and in the process of being constructed and how these identities are internally formed through personal experiences, while being impacted by social relationships and politics.

A sense of the diversity of experiences among Asian American college students is introduced in this study, which sheds light on the multiple constructions of Asian American identities and communities, challenging the homogenizing discourse of racial identity politics and the conceptualization of identity as a product of linear stage models. Future research on Asian American students should consider not only diversity of ethnicities and cultures, but also the dynamic and complex nature of Asian American identities and communities.

Faculty and student affairs practitioners must help Asian American students appreciate the diversity of experiences and worldviews of all Asian Americans and to incorporate them into their classrooms, events, and programs. They must work diligently to dismantle the assumptions of Asian Americans, as well as other communities of color, as homogeneous and foster an inclusive climate that welcomes difference among Asian American students and with their non–Asian American peers. More opportunities for Asian American students to talk with each other across ethnic and cultural groups, as well as within ethnic and cultural groups, are needed. Moreover, where possible, faculty and staff, who can help students explore their individual identities within broader political and social contexts, should guide these efforts. Students must also be challenged and encouraged to broaden their perspectives, understanding that they will change both in how they see others and in how they see themselves. This ambiguity of identity should be embraced, and a holistic sense of being can be nurtured.

References

Alvarez, A. N. (2002). Racial identity and Asian Americans: Supports and challenges. In M. E. McEwen, C. J. Kodama, A. N. Alvarez, S. Lee, & C. T. H. Liang (Eds.), *Working with Asian American college students: New directions for student services* (No. 97, pp. 33–43). San Francisco, CA: Jossey-Bass.

Alvarez, A. N., & Helms, J. E. (2001). Racial identity and reflected appraisals as influences on Asian Americans' racial adjustment. *Cultural Diversity and Ethnic Minority Psychology, 7*(3), 217–231.

Asher, N. (2000). *Transforming multicultural knowledge: Attending to the stories of Indian American high school students' efforts to negotiate self-representation.* Paper presented at the annual meeting of the American Educational Research Association, New Orleans, LA.

Chan, S., & Wang, L. (1991). Racism and the model minority: Asian-Americans in higher education. In P. Altbach & K. Lomotey (Eds.), *The racial crisis in American higher education* (pp. 43–67). Albany: State University of New York Press.

Chang, M. J., & Kiang, P. N. (2002). New challenges in representing Asian American students in U.S. higher education. In W. A. Smith, P. G. Altbach, & K. Lomotey (Eds.), *The racial crisis in American higher education* (Rev. ed., pp. 137–158). Albany: State University of New York Press.

Denzin, N. K., & Lincoln, Y. S. (2003). *The landscape of qualitative research: Theories and issues.* Thousand Oaks, CA: Sage.

Espiritu, Y. L. (1992). *Asian American panethnicity: Bridging institutions and identities.* Philadelphia, PA: Temple University Press.

Inkelas, K. K. (2004). Does participation in ethnic cocurricular activities facilitate a sense of ethnic awareness and understanding? A study of Asian Pacific American undergraduates. *Journal of College Student Development, 45*(3), 285–302.

Kawaguchi, S. (2003). Ethnic identity development and collegiate experience of Asian Pacific American students: Implications for practice. *NASPA Journal, 30*(3), 13–28.

Kibria, N. (1998). The contested meanings of "Asian American": Racial dilemmas in the contemporary U.S. *Ethnic and Racial Studies, 21*(5), 939–958.

Kibria, N. (2002). College and notions of "Asian Americans": Second-generation Chinese Americans and Korean Americans. In P. G. Min (Ed.), *The second generation: Ethnic identity among Asian Americans* (pp. 183–208). Walnut Creek, CA: AltaMira Press.

Kim, A., & Yeh, C. J. (2002). *Stereotypes of Asian American students* (Report No. EDO-UD-02-1). New York: ERIC Clearinghouse on Urban Education. (ERIC Document Reproduction Service No. ED462510)

Kim, J. (1981). *Processes of Asian American identity development: A study of Japanese American women's perceptions of their struggle to achieve positive identities as Americans of Asian ancestry* (Unpublished doctoral dissertation). University of Massachusetts, Amherst.

Kim, J. (2001). Asian American identity development theory. In C. L. Wijeyesinghe & B. W. Jackson III (Eds.), *New perspectives on racial identity development: A theoretical and practical anthology* (pp. 67–90). New York: New York University Press.

Kuo, E. W. (2001). *Apart and a part: The development of individual and group identity of Asian American college students.* Paper presented at the annual meeting of the American Educational Research Association, Seattle, WA.

Lee, R. M., & Yoo, H. C. (2004). Structure and measurement of ethnic identity for Asian American college students. *Journal of Counseling Psychology, 51*(2), 263–269.

Lee, S. (1996). *Unraveling the "model minority" stereotype: Listening to Asian American youth.* New York: Teachers College Press.

Lei, J. L. (2003). (Un)necessary toughness: Those "loud Black girls" and those "quiet Asian boys." *Anthropology and Education Quarterly, 34*(2), 158–181.

Lewis, A. E. (2003). Everyday race-making: Navigating racial boundaries in schools. *American Behavioral Scientist, 47*(3), 283–305.

Marshall, C., & Rossman, G. B. (1999). *Designing qualitative research* (3rd ed.). Thousand Oaks, CA: Sage.

McEwen, M. K., Kodama, C. M., Alvarez, A. N., Lee, S., & Liang, C. T. H. (Eds.). (2002). *Working with Asian American college students.* San Francisco, CA: Jossey-Bass.

Museus, S. D. (2009). A critical analysis of the exclusion of Asian Americans from higher education research and discourse. In L. Zhan (Ed.), *Asian American voices: Engaging, empowering, enabling* (pp. 59–76). New York: NLN Press.

Museus, S. D., & Chang, M. J. (2009). Rising to the challenge of conducting research on AAPIs in higher education. In S. D. Museus (Ed.), *Conducting research on AAPIs in higher education: New directions for institutional research* (No. 142, pp. 95–105). San Francisco, CA: Jossey-Bass.

Omi, M., & Winant, H. (1994). *Racial formation in the United States: From the 1960s to the 1990s.* New York: Routledge.

Osajima, K. H. (1991). Breaking the silence: Race and the educational experiences of Asian American students. In M. Foster (Ed.), *Readings on equal education: Qualitative investigations into schools and schooling* (Vol. 11, pp. 115–134). New York: AMS Press.

Osajima, K. H. (1995). Racial politics and the invisibility of Asian Americans in higher education. *Educational Foundations, 9*(1), 35–53.

Patton, M. (1990). *Qualitative research & evaluation methods.* Thousand Oaks, CA: Sage.

Phinney, J. S. (1992). The multigroup ethnic identity measure: A new scale for use with diverse groups. *Journal of Adolescent Research, 7,* 175–176.

Phinney, J. S. (1996). Understanding ethnic diversity: The role of ethnic diversity. *The American Behavioral Scientist, 40*(2), 143–152.

Phinney, J., & Alpuria, L. (1997). *Ethnic identity in older adolescents from four ethnic groups.* Paper presented at the biennial meeting of the Society for Research in Child Development, Baltimore, MD. Retrieved from http://www.eric.ed.gov/

Sears, D. O., Fu, M.-Y., Henry, P. J., & Bui, K. (2003). The origins and persistence of ethnic identity among the "new immigrant" groups. *Social Psychology Quarterly, 66*(4), 419–437.

Smith, L. T. (1999). *Decolonizing methodologies: Research and indigenous peoples.* London: Zed Books.

Strauss, A., & Corbin, J. (1998). *Basics of qualitative research: Procedures and techniques for developing grounded theory* (2nd ed.). Thousand Oaks, CA: Sage.

Teranishi, R. (2002). Asian Pacific Americans and critical race theory: An examination of school racial climate. *Equity and Excellence, 35*(2), 144–154.

U.S. Census Bureau. (2002, February). *The Asian population: 2000.* Retrieved from http://www.census.gov/prod/2002pubs/c2kbr01-16.pdf

Weiss, R. (1994). *Learning from strangers: The art and method of qualitative interview studies.* New York: The Free Press.

Yeh, C., & Huang, K. (1996). The collectivistic nature of ethnic identity development among Asian-American college students. *Adolescence, 31*(123), 645–662.

5

ENGAGING ASIAN AMERICAN AND PACIFIC ISLANDER CULTURE AND IDENTITY IN GRADUATE EDUCATION

Samuel D. Museus, M. Kalehua Mueller, and Kamakana Aquino

Although Asian American and Pacific Islanders (AAPIs)[1] are often viewed as model minorities who achieve universal and unparalleled academic and occupational success (Museus, 2009, 2011a; Museus & Kiang, 2009; Suzuki, 1977, 1989, 2002), many AAPI subpopulations suffer from racial and ethnic disparities in educational attainment and socio-economic status (Chapter 1, this text). Despite the fact that several AAPI subgroups face significant racial and ethnic inequalities in postsecondary education, researchers have rendered these populations virtually invisible in higher education scholarship (Museus, 2009; Museus & Chang, 2009; Museus & Kiang, 2009). In 2009, for example, Museus conducted an analysis of five of the most widely read peer-reviewed academic journals in the field of higher education and revealed that less than 1% of the articles published in these journals in the past decade included an explicit focus on Asian Americans.[2] In the context of the current chapter, it is important to note that this review also revealed that only one out of approximately 1,500 published articles in these journals gave explicit attention to Pacific Islander populations, and no articles published in these five journals gave explicit attention to AAPI graduate students.

The invisibility of AAPIs in higher education research is problematic, especially given the growth of this population and the fact that they are among the most misunderstood groups on college and university campuses (Chapter 1, this text; Chang, 2008). Indeed, Asian Americans and Pacific Islanders are the first- and second-fastest-growing racial groups in the nation, respectively, and are enrolling in colleges and universities in rapidly increasing numbers (Chapter 1, this text). Yet, common perceptions of AAPI students are still based largely on widespread misconceptions that they are not really racial and ethnic minorities, do not face race-related challenges, and do not require resources or support (Museus & Kiang, 2009). Such misconceptions can have detrimental consequences for AAPI students in postsecondary education, because they can lead to college faculty and staff ignoring the needs of this population (see Suzuki, 2002). Given the increasing presence of AAPIs in higher education, limited existing authentic knowledge of this population, and potential negative ramifications that can result from persisting misconceptions about this group, higher education scholars have a responsibility to increase authentic understandings of AAPIs in postsecondary education (Museus, 2009; Museus & Chang, 2009).

Much of the scholarship that does exist seeks to break down model minority stereotypes and underscores the diversity within this population. And, although research that challenges problematic misconceptions is important, equally critical is literature that helps educators who aim to serve AAPI students understand how they can do so effectively. Yet, with few exceptions (e.g., Chhuon & Hudley, 2008; Kiang, 2002, 2009; Museus, 2008b; Museus, Lam, Huang, Kem, & Tan, 2012; Museus & Maramba, 2011; Museus, Maramba, Palmer, Reyes, & Bresonis, in press), empirical inquiries that help us to understand the factors that shape the success of AAPI college students are difficult to find.

To address the dearth of knowledge regarding AAPI success in higher education, the current chapter is focused on understanding how culture can inform the construction of academic and social environments that are conducive to AAPI graduate student success. In the next section, we discuss key concepts in the literature on how culture influences the success of students of color. Owing to the paucity of research on culture and AAPI student success and the dearth of literature on culture and graduate student success, we borrow heavily from the literature on culture and success among students of color in general. Then, the two graduate student coauthors discuss how traditional cultural values shape their identities and experiences in graduate education. Both sections provide important knowledge for graduate educators hoping to engage the cultures and identities of their AAPI students—whereas the literature on culture provides important knowledge for understanding how educators can engage students' cultures and identities, graduate students' voices provide important cultural knowledge that educators can focus on. Together, these two bodies of knowledge offer the context for the final section of the chapter, which focuses on discussing how higher education faculty and staff can use understandings of culture to enhance the success of AAPI graduate students. However, before moving forward, it is important to note that, although we use Native Hawaiian culture and identity as a focal example, the lessons shared herein can inform educational policies and practices relevant to other AAPI undergraduate and graduate populations as well.

Cultures of Immersion and Origin

It is difficult to deny that culture plays a powerful role in shaping the experiences of college students of color. In this section, we discuss ways in which culture influences success among students of color in college. First, we discuss and define the two main types of culture (i.e., cultures of immersion and cultures of origin) that are central to our discussion, because they mutually shape the experiences and success of students of color. Then, we discuss the evolution of research on the impact these cultures have on success among students of color, highlighting key cultural concepts in the knowledge base that are most relevant to our discussion.

Cultures of Immersion

Cultures of immersion refer to the cultures that exist on students' respective campuses, or those in which students become immersed as they enter and navigate their institutions of higher education (Kuh & Love, 2000). These cultures of immersion are deeply embedded in the history and fabric of colleges and universities. Moreover, cultures of immersion drive behavior within postsecondary institutions in profound ways, and it has been argued that they influence just about everything that happens at their respective colleges and universities (Kuh, 2001/2002). The term *cultures of immersion* encompasses both dominant campus culture and campus subcultures that exist within the culture of the larger institution.

Several scholars have defined and demarcated the components of dominant campus cultures (e.g., Kuh & Hall, 1993; Kuh & Whitt, 1988). Kuh and Whitt (1988), for example, discussed culture in the context of higher education and defined *campus cultures* as the "collective, mutually shaping patterns of norms, values, practices, beliefs, and assumptions that guide the behavior of individuals and groups in higher education and provide a frame of reference within which to interpret the meaning of events and actions" (pp. 12–13). Schein (1992), however, provides a particularly useful framework for understanding the different elements of campus culture. The framework is composed of three levels of culture that range from the most to least visible elements: artifacts, values, and assumptions. *Artifacts* constitute the most visible elements of organizational culture, and they include its history, traditions, stories, and interactions (Schein, 1992). *Values* make up the second level of organizational culture in Schein's model, and they can both be espoused and enacted. *Espoused values* are the shared beliefs that members of a particular organization consider important (Whitt, 1996), and *enacted values* constitute those values that manifest in organizational members' actions (Museus, 2007). Finally, cultural *assumptions* refer to the most implicit aspects of organizational culture, and they compose the underlying system of beliefs "that influences what people in the culture think about, how they behave, and what they value" (Whitt, 1996, p. 191).

Although most colleges and universities arguably have a dominant culture that spans the diverse environments that exist across the larger institution, it is important to note that many diverse subcultures exist within subsystems of the larger campus. A *campus subculture* is defined as "a distinct system that is developed by a subset of members of an institution and consists of specific norms, values, beliefs, and assumptions that differ from the dominant culture of the campus and guide the thought and behavior of its group members" (Museus et al., 2012, pp. 107–108). Extant research indicates that campus subcultures, such as ethnic studies programs and ethnic student organizations, can influence the success of students of color in multiple ways (Guiffrida, 2003; Harper & Quaye, 2007; Kiang, 2002, 2009; Museus, 2008b; Museus et al., 2012; Museus & Quaye, 2009). For example, Museus et al. (2012) identified three primary functions that subcultures serve for students of color at predominantly White institutions: (1) providing safe havens for those students within unwelcoming dominant campus cultures; (2) serving to foster critical connections between institutional agents and students of color; and (3) constituting spaces in which college students can integrate the academic, social, and cultural spheres of their lives.

Cultures of Origin

Cultures of origin refer to the range of cultures in which students of color were engaged prior to college (Museus et al., 2012). Like cultures of immersion, cultures of origin consist of cultural artifacts, values, and assumptions that shape the perspectives, norms, and behaviors of members of these cultures. Understanding the cultures of origin of students of color is important in efforts to comprehend their college experiences and outcomes, because these precollege cultures shape the worldviews that these students bring to higher education and the meaning-making systems that they use to make sense of and navigate the postsecondary environments in which they are immersed (Kuh & Love, 2000; Museus & Quaye, 2009).

Although researchers sometimes refer to cultures of origin without considering the complexity of this concept, it is important to note that students may originate from and navigate several cultures prior to entering higher education, including those that exist within their families, peer groups, ethnic communities, and primary and secondary schools (Museus et al., 2012). This multiplicity of cultures complicates the study of cultures of origin and how they shape the experiences and outcomes of students of color in college. Much of the small but growing body of research on the impact of culture on college students of color has begun to examine the ways in which cultures of immersion and cultures of origin interact to shape their experiences and outcomes (Dee & Daly, 2012; Gonzalez, 2003; Guiffrida, 2003, 2006; Guiffrida, Kiyama, Waterman, & Museus, 2012; Hurtado & Carter, 1997; Jayakumar, 2012; Jayakumar & Museus, 2012; Kuh & Love, 2000; Museus, 2008b, 2011b; Museus et al., 2012; Museus & Harris, 2010; Museus & Maramba, 2011; Museus & Quaye, 2009; Rendón, 1994; Rendón, Jalomo, & Nora, 2000; Tierney, 1999; Tinto, 1975, 1987, 1993), and it is this literature to which we now turn.

Cultural Frameworks for Understanding College Success

It has been more than 35 years since Tinto (1975, 1987, 1993) first proposed his student integration model to help explain undergraduate student departure. Tinto's theory of student integration is the most widely cited perspective of college student departure and is based on a set of cultural foundations from the fields of anthropology and sociology (Durkheim, 1951; Van Gennep, 1960). Specifically, Tinto (1987, 1993) posited that students must dissociate from their cultures of origin and adopt the values and norms of dominant cultures on their respective campuses in order to integrate into the academic and social subsystems of their institutions and maximize their likelihood of success in college.

Several scholars have critiqued the cultural bias inherent in the underlying cultural assumptions of Tinto's theory and its inadequacy in explaining the experiences or success of students of color (Attinasi, 1989; Rendón et al., 2000; Tierney, 1992, 1999). The problem with the underlying assumptions of Tinto's theory is that most institutions of higher education are founded on Eurocentric cultural values, assumptions, and norms, and the theory suggests that students of color, who are likely to come from cultures incongruent with those on their respective campuses, must sever ties with their cultural heritages and assimilate into the Eurocentric cultures of their campuses to succeed. Tierney (1992, 1999) asserted that the expectation for students of color to assimilate into the cultures of their institutions was a form of *cultural suicide* that places a disproportionate share of the burden of adjustment on undergraduates of color and ignores the responsibility of colleges and universities to foster success among these students. The expectation of students of color to commit cultural suicide also ignores evidence that when they are more secure in their cultural identities and maintain ties with their cultural heritages they are more likely to have more positive educational experiences and outcomes (Deyhle, 1995; Museus & Maramba, 2011; Tierney, 1992). Thus, borrowing from the work of Deyhle (1995), Tierney advocated for institutions to focus on *cultural integrity*, or institutional programs and practices that engage the cultural backgrounds and identities of students of color.

Alternative concepts and models for understanding the impact of culture on the experience and success of students of color have emerged (e.g., Guiffrida, 2006; Kuh & Love, 2000; Museus, 2011b; Museus et al., 2012; Museus & Maramba, 2011; Museus & Quaye, 2009; Rendón, 1994; Rendón et al., 2000). These perspectives suggest that students are more likely to succeed when they establish more meaningful connections to their institutions. Thus, existing research on culture and students of color indicates that students' connections to both their cultures of immersion and cultures of origin are critical to their success. In the remainder of this section, we discuss cultural concepts that can help explain how faculty and staff can construct programs, practices, and curricula that foster the connections that students of color have to both their cultures of immersion and cultures of origin: cultural (in)congruence, cultural dissonance, cultural community connections, and cultural integration.

Cultural (In)congruence and Cultural Dissonance

Higher education scholars have underscored the important role of *cultural (in)congruence* and cultural dissonance. Specifically, Kuh and Love (2000) developed a cultural perspective of minority student departure and proposed that the cultural distance between students' cultures of immersion and origin is inversely related to college success among students of color. Because Kuh and Love's perspective was not empirically grounded, Museus and Quaye (2009) analyzed their cultural perspective in conjunction with literature on racial minority student success and interviews that illuminated the voices of 30 undergraduates of color. From this analysis, Museus and Quaye developed an intercultural perspective of minority student success, and one proposition in this perspective posits that cultural incongruence is positively associated with *cultural dissonance*—the tension that students feel when they encounter cultural knowledge that is incongruent with their cultural meaning-making system—and significant amounts of cultural dissonance experienced in a particular campus environment can pressure students of color to disengage from those institutional cultures.

Many inconsistencies between cultures of immersion and origin can contribute to cultural dissonance. For example, there is some evidence that AAPI students and other students of color are more likely than their White peers to come from collectivist-oriented communities and to encounter challenges navigating competitive or individualistic campus cultures (Guiffrida, 2006; Guiffrida et al., 2012). Indeed, if students of color from collectivist traditions are consistently confronted with individualistic expectations and norms that are incongruent with those with which they are most familiar, it could cause significant tensions that lead to increased discomfort, lower levels of satisfaction, disengagement, and lower likelihood of success (Museus, 2008a; Museus & Quaye, 2009).

One reason that cultural incongruence and dissonance could be negatively related to success is that when students' cultures of immersion and origin are incongruent those undergraduates may have a difficult time maintaining strong connections to both their culture of immersion and their culture of origin. Thus, institutions of higher education can diminish students' pressure to choose to maintain connections with one of those cultures, by creating spaces, programs, and activities that permit undergraduates of color to simultaneously foster connections with their institutions and their cultural communities. In the next section, we discuss concepts that can help explain the ways that educators can rethink and (re)construct educational environments in ways that can facilitate such connections.

Cultural Community Connections and Cultural Integration

Connections to cultural communities and cultural integration are two concepts that are useful in thinking about how educators can foster stronger connections between students of color with both their culture of immersion and their culture of origin. In a forthcoming paper, Museus, Shiroma, Dizon, and Nguyen examine the different connections between students of color and their communities of origin that shape the experiences of those undergraduates, and they outline three types: motivational, epistemological, and transformational connections. *Motivational connections* refer to the motivational forces that originate from the community to facilitate students' success, such as community and family members' encouragement and pressure to succeed. *Epistemological connections* refer to connections that permit students to acquire knowledge and understanding of their cultural communities, such as students' connections to ethnic studies curriculum and courses that allow them to learn about their communities' histories and social conditions. And, *transformational connections* are those connections through which students of color engage in efforts to positively transform their cultural communities, such as community service and service-learning activities that are focused on improving the conditions of those communities.

In higher education circles, the term *integration* is most frequently associated with Tinto's concepts of academic and social integration. However, in an effort to reclaim the term *integration* and reframe it in a more productive way, scholars have introduced the concept of *cultural integration* to describe the integration of the academic and social spheres of students' lives with their cultural backgrounds (Museus, 2011b; Museus et al., 2012). They argue that college educators can move beyond cultural fragmentation (i.e., the fragmentation of students' academic, social, and cultural lives) and intentionally incorporate cultural integration into spaces, programs, practices, events, and activities that bridge the different spheres of students' lives and forge stronger connections between the students and their institutions (figure 5.1). Empirical evidence suggests that cultural integration can shape the experiences of Asian American students in positive ways, because it allows students to academically, socially, and culturally connect to their institutions and academic programs simultaneously (Museus et al., 2012). Therefore, by creating environments and activities that foster cultural community connections and cultural integration, college educators can maximize the success of their students of color.

Despite the growing body of evidence regarding the importance of culture in understanding college experiences and outcomes among students of color, research on the role of culture in the experiences of AAPI graduate students is difficult to find. In the next section, we turn to the narratives of the two Native Hawaiian graduate student authors, to illuminate the ways

FIGURE 5.1
Cultural Fragmentation and Cultural Integration

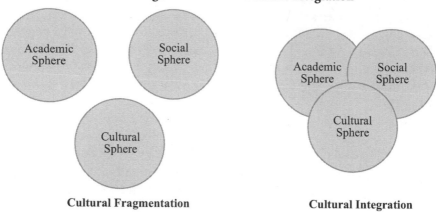

Source: Museus (2011b).

in which Hawaiian culture permeates their identities and experiences. Then, we use the concepts discussed in the current section and the experiences discussed in the following narratives to offer recommendations for higher education research and practice.

Native Hawaiian Culture and Identity

Although there is a paucity of literature on Native Hawaiian college students' experiences, the research that does exist on this population highlights the important role of culture and identity in these undergraduate Native Hawaiian students' experiences (e.g., Hokoana & Oliveira, 2012; Kupo, 2010), but cultural values and beliefs are equally relevant to Native Hawaiian graduate students. In this section, authors Kalehua Mueller and Kamakana Aquino discuss the roles of culture and identity in their experiences in graduate education.

Kalehua Mueller

I am the first child in my generation—a daughter of Japanese, Native Hawaiian, Chinese, and White parents. I come from a long line of salt farmers, fishermen, store owners, and chefs. This is important, because these ancestors shape my identity and purpose in life. My relatives, those living and deceased, have taught me the importance of family, responsibility, and working together. These three values guide and influence my experiences.

Family, or *'ohana*, is my foundation. Although my immediate family now lives outside of Hawaii, I juggle my time to meet the expectations and needs of my grandparents, many aunties and uncles, and numerous cousins. As the oldest child in my generation, I also understand that I have a specific responsibility, or *kuleana*, to my younger cousins. It is important for me to attend their various extracurricular activities, offer emotional support and relationship advice, and also be a positive role model for them. In my long educational journey through college and in starting graduate school, I have shared my successes and failures with my younger cousins, insisting they learn from my mistakes and repeat my accomplishments. Despite my obligations and responsibilities, my extended family supports me and has encouraged me to further my education in graduate school, all the while reminding me who I am and where I come from. My grandmother, in particular, always tells me that, because I have been given these educational opportunities, much is expected of me. She demands that, after I graduate, I have not only a commitment to my family, but also a responsibility to make a contribution to the community with my education and leave my own legacy for the next generation.

Beyond my relatives, I consider a close-knit group of individuals in my professional life my family. These Native Hawaiian educators and college administrators are more than just mentors. They purposely take time to *mālama*, or care for, younger educators and students like myself. They see me as their own child, or *keiki*, and they talk with me about my graduate classes, inspire my studies and research, and give sound advice as needed. Although these mentors are directors of a college access program and administrators at the community college, they believe in and are committed to a greater sense of family. As a part of their professional family, I often spend the night at their houses, am invited to important family gatherings, and even join them on family vacations. Thus, this broad and inclusive definition of family means that I have more opportunities to interact, learn from their experiences, and ultimately work together to help more Native Hawaiians.

My family, both extended and professional, has taught me the importance of service to our community through *laulima*, or cooperation. By following their example, I have learned that when people are united by a shared passion to affect and serve a community great things can happen. True cooperation is achieved, and we have collectively helped to design and implement programs to foster success for Native Hawaiian students.

It is this understanding of kuleana, commitment, and cooperation within the Native Hawaiian community that shapes my purpose and defines my passion. I look forward to fulfilling my responsibilities, as outlined for me by the previous generations, and leaving a legacy for the next generation. It is my goal to build upon what others in the community have established and use all I have learned to create even more opportunities for more Native Hawaiian students. I will have the support of not only my own biological family, but also my professional family to encourage me to develop new programs, pursue more research, and help further advocate for future generations. I am a part Hawaiian granddaughter, daughter, sister, niece, cousin, counselor, and student, and I have a family and community who are expecting great things from me.

Kamakana Aquino

ʻOhana is the Hawaiian word for family. It is my genealogy, my foundation, and my identity. Genealogy is to know, understand, and recognize from whom I descend and from where I come. I am descended from the first peoples who lived in the Hawaiian Islands more than 200 years ago. I am a product of my Hawaiian, Filipino, and Chinese ancestors. When I look into the mirror, I not only see myself, but I see my ancestors.

I am the youngest of three boys, come from a low-socioeconomic background, and currently live on Hawaiian homestead land in Waimānalo, ʻOahu. I am the first in my family to graduate from college, a huge accomplishment for me and for my ʻohana. My ʻohana is my foundation outside of the school environment and supports my journey through higher education. It is the relationship with my family that sustains my daily life. Without it, I would not have received the support needed to obtain a degree from college, nor would I be where I am today. ʻOhana is vital in Hawaiian society and to the greater Pacific family.

Within the ʻohana, there is *kuleana*, or responsibility. There is responsibility to oneself, to family, and to the community. While growing up, I was tasked with many responsibilities. For example, I was responsible for getting good grades in school and staying out of trouble. The greatest moment for any Hawaiian family is to have their child graduate from high school, and I did. After graduation, there were only two choices—getting a job or going to college. Getting a job would have been easier. However, succeeding in college is now my kuleana, because neither of my parents or brothers graduated from college. I, therefore, decided that I needed to pursue this journey of higher education for myself, my ʻohana, and my community.

There is also kuleana to my 'ohana, by helping around the house and providing financial support for the family, for food and other necessities. College is also a means of providing guidance to my family. I am able to think critically and analyze various issues and situations to better prepare or improve the well-being of my 'ohana.

And finally, there is kuleana to my community. As my brothers and I were raised, my parents and grandparents were active in the community—my parents were active within our elementary and secondary schools, and my grandparents within the neighboorhood. This is where my kuleana to the community originates, and my kuleana to my community includes being an active member in many different organizations, within both the university and the Hawaiian community. Simply giving back, or serving our community, is what we call it. Yet, it is more than that. It is also about actively pursuing the betterment of peoples' lives. My particular focus is the betterment of my Hawaiian people.

When kuleana is defined, then there is *laulima*. Laulima is the action of working together cohesively. Laulima, then, becomes a means of support through the active participation of all who seek a common goal. Because I still attend college, my family and I work together. Therefore, I am able to concentrate on my studies, and, when appropriate or needed, I tend to my family responsibilities. 'Ohana, kuleana, and laulima are three Hawaiian values that shape my identity and purpose in life. Although there are many other Hawaiian values, these are the three that I use to describe myself. They also shape my view of the world and how I interact with it.

Implications for Graduate Education Programs and Practices

If educators are equipped with knowledge of how culture shapes the experiences of college students and how specific cultural values shape the identities and experiences of students, they can begin to (re)think and (re)construct educational environments and activities to help those students flourish. The early sections of this chapter discussed literature on how culture shapes the experiences of students of color and the previous section revealed some of the core Hawaiian values that shape the experiences of two Native Hawaiian graduate students. In this section, we merge those two sets of knowledge to create and offer recommendations for educational practice, particularly for faculty who teach in graduate programs.

Foster Academic Families

The importance of considering the collectivist community orientations from which AAPI graduate students of color are likely to come and the value of 'ohana that Kalehua and Kamakana discuss in their narratives underscore the importance of family and community in understanding the experiences of AAPI graduate students. They also help us to understand how to foster meaningful connections with those students and how to bridge the divide between academic environments and cultural communities. Graduate faculty should work to foster a sense of family and community within their programs. This might involve making efforts to achieve cultural integration in the creation of academic environments and activities to allow students to simultaneously strengthen academic, social, and cultural ties with their graduate programs. If such a sense of family and community can be achieved, then AAPI students may develop their own sense of responsibility for the success of their program, their peers, and themselves.

Create Space to Develop Epistemological and Transformational Connections

To develop a sense of purpose or responsibility among their AAPI students, graduate programs should aim to foster epistemological and transformational connections. Regarding epistemological connections, graduate faculty should make concerted efforts to seek out and incorporate literature and knowledge from their AAPI students' cultural communities into their curriculum. They should also work with AAPI students to co-construct research projects and extracurricular professional development activities that focus on issues relevant to these students' communities. In regard to transformational connections, faculty should pursue research and other service projects with their AAPI students that are specifically aimed at understanding and solving problems within these students' communities. This would enable students to apply theories and topics covered in coursework to improve their communities, while further strengthening bonds between faculty advisors or mentors and their AAPI students.

Focus on Collaborative Education

In congruence with the collectivist orientations of many AAPI communities and the Hawaiian value of laulima that shapes Kalehua's and Kamakana's identities and experiences, graduate faculty can emphasize group projects and collaborative work within courses. These assignments would build on the strengths and cultural knowledge of collectivist-oriented AAPI students and help them further develop their skills in the areas of collaboration and cooperation. Although group projects are usually carried out by a handful of students within one course, faculty can broaden their conceptualization of group work and create interconnected course projects and activities that encourage students across courses to approach learning from a more holistic and cooperative perspective. For example, by creating a mock conference at the end of the semester, AAPI and other students can gain practical professional experience in proposing conference presentations, presenting their final projects and papers, and engaging in purposeful discussion with other students about research and other important higher education topics. Program requirements can also include an internship component to connect AAPI and other students with other professionals across campus to develop strong and beneficial mentoring relationships.

(Re)establish Culturally Relevant Programmatic Missions

Most, if not all, graduate programs have missions that drive the values, beliefs, assumptions, and behaviors that exist within them. However, rarely do graduate programs consistently and introspectively examine their missions and question whether they reflect the values and needs of their students' cultures of origin. If graduate faculty members consider incorporating the cultural values of the diverse communities from which their AAPI and other students come into the missions of their academic programs, it would facilitate stronger connections between their AAPI students and their programs. In the case of Native Hawaiian students, for example, faculty might consider incorporating 'ohana, kuleana, and laulima into the mission and goals of the program. If they do, they should select values that are relevant to and reflect the various cultures of origin from which their students come. For example, cooperation and working together is valued in many cultures and communities of color, and incorporating the value of laulima into the foundation of an academic program might benefit not only Native Hawaiian students, but all of those who enroll in and navigate the graduate program.

Notes

1. The term *Asian American* refers to people with origins in Asia, including Cambodia, China, India, Japan, Korea, Laos, Malaysia, Pakistan, the Philippines, Thailand, and Vietnam. The *Pacific Islander* category includes those with origins in

the Pacific, including Hawaii, Fiji, Guam, Samoa, Tahiti, Tonga, and other Pacific Islands.

2. The five journals reviewed were *Journal of College Student Development, The Journal of Higher Education, NASPA Journal, Research in Higher Education,* and *The Review of Higher Education.*

References

Attinasi, L. C., Jr. (1989). Getting in: Mexican Americans' perceptions of university attendance and the implications for freshman year persistence. *The Journal of Higher Education, 60*(3), 247–277.

Chang, M. (2008). Asian evasion: A recipe for flawed solutions. *Diverse Issues in Higher Education, 25*(7), 26.

Chhuon, V., & Hudley, C. (2008). Factors supporting Cambodian American students' successful adjustment into the university. *Journal of College Student Development, 49*(1), 15–30.

Dee, J. R., & Daly, C. J. (2012). Engaging faculty in the process of cultural change in support of diverse student populations. In S. D. Museus & U. M. Jayakumar (Eds.), *Creating campus cultures: Fostering success among racially diverse student populations* (pp. 168–188). New York: Routledge.

Deyhle, D. (1995). Navajo youth and Anglo racism: Cultural integrity and resistance. *Harvard Educational Review, 65*(3), 403–444.

Durkheim, E. (1951). *Suicide.* Glencoe, NJ: The Free Press.

Gonzalez, K. P. (2003). Campus culture and the experiences of Chicano students in a predominantly White university. *Urban Education, 37*(2), 193–218.

Guiffrida, D. A. (2003). African American student organizations as agents of social integration. *Journal of College Student Development, 44*(3), 304–319.

Guiffrida, D. A. (2006). Toward a cultural advancement of Tinto's theory. *The Review of Higher Education, 29*(4), 451–472.

Guiffrida, D. A., Kiyama, J. M., Waterman, S., & Museus, S. D. (2012). Moving from individual to collective cultures to serve students of color. In S. D. Museus & U. M. Jayakumar (Eds.), *Creating campus cultures: Fostering success among racially diverse student populations* (pp. 68–87). New York: Routledge.

Harper, S. R., & Quaye, S. J. (2007). Student organizations as venues for Black identity expression and development among African American male student leaders. *Journal of College Student Development, 48*(2), 127–144.

Hokoana, L. K., & Oliveira, J. K. (2012). Factors related to Native Hawaiian student success in college. In D. Ching & A. Agbayani (Eds.), *Asian Americans and Pacific Islanders in higher education: Research and perspectives on identity, leadership, and success* (pp. 195–212). Washington, DC: National Association of Student Personnel Administrators.

Hurtado, S., & Carter, D. (1997). Effects of college transition and perceptions of the campus racial climate on Latino college students' sense of belonging. *Sociology of Education, 70*(4), 324–345.

Jayakumar, U. M. (2012). Social praxis in shaping supportive cultures and traditionally White institutions. In S. D. Museus & U. M. Jayakumar (Eds.), *Creating campus cultures: Fostering success among racially diverse student populations* (pp. 130–149). New York: Routledge.

Jayakumar, U. M., & Museus, S. D. (2012). Mapping the intersection of campus cultures and equitable outcomes among racially diverse student populations. In S. D. Museus & U. M. Jayakumar (Eds.), *Creating campus cultures: Fostering success among racially diverse student populations* (pp. 1–27). New York: Routledge.

Kiang, P. N. (2002). Stories and structures of persistence: Ethnographic learning through research and practice in Asian American Studies. In Y. Zou & H. T. Trueba (Eds.), *Advances in ethnographic research: From our theoretical and methodological roots to post-modern critical ethnography* (pp. 223–255). Lanham, MD: Rowman & Littlefield.

Kiang, P. N. (2009). A thematic analysis of persistence and long-term educational engagement with Southeast Asian American college students. In L. Zhan (Ed.), *Asian American voices: Engaging, empowering, enabling* (pp. 21–58). New York: NLN Press.

Kuh, G. D. (2001/2002). Organizational culture and student persistence: Prospects and puzzles. *Journal of College Student Retention: Research, Theory & Practice, 3*(1), 23–39.

Kuh, G. D., & Hall, J. E. (1993). Using cultural perspectives in student affairs. In G. D. Kuh (Ed.), *Cultural perspectives in student affairs work* (pp. 1–20). Lanham, MD: American College Personnel Association.

Kuh, G. D., & Love, P. G. (2000). A cultural perspective on student departure. In J. M. Braxton (Ed.), *Reworking the student departure puzzle* (pp. 196–212). Nashville, TN: Vanderbilt University Press.

Kuh, G. D., & Whitt, E. J. (1988). The invisible tapestry: Culture in American colleges and universities. *ASHE-ERIC Higher Education Report, 17*(1). Washington, DC: Association for the Study of Higher Education.

Kupo, V. L. (2010). *What is Hawaiian? Explorations and understandings of Native Hawaiian college women's identities* (Doctoral dissertation) Bowling Green University, Bowling Green, OH.

Museus, S. D. (2007). Using qualitative methods to assess diverse campus cultures. In S. R. Harper & S. D. Museus (Eds.), *Using qualitative methods in institutional assessment: New directions for institutional research* (No. 136). San Francisco, CA: Jossey-Bass.

Museus, S. D. (2008a). Focusing on institutional fabric: Using campus culture assessments to enhance cross-cultural engagement. In S. R. Harper (Ed.), *Creating inclusive environments for cross-cultural learning and engagement in higher education* (pp. 205–234). Washington, DC: National Association of Student Personnel Administrators.

Museus, S. D. (2008b). The role of ethnic student organizations in fostering African American and Asian American students' cultural adjustment and membership at predominantly White institutions. *Journal of College Student Development, 49*(6), 568–586.

Museus, S. D. (2009). A critical analysis of the exclusion of Asian Americans from higher education research and discourse. In L. Zhan (Ed.), *Asian American voices: Engaging, empowering, enabling* (pp. 59–76). New York: NLN Press.

Museus, S. D. (2011a). Mixing quantitative national survey data and qualitative interview data to understand college access and equity: An examination of first-generation Asian Americans and Pacific Islanders. In K. A. Griffin & S. D. Museus (Eds.), *Using mixed-methods approaches to study intersectionality in higher education: New directions for institutional research* (pp. 63–75). San Francisco, CA: Jossey-Bass.

Museus, S. D. (2011b). Using cultural perspectives to understand the role of ethnic student organizations in Black students' progress to the end of the pipeline. In D. E. Evensen & C. D. Pratt (Eds.), *The end of the pipeline: A journey of recognition for African Americans entering the legal profession* (pp. 162–172). Durham, NC: Carolina Academic Press.

Museus, S. D., & Chang, M. J. (2009). Rising to the challenge of conducting research on Asian Americans in higher education. In S. D. Museus (Ed.), *Conducting research on Asian Americans in higher education: New directions for institutional research* (No. 142, pp. 95–105). San Francisco, CA: Jossey-Bass.

Museus, S. D., & Harris, F. (2010). The elements of institutional culture and minority college student success. In T. E. Dancy, II (Ed.), *Managing diversity: (Re)visioning equity on college campuses* (pp. 25–44). New York: Peter Lang.

Museus, S. D., & Kiang, P. N. (2009). The model minority myth and how it contributes to the invisible minority reality in higher education research. In S. D. Museus (Ed.), *Conducting research on Asian Americans in higher education: New directions for institutional research* (No. 142, pp. 5–15). San Francisco, CA: Jossey-Bass.

Museus, S. D., Lam, S., Huang, C., Kem, P., & Tan, K. (2012). Cultural integration in campus subcultures: Where the cultural, academic, and social spheres of college life collide. In S. D. Museus & U. M. Jayakumar (Eds.), *Creating campus cultures: Fostering success among racially diverse student populations* (pp. 106–129). New York: Routledge.

Museus, S. D., & Maramba, D. C. (2011). The impact of culture on Filipino American students' sense of belonging. *The Review of Higher Education, 34*(2), 231–258.

Museus, S. D., Maramba, D. C., Palmer, R. T., Reyes, A., & Bresonis, K. (in press). An explanatory model of Southeast Asian American college student success: A grounded theory analysis. In R. Endo & Xue Lan Rong (Eds.), *Asian American educational achievement, schooling, and identities.* Charlotte, NC: Information Age.

Museus, S. D., & Quaye, S. J. (2009). Toward an intercultural perspective of racial and ethnic minority college student persistence. *The Review of Higher Education, 33*(1), 67–94.

Museus, S. D., Shiroma, K., Dizon, J. P. M., & Nguyen, P. C. (Forthcoming). *Understanding community cultural connections and their impact on college success.* Paper presented at the 2013 Annual Meeting of the American Educational Research Association, San Francisco, CA.

Rendón, L. I. (1994). Validating culturally diverse students: Toward a new model of learning and student development. *Innovative Higher Education, 19*(1), 33–51.

Rendón, L. I., Jalomo, R. E., & Nora, A. (2000). Theoretical considerations in the study of minority student retention in higher education. In J. Braxton (Ed.), *Reworking the student departure puzzle* (pp. 127–156). Nashville, TN: Vanderbilt University Press.

Schein, E. H. (1992). *Organizational culture and leadership* (2nd ed.). San Francisco, CA: Jossey-Bass.

Suzuki, B. H. (1977). Education and the socialization of Asian Americans: A revisionist analysis of the "model minority" thesis. *Amerasia Journal, 4*(2), 23–51.

Suzuki, B. H. (1989, November–December). Asian Americans as the "model minority": Outdoing Whites? Or media hype? *Change,* pp. 13–19.

Suzuki, B. H. (2002). Revisiting the model minority stereotype: Implications for student affairs practice and higher education. *Working with Asian American college students: New directions for student services* (No. 97, pp. 21–32). San Francisco, CA: Jossey-Bass.

Tierney, W. G. (1992). An anthropological analysis of student participation in college. *The Journal of Higher Education, 63*(6), 603–618.

Tierney, W. G. (1999). Models of minority college-going and retention: Cultural integrity versus cultural suicide. *The Journal of Negro Education, 68*(1), 80–91.

Tinto, V. (1975). Dropout from higher education: A theoretical synthesis of recent research. *Review of Educational Research, 45*(1), 89–125.

Tinto, V. (1987). *Leaving college: Rethinking the causes and cures of student attrition.* Chicago, IL: University of Chicago Press.

Tinto, V. (1993). *Leaving college: Rethinking the causes and cures of student attrition* (2nd ed.). Chicago, IL: University of Chicago Press.

Van Gennep, A. (1960). *The rites of passage* (M. B. Vizedom & G. I. Chaffee, trans.). Chicago, IL: University of Chicago Press.

Whitt, E. J. (1996). Assessing student cultures. In M. L. Upcraft & J. H. Schuh (Eds.), *Assessment in student affairs: A guide for practitioners* (pp. 189–216). San Francisco, CA: Jossey-Bass.

6

NAMING OUR IDENTITY

Diverse Understandings of Asian Americanness
and Student Development Research

*Jane E. Pizzolato, Tu-Lien Kim Nguyen,
Marc P. Johnston, and Prema Chaudhari*

I n our research, we study the relationship between cultural selfways and various college student development trajectories. Cultural selfways represent a group's socialization goals toward culturally agreed upon ways of knowing and being (Markus, Mullaly, & Kitayama, 1997). Families, neighborhoods, and schools socialize individuals toward particular and sometimes divergent cultural selfways. Bringing this notion of cultural selfways to understanding college student development seems useful in three key ways: (1) It encourages focus on (in)congruence between entering cultural selfways and those valued by the university in understanding experiences and transitions to and through college, rather than looking at student deficits; (2) because of such a focus, cultural selfways research may be more useful in identifying more effective ways of supporting a diverse student body; and (3) cultural selfways research points out the psychological pervasiveness of precollegiate socialization. This pervasiveness means that college students do not leave behind ways of thinking or being when they physically move. Because students may have a diverse collection of selfways they are trying to balance, issues regarding identity development emerge, with identification (who one claims to be) being a consequence of how the student understands and balances diverse cultural selfways.

With respect to Asian American students, cultural selfways may be particularly important for the reasons just mentioned, but also because cultural selfways research may help clarify how and why Asian American students self-identify in relation to their Asianness (e.g., Vietnamese; Filipino; Korean American; Asian Indian; Asian American; Whitewashed Asian; F.O.B., or fresh off the boat) and what these forms of identification say about both their ethnic identity and how and which contextual variables seem to most heavily impact identification, belonging, and commitment to some part of their Asian American self. At this point, however, the literature on cultural selfways is limited in that it includes both descriptive and comparative research, but across all existing literature, the selfways under investigation are tied to a sense of national or geographic culture (e.g., Korean or East Asian), rather than embedded subcultures (e.g., Korean American, Asian American).

In our first cultural selfways study, we focused on self-identifying Asian students enrolled at two American universities (Pizzolato, Chaudhari, & Nguyen, 2008). This was an exploratory qualitative study. Consequently, we wanted to recognize our own identities as Asian American researchers and the potential impact of our phenotypical characteristics and cultural identities on the data collected and analyzed. However, we encountered an obstacle. What do we call ourselves? Although we are all of Asian descent and American citizens, our ethnicities are different. We identify differently with respect to being Asian American. The diversity of our own identities and identifications mirrors that of our participants—all of whom are Asian American. Based on our work to deconstruct and delineate different Asian American experiences by ethnicity, here we present some limitations of and implications for Asian American research and development theory. But first, and in the spirit of qualitative research, we provide some information about our own identities, especially because it was our conflict over naming our Asian Americanness that started this work. Next, we present our identity sections individually, then come together in a collective voice for the remaining sections of the chapter.

Jane

When we had that first discussion about what to call ourselves, I was the one most opposed to being labeled Asian American. I was born in Seoul, South Korea, a decade before the summer olympics were held in that city in 1988. I was adopted by White American parents and immigrated to America in 1979. I grew up in a university town on the East Coast and before I came to

Jane: ★ interesting

the States my parents constructed a community of other families with adopted Korean children in which I could grow up. As a group, the other children and I grew up thinking of ourselves as adopted Korean, not Korean. Korean was always modified by the word *adopted*. Later, we began to make sense of our ethnic identities by talking about ourselves as Asian, but not "real Asians." To us, the real Asians were the Asian kids who had Asian parents. There were a fair number of these children in our schools, and we all had friends who were "real." The term *American* never entered our vocabulary in referring to the real Asians or ourselves.

Today, I believe I am Asian American to the extent that I am Asian and have spent most of my life in America. Because of my experiences and work to understand what it means to be a person of color and an Asian person in America, my politics and social views are colored by my Asian Americanness. However, because I grew up in a multiethnic and mixed-race family, and with a father quite close to the immigrant experience himself (second-generation Italian American), how I make meaning of being Asian American is mediated by my experiences around being a cross-racial adoptee. Although I have been hurt by racist actions and words from people and organizations reacting to my race, I have been more deeply affected by others' reactions to the intersection of my race and my ethnicity. I am monoracially Asian, but because I'm from a multiethnic and mixed-race family, and am a cross-racial adoptee in this family, I am not just Korean American. I am multiethnic.

Who I am is informed by growing up at the intersection of different races, ethnicities, faiths, immigrant generations, and cultural communities. Others, however, very rarely recognize this complexity. More often, people (e.g., customs officials, border patrol agents, grocery clerks, strangers) have publicly questioned how my sister and I could belong to our White family. I've been told that I'm not Asian enough, or even that being adopted means that I'm essentially White. Strangers, peers, and my own students have told me these things. And, Korean immigrant adults have routinely stopped my parents when they see us together to thank them for adopting me and to tell them they are good people for taking in a Korean child. Taken together, these experiences have encouraged me to see myself as more Asian than Asian American. I prefer to be Asian in race and multiethnic in terms of ethnicity, in order to recognize that I am Asian but I'm also an adoptee who grew up in a multiethnic family. I claim Asian American now, but I do it while clarifying that I'm multiethnic. I want people to know that Asian American comes in all forms and it's messier than it seems, and I want to reject the way that the term *Asian American* conjures up an idea of a congruent racial and ethnic identity.

Tu-Lien

In 1980, an oppressive Vietnamese government forced my parents to risk their lives and flee Southern Vietnam by boat. After an arduous journey and staying in a refugee camp for a few months, they were sponsored to relocate to the United States. As the first child of Vietnamese refugees, the experiences that I faced early on set the foundation for who I am today. Born to two Vietnamese parents and initially living with my Christian, White grandparents (my parents' sponsors) in Iowa, I was immediately faced with cultural clashes I had to adapt to. Not only were my parents trying hard to keep Vietnamese traditions and language alive, the predominantly White setting of the Midwest put me in a place where I felt like I needed to choose between Vietnamese and American cultures.

Today, I identify as Asian American. (No hyphen, as I am fully Asian and American. Not 50% Asian, 50% American.) More specifically, I identify as Southeast Asian American, perhaps even more so than Vietnamese American. I believe that the term *Southeast* distinctly separates me from the dominant East Asians who tend to be thought of when (most) people refer to Asians in everyday conversation, in research, in stereotyping. I also believe that identifying as Southeast Asian American portrays a very specific experience—one of being associated with the Vietnam War, having a refugee experience, and struggling.

I identify as Southeast Asian American more so than Vietnamese, because I strongly identify with this idea of struggle. In the research on education, it so often seems like Vietnamese are becoming more and more like the stereotypical East Asians (model minority, high academic achievement, etc.), while other Southeast Asian ethnic groups, who may or may not be as successful, are overlooked. The Vietnamese are sometimes used as the example to which other groups should emulate. There seems to be a consistent emphasis on the idea of having experienced severe hardships, but still pulling oneself up by oneself's own bootstraps, never having to deal with such hardships again, and essentially becoming the American Dream. I fully acknowledge that I probably look like those students in a number of ways, but I never forget the struggles from which I came. This mind-set has shaped my approach to researching and understanding students holistically and allowing academic space for these students' perspectives and personal ways of understanding their experiences.

My professional background working as a counselor or therapist, with all sorts of students, has allowed me to learn from and find value in what is different from the "norm" or stereotype. High-achieving East Asians have often overshadowed Southeast Asian and Pacific Islander perspectives. Because I've had the privilege of not only identifying with the underrepresented but also working with them, I've developed a great sense of pride in this idea of not being the model minority. I find great pride in this idea of "coming from nothing" and understanding the ways in which individuals become savvy to get to a place or reach a goal that they may not have had access to otherwise attain. I am fascinated by this idea of struggle and the character that it builds in college-aged students.

Marc

My Asian Americanness has changed over time and continues to change given the contexts in which I find myself. I currently identify myself as a mixed-race Pilipino American, but that has not always been the case. When I was growing up in a suburban college town in the Midwest, most White people I encountered thought I was "some sort of Latino," and other Latinos often approached me speaking Spanish. Although I had visited the Philippines with my Filipina mother when I was 11, I never really related being Filipino with being Asian. Owing to the lasting impact of Spanish colonization, I felt like a Filipino could truly be "some sort of Latino." It was not until I transferred to Michigan State University that I found out that Filipino was categorized under a massive "Asian Pacific American" conglomerate, all with corresponding student organizations. I became highly involved in the pan–Asian American umbrella group on campus, where I learned that I wasn't "Asian" but was rather *Asian American*, a term that I internalized and proudly claimed, because I did not want to fit the perpetual foreigner stereotype and subsequently be relegated to the singular "Asian" with my Asian international classmates.

From my involvement in the pan–Asian American club, I also became involved in our Filipino American association, taking on leadership roles and enrolling in Filipino American studies courses. It was in these experiences that I started identifying as Pilipino, with *P* as a sign of empowerment and to make a political statement against Spanish colonization and the imposition of the *F* into "our" indigenous Filipino language. I also started to recognize flaws in the larger Asian American and Pacific Islander (AAPI) category and questioned whether Filipinos fit into the Asian category, as the census classifies us, or whether we fit into the Pacific Islander category, owing to the Philippines being an archipelago in the Pacific Ocean and sharing a more relatable history of colonization to other Pacific Islander populations. This struggle for finding a fit within the AAPI racial constructs has led me to conceptualize Pilipino Americans as our own distinct group outside of either Asian American or Pacific Islander.

In addition, as I found myself fully immersed in a Pilipino American identity, I started noticing subtle differences in the way I was treated or viewed as a legitimate Filipino, because of only being "half." I shared my concerns with a mentor who told me about the term *Hapa*, and I loved it. Claiming a "Hapa" identity felt empowering because it felt like I finally had a term that fit my experiences being mixed "Asian." Little did I know that there was a group of Native Hawaiians who did not appreciate the term *Hapa* being stolen from their indigenous language and used without regard to its historical context. I also realized that using the term *Hapa* to exclusively mean of mixed Asian decent was inadvertently modeling an elitist attitude within the broader multiracial landscape. Why did mixed Asians have our own term when other multiracial people did not? Thus, I dropped my use of the term *Hapa* and found the broader term *mixed* as a building block for solidarity among multiracial people and a more inclusive term for anyone of any mixed heritage (e.g., multiethnic, bicultural). Looking back, I realize the terms I used to identify myself resulted from my understanding of Asian Americanness. I bring these experiences in negotiating my own identity as a mixed-race Pilipino American into my research.

Prema

Who I am as an individual and as a professional conducting research on and working with Asian American students is characterized by my affiliation with Asian Americans and South Asian Americans, my Indian nationality, my ethnic backgrounds of Gujarati and Marathi, and my first-generation status. I am the daughter of parents who immigrated to the United States 30 years ago from India. I was raised in West Virginia, a state widely known for its reputation of being inhabited by hicks, country roads, and flannel. Growing up in racially homogeneous bubbles, whether it was within my predominantly White community or my Indian community, limited my view of what it truly meant for me to be a first-generation South Asian American, Gujarati, Marathi, Indian. Throughout my childhood and adolescent years, I was naturally oriented to taking on my American identity during the week and embracing my Indian identity on weekends. The former was defined by my ability to speak fluent English and expectation to accustom myself to the American norms, and the latter was defined by my *mandir* (temple) attendance, my speaking Gujarati at home, a dash of curry smell on every piece of clothing, and frequent trips to India. This was my norm. Though conflicted at times during high school because I was forced to wear both "hats" at once, for the most part, I took pride in my unique bicultural identity.

Nonetheless, this bicultural lifestyle eventually began taking a toll on me after I left for college. I found refuge in the Indian Subcontinent Association on campus, allowing me to fully embrace my ethnic backgrounds with ease. Shortly thereafter, I became immersed in a pan-Asian student group called the Asian Students' Alliance, as a means to explore and negotiate what it meant to be a South Asian American as part of the larger Asian American racial group. At this point in my life, Gujarati, Marathi, and Indian were more salient components of my identity than American, and South Asian more than Asian American. My American identity took a backseat to these other aspects of my identity. All too soon, this ethnic pride came to a halt when my affiliation with my American identity was constantly reinforced during my trips to India. I was a foreigner in my own "motherland." My trips to India reinforced the American dimension of who I was. In this context, I was forced to consider what it meant to be American. In America, others deemed me as an Indian or South Asian, and in India others saw me as an American. It was always one or the other, but never both. I perceived myself as both, and to this day, I still do. They are aspects of my identity that are distinctly different, but intertwine in a way that makes up my whole racial and ethnic identity. Although I am okay with identifying this way personally, it was not something I consciously considered in regard to my professional identity.

Only recently, through my professional experiences working with Asian American undergraduates, I began to comprehend my South Asian American background as a factor in my work. I never took into account my racial and ethnic background as a perception that others might consider in conjunction with my professional role. I recognized that I would always inherently be perceived as an insider within the Asian American community, regardless of what role I took on. Internally, I renegotiated how being a South Asian American professional working with Asian American students defined me and eventually found solace in a balanced understanding. By fully embracing my personal identity as a South Asian American and infusing it with my professional identity, I continue to embark on my journey as a researcher and practitioner working with Asian American college students.'

What We Know About Asian American College Student Development

As we found in discussing our own preferred identifications, the terms *Asian* and *Asian American* tend to be conflated, and their combination and separation are problematic in different ways. It is important to be aware that, although the terms can refer to a larger group of people that may be phenotypically similar in some ways, the choice to identify as Asian, Asian American, or AAPI is a personal one. Regardless of the personal identification choices made, AAPIs are one of the fastest growing racial/ethnic groups in the United States and among college student populations (Kodama, McEwen, Liang, & Lee, 2002; Suzuki, 2002). Despite their large numbers, AAPIs are consistently left out of much of the research in education, often being considered "model minorities" and not in need of attention (Kodama et al., 2002; Yu, 2006). Despite the hardships that Asian Americans and Pacific Islanders continue to face as minorities in the United States, the model minority myth categorizes Asian Americans as a homogeneous group of high-achieving students who inherently possess the skills and knowledge needed to succeed at all levels of education (Kim & Yeh, 2002; Omi & Takagi, 1998).

Psychosocial Development

Unsurprisingly then, there is little empirical research that helps clarify what Asian American college student development might look like (Evans, Forney, & Guido-DiBrito, 1998; Kodama et al., 2002). Kodama et al.'s Psychosocial Student Development Model is one of the few developmental models that offers insight into the cultural limitations of extant college student development theories. Kodama et al.'s model focuses on Asian American students' development in light of the issues related to race, racism, and stereotypes that may influence the ways in which they view themselves, their relationships, and their purpose in life. They frame their model in the context of two external domains that affect Asian American college students' lives: (1) Western values and racism in U.S. society, and (2) Asian values from community and family. Development occurs as Asian American students negotiate the tensions between these domains. Although useful in highlighting specific struggles that some Asian American students might face, we note that the model itself is predicated on two external domains that exert influence on Asian American students. These domains of "Western values and racism" and "Asian values from family and community" (Kodama et al., 2002, p. 46) are presented in a way that assumes these domains are mutually exclusive. However, our own narratives illuminate the complexities that exist in negotiating these different, yet often overlapping, psychological contexts—notions of appropriate methods of meaning-making that arise from different physical contexts and are then available methods of meaning-making to students as they travel across physical contexts (Pizzolato, Nguyen, Johnston, & Wang, 2012). In addition, the Asian values presented by Kodama et al., such as collectivism, interdependence, filial piety, and deference to authority, may not reflect the variety of distinct Asian American cultural and ethnic groups. For instance, Filipino Americans have been argued to have different cultural values than other Asian American groups because of the long history of Spanish colonization and U.S. dominance (Nadal, 2009). Furthermore, a study on group differences found that Filipino American college students maintained different levels of "Asian cultural values," compared with their Chinese, Korean, and Japanese American peers (Kim, Yang, Atkinson, Wolfe, & Hong, 2001).

Cultural Selfways

In order to better account for and understand the diverse developmental experiences and trajectories of Asian American college students, we find it useful to consider the social psychology literature on cultural selfways (Markus et al., 1997). Cultural selfways recognize that the notions of self and cultural context are inextricably related, and these selfways represent the socialization of individual selves toward culturally agreed upon ways of knowing and being. Cultural context shapes individuals' conceptions of and importance ascribed to the self (Goodnow, 1990; Heine, Lehman, Markus, & Kitayama, 1999; Hoshino-Browne, Zanna, Spencer, Zanna, & Kitayama, 2005; Shweder et al., 1998).

Research on Asian cultures, for example, reveals a distinctly different selfway than that found in Western culture, where the selfway focuses on the development of autonomous individuals. In Asian cultures, selfways convey values of interdependence and relationships. The self in Asian cultures is seen not as autonomous but as developed through, valued in, and inextricably tied to relationships with others (Heine et al., 1999; Hoshino-Browne et al., 2005; Markus & Kitayama, 1991; Shweder et al., 1998; Zhang, 1999). Consequently, the goal of the self in Asian cultures is to develop and maintain the equilibrium of relationships through appropriate control of individual desires and emotions that have the potential to disrupt the relationship.

Although the cultural selfways literature presents a helpful way to understand college students' sense of self in relation to their familial and cultural values, it is important to note that most of the literature references "Asian" cultures, which may be different from Asian American cultures. For students who are Asian and live in the United States, their selfways may not reflect the cultures of their "motherland," especially if they are third- or fourth-generation American. Extant literature does not address the potential differences between Asian cultural values and Asian American cultural values, which can be reflected in college students' diverse understandings of Asian Americanness.

Moreover, there is a tendency to use Eurocentric or Western frameworks of understanding development when studying Asian Americans, rather than using or creating more culturally sensitive approaches (Leong et al., 2007). This practice does not allow for the individual experiences of Asian American college students and diverse understandings of Asian Americanness to be examined. Additionally, although efforts are being made toward trying to understand the psychology of Asian Americans, these efforts often include the aggregation of Asian American ethnic subgroups and work to diminish the culturally specific experiences and perspectives that exist within them.

Because research has largely failed to recognize the uniqueness of specific AAPI ethnic groups, emergent generalizations have contributed to a homogenized view of Asian Americans. The development of a greater awareness of the experiences of AAPI students in the pursuit of higher education is necessary. According to the U.S. Census Bureau (2000), the Asian American population includes more than 30 ethnic groups who speak more than 300 languages. Great variations in immigration, socioeconomic status, and educational attainment, both before and after migration, exist among individuals, families, and communities (Teranishi, Ceja, Antonio, Allen, & McDonough, 2004). This internal diversity warrants closer study and a need for a deeper understanding of their diverse experiences and developmental courses relative to postsecondary education. The lumping of these unique ethnic groups into one category blurs important differences of which professionals in all relevant fields should be aware.

Implications for How to Study Asian American College Students

Despite the progress that has been made in identifying that Asian American college students face obstacles in college, have culturally specific needs, and may have different developmental pathways, there has been remarkably little in the way of an effort to truly understand Asian American students from an Asian American perspective. Research that examines Asian American students' lived experiences and gives attention to the differences in Asian American ethnicities, generation statuses, and specific challenges and cultural forces involved in being Asian American is needed. Consequently, we propose three guidelines for future research so that future inquiry can better take into account the diversity of Asian American experiences, as well as attempt to truly capture the Asian American experience in navigating higher education.

Recognizing the Diversity Within the "Asian American" Category

First, it seems important to start by asking students how they identify racially and ethnically and how they describe who they are to other people. Beginning with these questions can help clarify who thinks they are Asian and Asian American and whether we're even using the most salient term for labeling when talking about Asian American students. In our own work, by not specifying which ethnicities counted as Asian American, but instead asking for students to participate in a study on Asian American culture and student development, we were able to amass a large sample. Then, by asking, "How do you culturally identify?" in our interviews, we learned much about who thought they were Asian American and why. We had a critical mass of Iranian American students in this sample, and almost all of them described themselves as Asian American and disliked that the federal government and their university excluded them from that category. Cultural centers and ethnic studies (e.g., majors, minors, and areas of concentration) tend to label the group they focus on, but then rely on students self-selecting into these centers and studies, understanding who thinks they fit where is important, so that higher education can assess whether they have appropriate services to meet the diverse needs and cultural experiences of Asian American students.

From a research perspective, understanding who thinks they fit into the category "Asian American" seems important for knowing if and how existing research needs to be revised and refined to account for the diversity of this group.

Learning by Listening

Researchers cannot hope to capture the development and experiences of Asian American students without first stopping to listen to these students. Rather than entering studies armed with survey instruments or interview questions derived from past research and hoping to collect useful data, we must suspend assumptions about what we think we know and instead ask broad, open-ended questions that are designed to elucidate what the Asian American college experience feels like and what Asian American development feels like. For example, instead of assuming there is an East–West conflict raging inside Asian American students, ask about values, socialization practices, and relationships at home and at school. Furthermore, it seems important to take cues from research that has shown that Asian American students and White American students show distinct differences in what causes dissonance for them (see Heine et al., 1999). This is important to note, because dissonance is the mechanism for change in many development theories (Baxter Magolda, 1992, 2001; Belenky, Clinchy, Goldberger, & Tarule, 1986; Chickering & Reisser, 1993; King & Kitchener, 1994; Perry, 1968). If we continue to use existing surveys, we may fail to accurately describe Asian American students' development, because we are asking questions or posing scenarios that are less likely to be development-inducing for Asian American students.

In our own work on cultural selfways and epistemological development, we've moved away from asking only the typical questions that researchers use to evaluate epistemological development. Such research tends to ask about experiences or decisions and then probe for how the participant made meaning of the experience (Baxter Magolda, 1992, 2001; Belenky et al., 1986; Perry, 1968), or about learning preferences and strategies (Baxter Magolda, 1999). Although useful, these questions do not provide opportunities or clear probes for how to understand how precollegiate and cultural socialization play into the epistemological development process and products. Consequently, in addition to asking these common questions, we ask questions about cultural selfways that have come from different parts of the participants' lives (e.g., home and school). In addition, eliciting participants' descriptions about and identification with family, home community, racial group membership(s), ethnic group membership(s), and immigration statuses is especially important. In so doing, we are moving toward proposing a developmental model that better captures epistemological development and developmental influences than those that exist. Furthermore, we should be able to contribute to the literature on cultural selfways of Asian Americans by clarifying both the diversity of selfways in this pan-ethnic group and how Asian American selfways, in terms of both content and diversity, may differ from Asian selfways.

(Re)Constructing and Calibrating Instruments

In the interest of emerging and future interpretivist, qualitative research on Asian American students, we suggest revisiting, reconsidering, and revising existing surveys that aim to capture cultural, racial, and ethnic differences in both development and experiences. Such revisiting is important, because researchers rely on these surveys to tell them about racial patterns in development, experiences, and achievement. Given the consistent and pervasive East–West binary used to understand Asian American students and reliance on understanding of Asians in Asia to construct understandings of Asian Americans, it is possible that current measures rely too much on language, behaviors, and ideas specific to Asians. These may not be relevant to Asian Americans and thus may skew the current understanding of Asian Americans. Also, because immigration generation may impact the degree to which Asian American students look like Asians, and thus respond in particular ways to surveys and survey items based on understandings of Asians in Asia, it may be necessary to provide information about the immigration generation of samples when talking about Asian Americans. On a related note, reexamination of items designed to solicit racial group membership should be undertaken. Are all Asian Americans aggregated under a choice of "Asian"? Or are there ethnicity options? Gathering ethnicity information may be useful in examining whether what we know about Asian Americans is actually just a representation of what we know about some Asian Americans.

Conclusion

This chapter addresses limitations and presents implications for Asian American research and student development theory. Little is known about Asian American college student development (i.e., psychological, cognitive, social).

Our consideration for the complex nature of Asian Americanness in this area of inquiry challenges the current way of approaching and thinking about Asian American college students' experiences and development.

As seen through the authors' personal accounts of Asian Americanness and the participants in our studies, there is something deeper that warrants attention to the ways we are approaching this research. We know that Asian Americans are often aggregated into a single group. We also know that a variation of identities and identifications exists within the "Asian American," and that that variation might not be truly considered, using existing frameworks. Thus, we propose the use of more culturally sensitive conceptual frameworks. We also call researchers to revisit and revise our methods and instruments to make sure that we are grounding our findings in the experiences and development of Asian American college students. Grounding our findings in the actual experiences of Asian Americans means breaking away from the East–West mentality to recognize the intersectionality and diversity of Asian American identities and experiences. To these ends, we encourage researchers to consider whether their interview questions, coding schemes, and survey items adequately elicit and capture the diversity of experiences of Asian Americans, not just Asians in Asia, or immigrant Asian Americans.

References

Baxter Magolda, M. B. (1992). *Knowing and reasoning in college*. San Francisco, CA: Jossey Bass.

Baxter Magolda, M. B. (1999). *Creating contexts for learning and self-authorship: Constructive-developmental pedagogy*. Nashville, TN: Vanderbilt University Press.

Baxter Magolda, M. B. (2001). *Making their own way: Narratives for transforming higher education to promote self-development*. Sterling, VA: Stylus.

Belenky, M. F., Clinchy, B. M., Goldberger, N. R., & Tarule, J. M. (1986). *Women's ways of knowing: The development of self, voice, and mind*. New York: Basic Books.

Chickering, A., & Reisser, L. (1993). *Education and identity* (2nd ed.). San Francisco, CA: Jossey-Bass.

Evans, N. J., Forney, D. S., & Guido-DiBrito, F. M. (1998). *Student development in college: Theory, research, and practice*. San Francisco, CA: Jossey-Bass.

Goodnow, J. (1990). The socialization of cognition: What's involved? In J. W. Stigler, R. A. Shweder, & G. Herdt (Eds.), *Cultural psychology: Essays on comparative human development* (pp. 259–286). New York: Cambridge University Press.

Heine, S. J., Lehman, D. R., Markus, H. R., & Kitayama, S. (1999). Is there a universal need for positive self-regard? *Psychological Review, 106*(4), 766–794.

Hoshino-Browne, E., Zanna, A. S., Spencer, S. J., Zanna, M. P., & Kitayama, S. (2005). On the cultural guises of cognitive dissonance: The case of Easterners and Westerners. *Journal of Personality and Social Psychology, 89*(3), 294–310.

Kim, A., & Yeh, C. J. (2002). *Stereotypes of Asian American students. ERIC Digest,* ERIC Clearinghouse on Urban Education, Institute for Urban and Minority Education, Teachers College, Columbia University, New York.

Kim, B. S. K., Yang, P. H., Atkinson, D. R., Wolfe, M. M., & Hong, S. (2001). Cultural value similarities and differences among Asian American ethnic groups. *Cultural Diversity and Ethnic Minority Psychology, 7*(2), 343–361.

King, P. M., & Kitchener, K. S. (1994). *Developing reflective judgment.* San Francisco, CA: Jossey-Bass.

Kodama, C. M., McEwen, M. K., Liang, C. T. H., & Lee, S. (2002). An Asian American perspective on psychosocial student development theory. *New Directions for Student Services, 97,* 45–59.

Leong, F. T. L., Ebreo, A., Kinoshita, L., Inman, A. G., Hisn Yang, L., & Fu, M. (Eds.). (2007). *Handbook of Asian American psychology* (2nd ed.). Thousand Oaks, CA: Sage.

Markus, H. R., & Kitayama, S. (1991). Culture and the self: Implications for cognition, emotion, and motivation. *Psychological Review, 98,* 224–253.

Markus, H. R., Mullaly, P., & Kitayama, S. (1997). Selfways: Diversity in modes of cultural participation. In U. Neisser & D. Jopling (Eds.), *The conceptual self in context: Culture, experience, self-understanding* (pp. 89–130). Cambridge, UK: Cambridge University Press.

Nadal, K. L. (2009). *Filipino American psychology: A handbook of theory research and clinical practice.* Bloomington, IN: Authorhouse.

Omi, M., & Takagi, D. Y. (1998). Situating Asian Americans in the political discourse of affirmative action. In R. Post & M. Rogin (Eds.), *Race and representation: Affirmative action.* New York: Zone Books.

Perry, W. P. (1968). *Forms of intellectual and ethical development.* New York: W. W. Norton.

Pizzolato, J. E., Chaudhari, P., & Nguyen, T.-L. K. (2008, November). *Cultural selfways & self-authorship: The case of Asian students.* Paper presented at the annual meeting of the Association of Higher Education, Jacksonville, FL.

Pizzolato, J. E., Nguyen, T. K., Johnston, M. P., & Wang, S. (2012). Understanding context: Cultural, relational, & psychological interactions in self-authorship development. *Journal of College Student Development, 53*(5), 656–679.

Shweder, R. A., Goodnow, J., Hatano, G., LeVine, R. A., Markus, H. R., & Miller, P. (1998). The cultural psychology of development: One mind, many mentalities. In R. M. Lerner (Ed.), *Handbook of child psychology: Vol. 1 Theoretical models of human development* (5th ed., pp. 865–937). New York: Wiley.

Suzuki, B. H. (2002). Revisiting the model minority stereotype: Implications for student affairs practice and higher education. *Working with Asian American College Students: New Directions for Student Services* (No. 97, pp. 21–32). San Francisco: Jossey-Bass.

Teranishi, R. T., Ceja, M., Antonio, A. L., Allen, W. R., & McDonough, P. M. (2004). The college-choice process for Asian Pacific Americans: Ethnicity and socioeconomic class in context. *The Review of Higher Education, 27*(4), 527–551.

U.S. Census Bureau. (2000). *United States Census 2000.* From http://wwwcensus .gov/main/www/cen2000.html

Yu, T. (2006). Challenging the politics of the "model minority" stereotype: A case for educational equality. *Equity & Excellence in Education, 39*(4), 325–333.

Zhang, L.-F. (1999). A comparison of U.S. and Chinese university students' cognitive development: The cross-cultural applicability of Perry's theory. *The Journal of Psychology, 133*(4), 425–439.

7

THE ROLE OF CONTEXT, CRITICAL THEORY, AND COUNTER-NARRATIVES IN UNDERSTANDING PACIFIC ISLANDER INDIGENEITY

Erin Kahunawaika'ala Wright and Brandi Jean Nālani Balutski

Because of colonization, the question of *who* defines *what* is Native, and even *who* is defined as Native has been taken away from Native peoples by Western-trained scholars, government officials, and other technicians. The theft itself testifies to the pervasive power of colonialism and explains why self-identity by Natives of *who* and *what* they are elicits such strenuous and sometimes vicious denials by the dominant culture.

(Trask, 1999, p. 43)

L ike the Pacific Ocean encompasses varying topographies, myriad life forms, and shifting geopolitics, the term *Pacific Islanders*[1] represents people from incredibly diverse cultural groups (Chapter 1). Each Pacific Islander ethnic group comes from unique sociohistorical contexts and exists within particular sociopolitical conditions that, in turn, create distinctive narratives of racialization in the United States. Over the last three decades, robust conversations about who should be included or considered Pacific Islander have created a body of scholarship that endeavors to understand, articulate, and test the ideological, political, intellectual, and even practical boundaries of identity (Diaz, 2004; Diaz & Kauanui, 2001). Identity discussions have also emerged around disaggregating Pacific Islanders from Asian Americans in data collection to better understand the unique situations and needs of Pacific Islander populations (Hune, 2011; Kanaʻiaupuni, 2011; Panapasa, Crabbe, & Kaholokula, 2011; Taualii, Quenga, Samoa, Samanani, & Dover, 2011).

In the context of higher education, these conversations can help us better understand the multidimensional nature of Pacific Islander identities and their pragmatic implications for successful participation in higher education. In this chapter, we focus on indigenous Pacific Islanders, whom we distinguish from other Pacific Islanders, because of their shared experience of U.S. colonization and its differential historical and contemporary impacts on indigenous lands and resources, culture, citizenship, and sovereignty (Alfred & Corntassel, 2005, p. 597). Our narrative focuses on the indigenous cultural groups within the Pacific Islander classification from Hawaii, the Federated States of Micronesia (FSM), the Republic of the Marshall Islands (RMI), the Republic of Palau, the Territory of Guam, the Commonwealth of the Northern Mariana Islands (CNMI), and American Samoa.

The purpose of the current chapter is to demonstrate how postsecondary institutions can create and help perpetuate indigenous Pacific Islander counter-narratives on their campuses. First, we present Critical Race Theory (CRT) and Tribal Critical Theory (TribalCrit) as a framework for understanding the importance of historical and political context, as well as creating spaces for Pacific Islander counter-narratives. Second, we provide critical contextual information for this discussion by offering a brief overview of the historical context of the Pacific and the current political context of the U.S. government's involvement in and militarization of Pacific territories. This historical and political context is critical because it helps develop a more complex and holistic understanding of Pacific Islander identities and experiences. Third, we offer an example of how colleges and universities can create spaces for indigenous counter-narratives to flourish on college campuses that serve indigenous Pacific Islander populations. Before moving forward in this discussion, we find it useful to clarify our positionalities as Native Hawaiians, researchers in higher education, and authors of this chapter.

Our Positionalities

Erin Kahunawaikaʻala Wright

On her first day of kindergarten at Fern Elementary School in Kalihi, Oʻahu, my maternal grandmother was named "Dorothy" by her teacher. Her given name is Tung Kyau, but her teacher, she told me, could not pronounce it. Although my grandmother did not change it legally, *Dorothy* is the name on all of her government-issued forms of identification. When my mother was born in the mid-1940s in the territory of Hawaii, her paternal great-grandmother and great-grandaunt, Leilehua and Ana Kamakea, named her Kahunawaikaʻala to commemorate the story of a hidden spring that our family cared for at Mount Kaʻala on the Waiʻanae Coast of the Hawaiian island of Oʻahu. My grandmother ʻoki (cut) the name to Hunawaikaʻala, not wanting my mother to carry a name with "kahuna" because, at the time, the only meaning people associated with it was kanaka who practiced the "old ways," traditional rituals for prayer and worship, which were seen as primitive by most people in Hawaii. When I was born in 1973, my family named me Kahunawaikaʻala as a way to heal the ʻoki and honor our kūpuna (elders). I share these family stories on naming as part of my positionality, because they address the core of our discussion about Pacific Islanders and highlight our understanding of the power to name and define colonial influences and lasting impacts, engage in resistance and reclaim power to name ourselves, and tell our own stories in our own voices. As with the names of other indigenous peoples, Hawaiian names carry a family's history and hopes for a child. So, I have endeavored to embrace and enact the kuleana (responsibility, privilege) that comes with my name.

Brandi Jean Nālani Balutski

A few weeks before starting the Hawaiian studies graduate program at the University of Hawaiʻi at Mānoa, I attended a mandatory orientation, during which a senior faculty member in the department asked a question that, for the first time, made me question my kuleana and made me consider my positionality—"Why are you here?" I panicked. I struggled with the simple question, because I just did not have an answer. Even then, weeks before school started, I couldn't explain to my family or myself why I was there— why, despite earning a bachelor's degree in business, I was choosing Hawaiian studies over a master's in business administration. I quickly snapped out of my panic mode when the man next to me eloquently said, "I don't know why I'm here, but I know I have to be." At that very moment, amid my tears, I knew I was where I had to be. I share this story as part of my positionality, because this was a defining moment for me and my coming to understand my kuleana and the summation of my convictions, passion, and career. Looking back almost six years later, I find this question is not so intimidating. I am here because my kūpuna have a plan for me to serve and help rebuild our beloved Hawaiian nation.

Critical Race Theory and Tribal Critical Race Theory

Although CRT emerged in the field of law, it is a useful framework for examining and understanding the racialization of Pacific Islanders because it foregrounds race, racism, and power, as well as interrogates intersections of various forms of oppression and centers the experiences of Pacific Islanders (Labrador & Wright, 2011). Matsuda, Lawrence, Delgado, and Crenshaw (1993) identify six core tenets of CRT:

1. CRT asserts that racism is endemic to American society;
2. CRT expresses skepticism at dominant legal claims of neutrality, meritocracy, and color-blindness;
3. CRT challenges ahistoricism and insists on a contextual and historical analysis of the law;
4. CRT insists on the recognition of the experiences of people of color and communities of color in analyzing law and society;
5. CRT is interdisciplinary; and
6. CRT scholarship works toward eliminating racial oppression as part of the broader goal of ending all forms of oppression. (pp. 6–7)

In particular, CRT also helps us imagine the ways in which we can support the creation of indigenous Pacific Islanders' counter-narratives in higher education through its dedication to liberatory scholarship. Such counter-narratives are necessary for challenging oppressive dominant narratives and shedding light on the voices of people of color who have historically been silenced. Brayboy (2005) extends the work of CRT to include the political conditions and historical circumstances of indigenous peoples in the United States into a framework that he calls TribalCrit. Brayboy outlines nine tenets of TribalCrit, five of which we delineate here, because they are most applicable to our discussion:

1. Colonization is endemic to society;
2. U.S. policies toward Indigenous peoples are rooted in colonialism, White supremacy, and a desire for material gain;

3. Indigenous peoples occupy a liminal space that accounts for both the political and racialized natures of our identities;
4. Indigenous peoples constantly seek ways of expressing self-determination, sovereignty, and autonomy; and
5. Reframing culture, knowledge, research and power through an Indigenous perspective is imperative. (p. 429)

Brayboy's analysis is applicable to examinations of indigenous Pacific Islanders, because they are indigenous peoples by virtue of U.S. colonialism and imperialism in the Pacific. Articulating the Pacific-specific context of U.S. colonialism and imperialism is fundamental to our discussion, because it has lasting impacts on the current conditions of indigenous Pacific Islanders, including their lack of higher educational attainment (UCLA Asian American Studies Center et al., 2006). These tenets of CRT and TribalCrit provide analytical guides to frame indigenous Pacific Islander experiences while emphasizing the importance of building counter-narratives. They underscore the importance of considering historical and political contexts as well as underscore the power of counter-narratives, both of which we discuss in the following sections.

Historicizing the Pacific

To understand the experiences of Pacific Islanders, one must understand the historical and social contexts within which they exist. For more than 400 years, Oceania[2] has survived Western colonialism. Functioning under the ideology that Western expansionism was "inevitable, natural, and desirable," Western explorers set their sights on the Pacific in the early nineteenth century (Blaut, 1993, p. 19). Their initial interest in the Pacific was scientific, as well as economic. One historian noted that Captain James Cook, the British captain credited with "discovering" Hawaii, embarked on a 1774 voyage to Kanaky (New Caledonia), which was motivated as much by scientific interest as by the possibility of riches (Connell, 1987). Despite this seemingly benign interest, these inaugural voyages left an indelible mark on indigenous lands and peoples of the Pacific and opened up the Pacific to the rest of the world (Trask, 1999).

Akin to the experiences of islands in the Caribbean and the African continent, the Pacific was divided among imperialist powers of the West, like Spain, France, England, and the United States. Scientific interest eventually dissolved, and the promise of economic fortune and military interest prevailed, with each nation claiming different regions of the Pacific, in a quest to outdo the others (Robie, 1990). The nineteenth-century Pacific became a stomping ground for the West, including anyone from the Christian missionary to the blackbirder.[3] However, to the disappointment of the colonial powers, the economic gain was largely illusionary. At the time, the Pacific Islands held nothing of real value to Western nations, other than a beautiful place to rest and replenish supplies during voyages. Nevertheless, they maintained and defended their occupation of the Pacific against indigenous populations as well as other colonizers. And, as a result, Pacific Islanders' cultures—including their social structures, knowledge systems, and spiritual beliefs—were forever changed by Western colonialism and imperialism.

Identity Politics, Racial Categorization, and Pacific Islander Indigeneity

The terms *Asian Pacific Islanders* (APIs), *Asian and Pacific Americans* (APAs), and *Asian Americans and Pacific Islanders* (AAPIs) have been used for several decades to lump Pacific Islanders under an umbrella racial category. For years, Pacific Islander communities, especially those working in areas like social work and public health, have advocated for the disaggregation of Pacific Islanders from Asian Americans, in large part because of the inability to access accurate health data on Pacific Islanders (U.S. Office of Minority Health, 2007).

In 1997, the U.S. Office of Management and Budget (OMB) released OMB 15, which was designed to offer "standard classifications for record keeping, collection, and presentation of data on race and ethnicity in Federal program administrative reporting and statistical activities." A significant part of OMB 15 was the disaggregation of the API category into two distinct categories: (1) Asian and (2) Native Hawaiian or Other Pacific Islander (NHOPI). *Native Hawaiian or Other Pacific Islander* is defined as the following:

> A person having origins in any of the original peoples of Hawaii, Guam, Samoa, or other Pacific Islands. (The term "Native Hawaiian" does not include individuals who are native to the State of Hawaii by virtue of being born there.) In addition to Native Hawaiians, Guamanians, and Samoans, this category would include the following Pacific Islander groups reported in the 1990 census: Carolinian, Fijian, Kosraean, Melanesian, Micronesian, Northern Mariana Islander, Palauan, Papua New Guinean, Ponapean

(Pohnpean), Polynesian, Solomon Islander, Tahitian, Tarawa Islander, Tokelauan, Tongan, Trukese (Chuukese), and Yapese. (OMB, 1997)

Several rationales prompted the separation of Native Hawaiians and Other Pacific Islanders from Asians. OMB 15 states, "The Native Hawaiians presented compelling arguments that the standards must facilitate the production of data to describe their social and economic situation and to monitor discrimination against Native Hawaiians in housing, education, employment, and other areas" (OMB, 1997). Panapasa et al. (2011) offer key justifications for disaggregation:

1. NHPIs, compared to Asians, have higher rates of many chronic diseases and are more socio-economically and socio-culturally disadvantaged—issues masked by aggregation with Asians;

2. Asians were overrepresented in higher education, many NHPI college students were adversely affected by graduate schools' admission policies to limit the enrollment of Asians and were bypassed for scholarships; and

3. Disproportionate allocation of federal resources and support did not match the extent of the medical, social, and economic issues faced by NHPIs given their population size relative to Asians. (pp. 217–218)

Despite the federal law to disaggregate, Panapasa et al. (2011) found that a number of national surveys and administrative data were not compliant in reporting disaggregated NHOPI information. For example, vital health data from the National Center for Health Statistics for most states was noncompliant with OMB 15 as of 2005, which was eight years after the policy was instituted (Taualii et al., 2011). The implications for Pacific Islanders are fairly evident—existing data are unreliable and inadequate to accurately identify and address specific issues impacting these populations.

Currently, Pacific islands like Guam, Hawaii, Tahiti, and American Samoa continue to be occupied by colonizing countries, often being given the political status of territory, trusteeship, protectorate, free-association, and state. Despite titles appearing to signify degrees of sovereignty, these islands remain economically and politically tied to their colonizer. Trask (1999) defines this status as "neocolonialism." Neocolonialism is "the experience of oppression at a stage which is nominally identified as autonomous or independent" (p. 132). She uses the term *nominally* to signify that although many former colonies (like the FSM and RMI) are politically independent they are not economically independent. The citizens[4] of U.S. colonies assume liminal identities, legally and politically, as "full" citizens of neither the United States nor their island nation. Furthermore, these groups are then identified in the United States as "Native Hawaiian and Other Pacific Islanders," which classifies them racially but erases (or obscures) the legal and political aspects of their identities that impact, for example, issues of access to higher education.

In their writings about Pacific Islanders—especially in relation to Asian Americans, Asian American studies, and Pacific Islands studies—Diaz and Kauanui (2001) emphasize that a fundamental element of asserting Pacific Islander indigeneity is the connection between identity and place: They state that the "land and sea constitute our genealogies. . . . Land and sea are ways by which peoplehood is constituted" (pp. 318–319). The authors also locate Pacific Islander indigeneity within the international narrative of colonialism and Indigenous Peoples. In addition, Brayboy (2005) states that U.S. colonialism can also become a tool for analysis. Connecting Pacific Islanders to this broader Indigenous narrative, in part, distinguishes Pacific Islanders from ethnic minorities, while articulating the particular issues that impact many Indigenous communities, like nationhood and self-determination, cultural revitalization, and the recovery of resources like native lands, seas, and water. In particular, Diaz (2004) identifies these differentiations and connections between indigenous peoples:

> Often couched as an opposition between the quest for equality or civil rights on the one hand, and equity and sovereignty on the other—and even these are not unproblematic or unproblematized—Native Pacific struggles, unlike those of U.S. ethnic minorities, but much more similar to the struggles of Native Americans, are typically regarded as a quest for regaining lands and seas lost through colonialism and imperialism. (pp. 197–198)

As Labrador and Wright (2011) suggest, this liminal identity "points to the dual, simultaneous, overlapping, and sometimes contradictory processes of being race-d and indigenized, the nexus of racialization and indigenization where the 'rooted' and 'routed' meet" (p. 139).

U.S. Militarism and "Citizenship" in the Pacific

> We, the people of the Pacific, have been victimised too long by foreign powers. The Western imperialistic and colonial powers invaded our defenseless region, they took over our lands and subjugated our people to

their whims. . . . We call for an immediate end to the oppression, exploitation and subordination of the indigenous peoples of the Pacific. (Robie,
1990, p. 147)

U.S. militarization is an important part of colonization. The U.S. military
has had an active presence in the Pacific Islands since the mid-nineteenth
century and continues to shape the geopolitical contours of the Pacific and
its peoples. In this section, we discuss some of those influences.

World War II was critical to the U.S. military and its exploitation of the
Pacific. Trask (1999) explains, "As the preeminent military power in the
world, the U.S. has dealt with the Pacific, since World War II, as if it were
an American Ocean" (p. 48). In effect, the impact of U.S. militarization on
indigenous lands, natural resources, and the lives and societies of Pacific
Islanders has been, and continues to be, catastrophic.

According to the U.S. Department of the Interior Office of Insular
Affairs (OIA), the U.S. Pacific Command (USPACOM) is the embodiment
of U.S. military presence in the Pacific. Headquartered in Hawaii and made
up of a fleet of approximately 678,200 civilians, personnel, contractors, and
airmen, USPACOM represents one-fifth of the total U.S. military strength
and two-thirds of the total U.S. Marine Corps combat strength. USPACOM's
(2012) mission is to enhance "stability in the Asia-Pacific region by promoting security cooperation, encouraging peaceful development, responding to
contingencies, deterring aggression, and, when necessary fighting to win.
This approach is based on partnership, presence, and military readiness."
The term *partnership* comes in the form of different political arrangements
like Compacts of Free Associations (Micronesia) and prolonged American
occupation (Hawaii), where the lure of U.S. funding, protection, and liminal
"citizenry" is often negotiated at the expense of indigenous control over
lands and resources.

Over the last 70 years, the U.S. military has treated the Pacific as its
personal weapons testing laboratory. In Hawai'i, the U.S. military seized the
island of Kaho'olawe on December 8, 1941, the day after the Japanese
bombed Pearl Harbor on the Hawaiian island of O'ahu. Over the next several decades, it (and its allies) used Kahoolawe to test torpedoes, bombs,
surface explosions, and other weapons, nearly destroying the island's natural
geography (including its freshwater table) and surrounding reef. In 1976,
Protect Kaho'olawe 'Ohana, a Native grassroots organization formed to
defend Kahoolawe, filed a suit in federal district court to stop the navy's
bombing. In 1990, the island was conveyed back to the state of Hawaii, yet

the military's waste was left behind. And, 22 years later, cleanup of military ordnance, replanting of native vegetation, and spiritual healing for Native Hawaiians continues.

During the 12-year period between 1946 and 1958, a total of 66 atomic and hydrogen bombs were tested in the Marshall Islands. Robie (1990) explains, "Many islanders claimed they were used as guinea pigs for the experiments. Now, more than 40 years after the first Bikini tests, many islands are still uninhabitable because of the high radiation levels while the Bikinians and Rongelap islanders remain exiled people" (p. 2). As a result of the testing and its impact on the people, land, and ocean, people from the Marshall Islands and surrounding areas have left their homelands to access cancer treatments, follow sick family members, and find work in places like Hawaii and California.

There are five different U.S.-affiliated political entities in Micronesia: the Federated States of Micronesia (FSM), the Republic of the Marshall Islands (RMI), the Republic of Palau, the Territory of Guam, and the Commonwealth of the Northern Mariana Islands (CNMI). Since World War II, these political entities, excluding Guam, were Trust Territory of the Pacific Islands protectorates of the United States. However, these nations sought more autonomy from the United States and entered into the Compacts of Free Association (CFA) or commonwealth status in 1986 (1994 for Palau), most of which were renewed in 2003.

The CFA between the United States and FSM, RMI, and Palau have provided Micronesians with legal provisions, like the right to immigrate freely to, establish residency in, accept employment in, and attend school in the United States. The CFA also provides millions of dollars annually to these entities for infrastructure, alternative energy, education, health care, and other areas, in exchange for the "full authority and responsibility for security and defense matters" as well as the imposed consultation and collaboration on economic development affairs (OIA, 1986). These U.S.-affiliated political entities are managed by the U.S. Department of the Interior Office of Insular Affairs (OIA), whose operations eerily resemble a neocolonial hegemonic structure meant to dictate the political and social affairs of independent nations through funding priorities and legal provisions. For example, a budget of $575.3 million was allocated "to empower U.S.-affiliated insular communities and encourage economic activity and growth" for fiscal year 2013 (OIA, 2012). Consequently, accepting U.S. aid also means accepting prolonged U.S. occupation, including military control over native lands and seas. As a result, we contend that college educators who serve indigenous

Pacific Islander populations have a moral obligation to understand these sociohistorical contexts and to use that knowledge to develop programs and practices to support indigenous Pacific Islanders in higher education. In the remainder of this chapter, we discuss a framework and example that educators can use to pursue such efforts.

An Example of Indigenous Counter-Narrative: Creating a "Hawaiian Place of Learning" in Higher Education

Examples of Pacific Islander counter-narratives and anticolonial projects are abundant across the Pacific. In Guam, Chamorros are actively resisting further U.S. military occupation and fighting for independence. Although often seen as simply victims, indigenous Marshall Islanders have a rich history of resisting nuclear testing and supporting a nuclear-free and independent Pacific. But, given our professional knowledge and experience, we decided to construct our counter-narrative around what we know best, and that is the work of Hawai'inuiākea School of Hawaiian Knowledge at the University of Hawai'i at Mānoa (UHM). In particular, we will focus on the school itself, because its establishment, presence, and work continually express sovereignty, self-determination, and autonomy and reframe culture, research, knowledge, and power through an indigenous perspective, as identified in TribalCrit.

University of Hawai'i at Mānoa

Located in Mānoa Valley on the island of O'ahu, the University of Hawai'i at Mānoa was founded in 1907 under the Morrill Act as a land-grant college. In 1965, the state legislature created a statewide system of community colleges and eventually two more four-year campuses and placed them within the University of Hawai'i (UH) system. Currently, UHM is the only Research I institution and the largest campus in the system. UHM serves more Native Hawaiian students than any other campus in the system, reaching 3,004 undergraduates in 2011.

In 2002, UHM adopted a strategic plan entitled "Defining Our Destiny." Designed to guide the campus through the first decade of the millennium, the plan highlights the importance of Hawaiian culture, language, practices, and place to this institution's identity. This focus emerged in response to the severe underrepresentation of Native Hawaiians in higher education in Hawai'i and the specific problems encountered at the flagship campus by Native Hawaiian faculty, staff, and students. In its most recent strategic plan, which was published in 2011, UHM continues to underscore the institution's explicit commitment to Native Hawaiians and to creating a "Hawaiian place of learning."

Eia Hawai'inuiākea: Hawai'inuiākea School of Hawaiian Knowledge

The "Hawaiian Renaissance," a political and social movement in the 1970s, which helped problematize our liminal identity and revitalize many of our cultural practices, birthed the establishment of several indigenous spaces and places of resistance among, against, and often within neocolonial systems. During this time, the Center for Hawaiian Studies[5] was created at UHM in 1977. In addition, the first Hawaiian language course was taught in 1921, and a bachelor of arts in Hawaiian was available in 1979 as a provisional degree, but was given permanent status in 1985. Congruent with TribalCrit, the Center for Hawaiian Studies' mission speaks directly to cultural and political autonomy for Native Hawaiians:

> To achieve and maintain excellence in the pursuit of knowledge concerning the Native people of Hawai'i, their origin, history, language, literature, religion, arts and sciences, interactions with their oceanic environment and other peoples; and to reveal, disseminate and apply this knowledge for the betterment of all peoples. Kamakakūokalani is committed to Native Hawaiian self-determination and honoring the thousands of Hawaiians who one hundred years ago signed the Kū'ē petition opposing annexation by the U.S. The mandate of these kūpuna to their descendants is to forever retain Hawaiian national identity and seek reclamation of Hawaiian sovereignty. Kamakakūokalani provides "Education for the Nation," empowering students' identities and preparing them to lead Hawai'i into a sustainable future. (Kamakakūokalani, 2012).

On May 16, 2007, the University of Hawai'i Board of Regents approved the establishment of the Hawai'inuiākea School of Hawaiian Knowledge (HSHK), the only college of indigenous knowledge in a U.S. Research I institution. Although HSHK's establishment is recent, the idea was conceptualized nearly 30 years ago in the Ka'ū Report, a report of recommendations and research compiled by a task force of Native Hawaiian faculty and staff in the UH system.

HSHK is composed of four units: Kamakakūokalani Center for Hawaiian Studies, Kawaihuelani Center for Hawaiian Language, Ka Papa Lo'i 'O

Kānewai Cultural Garden, and Native Hawaiian Student Services. HSHK defines its mission as the following:

> With respect and reverence for our Native Hawaiian ancestors, the mission of Hawai'inuiākea is to pursue, perpetuate, research, and revitalize all areas and forms of Hawaiian knowledge, including its language, origins, history, arts, sciences, literature, religion, education, law, and society, its political, medicinal, and cultural practices, as well as all other forms of knowledge. (Hawai'inuiākea School of Hawaiian Knowledge. 2012)

HSHK preserves, perpetuates, generates, and disseminates indigenous knowledge. Each unit within HSHK further articulates its commitment to Native Hawaiian people, places, perspectives, knowledge, and nationhood. Kamakakūokalani Center for Hawaiian Studies (KCHS) (2012) identifies its kuleana to do the following:

1. Present the interplay of history, culture, and politics as well as the interconnectedness of all knowledge, contemporary and ancestral, from Kanaka Maoli perspectives in order that students will understand Kanaka Maoli experiences in the context of world indigenous peoples.
2. Nurture and educate our students to become community leaders, teachers and scholars who will make a positive contribution to our people and our island homeland into the future.
3. Strengthen genealogical ties to Papahānaumoku, our earth mother, and Hawai'i as our ancestral homeland in order that our students will know Kanaka Maoli are a Lāhui connected by our ancestor Hāloa across Nā Kai 'Ewalu.

Of course, the discipline is open to students of all ancestries, but KCHS is very clear and deliberate in its motivations and focus.

The motto of Kawaihuelani Center for Hawaiian Language (KCHL), "I Pono Nā Mamo a Hāloa," "recognizes Hāloa, the common ancestor of the Hawaiian people, thereby honoring the connection between genealogy and language revitalization as an appropriate balance for our future as a people" (Kawaihuelani, 2012). The mission of KCHL is to do the following:

> [R]evitalize the Hawaiian language and culture through quality Hawaiian education. . . . Education and revitalization of Hawaiian language result in additional research and contributions to the Hawaiian knowledge base,

thereby creating new ways of knowing and understanding the past, present, and future of the Native people of these islands. (Kawaihuelani, 2012)

Again, the discipline is open to all students, but KCHL is clear in its perspective as an indigenous unit and its intended audience of Native Hawaiian students.

Ka Papa Lo'i 'O Kānewai (Kānewai, 2012) provides HSHK with hands-on experience, especially as it relates to Native Hawaiian traditional farming and cultivation practices. In one sense, Kānewai provides the context for people to experience a surface level of Hawaiian cultural concepts like "mālama 'āina" (caring for the land) by helping to, for example, weed the lo'i (taro pond). In another, Kānewai also provides an opportunity to learn deeply from the land. The mission of Kānewai is a well-known traditional Hawaiian proverb, "ma ka hana ka 'ike," or one learns by doing, or true knowledge comes from experience (Kānewai, 2012).

Native Hawaiian Student Services (NHSS) provides holistic support to Native Hawaiians pursuing higher education. NHSS's efforts, resources, programs, and initiatives are specifically designed to increase the recruitment and retention of Native Hawaiian students. NHSS identifies the following core values, which drive the program:

1. Encourage the exploration of students' Hawaiian identity;
2. Being grounded in Native Hawaiian knowledge systems;
3. Recognize our kuleana (responsibility) to honor the traditions of our indigenous people;
4. Promote social justice for Native Hawaiians;
5. Promote the creation and maintenance of Hawaiian spaces of learning, or pu'uhonua (i.e., places of refuge) for students to feel safe, welcomed and encouraged;
6. Advocate for Hawaiian places of learning, or institutional environments, that are receptive to being change agents in supporting Native Hawaiian students;
7. Educate a highly knowledgeable, skilled, flexible, world-class Native Hawaiian workforce through academic and career preparation for the Hawaiian nation. (Kauhale, 2012)

In addition, NHSS is actively engaged in developing research on Native Hawaiian students and around its services to not only inform its practice but also to add to the scholarship on Native Hawaiians and higher education and developing (and assessing) indigenous student services. Unlike other colleges and schools at UHM, HSHK is the only one that targets Native Hawaiians as a priority and nation-building as central to their work and affirms Native Hawaiian knowledge systems as pioneering, legitimate, and relevant.

Toward Supporting Indigenous Pacific Islanders in Higher Education

In this chapter, we have provided a foundation for understanding Pacific Islanders as indigenous peoples by framing our discussion and analysis using TribalCrit, as well as discussing the historical and sociopolitical context of the United States in the Pacific to contextualize indigenous Pacific Islanders' experiences. Given this lens, TribalCrit also provides a way for us to push our collective thinking to identify real ways in which higher education can actively support indigenous Pacific Islanders in scholarship and practice. A critical first step for those with limited knowledge of indigenous Pacific Islander populations involves understanding and acknowledging the importance of data disaggregation on their respective campuses, the importance of which several chapters in the current book underscore.

Regarding other implications for research, researchers should consider conducting research on indigenous Pacific Islanders using indigenous theoretical frameworks, such as TribalCrit. Such frameworks provide ways to understand and contextualize Pacific Islander indigeneity, because these frameworks are rooted in place, experience, and survivance. There is also a need for research that examines the development and impact of indigenous counter-spaces in higher education, such as HSHK, on indigenous Pacific Islanders as well as the institution itself. Researchers who study indigenous Pacific Islanders should recognize the complexity of Pacific Islanders' identities and the fact that they are people of color but also have indigenous identities to be embraced and developed.

Regarding implications for practice, college educators can learn about indigenous Pacific Islander populations through existing scholarship and conversations with indigenous Pacific Islander students, staff, and community members. They can also engage in efforts to create counter-spaces, where indigenous Pacific Islander faculty, staff, and students can embrace their cultural identities, learn about and create culturally familiar spaces, and co-construct counter-narratives. And, college educators should consider incorporating discussions about the historical and sociopolitical context of the Pacific into curricula to educate Pacific Islander students about how these contexts shape their existence. Hopefully by investing in these small actions we can start to build more understanding about indigenous Pacific Islanders in higher education and, in turn, cooperatively create higher education environments for us to thrive.

Notes

1. Our operational definition of *Pacific Islanders* is individuals who have genealogical ties to the indigenous peoples of Micronesia, Melanesia, and Polynesia. Throughout this chapter, this population will be referred to as "Pacific Islanders," "Native Hawaiians and Other Pacific Islanders" (NHOPI), "Native Hawaiian and Pacific Islanders" (NHPI), and "Native Pacific Islanders" depending on the reference. In our general discussion, we intentionally use "Pacific Islanders" in our narrative to speak to the collective spirit of the discussion rather than isolating, preferencing, or "othering" Pacific Islander cultural groups.

2. In this context, the term *Oceania* is used as Hau'ofa (1994) does, which is to link the three anthropologically defined cultural areas of the Pacific: Melanesia, Micronesia, and Polynesia.

3. Blackbirding was the practice of acquiring slaves through kidnapping or deception. It was a common practice for British ships to travel to islands like Tuvalu, Kiribati, Tonga, Vanuatu, and Kanaky to capture indigenous Pacific Islanders and take them to work on plantations in South America.

4. Indigenous and nonindigenous citizens, though for indigenous peoples, the status of "indigeneity"—the connection as "first people" to place and political status—is different in its legislation, akin to that of ethnic minorities and American Indians or Alaska Natives in the United States.

5. In 2002, the Center for Hawaiian Studies was renamed Kamakakūokalani Center for Hawaiian Studies in honor of Gladys 'Ainoa Kamakakūokalani Brandt, a former regent for the University of Hawai'i Board of Regents, who lobbied the Hawaii legislature to fund the Center for Hawaiian Studies and its building.

References

Alfred, T., & Corntassel, J. (2005). Being indigenous: Resurgences against contemporary colonialism. *Government and Opposition, 40*(4), 597–614.

Blaut, J. M. (1993). *The colonizer's model of the world: Geographic diffusionism and Eurocentric history.* New York: The Guilford Press.

Brayboy, B. M. J. (2005). Toward a tribal critical race theory in education. *The Urban Review, 37*(5), 425–446.

Connell, J. (1987). *New Caledonia or Kanaky? The political history of a French colony.* Canberra: Australian National University Press.

Diaz, V. M. (2004). To 'P' or not to 'P'? Marking the territory between Pacific Islander and Asian American studies. *Journal of Asian American Studies, 7*(3), 183–208.

Diaz, V. M., & Kauanui, J. K. (2001). Native Pacific cultural studies on the edge. *The Contemporary Pacific, 13*(2), 315–342.

Hau'ofa, E. (1994). Our sea of islands. *The Contemporary Pacific, 6*(1), 148–161.

Hawai'inuiākea School of Hawaiian Knowledge. (2012.). About Hawai'inuiākea. Retrieved from http://manoa.hawaii.edu/hshk

Hune, S. (2011). Educational data, research methods, policies, and practices that matter for AAPIs. *AAPI Nexus, 9*(1&2), 115–118.

Kamakakūokalani Center for Hawaiian Studies. (2012.). Kamakakūokalani Center for Hawaiian Studies. Retrieved from http://manoa.hawaii.edu/hshk/index.php/site/acad_studies/en/

Kana'iaupuni, S. M. (2011). Lots of aloha, little data: Data and research on Native Hawaiian and Pacific Islanders. *AAPI Nexus, 9*(1&2), 207–211.

Kānewai. (2012). Ka Papa Lo'i o Kānewai. Retrieved from http://manoa.hawaii.edu/hshk/index.php/site/acad_language/en/

Kauhale. (2012). Kauhale (Native Hawaiian Student Services). Retrieved from http://manoa.hawaii.edu/hshk/index.php/site/acad_kauhale/en/

Kawaihuelani. (2012). Kawaihuelani Center for Hawaiian Language. Retrieved from http://manoa.hawaii.edu/hshk/index.php/site/acad_language/en/

Labrador, R. N., & Wright, E. K. (2011). Engaging indigeneity in Pacific Islander and Asian American studies. *AmerAsia Journal, 37*(3), 135–147.

Matsuda, M., Lawrence, C., Delgado, R., & Crenshaw, K. (Eds.). (1993). *Words that wound: Critical Race Theory, assaultive speech, and the First Amendment.* Boulder, CO: Westview Press.

Panapasa, S. V., Crabbe, M. K., & Kaholokula, J. K. (2011). Efficacy of federal data: Revised Office of Management and Budget Standard for Native Hawaiian and Other Pacific Islanders examined. *AAPI Nexus, 9*(1&2), 212–220.

Robie, D. (1990). *Blood on their banner: Nationalist struggles in the South Pacific.* Atlantic Highlands, NJ: Zed.

Taualii, M., Quenga, J., Samoa, R., Samanani, S., & Dover, D. (2011). Liberating data: Accessing Native Hawaiian and Other Pacific Islander data from national data sets. *AAPI Nexus, 9*(1&2), 249–255.

Trask, H. (1999). *From a native daughter: Colonialism and sovereignty in Hawai'i.* Honolulu: University of Hawai'i Press.

UCLA Asian American Studies Center, UC Asian American and Pacific Islander Policy Initiative, & the Asian Pacific American Legal Foundation. (2006, November 14). Pacific Islanders lagging behind in higher educational attainment. *Analytical Briefs on New Census Data.* Los Angeles: UCLA Asian American Studies Center.

U.S. Department of the Interior Office of Insular Affairs. (1986, January 14). Compact of Free Association Act of 1985. U.S. Public Law 99-239. Retrieved from http://www.doi.gov/oia/compact/compact.html

U.S. Department of the Interior Office of Insular Affairs. (2012). Retrieved from http://www.doi.gov/oia/index.html

U.S. Office of Management and Budget. (1997, October 30). Revisions to the standards for the classification of federal data on race and ethnicity. *Federal Register Notice.* Retrieved from http://www.whitehouse.gov/omb/fedreg_1997standards

U.S. Office of Minority Health. (2007). *Official report and resolutions for the California Native Hawaiian and Other Pacific Islanders town hall meeting: "And wish all good health."* Washington, DC: U.S. Government Printing Office.

PART TWO

THE DIVERSE VOICES OF ASIAN AMERICANS AND PACIFIC ISLANDERS

Karen K. Inkelas

Pernicious social stereotypes depict the Asian American and Pacific Islander (AAPI) experience as largely homogeneous, particularly in terms of educational success. That inaccurate historical narrative has slowly given way to an acknowledgment of the diversity within the AAPI population, and the discourse about AAPI diversity is still evolving. Initial discussions about AAPI diversity typically revolve around the many ethnic backgrounds that make up the category (e.g., Lee, 1998). Indeed, the 2010 census included 49 different ethnic categories (25 Asian and 24 Pacific Islander) under the "Asian and Pacific Islander" umbrella (see Chapter 1 of this volume). Moreover, the discourse typically moves on to discussing observable differences among the various ethnic groups, including cultural, linguistic, and generational variations. In addition, several authors have noted a bimodal distribution of socioeconomic status among AAPIs, with some Asian and Pacific Americans living in high socioeconomic situations, with advanced educational attainment and professional careers, and others in low socioeconomic circumstances, with only basic schooling and mundane work situations (see Chapter 1).

Yet, the chapters in Part Two introduce readers to a broader and deeper sense of diversity within the AAPI community. With these contributions, the literature on the AAPI college student population moves beyond racial generalizations and surface distinctions such as cuisine and manner of dress, and delves into topics that illuminate the previously hidden experiences of

AAPI students, who are becoming more and more prevalent on college campuses today. Moreover, bringing these diverse stories into the light aids faculty and staff in better understanding the complex social forces that influence AAPIs of all backgrounds. Finally, as all of the authors in this part describe, the college years are a time of heightened exploration of one's social identities, and AAPI students, like most undergraduates, often wrestle with multiple aspects of their identities. They illuminate the reality that, for AAPI students, this period of development is not only defined by the probing of racial or ethnic identity, but can also be defined by issues related to gender, citizenship status, socioeconomic status, sexual orientation, religious faith, and civic responsibility.

This part opens with "Hybrid Faith, Hybrid Identities: Asian American Evangelical Christian Students on Campus." In this chapter, Julie Park, Jonathan Lew, and Warren Chiang address the trend of increasing AAPI participation in Christian fellowships. First, the authors accurately point out that AAPI students can practice a wide variety of faiths, including Eastern and Western religions. Moreover, they note that a significant proportion of AAPI students also hold no religious beliefs. Yet, on many campuses, AAPIs represent the majority of the members of Christian fellowship groups, or attend fellowships that cater only to Asian Americans. Park et al. discuss the role that such fellowships may play in AAPI students' identity development, mental health, and cross-race interaction. They also include a new term, *homophily* (see further discussion of homophily in Chapter 12 of this part), that can be used to describe the phenomenon through which individuals of like backgrounds tend to gravitate toward one another. Finally, the authors illustrate the interplay among race, religion, and institutional policy when discussing the relative utility of these types of groups on college campuses.

In "Campus Contexts and Hmong Students' Experiences Negotiating Identity and Higher Education," using case study methodology, Rican Vue explores college environmental factors associated with identity formation among Hmong students. The study takes place on a West Coast campus with a large AAPI enrollment, and Vue notes that Hmong students feel invisible in the AAPI student community. With many Hmong participants coming from communities with turbulent immigration and refugee histories and low socioeconomic circumstances, they drew distinctions between their own experiences and those of the "model minority" stereotype, to which they are assumed to conform. Looking for a place on campus where they could learn more about their own backgrounds, some Hmong students in the study found no solace in the Asian American studies courses, as many questioned why their histories did not find a place in the Asian American studies curriculum. Instead, they turned to study-abroad experiences, and the Hmong Students Association on campus for ways to learn about themselves and what it means to be Hmong in America.

Add the circumstance that one must not stand out too much for fear of being exposed to the milieu of multiple social identities, and you have the single-person case study that is presented by Tracy Lachina Buenavista and Angela Chuan-Ru Chen in "Intersections and Crossroads: A Counter-Story of an Undocumented Asian American College Student." The authors conducted an in-depth case study of one AAPI individual who is undocumented and is a member of the AAPI group that constitutes roughly 10% of the entire undocumented U.S. population. They illuminate the silencing experienced by a student who faces the challenges associated with integrating multiple layers of social identities, such as race, gender, and socioeconomic status, but who is also constantly in fear of deportation if she speaks out or takes any public actions. Using Critical Race Theory, this contribution illuminates how oppression lingers socially, economically, legally, and politically.

Jean Ryoo and Rob Ho, in "Living the Legacy of '68: The Perspectives and Experiences of Asian American Student Activists," bring to light linkages between past Asian American activism and current efforts. The chapter begins with a solid review of historical Asian American activism, highlighting the stories that are counter to the "model minority" stereotype and how Asian Americans, like other persons of color, have stood up to prejudice and marginalization and are civically and politically engaged. Particularly noteworthy is the observation that many of the Asian American students in their study felt isolated, despite being on a campus at which AAPIs made up approximately 40% of enrollment. Ryoo and Ho suggest that this isolation leads to implications regarding campus climates, particularly in terms of formal structures, programming, and classroom environments on campus. Moreover, they ponder how activists on campuses with a much smaller AAPI enrollment must feel.

Ryoo and Ho conclude their study by focusing on three topics that actually cut across all of the chapters in this part: (1) the role and purpose of Asian American studies curricula at institutions of higher education; (2) the salience of cocurricular activities in helping students make meaning of their lives; and (3) the sense of higher purpose that some AAPI students feel toward their communities, both large and small. Indeed, these three points, I believe, represent the important future direction of research on diversity within the AAPI experience.

Finally, Sean Pepin and Donna Talbot pose an interesting question regarding homophily in "Negotiating the Complexities of Being Self-Identified as Both Asian American and Lesbian, Gay, or Bisexual." What happens when gravitation toward different identities within the same person is seemingly leading in opposite directions? The authors surveyed students in the Asian American lesbian, gay, or bisexual (LGB) community through a combination of purposive and snowball sampling. They found that AAPI LGB students felt as though they could express only one identity at a time, depending upon the space in which they found themselves at a given moment. Moreover, Pepin and Talbot argue that their participants might not have even wanted to fuse their AAPI and LGB identities together. In addition, the students describe how they are constantly being pressured to prove their legitimacy in either peer group: They are pressured to demonstrate that they are "Asian enough" among their AAPI friends and "gay enough" around their LGB friends. Knowledge of these struggles that conflicting social identities engender is precisely the kind of information needed by those who work directly with students and their growth and development.

Several of the studies in this part portray a double-edged perception that AAPI students hold of Asian American studies curricula at their institutions. On the one hand, AAPI students are grateful to have a curricular "home" in which they can learn about their histories and contributions to American culture. On the other hand, many wish that Asian American studies curricula would "broaden their tent" to include AAPI voices that remain marginalized, even within the study of Asian America, such as Hmong students, LGB students, undocumented students, and even Asian American activists. The next generation of discourse on the future of Asian American studies should pose the following questions: Who should be included in the study of Asian America, and how should that inclusion be captured within the curriculum? To what extent should Asian American studies programs cater to all subgroups within their umbrella, and to what extent should they focus on commonalities across subgroups? Answering these questions is surely a formidable task, but one that is gaining the attention of Asian American studies scholars as well (Lum, 2010).

Although the curriculum, including the Asian American studies curriculum, takes a large role in influencing AAPI college students, all of the chapters in this part underscore the critical importance that cocurricular activities play in developing AAPI students' views about themselves, their heritages, and their broader communities. Regardless of their focus, AAPI students are finding great personal meaning in their involvement with cocurricular campus organizations and activities. The contributions in this part have done the literature a great service by shedding light on how cocurricular organizations and activities influence students' growth and development. An important next step for scholarship is to nest these experiences in a broader set of theory, much like Park et al. begin to do in their chapter.

Finally, all of the works in this part allude to an unspoken tie that AAPI students feel to their home and broader communities. Integrating Asian American students' campus experiences into their home and community life will continue to break down outdated notions that external forces have little to no influence on student success in college and instead replace that line of thinking with ways in which their time on campus relates to their larger life circumstances. Scholarship in this realm might consider consulting the critical literature on dominant depictions of undergraduate success.

Together, these five chapters push our understanding of Asian American students in directions that force us to recognize that simplistic interactions with and treatment of Asian American students do them a great disservice. These contributions even challenge those who acknowledge that Asian America is diverse, by demonstrating that making such an acknowledgment is only a tiny step forward toward our understanding and building upon that recognition with more complex understandings of this population is critical. Although much more work in this area must be done, these five chapters represent a strong step in the right direction.

References

Lee, S. M. (1998). Asian Americans: Diverse and growing. *Population Bulletin, 53*(2). Retrieved from www.prb.org/source/53.2asianamerican.pdf

Lum, L. (2010). Asian American studies at a crossroads. *Diverse Issues in Higher Education*. Retrieved May 21, 2012, from http://diverseeducation.com/article/13825/

8

HYBRID FAITH, HYBRID IDENTITIES

Asian American Evangelical Christian Students on Campus

Julie J. Park, Jonathan W. Lew, and Warren Chiang

Asian American students represent a variety of religious traditions, including Islam, Christianity, Hinduism, Buddhism, and Sikhism. Some students self-identify as atheist, agnostic, or simply do not affiliate with a religious or spiritual identity. Moreover, Asian Americans have become the dominant force in the religious student organization scene at many selective institutions (Stafford, 2006). For instance, at the University of California–Los Angeles, researcher Sharon Kim (2000) counted 14 Christian campus groups catering specifically to Korean Americans and an additional 10 groups that catered to Asian Americans more generally.

Given these observations, it is clear that both religious and spiritual belief and identity are relevant to our understanding of Asian American college students. In this chapter, we review the literature on one significant facet of the Asian American religious community: Asian American evangelical[1] college students. We begin by reviewing past work on Asian American campus fellowships and why they exist. We then investigate implications that these groups have for students in three areas: racial and ethnic identity, mental health, and cross-racial interaction.

Although sociology and religious studies scholars have been studying the rise of Asian Americans in *campus fellowships*—the term many evangelical

Christian student organizations use to describe themselves—since the mid-1990s, this topic has received little attention from higher education audiences. A few higher education scholars have begun researching and writing about religion and spirituality among students in general (Astin, Astin, & Lindholm, 2010; Chickering, Dalton, & Stamm, 2006; Tisdell, 2003). Tisdell defines *religion* as "an organized community of faith that has written doctrine and codes of regulatory behavior" in contrast with *spirituality*, which she explains is a "personal belief and experience of a divine spirit or higher purpose, about how we construct meaning, and what we individually and communally experience and attend to and honor as the sacred in our lives" (p. 29). She asserts that these constructs are not the same but can be related. More recently, several scholars have studied evangelical campus groups as distinct student subcultures (Bryant, 2005; Magolda & Gross, 2009; Moran, 2007). Yet, the concepts of religion and spirituality are not "one size fits all" and cannot be uniformly applied to different groups. Accordingly, we draw attention to how Asian Americans are changing the face of religious engagement on many college campuses and, in turn, how religious engagement might affect Asian American student development and collegiate experiences.

The Emergence and Growth of Asian American Campus Fellowships

Since the 1980s, noticeable numbers of Asian American students have been joining existing evangelical campus ministries and forming new ones on colleges and universities across the United States. Major metropolitan newspapers have recognized the dramatic growth in the numbers of Asian American students who are active in campus fellowships (Cho, 1999; Hua, 2007; Swidey, 2003). In addition, several scholars have noted that on the West and East Coasts Asian Americans are often overrepresented in evangelical campus ministries compared with their percentage in the student body. At colleges and universities in New York City in 1997, for example, one-fourth of all evangelical college students were estimated to be Asian American (Carnes & Yang, 2004). At Yale University, the local chapter of Campus Crusade went from an entirely White student membership in the 1980s to being 90% Asian American by the early 2000s (R. Y. Kim, 2006). Noting this shift, a student affairs professional at UC Berkeley observed that the recruiting tables at Sproul Plaza on its campus were increasingly more likely to be populated by Asian American campus ministry groups in recent years (Chang, 2000).

This rise in participation can be attributed to at least four trends: demographics, the appeal of Christianity and Asian American campus ministries to Asian Americans, the "supply" of ethnic-specific ministries available to meet the demand, and the trend of homophily.[2] First, the growth in the numbers of Asian American evangelical students has paralleled the overall growth in Asian American enrollment and, in particular, East Asian American enrollment in higher education (*The Chronicle of Higher Education*, 2009). The increasing presence of Asian American students on college campuses makes these groups literally feasible (R. Y. Kim, 2006). As the Asian American student population grows, the greater the chance that those students will create their own subcultures to cater to different facets of the population. Indeed, even within one ethnic community, there can be numerous campus fellowships that meet the different needs of subpopulations, such as second-generation Korean Americans, international Koreans, and recently immigrated Korean Americans (Kim, 2006). Although Asian American evangelicals have the most options for religious community at large West Coast universities with large numbers of Asian American students, Asian American campus fellowships exist at institutions with smaller Asian American enrollments across the nation as well.

Second, there is something about the distinctive mix of faith and ethnic community that attracts many Asian American students. Various hypotheses have been proposed to explain the apparent popularity of evangelicalism among Asian American students, including (1) the fruitful legacy of Christian missionary efforts and church planting in Asia and among Asian immigrant communities in the United States (Busto, 1996; Hall, 2002; R. Y. Kim, 2006), (2) the appeal of a religion perceived as a step in the process of entering the mainstream of American culture (Busto, 1996; Hall, 2002), and (3) evangelicalism's compatibility with Asian cultural values that are rooted in Confucianism (Busto, 1996; Hall, 2002).

As ethnic churches continue to thrive, particularly within Chinese and Korean American communities (Rah, 2009), their young adults go to college looking for spiritual community. Some may join predominantly White or multiethnic groups, but when the option to gather with peers of the same ethnicity is available, many are drawn to ethnic-specific faith communities (R. Y. Kim, 2006). A few explanations for the appeal of Asian American evangelical groups include students' longing for family-like relationships away from home, their search for identity, and their desire for "safe" ways to exercise their newfound freedom (Ch'ien, 2000). Ethnic-specific ministries can provide a sense of belonging, create a sense of community, and give students a home away from home during the college years (R. Y. Kim, 2006; S. Kim, 2000; J. J. Park, 2011). These groups can also be places where ethnic identity is valued and issues of racism are discussed (Lum, 2007). Even without such discussions, ethnic-specific ministries can provide a safe space where students do not have to fear being stereotyped, marginalized, and misunderstood because of their ethnicity or culture (R. Y. Kim, 2006; S. Kim, 2000).

Students may also desire to be in communities where peers share similar experiences around parental expectations and cultural issues. In one interview, Paul Tokunaga, former national coordinator of Asian American ministry for InterVarsity Christian Fellowship, indicated that evangelical ministries can provide help, hope, and healing for Asian American students who struggle with the high expectations that their parents place on them (Kilpatrick, 1999). Because of the tendency within some Asian communities to be less verbally expressive about love and affection, some Asian American students may find exceptional comfort in the Christian message that God loves and accepts them for who they are and not what they do. Finally, some students may prefer Asian American ministries because of opportunities to assume leadership positions that might not be available in predominantly White ministries (R. Y. Kim, 2006; Stafford, 2006).

Third, given the appeal of these groups to a sector of the Asian American population, various organizations have worked to meet the rising demand for communities that support Asian American religious involvement. Churches and parachurch organizations have started new campus fellowships to meet the demand from students for culturally relevant ministry. Because of growing interest from Asian American students, the three major national campus ministries—Campus Crusade for Christ, InterVarsity Christian Fellowship, and The Navigators—have each formed separate Asian American ministries within their organizations.

Finally, although these structures support the demand for ministry that reaches Asian American students, the trend of homophily contributes to the continued growth and sustenance of these organizations. Homophily explains some of the growth of Asian American campus fellowships; it also explains how some fellowships have transitioned from being predominantly White to predominantly Asian American. Julie Park (2009b) describes how homophily can trigger a push-and-pull dynamic. Individuals attract others with similar ethnic backgrounds, contributing to an organizational culture that caters to the growing dominant ethnic group. Without intervention, individuals of other ethnic backgrounds will feel marginalized and leave, opening the door for the community to be dominated by a particular ethnic group. Lattin (2009) described how homophily played out on one campus, whereas some campuses have become so dominated by Asian Americans that White students generally avoid such groups.

In the end, we find no singular reason for why Asian American students gravitate toward evangelical groups. Instead, a number of intersecting forces, such as institutional demographics, the desire for a sense of belonging, and homophily, appear to influence these groups' growth. What seems clear is that among myriad options on today's college campus, Asian American students have an increasing number of choices regarding venues to explore religion and spirituality during the college years. Here, these students find a combination of a sense of belonging, an affirmation of their cultural heritage, and a safe space to exercise ethnic and religious identity. We now discuss implications of Asian American campus fellowships in three areas: how Asian American campus fellowships work as sites for identity development, their relationship to mental health concerns, and their influence on cross-racial interaction.

Campus Fellowships as Sites for Racial and Ethnic Identity Development

In enabling Asian American evangelical students to find or form new student subcultures, evangelical campus fellowships provide venues for identity development. These ministries work as experimental labs where students can resist or reshape the cultural and religious values and practices (e.g., gender relations) that they have inherited from their parents and intertwine those with the values and practices (e.g., musical worship styles) that they have selectively claimed from American society and other evangelical subcultures.

Some scholars have proposed that campus fellowships can reinforce the "model minority" image of Asian American students. In the first peer-reviewed article examining the rise of Asian American campus fellowships, Busto (1996) posited that involvement in evangelicalism may be attractive to Asian American students because it reinforces an "upwardly mobile middle-class ethic" and an accompanying religious stereotype as "God's whiz kids—exemplars of evangelical piety and action to which other evangelicals should aspire" (p. 140). Are campus fellowships just another example of Asian Americans "outwhiting the Whites" (Stokes, 1971, p. 24)? Do these groups simply duplicate existing mainstream evangelical structures and impose an Asian American title on them, or is something more complex at work?

In some ways, activities in predominantly Asian American campus fellowships may generally mirror the music style and teaching found in predominantly White fellowships (R. Y. Kim, 2006). In this way, Asian American campus fellowships could appear to miss opportunities to challenge Asian American students to fully develop an integrated sense of racial and ethnic identity. However, many Asian American campus fellowships are doing more than simply mimicking White American Evangelicalism in at least three spheres of identity development: pan-ethnic and collective identity development, individual racial and ethnic identity development, and the relationship among racial and ethnic and religious identity.

Pan-Ethnic and Collective Identity Development

Like pan–Asian American churches (Jeung, 2005) and secular Asian American student groups (Rhoads, Lee, & Yamada, 2002), Asian American campus fellowships can be sites where students negotiate an evolving sense of pan-ethnic Asian American identity as well as places for Asian Americans from diverse backgrounds to explore similarities and differences in their experiences. These groups can draw students who worshipped in ethnically homogeneous congregations prior to college under a pan-ethnic umbrella. For instance, in 2009, the Asian American InterVarsity chapter at the University of Wisconsin–Madison was made up of approximately 45% Korean American students, 25% Chinese or Taiwanese American students, 20% Hmong American students, and 10% of students from other Asian ethnic backgrounds (C. Chen, personal communication, October 2, 2009). The group also included international students, multiracial students, and Korean American adoptees.

Some researchers have found that Asian American campus fellowships provide unique sites for collective racial and ethnic identity development, departing from mainstream evangelicalism and enabling students to form what Sharon Kim (2000) termed a *hybrid culture*. In her study of Korean American students, Kim observed how students borrowed and combined aspects of American, Korean, evangelical, and generational values and practices. They balanced to varying degrees American individualism with a more collectivist orientation and American egalitarianism with Korean-influenced authority structure. Similarly, Rebecca Kim (2006) discussed how Asian American campus fellowships are sites for "emergent ethnicity." Unlike previous proponents of theories who predicted that racial and ethnic minorities would eventually assimilate into mainstream American society (R. E. Park,

1950) and scholars who believe that ethnicity for second-plus-generation Americans primarily holds symbolic value (Gans, 1979), Kim asserted that meaningful representations of ethnicity are continuously emerging as Asian Americans continue to derive meaning from ethnic or racial identity categories and communities. Thus, campus fellowships are environments in which second-plus-generation Asian Americans explore the continuing salience of race, ethnicity, and culture in their lives.

Individual Racial and Ethnic Identity Development

Whereas Asian American campus fellowships can work as sites for collective, group-based representations of race/ethnicity, they may also facilitate individual racial and ethnic identity development. Participation in campus fellowships can facilitate racial and ethnic identity development for Asian American students by providing an environment where awareness about identity is heightened by being around same-race or same-ethnicity peers, or through providing an environment where awareness of identity is heightened by difference. First, some proponents of ethnic-specific campus fellowships argue that these groups are particularly conducive to racial and ethnic identity development because they are safe spaces for Asian Americans to explore questions around identity (Tomikawa & Schaupp, 2001). Such ethnic-specific groups may provide students with opportunities to examine Asian American family dynamics, gender identity, and leadership development. For instance, InterVarsity Press, the publishing arm of InterVarsity Christian Fellowship, which includes many chapters that are ethnic-specific, has published books catering to Asian American students, such as *Following Jesus Without Dishonoring Your Parents* (Yep, Cha, Tokunaga, Jao, & Cho Van Riesen, 1998) and *More Than Serving Tea: Asian American Women on Expectations, Relationships, Leadership and Faith* (Toyama & Gee, 2006). Although such discussions can happen in multiethnic settings, ethnic-specific fellowships can speak more directly to these issues.

Multiethnic campus fellowships can also be fruitful sites for racial and ethnic identity development (Garces-Foley, 2007; J. J. Park, 2009b). In Julie Park's (2009b) study of a West Coast chapter of InterVarsity Christian Fellowship, Asian American students reported that being around peers of different racial and ethnic backgrounds made them more conscious of their own identities, opening the door to conversations around race, ethnicity, difference, and racial and ethnic reconciliation. Being in a racially heterogeneous environment made them aware of parts of their culture and upbringing that they had taken for granted. This group provided opportunities for students to dialogue both across and within racial and ethnic groups, giving them chances to process questions about their identity as Asian Americans and their role in the multiethnic community.

Relationship Among Racial and Ethnic and Religious Identity

Additionally, campus fellowships may influence students' identity development by helping them explore how racial, ethnic, and religious identities relate to one another. The relationship among racial, ethnic, and religious identities is complex, with some seeing religious identity as subordinate to racial and ethnic identity, or vice versa, and others seeing the two identities as mutually influential (Abelmann, 2009; J. Z. Park, 2004). Some religious communities may not totally discount the value of racial and ethnic identity but assert that faith trumps race and ethnicity. Alumkal (2004) argued that evangelical ministries promote an alternative, religiously based identity by promoting unity "in Christ" across racial and ethnic lines; emphasizing racial and ethnic reconciliation on a more individualistic, rather than systemic, level; and encouraging students to find their identities in Christ, rather than in their "Asianness" or "Americanness." In this fashion, some Asian American campus fellowships promote a "color-blind" approach to race and ethnic relations, in line with mainstream White evangelicalism (Emerson & Smith, 2000). By downplaying the significance of race and ethnicity, campus fellowships and religious organizations can "relegat[e] ethnic difference to secondary importance" (Busto, 1996, p. 138).

Alternatively, some campus ministries encourage students to see their racial and ethnic identities as highly relevant to their religious identity, and vice versa. Julie Park (2009b) described how a multiethnic but predominantly Asian American campus fellowship encouraged students to view race/ethnicity and faith as complementary realms. She quoted students who described how their views on racial issues and ethnic identity shifted from seeing such issues as irrelevant to Christianity to seeing them as extremely important components of their faith. Students discussed how they came to see racial and ethnic identities as created and valued by God, as well as how the fellowship encouraged them to reject a color-blind outlook. Although such groups may be less common, her research shows that not all evangelical campus fellowships seek to subsume racial and ethnic identity in favor of religious identity. Thus, despite the very real tension between racial and religious identity, it appears that campus fellowships are a venue for students to negotiate these complex realities. If such groups offer unique spaces within which to grow and develop, they also likely influence the psychological well-being of their members.

Asian American Campus Fellowships and Implications for Mental Health

Asian American students face a number of mental health challenges on college campuses, including depression, discrimination, and perfectionism in the college setting (Castro, 2003; Cress & Ikeda, 2002; Gloria & Ho, 2003). Suicide is the second leading cause of death for Asian American women ages 15 to 24 (Noh, 2007). Asian American mental health concerns are exacerbated by ethnic-specific factors in Asian cultures, such as privatizing of emotions and discouraging of self-advocacy, which complicate traditional Western-Eurocentric avenues for emotional processing (Kim & Omizo, 2005; Yeh & Huang, 1996). There is also a propensity for Asian Americans to underuse professional counseling services (Abe-Kim et al., 2007), and many campuses do little to address the unique mental health needs of Asian American students.

Campus fellowships can positively support students' mental health, as well as pose certain complications for colleges and universities. We begin with the possible benefits. These groups provide a "supportive and familial structure" (Busto, 1996, p. 140) that can function like a surrogate family for Asian Americans, especially those attending college away from home. They provide a social support system for Asian Americans who might otherwise feel isolated or alienated from the campus environment. Simply put, these groups offer a sense of belonging and community, which are strongly related to student satisfaction with college (J. J. Park, 2009a). As "well-structured and nurturing" communities, these groups can assist Asian American students in "surviving the anxieties (and) alienation of the college experience" (Busto, 1996, p. 142).

Campus fellowships are also uniquely poised to address particular Asian American–specific mental health issues in an accessible manner. For example, because of social stigma, an Asian American student may feel hesitant to sign up for a counseling session to talk about parental pressures, but he or she may feel comfortable attending a small group where such issues are discussed. Such groups can give students an avenue to process their racial and ethnic identities, family dynamics, balancing of the obligations of family with individual needs, and contemplation of a major or career change. Moreover, spirituality can potentially help students cope with mental distress and psychological disequilibrium when dealing with these issues, although spiritual and religious struggle may exacerbate disequilibrium (Bryant & Astin, 2008). Thus, engaging in the spiritual disciplines used by campus fellowships (e.g., prayer, meditation, prioritizing of community, and sharing about personal struggles) might also help students cope with stressors.

However, campus fellowships may complicate mental health concerns for Asian American students in areas such as student–parent relationships and the role of campus ministry staff. First, campus fellowships can possibly foster situations that exacerbate mental stress in student–parent relationships. Students may come from families that are suspicious of campus fellowship involvement, especially if such involvement in a campus fellowship appears to take precedence over their academic performance, or when they become spiritually motivated to change majors or career trajectories to options that are not as prominent or lucrative (Lum, 2007). This can cause undue mental stress, because many Asian American students are children of immigrants with strong expectations for academic and career success.

Second, the fact that campus ministry staff and leaders are generally not university employees complicates how such groups might handle mental health concerns. Asian American students may be more likely to seek help from religious leaders and peers within these organizations instead of a university counseling center when faced with emotional or family problems (Park & Millora, 2010). However, mental health issues have substantial liability concerns attached to them, and campus fellowships, which are sometimes largely student run, may not always be equipped to handle the concerns that their members bring to them. We encourage university counseling centers to work in partnership with campus fellowships to extend services to Asian American students (Cuyjet & Liu, 1999) and also to educate campus fellowships on when it may be prudent to refer students to professional counseling services.

Cross-Racial Interactions: Do Campus Fellowships Facilitate or Hinder Them?

Finally, campus fellowships can potentially affect Asian American evangelical student experiences with diversity during the college years. Campus fellowships are an excellent site for examining the phenomenon of cross-racial interaction, or lack thereof, on college campuses because of the general ethnic homogeneity of these groups. Campus fellowships face a unique quandary because their faith articulates a vision of unity that transcends racial and ethnic divisions. For instance, Matthew 28:19 commands Christians to "make disciples of all nations" and Galatians 3:28 states that "there is neither Jew nor Greek . . . for all are one in Christ Jesus." Yet, many fellowships are predominantly one ethnic group or another. Similarly, U.S. evangelical congregations are often ethnically stratified (Emerson & Chai-Kim, 2003).

Asian American evangelical students are sometimes forced to justify their involvement in ethnically homogeneous religious groups, given biblical passages that apparently endorse transcending or crossing racial and ethnic divides (J. J. Park, 2011). Second-generation Asian Americans often use a worship style similar to that used by non-Asians, do not have a language barrier like their parents, and have plentiful opportunities to interact with people from various racial and ethnic backgrounds (R. Y. Kim, 2006). These students, therefore, may have more difficulty justifying on religious grounds why they should maintain ethnically distinct fellowships.

How do Asian American students confront the tension between ethnicity-based separatism and religious-based universalism, and what do their attitudes tell us about how students are reacting to issues of diversity and cross-racial interaction on campus? Despite the attempt by fellowships to encourage students to prioritize religious identity over racial and ethnic identities, Soyoung Park (2004) noted a disparity between Korean American students' statements about the preeminence of their religious identity and the fact that they joined ethnic-specific groups that rarely reached out beyond racial and ethnic boundaries. She later described this tension as "sociological ambivalence," where students resigned themselves to not crossing racial and ethnic lines, even though they knew that their Christianity compelled them to extend their love and message to other racial and ethnic groups.

R. Y. Kim (2006) described how two Korean American ministries at one university attempted to reconcile the conflict between ethnic separatism and religious universalism. Students in both ministries expressed discomfort with the ethnic exclusivity of their groups. One of the ministries made efforts to be more inclusive by dropping the use of Korean terms and inviting non-Koreans to outreach events. The other ministry changed its name from "Korean Christian Fellowship" to "Christian Student Fellowship" and made conscious efforts to diversify its leadership and speakers. Despite those changes, the latter organization remained 95% Korean American at the time of her research and was still known on campus as a Korean American ministry.

Observing similar trends, Julie Park (2009b) argued that many students, Asian American and otherwise, have strong ideals around diversity, but campus demographics and organizational culture work in tandem to facilitate or hinder opportunities for cross-racial interaction for campus fellowships. The InterVarsity Christian Fellowship chapter that she studied at "West Coast University" evolved from a predominantly White group in the early 1990s to a racially heterogeneous group in the late 1990s to a predominantly Asian American group by 2006. As the group intentionally pursued multiethnic community in the mid-1990s, its efforts were rewarded by group diversification. However, by 2006, the focus on race in the group had lessened, and concurrently, the Black and Latino/a populations at the institution had dropped, following a state ban on affirmative action. Park documented how the community sparked open discussions about the implications of Asian Americans being the majority group in the fellowship. Although the group decided to become more intentional about pursuing multiethnicity, Park noted that its efforts would be limited by the demographics of the broader institution.

Although Christian student groups provide a valuable space for Asian American students to practice their faith while exploring ethnic identity, those gains may come at the expense of greater interracial dialogue. Ethnic-specific Christian groups appear to do much in affirming the background of their members, but face the inevitable question of how they will engage the broader campus. Is it possible to nurture ethnic-specific community while promoting cross-racial interaction? Anecdotally, we know of some examples. For instance, at the University of Texas–Austin, there are six InterVarsity Christian Fellowship groups that collaborate with Black, Latino/a, South Asian American, East Asian American, and Greek life students in order to host conferences, joint worship services, and leadership trainings together.

Areas for Future Research

There are still significant gaps in our knowledge about Asian American evangelical college students. As for research designs, most of the research conducted to this point has been qualitative; there is a need for quantitative analysis of this student population. Also, most studies were conducted at large universities on the West Coast or in the New York/New Jersey region, and the experiences of Christian evangelical students in other geographic regions have yet to be explored. Most of the studies focusing on specific ethnic group experiences have concentrated on Korean Americans, and more research is also needed on evangelicalism among students of Chinese, Filipino, Southeast Asian, and South Asian descent. There is also the need for research on the third and later generations (R. Y. Kim, 2003), and how racial and ethnic identity and group formation are affected by greater acculturation; some of that research can be conducted now with Chinese American and Japanese American students who have already reached that stage.

More studies are needed on how Asian American evangelical students are affected by these groups, as well as how the fellowships influence the racial and spiritual climate on college campuses. Finally, we would like to see how participation in these groups affects the religious and social communities that students affiliate with after college. Some studies have begun to explore how college experiences influence postcollege involvement with churches (Garces-Foley, 2007), and future research can further examine how involvement in ethnic-specific or multiethnic campus ministries affects individuals' cross-cultural understanding, sense of self, and relationships with people of different ethnic and religious backgrounds. We hope that advancing this area of research will benefit the larger conversations in higher education about campus diversity, student development, and the role of religion in academia.

Notes

1. There are some variations in the precise definition of the term *evangelical*, but for the purposes of this chapter, we use Bryant's (2005, p. 2) definition to describe individuals or organizations that generally agree to four basic principles: "(1) adherence to the authority of Biblical scriptures, (2) emphasis on the importance of sharing their faith with others (i.e., evangelizing), (3) belief in the significance of personal conversion when one is 'born again,' and (4) belief that salvation comes only through faith in Jesus Christ." Sociologically, evangelicals are considered a subset of Christianity and are often contrasted with "mainline" or "liberal" Protestants and Catholics, although evangelicals can be found within mainline Protestant and Catholic churches as well.

2. Researchers use the term *homophily* to describe how "likes attract likes"; that is, people of similar background traits tend to gravitate toward one another (McPherson, Smith-Lovin, & Cook, 2001).

References

Abe-Kim, J., Takeuchi, D. T., Hong, S., Zane, N., Sue, S., Spencer, M. S., . . . Alegría, M. (2007). Use of mental health–related services among immigrant and

US-born Asian Americans: Results from the National Latino and Asian American Study. *American Journal of Public Health, 97*(1), 91–98.

Abelmann, N. (2009). *The intimate university: Korean American students and the problems of segregation.* Durham, NC: Duke University Press.

Alumkal, A. W. (2004). American evangelicalism in the post–civil rights era: A racial formation theory analysis. *Sociology of Religion, 65*(3), 195–213.

Astin, A., Astin, H., & Lindholm, J. (2010). *Cultivating the spirit: How college can enhance students' inner lives.* San Francisco, CA: Jossey-Bass.

Bryant, A. N. (2005). Evangelicals on campus: An exploration of culture, faith, and college life. *Religion & Education, 32*(2), 1–30.

Bryant, A. N., & Astin, H. S. (2008). The correlates of spiritual struggle during the college years. *The Journal of Higher Education, 79*(1), 1–27.

Busto, R. V. (1996). The Gospel according to the model minority? Hazarding an interpretation of Asian American evangelical college students. *Amerasia Journal, 22*(1), 133–147.

Carnes, T., & Yang, F. (Eds.). (2004). *Asian American religions: The making and remaking of borders and boundaries.* New York: New York University Press.

Castro, J. R. J. (2003). Perfectionism and ethnicity: Implications for depressive symptoms and self-reported academic achievement. *Cultural Diversity & Ethnic Minority Psychology, 9*(1), 64–78.

Chang, C. (2000). Amen. Pass the kimchee. *Monolid: An Asian American Magazine for Those Who Aren't Blinking, 1*(1), 62–69.

Chickering, A. W., Dalton, J. C., & Stamm, L. (2006). *Encouraging authenticity and spirituality in higher education.* San Francisco, CA: Jossey-Bass.

Ch'ien, E. (2000). Evangels on campus: Asian American college students are making the grade with God. *A. Magazine.* Retrieved October 24, 2007, from the Pro-Quest Ethnic NewsWatch database.

Cho, D. (1999). One changing facet of Christianity: More Asian Americans are joining college prayer meetings and Christian clubs. *Philadelphia Inquirer.* Retrieved October 24, 2007, from the LexisNexis academic database.

The Chronicle of Higher Education. (2009). *College enrollment by racial and ethnic group, selected years.* Retrieved May 31, 2012, from http://chronicle.com/article/College-Enrollment-by-Racial/48038/

Cress, C. M., & Ikeda, E. K. (2002). Distress under duress: The relationship between campus climate and depression in Asian American college students. *NASPA Journal, 40*(2), 74–97.

Cuyjet, M. J., & Liu, W. M. (1999). Counseling Asian and Pacific Islander Americans in the college/university environment. In D. S. Sandhu (Ed.), *Asian and Pacific Islander Americans: Issues and concerns for counseling and psychotherapy* (pp. 151–166). Commack, NY: Nova Science.

Emerson, M. O., & Chai-Kim, K. (2003). Multiracial congregations: An analysis of their development and a typology. *Journal for the Scientific Study of Religion, 42,* 217–227.

Emerson, M. O., & Smith, C. (2000). *Divided by faith: Evangelical religion and the problem of race in America.* New York: Oxford University Press.

Gans, H. (1979). Symbolic ethnicity: The future of ethnic groups and culture in America. *Ethnic and Racial Studies, 2,* 1–20.

Garces-Foley, K. (2007). *Crossing the ethnic divide: The multiethnic church on a mission.* New York: Oxford University Press.

Gloria, A. M., & Ho, T. A. (2003). Environmental, social, and psychological experiences of Asian American undergraduates: Examining issues of academic persistence. *Journal of Counseling and Development, 81,* 93–105.

Hall, B. (2002). *Chinese American students at the border of Christian faith* (Doctoral dissertation) Rutgers State University, Newark, NJ. Dissertation Abstracts International. (UMI No. 3055055)

Hua, V. (2007). UC Berkeley evangelicals build flock on campus: At Cal, Christian groups find eager adherents among Asian American students. *San Francisco Chronicle.* Retrieved May 21, 2007, from http://www.sfgate.com/cgi-bin/article.cgi?f=/c/a/2007/05/21/BAG7RPUKRS1.DTL

Jeung, R. (2005). *Faithful generations: Race and new Asian American churches.* New Brunswick, NJ: Rutgers University Press.

Kilpatrick, J. (1999). Asian American students: Hungry for God. *Charisma,* p. 52.

Kim, B. S. K., & Omizo, M. M. (2005). Asian and European American cultural values, collective self esteem, acculturative stress, cognitive flexibility, and general self-efficacy among Asian American college students. *Journal of Counseling Psychology, 52*(3), 412–419.

Kim, R. Y. (2003). *Emergent ethnicity: Second-generation Korean American campus evangelicals' religious participation and ethnic group formation* (Doctoral dissertation) University of California, Los Angeles. Dissertation Abstracts International. (UMI No. 3089022)

Kim, R. Y. (2006). *God's new whiz kids? Korean American evangelicals on campus.* New York: New York University Press.

Kim, S. (2000). Creating campus communities: Second-generation Korean American ministries at UCLA. In R. W. Flory & D. E. Miller (Eds.), *GenX religion* (pp. 92–112). New York: Routledge.

Lattin, D. (2009). The new believers. *California Magazine.* Retrieved October 29, 2009, from http://www.alumni.berkeley.edu/California/200909/lattin.pdf

Lum, L. (2007). The "Asianization" of campus fellowships. *Diverse Issues in Higher Education, 24*(17), 16–19.

Magolda, P. M., & Gross, K. E. (2009). *It's all about Jesus! Faith as an oppositional collegiate subculture.* Sterling, VA: Stylus.

McPherson, M., Smith-Lovin, L., & Cook, J. M. (2001). Birds of a feather: Homophily in social networks. *Annual Review of Sociology, 27,* 415–444.

Moran, C. D. (2007). The public identity work of evangelical Christian students. *Journal of College Student Development, 48*(4), 418–434.

Noh, E. (2007). Suicide among Asian American women: Influences of racism and sexism on suicide subjectification. *American Journal of Public Health, 97*(7), 1269–1274.

Park, J. J. (2009a). Are we satisfied? A look at student satisfaction with the diversity at traditionally White institutions. *The Review of Higher Education, 32*(3), 291–320.

Park, J. J. (2009b). *When race and religion hit campus: An ethnographic examination of a campus religious organization* (Doctoral dissertation). University of California, Los Angeles.

Park, J. J. (2011). "I needed to get out of my Korean bubble": An ethnographic account of Korean American collegians juggling diversity in a religious context. *Anthropology & Education Quarterly, 42*(3), 193–212.

Park, J. J., & Millora, L. M. (2010). Psychological well-being for White, Black, Latino/a, and Asian American students: Considering spirituality and religion. *Journal of Student Affairs Research and Practice, 47*(4), 1–18.

Park, J. Z. (2004). *The ethnic and religious identities of young Asian Americans* (Doctoral dissertation). University of Notre Dame, South Bend, IN.

Park, R. E. (1950). *Race and culture.* London, UK: The Free Press.

Park, S. (2004). "Korean American evangelical": A resolution of sociological ambivalence among Korean American college students. In T. Carnes & F. Yang (Eds.), *Asian American religions: The making and remaking of borders and boundaries* (pp. 182–204). New York: New York University Press.

Rah, S. C. (2009). *The next evangelicalism: Freeing the church from Western cultural captivity.* Downers Grove, IL: InterVarsity Press.

Rhoads, R. A., Lee, J. J., & Yamada, M. (2002). Panethnicity and collective action among Asian American college students. *Journal of College Student Development, 43*(6), 876–891.

Stafford, T. (2006). The tiger in the academy: Asian Americans populate America's elite colleges more than ever—and campus ministries even more than that. *Christianity Today, 50*(4), 70–73.

Stokes, B. (1971). Success story: Outwhiting the Whites. *Newsweek,* 24–25.

Swidey, N. (2003). God on the quad: New England's liberal college campuses have become fertile ground for the evangelical movement, which is attracting students in record numbers, but after they graduate, will they keep the faith? *Boston Globe.* Retrieved March 5, 2005, from http://www.boston.com/news/globe/magazine/articles/2003/11/30/god_on_the_quad

Tisdell, E. J. (2003). *Exploring spirituality and culture in adult and higher education.* San Francisco, CA: Jossey-Bass.

Tomikawa, C. T., & Schaupp, S. (2001). *Two views regarding ethnic specific and multiethnic fellowships.* Retrieved October 8, 2009, from http://www.inter varsity.org/

Toyama, N. A., & Gee, T. (Eds.). (2006). *More than serving tea: Asian American women on expectations, relationships, leadership and faith.* Downers Grove, IL: InterVarsity Press.

Yeh, C. J., & Huang, K. (1996). The collectivistic nature of ethnic identity development among Asian-American college students. *Adolescence, 31*(123), 645.

Yep, J., Cha, P., Tokunaga, P., Jao, G., & Cho Van Riesen, S. (1998). *Following Jesus without dishonoring your parents.* Downers Grove, IL: InterVarsity Press.

9

CAMPUS CONTEXTS AND HMONG STUDENTS' EXPERIENCES NEGOTIATING IDENTITY AND HIGHER EDUCATION

Rican Vue

Asian Americans and Pacific Islanders (AAPIs) are racialized as over-achieving model minorities—or an overrepresented monolithic group that achieves unparalleled and universal academic and occu-pational success (S. S. Lee, 2006; Suzuki, 2002). This stereotype is so deeply ingrained in society that AAPIs are considered outside the purview of both social justice agendas and discourses surrounding them. Consequently, higher education research on "minorities" often excludes AAPIs (e.g., Astin, 1982), as do many educational support programs (Museus, 2009). Indeed, AAPIs are excluded from psychological, outreach, and retention services, because they are "overrepresented" and assumed to be problem-free (Hune, 2002; S. S. Lee, 2006; Suzuki, 2002).

In contrast to the misinformed notion that AAPIs are comprised of a homogeneous population, several scholars have discussed the fact that the AAPI category represents more than 40 ethnic groups that differ enormously in language, cultural background, and immigration experience (e.g., Hune, 2002; Museus, 2009; The National Commission on Asian American and Pacific Islander Research in Education [CARE], 2008). This research indi-cates that Southeast Asian Americans (SEAAs)[1] and Pacific Islanders exhibit lower levels of educational attainment than other AAPIs (Hune, 2002) and the national population (Museus & Kiang, 2009). Hmong Americans, one SEAA subgroup, are underrepresented in higher education and have one of the lowest educational attainment rates of all racial and ethnic groups: Only 7.4% of Hmong Americans over age 25 have at least a bachelor's degree, compared with approximately 25% of the overall national population (CARE, 2008; Museus, 2009; Museus & Kiang, 2009; Pfeifer & Lee, 2004).

In addition, SEAA students generally enter higher education with more characteristics associated with being at risk of school attrition (Yeh, 2002). These factors include their relatively recent entry into the United States and the lack of pre-migratory education (Ima & Rumbaut, 1995; S. J. Lee, 2005). SEAAs also face a host of psychological issues stemming from war-related trauma and their refugee experiences, which can have intergenerational effects (Han, 2005; Kiang, 2002; Koltyk, 1998). Finally, SEAAs exhibit high rates of poverty (Pfeifer & Lee, 2004), which increases the likelihood that they will live in segregated racial and ethnic enclaves, be concentrated in underserved K–12 schools, and encounter a host of barriers presented in urban contexts that limit their opportunities for success (CARE, 2008; Lei, 2003; Teranishi, 2004).

In recognition of vast educational attainment disparities among AAPIs and the unique challenges faced by SEAAs, scholars have called for research that closely examines specific groups' experiences with education in order to dislodge the assumption that AAPIs are problem-free (Hune, 2002; Museus, 2009; Suzuki, 2002; Yeh, 2002). Hmong Americans are often referenced as examples that counter model-minority assumptions, precisely because of the numerous educational challenges that they face. Yet, research on their experiences in college and the impact of higher education on their identity is difficult to find.

A Qualitative Inquiry Into Hmong American Students' College Experiences

In the remainder of this chapter, I discuss a qualitative study that explores the identity formation of Hmong college students and the environments that raise identity salience. *Identity salience* refers to the extent to which an aspect(s) or dimension(s) of a person's identity (e.g., race, ethnicity, gender) is a relevant part of his or her self-concept at a particular moment in time or in a given space (Philip, 2007; Sellers, Smith, Shelton, Rowley, & Chavous,

1998). Undergirding the present exploration of identity is the notion that identity is fluid and contextual (Abes, Jones, & McEwen, 2007; Jones & McEwen, 2000). Experiences or situations may raise the significance of various aspects of identity and shape the qualitative meaning of how one self-identifies. In the current study, I am concerned primarily with the salience of Hmong ethnic identity and how other social identities (e.g., gender and racial) inform the meaning of ethnic identity.

My data are drawn primarily from one-on-one individual interviews with students who self-identify as Hmong. The interview protocol included questions that specifically addressed ethnic identity and ethnic identity salience, including the following: (1) How often do you find yourself thinking about your ethnic identity? and (2) In what particular moments or situations do you think about your identity? The current analysis identified themes that emerged throughout participant narratives regarding issues of ethnic identity and ethnic identity salience.

It is important to note that this inquiry is intended to expand research beyond aggregate data and racial narratives that mask the experiences and voices of Hmong Americans. Therefore, a foundational layer of context that informs my inquiry is the notion that race and other social constructs that work to marginalize oppressed groups permeates institutional, group, and individual realities (Collins, 2005; Omi & Winant, 1994). Such a position necessitates the perspectives of people of color and the instructive value that their experiences hold in challenging dominant values, ideologies, and practices that have become normalized and codified as knowledge. A qualitative methodology that is concerned with how reality is lived or felt and how meaning is negotiated (Merriam, 1998) is appropriate for illuminating Hmong voices and realities—in this case, how they understand their identity and higher education experiences.

In keeping with the voices of my participants, I use the terms *Hmong* and *Hmong American* interchangeably, as my participants do in their interviews. A fluid use of the terms reflects how they think, view, and speak of themselves, and I therefore aim to project their understanding of identity in this chapter. Furthermore, the analysis is aimed at exploring complexities between particular context(s) and ethnic identity salience.

West Coast University and Participants

West Coast University (WCU) is a large selective public university at which AAPI students make up a plurality of the undergraduate population: 36% of the more than 20,000 undergraduate students enrolled. This percentage is larger than that of any other race: Caucasian (35%), Chicano or Mexican American (11%), Latino (4%), Filipino (4%), African American (3.5%), and American Indian (less than 1%). The number of Hmong students is unknown, owing to limitations in institutional data, but participants estimate that there are approximately 30.

A total of 13 Hmong students participated in this study. The majority of the sample is female (11), and the majority are upperclassmen (5 juniors and 5 seniors). The sample includes participants majoring in science (7), social sciences (3), and humanities (3). All participants are traditional college-aged, full-time students and current members of the Hmong student organization on campus. Eleven participants identify as second-generation immigrants and 2 as 1.5-generation (Rumbaut & Ima, 1988). Ten are among the first generation in their family to attend college, and three have at least one parent with some higher education. In the following sections, I provide an overview of the findings of the investigation.

Underrepresentation of Hmong at West Coast University

As previously discussed, essentialist notions of AAPIs assume that they are a culturally homogeneous and unified racial group. Under this premise, Hmong students might be expected to feel *naturally* integrated and at home at a university where AAPIs are a plurality of the undergraduate student demographic. However, participants' responses indicate that, despite the large number of AAPIs at their institution, the absence of Hmong students on campus operates as a defining feature of their experiences:

> I think about [my Hmong identity] a lot when it comes to my personal life, especially if I'm talking about maybe having friends here or family here, then I think about just being Hmong and how small the Hmong community is and you kind of . . . you don't meet a lot of people who are Hmong to be able to satisfy that feeling of having a family here. [Julie]

In fact, when participants were asked how they felt at the institution, many expressed feeling invisible, overlooked, small, lonely, and unacknowledged. They often described feeling misunderstood or dismissed as merely another AAPI. In contrast to these more negative expressions, other participants indicated feeling "special" and "proud" because they were among the few within their communities to matriculate to college. Nevertheless, despite their positive outlook and sense of self-efficacy, these expressions also signify their awareness of a grim reality: Hmong Americans' limited access to higher education.

Participants' narratives detail a nuanced account of AAPI experiences, illuminating critical challenges faced in their specific ethnic community. For example, Joy stated, "Our poverty rate is the highest among Asians, and no one's really going to school, the homicides, gangs, gender biases, and domestic violence, it's really bad." Participants' enumeration of such challenges underscores how ethnicity, race, class, and gender intersect to shape identity and experience. Participants' responses also illuminate how such challenges are marginalized within the larger university context. For example, Joy went on to critique the socially constructed nature of race in responding to a number of published pieces in the WCU newspaper concerning campus diversity, minority students, and AAPIs. Among the published pieces is an article discussing how Asian Americans have replaced Whites as the largest student group. A second piece is a controversial op-ed commentary, in which the author asserts his disadvantaged minority status as a White student on campus because of the large numbers of Asian Americans enrolled. Within her critique, Joy addresses the consequences of aggregate categorization for ethnic subgroups, particularly for Hmong Americans:

> There's so many different ethnic groups within the Asian category . . . with our org, we do contribute to that diversity. . . . This state has the most Hmong people, and yet, there's less than 30 students at WCU. . . . We do have a bunch of issues in our community that has been invisible because really nobody knows who we are and because we're Asian.

In her own words, Joy challenges assumptions that position AAPIs as a singular group that can be categorized as such. By acknowledging their ethnic identity, participants brought to bear how, experientially, diversity might look among AAPIs, therefore illustrating that issues of access and underrepresentation are relevant for select AAPI subgroups. Although many of the participants identified with a pan-ethnic identity, on the whole, being Hmong was a more salient identity for them than an AAPI racial identity. It is possible that this ethnic identity was more salient because it more closely represented their day-to-day lived realities, and their Hmong identities enabled them to account for their unique ethnic-specific experiences, which are often overlooked within the larger AAPI community.

The Exclusion and Misrepresentation of Hmong Culture and Issues in Curriculum

Participants underscored the importance of a culturally relevant curriculum, because they believed that a Hmong course is necessary for their own education and development, as well as the education of the larger campus community. Linda's critique of WCU is, "You go to one of the top schools, and you want to be able to learn about yourself, and you can't." Whereas the absence of Hmong culture and history from the curriculum affected participants' self-understandings, it also shaped their interactions with college peers, the majority of whom had limited knowledge of Hmong Americans. Participants described continually being asked about their identity, which became a basis for their critique of education. For example, Sue passionately explains that, everywhere she goes, people are always asking her, "'What is that?' [Hmong] or 'what are you?' Like, I think it's really sad because the reason why we're here is because of the war in the Vietnam with America . . . and so I don't feel justified because they don't really teach about why we're here and who we are." Sue's statement challenges what is included and legitimated as part of history in American education systems and highlights the denial of Hmong people's place within U.S. history. Overall, participants expressed frustration and anger regarding the exclusion of Hmong from the curriculum.

In addition to critiquing their education, participants discussed internal reflection and disappointment regarding limited understandings of self. Indeed, although participants in this study emphasized the centrality of a Hmong identity to their lives and educational experiences, many struggled in defining it for others. Lisa painfully shared, "I find it really difficult to try to explain what Hmong is, because I myself don't really know the full history." Additionally, participants like Sue, who displayed a keen awareness of institutions' lack of culturally relevant content in their curriculum, still expressed disappointment with themselves for having limited knowledge about their history and culture:

> I feel bad because I don't know too much about the history. I have this kind of vague description of who we are and where we came from, but I can't really tell them the exact dates or where the places our parents were in like the refugee camps and all that stuff.

Consequently, the absence of Hmong history from their education limited participants' ability to remedy their invalidation on campus and led participants to question their own identities as well as encounter challenges integrating their "Hmong" and "American" identities.

Asian American Studies Courses and Ethnic Identity

One place participants learned more about themselves was in Asian American studies (AAS) courses, in which students were able to develop meaningful connections with the curriculum. For example, Joy, who originally majored in science and eventually transferred into AAS, often emphasized the importance of being able to "relate" to what she is learning as the primary reason for her change in major:

> I think a lot of people are afraid. . . . They're like, "What are you going to do with that [AAS degree]?" I'm just like, "Well, I'm just really glad that I'm learning about something I really like, something I can relate to," and in a lot of the Asian American courses, they really teach you how to pretty much speak up and be critical, so I think that's pretty beneficial.

The curriculum resonated with participants because it provided a means for acquiring knowledge about AAPI community history and issues. For Joy, in particular, it was both valuable and empowering to be cognizant and critical of her place as a person of color in a stratified society.

Although participants were able to connect with the AAS curriculum and benefit from the instructive value it had for their racial identity as AAPIs, some also felt the class content was lacking in speaking to some of their specific experiences as Hmong Americans, which they viewed as consisting of distinct issues given their pre-migratory conditions and immigration history. Joy, one of the most vocal advocates for AAS courses, insisting on its importance, because "You learn about your Asian American experience," reveals that she also desired to see more of her specific ethnic history addressed:

> But it would be nice to have a class where you could learn about *your history* and *your parents*, where they come from. Because again, it goes back to, people ask me, like, "Where are you from? Who are you?" . . . I can say I'm Hmong, but other than that . . .

As Joy's comment illustrates, AAS classes helped participants understand different dimensions of their identity (i.e., Hmong and Asian American identities), even if they were unable to fully accommodate each one.

Despite this absence, many students expressed how AAS courses were the only contexts in which culturally relevant issues were presented in their classes. Moreover, many of the Hmong females exhibited an increased awareness of gender issues within their community as a result of AAS courses. Indeed, female participants often spoke about the gender conscious-ness fostered by AAS courses. For example, Sue indicated that her AAS classes allowed her to explore and better understand gender dynamics in her community, when she stated, "All my papers have something to do with the Hmong community, whether it's women, whether it's young marriages or interracial dating." Thus, AAS courses provided opportunities to explore and understand how intersections between race and gender shape the experiences of Hmong women.

Study-Abroad Experiences and Ethnic Identity

In addition to AAS courses, participants turned to study-abroad programs to satisfy the desire to learn about themselves and connect their learning to their own lives. This desire was evident in the relatively large number of Hmong students at WCU, including more than half of the study partici-pants, who studied or planned to study abroad in Thailand during their tenure as undergraduates. Although first-generation Hmong Americans are predominantly refugees displaced from Laos, many spent several years in the refugee camps of Thailand before migrating to other nations. For Hmong people, the dire refugee camp experience resulted in "a loss of status, iden-tity, and autonomy" because of the symbolic representation of their grim physical circumstances (Koltyk, 1998), consequently highlighting the salience of their ethnic minority status as a diasporic community with no presumable ethnic homeland of their own. However, because of its role as a gateway for Hmong to the United States, Thailand might be considered a heritage coun-try where second-generation Hmong Americans might go in search of a sense of identity and culture, or acquire an impression of their parents' lives before they migrated to the United States.

Across participants, studying in Thailand was motivated by a sense of incompletion they experienced in their education. Mai, a history major explains, "I was taking a class on Southeast Asian history, but then I still felt like there was something missing, that I wanted more . . . like WCU wasn't giving me enough." In her courses, Mai described herself as always "trying to look for connections," which she found in a broader context. She stated, "When you look at all the broad things . . . colonization and the Vietnam War . . . I could relate everything back to my parents and their story and their struggles now, just because of things that have happened in Southeast Asia." Like Mai, other participants who studied in Thailand desired to learn more about themselves through their parents' experiences and viewed studying abroad in a heritage country as an opportunity to do so.

Studying abroad in Thailand also allowed participants to draw parallels between international Hmong communities and their communities at home. For example, Mai discussed how, during her trip abroad, she discovered commonalities with her own life that provided perspective on the meaning of ethnic identity:

> In this one village, I was talking to one of the older men, and he was just saying how a lot of the younger Hmong, they're getting a better education. But, then at the same time, they're taking that education and they're going to work in the cities, and so they don't come back to the villages anymore and actually give back. And, he's just like, they're losing their Hmong identity there, too, and so I was like, "Wow. We thought we were the only ones going through that," but they're going through it here, too, in Thailand.

Mai's experiences illustrate how her ethnic identity was continually being negotiated. They also illuminate how studying abroad provided an important context for students to connect with Hmong history, community, and culture, as well as facilitate their identity exploration and development.

Reconstructing Ethnic Identity and Developing Purpose

Ethnic identity was a salient factor in participants' development of purpose, which includes several interrelated priorities: vocational goals and aspirations, interpersonal interests, and family commitments. For participants, challenges associated with race and ethnicity became a foundation for understanding the value of an education beyond individual concerns or interests. Specifically, students' ethnic identity served as a reference point that provided motivation to persevere in college, especially under challenging circumstances such as academic difficulty or moments of uncertainty. Joua, for example, articulated the following:

> I have something to hold me back if I want to go and do something extreme like, just forget about school, quit, because I can't. Because I have to think about my parents, they put so much effort to get here and they're making ends meet. I see them struggle sometimes to just pay the bills.

Like other participant narratives, Joua's desire to overcome the inequities that her parents faced kept her motivated. Therefore, the purpose of education resonated not only as a personal undertaking, but also within the larger context of family and community.

Many of the students viewed their personal goals as aligned with their aspirations for their community. When asked about personal goals and aspirations, discourses of community ranging from the well-being of Hmong youth, to caring for the aging first generation, and facilitating the adjustment and success of the most recent Hmong refugee arrivals were often significant and even central in participants' vision of personal success. Julie described that her "dream" was to open up her own pharmacy so that "Hmong parents who don't speak English can get the help they need without always having to have a translator or be frustrated" and she stated, "I think that's my biggest contribution." In reflecting on her motivations, she shared that her own childhood experiences translating for her parents and witnessing their disempowerment were instrumental in the formation of her aspirations. For many participants, career choices stemmed from their own experiences growing up in a refugee community, and aspirations for succeeding were motivated by being able to someday serve as an instrument of societal change for the collective benefit of the Hmong community. Thus, participants described how their career choices and motivations for success are guided by the needs of, and commitment to, their community.

Hmong Student Association as Space for Developing Identity and Purpose

The Hmong Student Association (HSA) served as a space in which participants engaged in activities that directly addressed issues and experiences they shared as Hmong Americans. One example is their annual campus culture show, which narrated the experiences of a fictional character named Bee, who is a Hmong boy coming to terms with his ethnic identity. Initially, Bee rejects Hmong identity and culture; however, both Hmong identity and culture eventually become central to his self-identification. The ethnic identity development of Bee's character reflects participants' own experiences with identity. Amy, a first-year student, explained the following:

> With Bee, I felt like he . . . in the beginning, he was trying to escape, and then he found himself in the end. . . . I think I'm still finding myself, finding out where I come from. . . . I think it is where I'm headed, too.

For Amy and other students, Bee's character symbolized reconnecting to Hmong identity and regaining new appreciation for how history and culture have continued to play a role in their lives.

As participants found themselves isolated in a new environment, where Hmong students are largely absent and invalidated, the meaning and value of ethnic identity and community became apparent. Being connected to a community of Hmong students at WCU provided an affirming presence for students on campus that cultivated community and ethnic identity, thereby bolstering their academic and cultural sense of belonging at the institution. In particular, Sue described the importance of HSA for her academic identity and ethnic/cultural identity:

> It [HSA] gives you a sense of who you are and helps you identify you. It helps you experience what you're going through with other people. And helps to build that bond and commitment to the other members . . . to let you know that you do belong here, and that there is a support group for you. I was lost basically for most of my first year, because there's, like, no one here. Coming from a place where there's Hmong people everywhere and, like, honestly, I just wanted to get away. But I came here, and there were no Hmong people, it's like, I miss Hmong people.

For Sue, the shift in environment, from one where Hmong were "everywhere" to one where they were virtually nonexistent, changed the meaning attached to her ethnic identity. Whereas ethnic identity previously existed as a constraint for individual exploration, it became an affirming buffer from isolation, misunderstanding, and external hostility. Moreover, participation in the HSA provided participants with their primary coping mechanisms and a space to reflect on their dynamic experiences as Hmong Americans, addressing both the similarities and variations in experiences among those in the group.

In addition to being a safe space to negotiate identity without misunderstanding and feel a sense of belonging, the HSA enabled participants to envision how their education might be applied to their communities. Whereas the formal curriculum often lacks cultural relevancy, ethnic organizations supplement this void in students' education (Museus, 2008). Jason, for example, stated, "I think HSA is really different. . . . It's more about my identity and who I am and what I can give back to the community and to other students." HSA's role in helping students find meaning as it relates to their place in their community and society is demonstrated through its members' engagement in various activities, including educational outreach, community advocacy, and campus awareness activities. These activities enable students to utilize their position as university students to address their marginalization in the mainstream culture of campus and in society. Many of the issues in which students involve themselves directly challenge or bring awareness to inequities that Hmong Americans experience in U.S. society.

Implications for Research and Practice

This chapter explored Hmong students' identity exploration and negotiation in college. For participants, ethnicity was salient for their experiences and sense of belonging on campus. Although not the only salient dimension, ethnicity was a central theme, because of the ways that it interacted with other identity dimensions in shaping their experiences. For example, understandings of a Hmong identity were intricately interconnected with their experiences of class and gender. Furthermore, dynamics of environmental context appear to influence the salience of identity dimensions or experiences of identity. In particular, ethnic identity was salient owing to the ways the institution invalidated Hmong history, culture, and experiences. Nevertheless, specific campus contexts were instrumental in participants' negotiations of identity and education. Such findings have a number of implications for research and practice.

In regard to research, although it is clear that Hmong student experiences are heterogeneous, the diversity of experiences within this population was not the focus of the current analysis. Future research should attempt to further examine how multiple identity and intersections (of ethnicity, gender, class, and religion) mutually shape the experiences of Hmong and other AAPI students, faculty, and academic service personnel in higher education.

In addition, this study's focus examined Hmong students' experiences at one institution, specifically a highly selective public institution where AAPIs are a racial plurality. As a result, this study raises compelling questions for future research. For example, how would differences in selectivity or structural diversity, specifically ethnic and racial breakdown, shape how racial and ethnic identities are shared? It might be understood that WCU's institutional type as a highly selective university contributed to participants' feelings of invisibility and efficacy. Furthermore, it might be expected that students at an institution with a larger critical mass of students from shared ethnic backgrounds may experience less ethnic salience or experience race and ethnicity in different ways. Thus, how do these and other institutional contexts influence how identity is experienced and negotiated? A larger and broader sample, which includes varying institutional types, may be able to help answer these questions.

Regarding practice, faculty and academic service personnel should engage students in discussions of ethnic identity and its relationship to course learning and major decisions. Self-reflection that is generated from such conversations may lead students to better understand their own racial and ethnic identity and to develop a sense of purpose. Additionally, given that Hmong students must simultaneously negotiate cultural expectations and dominant cultural systems in college, such activities may lead students to find purpose that meets the expectations of both individual and collectivist goals that *they* construct, rather than by the definitions of others.

Student affairs officers can also make students aware of opportunities to explore identity through student organizations, ethnic studies courses, and study-abroad programs. Participation in such activities yielded benefits for the current study's participants. These findings support previous studies on the positive role of ethnic organizations and ethnic studies for AAPIs' educational experiences (Inkelas, 2004; Kiang, 2002; Museus, 2008) and offer new insights into the role of study abroad for Hmong students who study in a country of heritage.

Another implication for student support personnel is to make services more inclusive by acknowledging intra-race diversity when advertising and constructing programs and activities, especially for services geared toward AAPIs. Indeed, given participants' frustrations with peer and faculty's limited awareness of ethnic diversity within the AAPI community, Hmong and other AAPI students who identify more strongly with their ethnic community than the pan-ethnic AAPI racial group may be more likely to respond to support programs and services that demonstrate an awareness of ethnic differences within the AAPI category.

On a related note, faculty and staff should increase their knowledge of specific ethnic populations and therefore increase their levels of cultural competency. Such increased cultural competency among faculty and staff could lead to programs and services that are more accessible by Hmong and AAPI students on their respective campuses. This is a critical consideration, given the fact that AAPIs tend to underuse social services (Liang & Sedlacek, 2003), despite their increasing need for such support (Hsu, Davies, & Hansen, 2004; Okazaki, 1997).

Indeed, it is critical that educators who are working with AAPI undergraduates not assume that students share similar experiences and backgrounds simply because of their shared racial identity. Beyond race, other identities and experiences are important in shaping students' experiences in college. And, different experiences may require different types of support in development and engagement. For example, students who grow up in primarily White neighborhoods may be in search of affirming ethnic identity, whereas others may need support in redefining themselves independent of their ethnic community.

Beyond individual experiences, initiatives at the institutional level can create opportunities for meaningful involvement and profoundly influence how students experience identity. Campus-administered forums on identity, diversity, and leadership should be encouraged, offered, and possibly instituted as part of residence hall activities, community program offices that work with student organizations, and orientation for new students. These programmatic offerings may serve as venues for campuswide dialogue about different identity issues, raising awareness, and promoting an inclusive climate for student learning.

Notes

1. For the purpose of this chapter, the term *Southeast Asian Americans* refers to Cambodian, Hmong, Laotian, and Vietnamese Americans.

References

Abes, E. S., Jones, S. R., & McEwen, M. K. (2007). Reconceptualizing the model of multiple dimensions of identity: The role of meaning-making capacity in the construction of multiple identities. *Journal of College Student Development, 48*(1), 1–22.

Astin, A. (1982). *Minorities in American higher education: Recent trends, current prospects, and recommendations.* San Francisco, CA: Jossey-Bass.

Collins, P. H. (2005). *Black sexual politics: African Americans, gender, and the new racism.* New York: Routledge.

Han, M. (2005). Relationship among perceived parental trauma, parental attachment, and sense of coherence in Southeast Asian American college students. *Journal of Family Social Work, 9*(2), 25–45.

Hsu, E., Davies, C. A., & Hansen, D. J. (2004). Understanding mental health needs of Southeast Asian refugees: Historical, cultural, and contextual challenges. *Clinical Psychology Review, 24,* 193–213.

Hune, S. (2002). Demographics and diversity of Asian American college students. In M. K. McEwen, C. M. Kodama, A. N. Alvarez, S. Lee, & C. T. H. Liang

(Eds.), *Working with Asian American college students: New directions for student services* (No. 97, pp. 11–20). San Francisco, CA: Jossey-Bass.

Ima, K., & Rumbaut, R. G. (1995). Southeast Asian refugees in American schools: A comparison of fluent-English-proficient and limited-English-proficient students. In D. T. Nakanishi & T. Y. Nishida (Eds.), *The Asian American educational experience: A source book for teachers and students.* New York: Routledge.

Inkelas, K. K. (2004). Does participation in ethnic cocurricular activities facilitate a sense of ethnic awareness and understanding? A study of Asian Pacific American undergraduates. *Journal of College Student Development, 45*(3), 285–302.

Jones, S. R., & McEwen, M. K. (2000). A conceptual model of multiple dimensions of identity. *Journal of College Student Development, 41,* 405–414.

Kiang, P. (2002). Stories and structures of persistence: Ethnographic learning through research and practice in Asian American studies. In Y. Zou & E. T. Trueba (Eds.), *Ethnography and schools: Qualitative approaches to the study of education* (pp. 223–255). Lanham, MD: Rowman & Littlefield.

Koltyk, J. (1998). *New pioneers in the heartland: Hmong life in Wisconsin.* Boston, MA: Allyn & Bacon.

Lee, S. J. (2005). *Up against Whiteness: Race, school, and immigrant youth.* New York: Teachers College Press.

Lee, S. S. (2006). Over-represented and de-minoritized: The racialization of Asian Americans in higher education. *InterActions: UCLA Journal of Education and Informational Studies, 2*(2). Retrieved from http://repositories.cdlib.org/gseis/interactions/vol2/iss2/art4

Lei, J. L. (2003). (Un)Necessary toughness? Those "loud Black girls" and those "quiet Asian boys." *Anthropology and Education Quarterly, 34*(2), 158–181.

Liang, C. T. H., & Sedlacek, W. E. (2003). Organizing services for incoming Asian American students. *Journal of College Student Development, 44,* 260–266.

Merriam, S. B. (1998). *Qualitative research and case study applications in education.* San Francisco, CA: Jossey-Bass.

Museus, S. D. (2008). The role of ethnic student organizations in fostering African American and Asian American students' cultural adjustment and membership at predominantly White institutions. *Journal of College Student Development, 49*(6), 1–19.

Museus, S. D. (2009). A critical analysis of the exclusion of Asian American from higher education research and discourse. In L. Zhan (Ed.), *Asian American voices: Engaging, empowering, enabling* (pp. 59–76). New York: NLN Press.

Museus, S. D., & Kiang, P. N. (2009). The model minority myth and how it contributes to the invisible minority reality in higher education research. In S. D. Museus (Ed.), *Conducting research on Asian Americans in higher education: New directions for institutional research* (No. 142, pp. 5–15). San Francisco, CA: Jossey-Bass.

The National Commission on Asian American and Pacific Islander Research in Education. (2008). *Asian Americans and Pacific Islanders in higher education—Facts, not fiction: Setting the record straight.* New York: College Board.

Okazaki, S. (1997). Sources of ethnic differences between Asian American and White American college students on measures of depression and social anxiety. *Journal of Abnormal Psychology, 106*(1), 52–60.

Omi, M., & Winant, H. (1994). *Racial formation in the United States: From the 1960s to the 1990s.* New York: Routledge.

Pfeifer, M. E., & Lee, S. (2004). Hmong population, demographic, socioeconomic, and educational trends in the 2000 census. In H. HCRC (Ed.), *Hmong census publication: Data and analysis* (pp. 3–11). Washington, DC: Hmong National Development & Hmong Cultural and Resource Center.

Philip, C. (2007). *Asian American identities: Racial and ethnic identity issues in the twenty-first century.* Youngstown, NY: Cambria Press.

Rumbaut, R. G., & Ima, K. (1988). *The adaptation of Southeast Asian refugee youth: A comparative study.* Final report to the Office of Resettlement. San Diego, CA: San Diego State University. (ERIC Document Reproduction Service No. ED299372).

Sellers, R. M., Smith, M. A., Shelton, J. N., Rowley, S. A. J., & Chavous, T. M. (1998). Multidimensional model of racial identity: A reconceptualization of African American racial identity. *Personality and Social Psychology Review, 2*(1), 18–39.

Suzuki, B. H. (2002). Revisiting the model minority stereotype: Implications for student affairs practice and higher education. In M. K. McEwen, C. M. Kodama, A. N. Alvarez, S. Lee, & C. T. H. Liang (Eds.), *Working with Asian American college students: New directions for student services* (No. 97, pp. 21–32). San Francisco, CA: Jossey-Bass.

Teranishi, R. (2004). Yellow and brown: Emerging Asian American immigrant populations and residential segregation. *Equity and Excellence, 37*(3), 255–263.

Yeh, T. L. (2002). Asian American college students who are educationally at risk. In M. K. McEwen, C. M. Kodama, A. N. Alvarez, S. Lee, & C. T. H. Liang (Eds.), *Working with Asian American college students: New directions for student services* (No. 97, pp. 61–72). San Francisco, CA: Jossey-Bass.

IO

INTERSECTIONS AND CROSSROADS

A Counter-Story of an Undocumented Asian American College Student

Tracy Lachina Buenavista and Angela Chuan-Ru Chen

Higher education scholars and practitioners often debunk homogeneous depictions of a monolithic Asian American educational experience by highlighting the diversity of this group. In this chapter, we further advance this agenda by showcasing the experience of an undocumented Filipina student, Andresa Maypagasa.[1] Furthermore, we assert that efforts to understand the postsecondary experiences of Asian American students require a comprehension of how race, socioeconomic status, gender, immigration, and citizenship intersect to shape their marginalization, and the subsequent crossroads they must navigate.

In a report released by the Department of Homeland Security, researchers highlighted that the undocumented population in the United States has been steadily increasing in the past decade (Hoefer, Rytina, & Baker, 2009). In 2008, there were about 11.6 million undocumented people in the nation, which is an increase of 37% since 2000. Although there are a substantial number of undocumented people from non-Asian countries, such as Mexico, statistics reveal a presence of undocumented people from Asia—approximately 1.2 million in 2008. Four Asian countries were among the top 10 countries of origin of undocumented people: the Philippines, Korea, China, and India. It is understandable that the discourse on undocumented experiences is Latino-focused when one considers that the vast majority of the undocumented population is from Latin American countries. However, the significant and increasing numbers of undocumented people from Asian countries warrant paying attention to this group.

Undocumented students face unique struggles, but those challenges have only recently been brought into higher education discourse (Rincon, 2008). Indeed, only approximately 50% of undocumented people between the ages of 18 and 24 graduate from high school (Passel, 2005). Of those who do graduate, only 50% will go on to pursue some type of postsecondary education. Whereas college access is difficult for undocumented youth, persistence can also pose challenges. One barrier to college access and persistence for undocumented students is financial difficulties. The average family income for undocumented people is 40% less than that of their immigrant and "native" family counterparts (Passel, 2005), but their unauthorized status often renders them ineligible for state and federal financial aid (Rincon, 2008). Thus, although students from these families demonstrate a great need for financial aid, they remain ineligible to receive it.

Only 11 states have passed legislation granting undocumented students the ability to be eligible for in-state tuition (Luse, 2009). In California, where the majority of undocumented people reside, the educational policy is called Assembly Bill 540 (AB 540), which grants the ability to pay in-state tuition to any persons, undocumented or not, who (1) attended a California high school for three or more years, (2) graduated from a California high school or earned the equivalent of a high school diploma, (3) registers at a public college or university in California, and (4) files an affidavit promising to become a "lawful permanent resident" at the earliest possible opportunity (AB 540, 2001). As a result of this policy, the University of California system has been able to estimate the number of undocumented students through demographic data associated with AB 540 recipients. In a report released by the University of California Office of the President (2006), out of the 390 undocumented AB 540 recipients, 39.5% self-identified as "Asian." Considering that people of Asian descent are not as representative in the overall undocumented population, such a figure indicates that there may be racial differences in access among undocumented students, at least within the University of California.

Although there is some mention of the racial and ethnic diversity of undocumented students (Gonzales, 2009; Madera et al., 2008), there is a lack of attention paid to issues faced by undocumented Asian Americans. Moreover, although the majority of undocumented students are people of color, studies have yet to examine the ways in which race and racism shape the experiences of undocumented students. In response, we use Critical Race Theory (CRT) and case study methods to present the counter-story of an undocumented U.S. Filipina student, Andresa Maypagasa, whose story exemplifies how the lives of undocumented Asian Americans are simultaneously shaped by racism, poverty, sexism, and a lack of citizenship.

Current Undocumented Student Discourse

Within the past few years, scholarship that examines undocumented student experiences has emerged (Gonzales, 2009; Perez, 2009; Rincon, 2008). This literature has highlighted and brought national attention to the general issues that affect undocumented students and has been integral in framing the educational discourse on this population. Although such research provides rich descriptions of undocumented students' experiences, few offer an in-depth examination of Asian American perspectives or the relationship between undocumented status and educational marginalization as they are shaped by race, socioeconomic status, and gender.

Perez (2009), for example, presents undocumented student trajectories through narratives of undocumented Latino youth along the educational pipeline, from high school students to college graduates. Although he thoroughly describes how these students are firmly rooted in their Latino identity and community, as well as discusses their potential contributions as educated persons, he does not interrogate how Latinos are racialized. The analysis attributes immigration status as the central cause for the social barriers identified by participants, without sufficient discussion of the intersectionality of race, class, gender, and lack of citizenship in their experience.

Similarly, *Underground Undergrads: UCLA Undocumented Immigrant Students Speak Out* (Madera et al., 2008) is a student publication that features the narratives of high-achieving undocumented college students in their struggle to persist at a large public research university. This collection includes candid stories of hardship, resilience, and agency that humanize the emotional and financial distress that characterize their experiences. Accounts from both Latino and Asian students are profiled, each describing the unique transnational context surrounding their immigration experiences. Although this publication implicitly challenges the notion that immigration is strictly a "Latino" issue by including Asian American immigrant perspectives, it lacks a critical analysis of how students' experiences differ across racial identities. Thus, these undocumented college students' narratives are limited and undermine the significance of how race and racism shape their experiences.

One goal of the aforementioned works is to dispel the myth that undocumented people represent social and economic parasites, often focusing on their contributions to the United States. Aligned with this goal, Gonzales (2009) authored a report focused on the social and political barriers experienced by undocumented students and made a strong economic argument for the need to create a pathway to citizenship for high-achieving undocumented youth. Combining education and economic data with stories on undocumented students, Gonzales emphasizes the potential economic contributions of high-achieving undocumented students to the global economy. Gonzales acknowledges the growing number of undocumented Asian American students and problematizes their lack of visibility. However, his analysis is problematic when he suggests that Asian invisibility is self-imposed, and that they "remain hidden because their families enforce silence and secrecy for fear of being discovered and deported" (p. 10). By blaming undocumented Asian American students for their own silence, he overlooks the institutional factors, such as racism, that perpetuate their silence.

The scholarship on undocumented students' experiences highlights the barriers to higher education, such as the financial burden imposed upon these students because of their noncitizen status. Scholars have also used narratives of unique undocumented student achievement and resiliency to validate their entitlement to resources and eventual citizenship. These works, however, fail to critically examine the sociohistorical context of how these students are racialized and how racism is significant in shaping their experiences. For this reason, we rely on CRT to guide our data collection and analysis of the challenges faced by one undocumented Filipina's pathway to higher education. In doing so, we offer a more nuanced examination of one student's experiences, not only as they are shaped by undocumented status, but also as they are compounded by race, socioeconomic status, and gender.

Critical Race Theory and Case Study Methodology

CRT, within an educational context, is concerned with highlighting how race and racism are central in shaping the experiences of people of color and thus provides a useful framework to examine the higher education experiences of undocumented students—the majority of whom are students of color. Solórzano (1997) identified five tenets that characterize CRT research

in education: (1) asserts that race is socially constructed and racism serves to oppress those racialized as people of color, (2) challenges deficit and White supremacist ideology that often shape education discourse, (3) represents a commitment to advancing social justice within education, (4) relies on the experiential knowledge of marginalized people to highlight and transform oppressive practices in education, and (5) employs interdisciplinary methods and perspectives to examine and understand the experiences of people of color in education.

Using the tenets of CRT, we sought to understand Andresa's experiences through an in-depth examination of how historical and contemporary inequities shaped her educational context. Thus, we used a single case study design to conduct a detailed exploration of one "subject" within her context (Bogdan & Biklen, 2003; Yin, 1994). The value of this approach was our ability to gain a deep and nuanced understanding of Andresa's educational trajectory, through an intensive exploration of how her undocumented status intersects with her race, class, and gender to shape her experiences.

Solórzano and Yosso (2002) define counter-stories as a method of highlighting the experiences of people whose voices are often silenced. Counter-storytelling poses a direct challenge to contemporary color-blind discourse that attempts to downplay the role of race in people's lives. However, counter-storytelling does not just involve the description of particular life events, but rather locates the experiences of people of color within the social, historical, and political context that have shaped them. Thus, beyond solely providing a descriptive account of Andresa's experiences as an undocumented student, we illuminate the institutional racism that pervades her life and discuss how her race, socioeconomic status, and gender intersected with undocumented status to ultimately shape the barriers she faced in her pursuit of higher education.

We collected ethnographic data over a six-month period. There were three primary methods of data collection. First, data collection included observational notes and memos from (1) numerous informal interactions via in-person and e-mail correspondence with Andresa, (2) three formal visits with Andresa at spaces in the area where she was raised, and (3) attendance at one meeting for a support group for undocumented Asian American students. Second, she filled out two short questionnaires: one focusing on demographic information, and one regarding her experiences as an undocumented Asian American college student. Finally, one semi-structured interview was conducted at her home. The audio-taped interview lasted two hours, was transcribed verbatim, and was edited to include additional thoughts Andresa shared after reflecting on the interview experience. For confidentiality purposes, we have removed information that could potentially be used to reveal Andresa's real identity from interviews and ethnographic notes. Our work with Andresa is part of a larger project on undocumented Asian American college students' experiences. In the following, we briefly describe Andresa's immigration process and present her subsequent experiences as a counter-story to the current research that does not highlight the relationship between undocumented student issues and race, socioeconomic status, and gender.

Contextualizing Undocumented Asian American Student Experiences

Andresa's experience as an undocumented Filipina is part of a larger story of Filipino immigration, in which U.S. and Philippine immigration policies combined with the neocolonial relationship between the two countries have produced the systematic movement of Filipinos to, and subsequent marginalization of Filipinos in, the United States (San Juan, 2009). Andresa arrived in the United States from the Philippines in December 1991, at the age of 10. Andresa's migration occurred during a two-year chain migration process that began with her mother, continued with her and her four siblings, and concluded with her father's arrival. All of them were permitted entrance into the United States through the acquisition of tourist visas. They would be characterized as "overstayers," or persons who acquire undocumented status through visa expiration. Overstayers represent 25–40% of undocumented people (Passel, 2005). Contrary to popular belief, overstayers legally enter the United States, although continued presence beyond the approved length of visit leads to unauthorized status. Andresa represents an interesting case, because she recently became eligible for a green card; her eligibility was gained through marriage to a U.S. citizen after she completed her undergraduate education. However, as she adamantly argued throughout our communication, her "papers" do not erase her 17 years of being an undocumented youth and navigating higher education as such.

While she was undocumented, Andresa attended public schools from grades 5 to 12 and community college for three years, before transferring and graduating with a bachelor's degree in ethnic studies from a large public university. From middle school to college, she attended school full-time and worked multiple jobs alongside her family, which included newspaper delivery and child care. Although her undergraduate experiences as an undocumented student are the focus of this chapter, it is important to note that she is currently enrolled as a graduate student in ethnic studies at the same institution where she earned her bachelor's degree.

Andresa's story revealed the multilevel trauma inflicted upon undocumented Asian Americans. Although she was poignantly open about sharing her stories, her accounts were simultaneously characterized by sadness, laughter, fear, and resilience. During both formal and informal discussions, Andresa described the emotional turmoil that she felt because of the lack of access to basic civil rights, which heightened her awareness of her marginalization as not only a noncitizen, but also a poor woman of color. It was exactly her ability to highlight the intersections between race, socioeconomic status, gender, and undocumented status that influenced us to focus on her narrative. In the following, we use CRT to show how Andresa's complex pathway to and through college exemplified and was a result of these intersections.

Race and Undocumented Status in Higher Education

Andresa's path to higher education was one that she described as "lonely." She independently pursued her postsecondary goals, while fearing that people would not understand her situation as an undocumented student or might even reveal her unauthorized status to others. When asked if she sought any assistance from anyone, Andresa replied, "No, I never confided in anybody. Not even counselors." Although she credited her family with encouraging her to pursue higher education, their participation was constrained by work and unfamiliarity with the mechanics of the college choice process. Andresa described how she became overreliant on the Internet in her efforts to find information about college, because there was no threat of having to share with anyone her status online. In doing so, she repeatedly encountered difficulty finding information that acknowledged undocumented Asian American experiences and resources. For example, many websites for undocumented students explicitly addressed a Latino audience, often having information available in both English and Spanish. Although she still found these sources informative, they seemed only to validate that she was a racial anomaly within the undocumented community.

In particular, Andresa described her perception that, among the undocumented student population, Latinos had greater access to college-going resources. She explained:

I think there's just more resources like scholarships and organizations for Latinos. It's harder to find a scholarship for an undocumented Asian American person . . . because I think there are more Latinos. Just their population size, they're just a lot bigger. They're [geographically] closer to the United States, so there's more people. Having that they have more people, I think they have more support.

She further discussed her experience trying to find support within the larger undocumented population and how her attempts often highlighted her racial difference among those she considered to be her peers: "You're like part of this group. There's this anonymous aspect to it. But if you're Asian, you just stick out like a sore thumb!" An important aspect to supporting undocumented students is anonymity. When Andresa attempted to find support from other undocumented students, her racial background often only drew attention to her, which left her feeling marginalized and led her to develop the perception that resources for undocumented students primarily supported those who were Latino—a sentiment that she often expressed throughout our interactions.

Andresa offered her analysis that undocumented Asian Americans are often left out of discussions about undocumented students because the media has done a good job putting a "Latino face" on undocumented people. Undocumented people, including youth, are often racialized as criminal and economically parasitic (Bacon, 2008). Oppositely, Asian Americans are often racialized to be model minorities: academically and economically successful regardless of race. Model-minority success is often attributed to the hard work of Asian Americans coupled with culturally inherent characteristics of being quiet and complacent (Chou & Feagin, 2008). These assumptions of Asian American culture are often used to explain why Asian Americans do not seek out the institutional support to facilitate college access and persistence and subsequently misdirect attention away from the racial hostility that often imposes silence on Asian Americans. In the context of Andresa's experiences, she expressed how such Asian American racialization is compounded by undocumented status.

On multiple occasions, Andresa shared that, from a very early age, her mother informed her of her undocumented status. In her interview, Andresa explained that she used silence as a way to avoid revealing her status. Consequently, this strategy only served to reinforce racialized stereotypes of Asian Americans:

I always have to be careful about what I say, because if I get into a certain topic, I might have to reveal something about myself that I don't want to. . . . I'm very secretive, and I'm already introverted [from the time] when I was little, so it kind of reinforced that [stereotype], and made me really quiet and silent. . . . You couldn't trust the person next to you.

Sociologists Chou and Feagin (2008) explain how silence is not necessarily an Asian American cultural trait, but rather a strategic response to racism imposed upon Asian Americans. They argue that beyond the countless number of Asian Americans who demonstrate qualities counter to the stereotype, those who exhibit silence often do so to cope with anti-Asian discrimination. Aligned with this analysis, Andresa's early knowledge of her undocumented status fostered her tendency to be "secretive" through nondisclosure. Undocumented persons often experience a constant fear of their status being exposed and feel pressure to avoid revealing that status. Unfortunately, as an undocumented Asian American, this protective measure only affirmed racial stereotypes of how Andresa was expected to act: "quiet and silent."

Socioeconomic and Undocumented Status in Higher Education

Undocumented people are often from low-income families and subjected to poor labor conditions. They experience high rates of unemployment, unstable work situations, abusive labor conditions, and policing of workplaces (Valenzuela, Theodore, Melendez, & Gonzalez, 2006). Regardless of their student status, many undocumented undergraduates also work and, therefore, face such poor labor conditions. Andresa described the relationship between work and school and how this relationship affected her college success. During a conversation about why she did not become involved in campus organizations, she explained, "I worked. I would be at school full-time and then go to work full-time. What I would do is commute. I was always on [public transportation]. That's how I paid for [school]." Andresa consistently reminded us of the inability to separate her status as a student from that of a worker.

Undocumented students are ineligible for both state and federal financial aid. Thus, their pathway to and through higher education is dependent on their familiarity with constantly changing educational policies that affect their access to financial resources. Andresa recalled how citizenship and socioeconomic status factored into her decision to attend community college for three years instead of two:

In high school, I got into [community college] because I lied. I put that I was a citizen just because everyone was taking the same test, and I was scared and nervous and didn't want to be like, "What if you're not a citizen?" I didn't want to draw attention to myself so I just put "yes." . . . With transferring to a four-year university, it is a little more complicated, so it took me an extra year to transfer, because they didn't have AB 540 yet. I didn't want to lie anymore and say I was a citizen. So I had to wait for the AB 540 thing.

As previously described, AB 540 grants eligible undocumented students the ability to pay in-state tuition in California. Initially, Andresa lied about her citizenship out of fear and as a way to avoid drawing attention to her undocumented status. Upon the transfer process, she learned about AB 540 and decided to attend the community college for one additional year and wait for the implementation of AB 540 before transferring to a four-year institution. It is important to note that Andresa became aware of such pending legislation through ethnic media outlets: "It was in the Philippine news. That's what I used to read. They would talk about it, so I was just waiting." Without AB 540, Andresa would have been subject to paying higher nonresident fees.

Furthermore, although she wanted to attend a college away from home, her first concern in choosing a college was money. She shared:

> The first college I applied to was [in southern California]. I got accepted, but I was like, what am I going to do [there]? I don't know anybody. I don't know what to do. It was always in the back of my head that I'm going to be on my own. How am I going to find a job? My mom is my only means of income, and if I'm far away from her, it's going to be hard for me to survive, and I don't want her to pay for my college. So I didn't go there. . . . It was romantic to go to college far away, so I wanted to try that. But I ended up [local].

Andresa looked forward to going away for college—the opportunity, in her words, was "romantic." However, her choice was limited because of the lack of financial security created by her status. As an undocumented person, employment is difficult to find and is often found through social networks. Andresa's concern of being separated from her mother had to do with the financial support each provided for the other. As previously mentioned, Andresa worked alongside her family providing child care. Andresa's mother established a day care business, from which she paid Andresa "under the table." Going away for college threatened not only Andresa's employment options, but it also meant her mother would have lost a worker, and her family would have lost an income contributor.

Although such a story of socioeconomic hardship is not unique to Andresa, her experiences highlight the labor difficulties to which undocu-. mented people are subjected and the impact that the intersecting socioeco- nomic and undocumented statuses can have on access and retention for undocumented students. Andresa also often discussed her experiences as an undocumented woman. In the next section, we describe how gender also played an important role in her experiences as an undocumented student.

Gender and Undocumented Status in Higher Education

Although research on undocumented students is primarily concerned with financial barriers that block their college access and retention, gender also plays an important role in their educational experiences. The intersection of gender, labor, and education played out in Andresa's outlook on higher education. She often spoke about the challenges faced by undocumented women and how they affected her attitude toward higher education.

In describing her postsecondary trajectory, Andresa shared how she began taking early childhood classes at a local community college while she was in high school, to better prepare herself for work that she deemed "realis- tic" because of her undocumented status. But that was counter to her aspira- tions to attend art school and become a visual artist:

> And I don't know how it is with other people, but I know I experienced depression. I stopped hoping, I stopped dreaming. If you can't even dream, what's the point? I can't go like, "one day I want to be a . . ." something . . . I felt like I couldn't really [become] what I wanted to be [an artist]. I couldn't really have that. I had to just be a preschool teacher. Not that I hate that, but you just end up loving the things that you do because that's what you have to do.

Andresa had the desire and the talent to become a visual artist, but success as an artist is, in part, defined by the ability to showcase your work and yourself. However, as an undocumented person, such visibility would make her vulnerable to threats of deportation. Because of that, she pursued an educational route that entailed formal preparation to continue her work as a child care provider, which seemed a more feasible and less dangerous employment option. Indeed, scholars have noted the need to examine the role of gender in shaping immigrant experiences (Chang, 2000; Parreñas,

2001). And, Andresa's decision to pursue early childhood education was facilitated by gendered factors that deemed child care to be a realistic option for her.

Beyond labor, Andresa signaled how gender is central to the lives of undocumented people, and discussed how marriage is often seen as the only viable option to establish legal residency. It is important to interrogate the impact that marriage can have on the postsecondary experiences of undocumented students. Andresa expressed that for her and other undocumented women marriage could impose limitations on their college aspirations. In discussing her family's experience, she reflected on how her sisters' decisions to get married prevented them from attending four-year universities:

> Like, I feel I was pretty blessed with the things I got to do in my life. I'm glad that I didn't get married [at a young age]. . . . I just feel bad for my sisters, because my older sisters were very smart. And they could've gone to colleges and done big things, but being married at such a young age is not fun.

Her sisters were married between the ages of 19 and 21, and Andresa married at 26, after she completed her undergraduate education. Andresa attributed her ability to pursue higher education to her decision to put off marriage. She discussed the difficulties that women face in supporting a family before they might be completely ready for such an endeavor and the challenges of balancing family responsibilities with college obligations. Thus, although marriage might lead to legal residency and eventual eligibility for financial aid for school, it can also make undocumented students' lives more complex and serve as a deterrent to higher education.

Andresa and her sisters' experiences highlight the role of gender and immigration in shaping work and opportunities for postsecondary education. Moreover, Andresa's reflection shows how undocumented women of color are often limited to domestic or service-sector work. Her narrative expresses the complexity of educational trajectories fostered by the intersection of gender and citizenship status and draws attention to the need to focus more on how gender might shape how undocumented students understand, approach, and make decisions about opportunities to pursue higher education.

Implications for Future Research

The main goal of this chapter is to demonstrate that, through an application of Critical Race Theory, undocumented students' experiences can be better understood as a complex phenomenon that results from the intersectionality among race, socioeconomic status, gender, and immigration. Through a case study approach, we presented an in-depth and nuanced analysis of how undocumented status permeated the different aspects of Andresa's understanding of, and experiences within, higher education. Yet, although her story demonstrated that undocumented status is independently a salient identity, it must be understood as intertwined with other factors shaping undocumented students' lives.

Undocumented students are multiply marginalized, based on their race, socioeconomic status, gender, and noncitizenship status. Andresa demonstrated how using silence as a strategy to prevent disclosure of her status only reinforced racialized stereotypes of silent Asian American model minorities and subsequently made her feel marginalized, even among other undocumented students. Furthermore, the perpetuation of these stereotypes obscured the harshness of her socioeconomic reality. Finally, through her discussion of how gendered constructions of immigration are tied to the potential of legality, Andresa also highlighted how heteronormative notions of marriage can play a role in shaping postsecondary aspirations and opportunities for undocumented students.

Filipinos represent one of the largest undocumented ethnic groups, but undocumented Asian Americans of other ethnicities do exist. Thus, one limitation of this chapter is our focus on an undocumented Filipina college student. Andresa's story is certainly an important step toward more critically understanding undocumented student experiences beyond their academic challenges and resiliency, but also in the context of the larger social, political, and economic conditions that define their realities. Nevertheless, the diversity of the Asian American community warrants research that examines how undocumented students from different Asian ethnic communities might experience the path to and through higher education in unique ways. As the interest and urgency to address undocumented student issues heightens, education scholarship that examines the racialized process of immigration is needed to understand the depth of undocumented students' experiences within higher education more holistically.

Although still a relatively recent phenomenon, research on undocumented students is characterized by descriptive accounts of undocumented student stories and policy-oriented reports that advocate for increased access to educational resources, such as state and federal financial aid (Gonzales, 2009; Passel, 2005; Perez, 2009; Rincon, 2008). The research is significant and timely. Each year, approximately 65,000 undocumented youth graduate from high school, but their academic, professional, and overall life prospects remain uncertain because of discrimination against undocumented people (Gonzales, 2009). However, as evidenced by Andresa's counterstory, scholarship on undocumented students needs to better account for the complexity of undocumented student experiences so that those responsible for creating and implementing more equitable education policies consider the racial diversity of this population.

Notes

1. A pseudonym is used to protect the identity of the participant. *Andresa* is derived from the name Andres Bonifacio, a Philippine revolutionary figure. *Maypagasa* means "hopeful" in Tagalog and is used to honor Andresa's perseverance and resilience as an undocumented woman of color.

References

AB 540 (2001). AB 540 Assembly Bill analysis. California Assembly Committee on Higher Education. Retrieved October 1, 2009, from http://info.sen.ca.gov/pub/01-02/bill/asm/ab_0501-0550/ab_540_cfa_20010502_124759_asm_comm.html

Bacon, D. (2008). *Illegal people: How globalization creates migration and criminalizes immigrants.* Boston, MA: Beacon Press.

Bogdan, R. C., & Biklen, S. K. (2003). *Qualitative research for education: An introduction to theories and methods.* Boston, MA: Pearson Education Group.

Chang, G. (2000). *Disposable domestics: Immigrant women workers in the global economy.* Cambridge, MA: South End Press.

Chou, R., & Feagin, J. R. (2008). *The myth of the model minority: Asian Americans facing racism.* Boulder, CO: Paradigm.

Gonzales, R. (2009). *Young lives on hold: The college dreams of undocumented students.* New York: College Board Advocacy.

Hoefer, M., Rytina, N., & Baker, B. C. (2009). *Estimates of the unauthorized immigrant population residing in the United States: January 2008.* Washington, DC: Department of Homeland Security Office of Immigration Statistics.

Luse, T. (2009). Illegal immigrants offered tuition: UW system gives undocumented residents in-state rates as part of Doyle's new law. *The Badger Herald.* Retrieved October 31, 2009, from http://badgerherald.com/news/2009/10/26/illegal_immigrants_0.php.

Parreñas, R. S. (2001). *Servants of globalization: Women, migration, and domestic work.* Stanford, CA: Stanford University Press.

Passel, J. S. (2005). *Unauthorized migrants: Numbers and characteristics.* Washington, DC: Pew Hispanic Center.

Perez, W. (2009). *We ARE Americans: Undocumented students pursuing the American dream.* Sterling, VA: Stylus.

Rincon, A. (2008). *Undocumented immigrants and higher education: Si se puede.* New York: LFB Scholarly Publishing.

San Juan, E., Jr. (2009). *Toward Filipino self-determination: Beyond transnational globalization.* Albany: State University of New York Press.

Solórzano, D. G. (1997). Images and words that wound: Critical race theory, racial stereotyping, and teacher education. *Teacher Education Quarterly, 24,* 5–19.

Solórzano, D. G., & Yosso, T. J. (2002). Critical race methodology: Counter-story-telling as an analytical framework for education research. *Qualitative Inquiry, 8*(1), 23–44.

Madera, G., Mathay, A. A., Najafi, A. M., Saldivar, H. H., Solis, S., Titong, A. J. M., . . . Monroe, J. (Eds.). (2008). *Underground undergrads: UCLA undocumented immigrant students speak out.* Los Angeles: UCLA Center for Labor Research and Education.

University of California Office of the President. (2006). *Annual report on AB 540 tuition exemptions, 2005–2006 academic year.*

Valenzuela, A., Theodore, N., Melendez, E., & Gonzalez, A. L. (2006). *On the corner: Day labor in the United States.* Los Angeles: UCLA Center for the Study of Urban Poverty.

Yin, R. K. (1994). *Case study research, design and methods* (2nd ed.). Thousand Oaks, CA: Sage.

II

LIVING THE LEGACY OF '68

The Perspectives and Experiences
of Asian American Student Activists

Jean J. Ryoo and Rob Ho

More than 40 years after the 1968 San Francisco State University student-led strike and the birth of the Asian American Movement—the last of the "ethnic-consciousness movements" in which diverse Asian Americans joined together on university campuses and called for solidarity, political empowerment, racial equality, and social justice (Wei, 1993)—very little is known about Asian American student activism today. This lack of understanding is not only because there is a dearth of research on student activism, but also because of the nation's Black–White race relations, which blind us to the exploitation of Asian Americans, who are viewed as a homogeneous "model minority" that is successfully integrated into American society without resistance. Yet, the Asian American Movement marked a critical turning point in student activism, during which an increase in the number of Asian American college students coincided with the politically charged anti–Vietnam War era (Wei, 1993). Similarly, today, Asian Americans constitute a growing proportion of America's postsecondary students, during a time when the largest number of college students mobilized to elect the nation's first African American president.

Nevertheless, little research describes what role Asian American college students play in current social activism and what motivates their engagement, despite their numerous academic responsibilities. Their stories remain

The authors wish to thank Jenifer Crawford, Chris Lee, and the editors of this volume for their constructive comments on earlier drafts of this chapter.

unheard, contributing to the model minority myth and suggesting that Asian American students are not politically engaged with the greater community. This myth is a lingering form of racist ideology that not only constructs Asian Americans as successful racial minorities with high levels of educational attainment and income, but also proves dangerous for Asian Americans when it is embraced as a normative standard to which they must aspire. Internalization of this construct can have devastating effects on a student's sense of lost identity, resentment, and self-limited occupational aspirations (Chun, 1995; Chun & Sue, 1998; Goodwin, 2003; Young, 1998). We conducted a case study to debunk this myth, fill a gap in the knowledge base, provide Asian American students with an opportunity to share their voices, and describe the current state of Asian American student social activism.

A Brief History of Asian American Activism—1960s to the 1980s

There is a long history of Asian American activism in the United States. Although it is beyond the purview of this chapter to provide a detailed account of this literature (for more details, see Ho, 2000; Louie & Omatsu, 2001; Wei, 1993), it is useful to briefly review the major developments that occurred over the past 40 years, to help contextualize current manifestations on college campuses. The late 1960s was a time of social and political upheaval, and it marked the beginning of a watershed period for Asian American activism, commonly referred to as the Movement. One pivotal moment in this Movement was the 1968 San Francisco State University (SFSU) student strike that led to the creation of the first School of Ethnic Studies and the emergence of a new generation of activists who fought for civil rights on university campuses and within their local communities (Wei, 2004). The establishment of the field of Asian American studies (AAS) was perhaps one of the most notable achievements of the Movement, because Asian American student activists at SFSU and the University of California–Berkeley protested the omission of their histories and experiences from the college curriculum.

Using their own voices, media publications, and protest marches, students collaborated to cultivate a sense of pan–Asian American solidarity and pushed for AAS programs in postsecondary institutions across the country, introducing students to the Asian American experience and fostering a generation of researchers who challenged Eurocentric texts and curricula that omitted and misrepresented the stories of their communities (Umemoto, 2007). AAS helped mobilize students to challenge hegemonic power structures that subordinated Asian Americans, galvanizing them to work for social change. At UCLA, such organizing led to the creation of the "Oriental Concerned" student group (Pulido, 2006) and the tenacious fight for AAS Center Director and Professor Don Nakanishi's tenure in the late 1980s (Minami, 1995).

More broadly, the Movement was instrumental in creating pan–Asian American coalitions at local, regional, and national levels to fight for bilingual/bicultural education, civil rights, fair immigration laws, and speaking out against anti-Asian violence while seeking justice for the victims of such crimes (Umemoto, 2007). Other examples of success include (1) the 1974 *Lau v. Nichols* court case, which involved non-English-speaking Chinese students whose parents filed a successful suit against the San Francisco Board of Education, resulting in bilingual education for Asian and Latino children; (2) the Japanese American redress movement in the late 1980s, which culminated in President Reagan signing the 1988 Civil Liberties Act, authorizing $1.25 billion in reparations payments to 70,000 Japanese Americans who survived U.S. concentration camps during World War II; and (3) a significant increase in Asian American participation in electoral politics and representation in public office (Wei, 1993).

Recent Asian American Activism—1990s to the Present

Asian American commitment to social change has not faltered since the late 1960s. Although many scholars debate about the nature of current activism—whether it should focus on civil rights issues alone or also embrace questions about Asian American identity politics—individuals of diverse Asian American backgrounds continue to join together against racial and class oppression. Pulido (2006) wrote: "Even though the movement itself has collapsed, its legacy and impact can be seen in the greater empowerment of people of color, as well as in the coalitions and organizations forged out of the experiences and networks of that era" (p. 216). She described how coalitions born during the Asian American Movement (e.g., the Action for Grassroots Empowerment, Neighborhood Development Alternatives, the Asian Pacific American Labor Alliance) continue to flourish despite challenges from conservatives and neoconservatives during the 1990s (Cho, 1994; Yoshikawa, 1994). Filipino American youth activist Steven De Castro (1994), for example, revealed how younger generations of Asian Americans were politically active long after the Asian American Movement of the 1960s.

In fact, Asian American students at the University of California–Los Angeles (UCLA) have been particularly active in the past five years. In 2006, Asian American student organizations across the University of California (UC) system—brought together by UCLA students from the Asian Pacific Coalition (APC)—united in a yearlong struggle against a UCLA student newspaper's anti-Asian sentiment that blamed Asian American students for the decreased number of African American and Latino students enrolled in UC schools. In an effort to dispel misconceptions that suggested all Asian Americans, whether Japanese American or Hmong American, were experiencing uniform educational access and success, the "Count Me In!" campaign successfully lobbied the UC system to increase the number of disaggregated Asian American ethnic categories from 8 to 23. Such disaggregation of data helped the UC system track the experiences of lesser-known Asian American student populations and more effectively illustrate differences in those students' experiences.

The aforementioned campaign demonstrated that Asian American activists are engaged in political and community organizing, yet their stories continue to be unfamiliar to broader audiences. To share these students' stories and learn from them, we asked the following questions: (1) What motivates Asian American students to engage in political or social activism? and (2) How have Asian American students been affected by their activist experiences?

Theoretical Framework

Asian American student activism at UCLA can be analyzed using Critical Race Theory (CRT) methodology in education and Transformational Resistance. This study drew directly from CRT methodology in education's five major tenets in educational research by (1) understanding the centrality of racism while recognizing its intersectionality with other forms of subordination, (2) attempting to challenge dominant ideology, (3) remaining committed to social justice, (4) privileging experiential knowledge, and (5) valuing interdisciplinary perspectives (Solórzano & Delgado Bernal, 2001; Yosso, 2005). CRT methodology was used to better understand UCLA Asian American student activists' perspectives through their narratives and lived experiences.

In conjunction with CRT, resistance theory, as described by Solórzano and Delgado Bernal's (2001) adaptation of Henry Giroux's (1983a, 1983b) notion of student resistance, can help make sense of Asian American student activism by illustrating how social oppression intersects with motivation based on social justice. More specifically, "Transformational Resistance"—in which a student is cognizant of how she is marginalized within her school environment and individually strives for change to improve either the institution or her social conditions—is valuable to consider when looking at the motivations and actions of Asian American student activists. For example, Asian American students in the 1968 SFSU student strike were acutely aware of being omitted from university admissions, classroom curricula, and the dominant Black–White racial discourse, which excluded their own experiences (criticism of oppression). Their critique led to the infamous SFSU student strike (desire for social justice), which, at the time, was the longest student strike in U.S. history. These two lenses—CRT and Transformational Resistance—help inform our methodological approach.

Methods

This narrative inquiry involved open-ended interviews that were recorded, transcribed, and coded for trends in beliefs, experiences, and practices of Asian American student activists. We recruited students from UCLA, where Asian American students made up 42% of all enrolled freshmen in 2007 and 40% of the entire undergraduate student population in 2008 (UCLA Office of Analysis and Information Management, 2008). Participants were students affiliated with Asian American ethnic student organizations and an AAS undergraduate course that focused on art as a political tool for social change.

We interviewed 10 students either individually or in focus groups. The 10 students consisted of 2 males and 8 females and included sophomores, juniors, and seniors. The students included were of Vietnamese, Hmong, Chinese, Japanese, Laotian, or Filipino descent, and most were U.S. citizens. They hailed from a range of different states and attended both public and private K–12 schools. To maintain confidentiality, the names of participants have been changed, and we refrained from discussing the specific details of their political work.

Findings

Although personal histories varied significantly among the Asian American students we interviewed, two common themes united their social activism experiences: (1) feelings of privilege, difference, and responsibility seemed to motivate students' political activism for Asian American rights; and (2) students experienced personal growth and new identity formation through political activism.

Recognizing Privilege, Difference, and Responsibility as Motivation

Most interviewees recognized that attending UCLA was a privilege that made them proud but also made them feel like they did not "fit in" with the larger student demographic. Although UCLA has a large Asian American population, most interviewees recognized class difference as an isolating marker and noted how UCLA's student population "looked" different from their home communities that had more African Americans and Latinos. Interestingly, such privilege and difference that student activists felt at UCLA functioned as a motivator for political activism. Many interviewees equated both the privilege of getting to study at a highly reputable, four-year university and the feeling of difference from more economically privileged peers with a responsibility to help others outside of UCLA and in their home communities.

This feeling of being an "outsider" at UCLA was described by one interviewee, who said she felt out of place because of her socioeconomic background, but this nonetheless motivated her to get involved in political activism:

> I feel like I've become a lot more aware of my financial background coming here, just because I guess a lot of people are a lot more well off . . . [and I] feel like I don't belong on this campus. . . . My roommates passed all these AP tests, whereas I didn't pass any, or they got high scores on their SATs . . . whereas I barely broke 1,000. So why am I here? Why was I chosen? So realizing how different I was, was a big shock for me . . . but also feeling proud that I was here . . . so I've felt like this isn't my community, even though [through] organizing, I've created a community for myself, but all the work I'm doing here isn't for L.A., it's for [my home city]. [Ligaya, Filipino American female]

This sense of feeling "like I don't belong on this campus" seemed to drive Ligaya's desire to get involved in organizing work—as the vice president of a leading UCLA Asian American political organization—and to share her new knowledge with those who were unable to come to this campus. She described future plans to fulfill this responsibility by becoming a teacher at her alma mater and changing its history curriculum to reflect the experiences of students of color. Without mentioning CRT, Ligaya's comments reflected its understanding of the centrality of racism, as well as a desire to challenge dominant ideologies through a commitment to social justice, as she described offering ethnic studies to students in K–12 schools.

Another interviewee reflected the same sentiment of outsider status motivating political activist work. Charlie, a Filipino American male, attended "a diverse, urban high school" and, although he was a fairly strong student, his school had few AP classes, and his SAT exam scores were low, so he did not originally consider applying to University of California schools. However, when his college counselor told him not to apply to UCLA and laughed at the idea, Charlie became angry, applied to the school, and was determined to get in. Upon receiving his acceptance letter, Charlie told his mother the following:

> I have to go, not only to say that I got accepted, but because I have to make something of myself, do something, and then come back and be able to say to [the college counselor] that I actually did it, I graduated, and [I need to] discontinue this kind of injustice in our high schools and universities.

However, Charlie experienced "a big culture shock" at UCLA, as he shared in the following remarks:

> Before, I was surrounded by diverse communities, but here there's barely any Black people or other people of color . . . and even people of color here are a different kind of student coming from upper-middle-class backgrounds, and relating to them wasn't the same.

In response to this realization, Charlie felt responsible for other people of color outside of UCLA, which he illustrated with the following statement:

> I think I always felt a responsibility to be involved and a responsibility to people who fought for me to be here and to give me the opportunity to attend such an institution. . . . If that meant wearing 16 hats and working 3 jobs, it was hard for me to question it because I thought I owed it to [them] . . . so knowing that this is what I need to do to make sure other people have the same opportunities as me, especially people of color, especially my family members, especially people who come from my old high school and have had college counselors who told them not to apply.

Thus, Charlie became involved in campaigns for increasing diversity at UCLA and for offering financial aid to undocumented immigrant students. Reflecting CRT's centrality of racism in his story, Charlie showed a strong identification with communities of color.

Other interviewees voiced similar feelings of privilege and responsibility as motivational in their social activism. As Nani, a Laotian American female, explained:

> Being able to give back to the space that I have taken so much out of was really important to me . . . and learning from other people about the things they have gone through and realizing you have a responsibility as a privileged college student in this position to be able to use that in a way that would be beneficial or at least helpful for others [was valuable to me].

This led to Nani volunteering more than 40 hours a week to various Asian American political groups. Similarly, Lan, a Chinese American female, described her political work at UCLA as a privilege that is only useful if shared with others. She stated, "A lot of times I say that I feel really privileged to have found stuff that I'm involved with now, but how much does that mean [unless I get others involved]? . . . That's why I realized that it's really important to get other people involved in [community activism work]." Lan worked with Southeast Asian American students in a high school retention program and made efforts to get other UCLA students involved with the Asian American community.

Reminiscent of CRT and Transformational Resistance, interviewees shared the sentiment that their positions of privilege as university students and feelings of race and class difference at UCLA were central to recognizing a responsibility to others who also feel difference, do not have such privilege, and are outsiders.

New Identity and Personal Growth Through Activism and Community Service

Recognition of privilege and difference at UCLA inevitably resulted in new perspectives of self for many of our interviewees. Indeed, interviewees noted how identity development and personal growth were powerfully influenced by their experiences in political activism. For example, May, a Hmong American involved in Southeast Asian peer counseling, equated her community work to finding her identity. She stated, "Peer counseling is more than just about reaching out to students in academic difficulty, but a lot about how we are helping out each other as a community and in understanding our identities." Thao, a Vietnamese American male, echoed this sentiment in the following statement:

I was big into developing myself. . . . I was *this close* [pinching his fingers together] to joining the Marines out of high school. . . . I felt like I was growing by joining [student organization] . . . [and by] building the community, raising awareness, building peoples' consciousness, and just getting involved in general.

Ligaya also described being transformed through activism, saying, "I feel like I've changed a lot . . . feeling like you're a part of something that is a lot bigger than yourself . . . knowing you have a purpose." As visible in their testimonies, students' activism was identity changing, because it led them to view the world from new perspectives.

It is important to note that, alongside political activism, taking AAS courses also powerfully influenced these students. A Laotian American, Janet, described how her political work and AAS courses were inherently tied to her Asian American identity:

Taking [AAS] classes and learning about my history has taught me to appreciate where I came from and what my parents had to go through . . . and it's pushed me to think about the community and give back and find that strength . . . because some people forget that we've been struggling, but we need to maintain it. . . . Finding your place here is how you're taking ownership of what's happening to you. . . . How are you in charge of understanding your own history and the history of your own people if it's not taught to you in your own classrooms? . . . How are you looking up your background and really discovering where your place needs to be at, who you need to be, and who you're advocating for?

Political activism allowed Janet to take ownership of her identity and find "her place" at the university. Chi Yan, a Chinese American, also described how taking classes in AAS and participating in a Chinatown high school retention program helped her grow in new ways. She located her identity development in her community work:

In high school, you just kind of get by, but here you can't just get by, you have to think about what you're here for. . . . Finding Asian American studies and finding [student organization] shows me how I had been running away from things that could have made me a better person. . . . By coming here [I've found] ways to stop making excuses for [my]self. . . . How much comfort do you take before you fall back into the whole ignorance is bliss?

Her activist work helped her remain committed to herself and her community. Michelle, a Japanese American, also described how her political activism and AAS coursework directly influenced both her identity formation and relationship to the community:

> A lot of it has to do with the understanding of self-identity. A little is ethnically, sexually . . . and from that identity, maybe from what students get from the work that they do or from the Asian American studies major/minor is they take . . . the experiences they have gone through, and are able to see how they themselves fit into that picture. So for me . . . I'm a Japanese American and then an Asian American and then so on and so forth. And then the question expands when you understand how you fit into not only your history but how you fit into your current situation that your community is in, sort of understanding your role as a student . . . and furthering that community.

Michelle recognized how understanding herself in relation to the world was an important aspect of her experiences as a student activist. She said political activism "is where I learned about the importance of internment in terms of the larger Japanese American community, and then that formed my identity as a Japanese American." Thus, political activism and AAS coursework proved central to developing a new sense of her Asian American identity and personal growth.

Involvement with political activism at UCLA helped students develop not only stronger political and Asian American identities, but also a greater sense of responsibility to the world beyond college. These students viewed their experiences as so enriching that many expressed the desire to push other undergraduates to engage in the same work.

Implications

Although this is not an exhaustive study of all Asian American student perspectives and although UCLA's social environment does not mirror that of all universities, our findings still have valuable implications for improving higher education for diverse Asian American student populations. The positive experiences and challenges described by interviewees are not unfamiliar to other Asian American students nationwide. In particular, higher education researchers and practitioners should pay particular attention to four key areas: the recognition of privilege, the alienation of Asian American students, the importance of Asian American studies, and the formation of Asian American identity.

Recognition of Privilege

The recognition of privilege is an unexpected theme that emerged from the data, pointing to how students saw themselves as fortunate to be attending a highly selective institution, and, thus, responsible to give back to others and ensure that they have the same opportunities. It would be valuable to examine to what extent this recognition of privilege is espoused by students at other elite schools and whether this motivates them to be active in their campus communities for the betterment of others, especially those from the same racial background. In a similar vein, Asian American students who attend less-selective institutions may or may not recognize any sense of privilege that can affect their participation levels in student activism and social justice activities. Is it possible that there are forms of boutique activism—activism involving small numbers of students who usually lack a detailed understanding of the background of the cause and who may be involved for other reasons—that attract more class-privileged Asian American students? Does that affect forms of political activism? This type of information could provide practitioners with additional understandings of how to serve these students.

Asian American Student Alienation

The students in our study described feeling isolated on a campus where 40% of undergraduates came from similar racial backgrounds. This leads to major questions regarding how institutional structures, programming, and classroom environments are contributing to their alienation and how American higher education reproduces social inequalities across race, class, gender, and sexuality. If these students are experiencing such isolation at a supposedly "socially progressive" and "racially diverse" school, what type of hostilities do Asian American students in less diverse schools face? As other chapters in this book demonstrate, Asian American students, despite being hailed as the model minority, continue to suffer the lingering effects of exclusion from the wider student body and their respective institutions of higher learning.

Nationwide, Asian American students have legitimate concerns that chilly campus climates—whether at public or private institutions, highly or less-selective institutions, or four-year or community colleges—adversely affect their ability to receive a quality education unfettered by hostile racial environments. Professors, university administrators, and student affairs personnel need to pay particular attention to these issues, not just for Asian American undergraduates, but for all racial minority students.

The Importance of Asian American Studies

Students highlighted the influence of AAS and their classes in ethnic studies. Such coursework played a crucial role in their "conscientization" and awareness of racial oppression by introducing students to their own Asian American history, facilitating social justice awareness and their participation in related causes. This participation, often in Asian American student groups, also supported leadership development, which helped foster additional organizational, public-speaking, and communication skills that supplemented students' formal learning. Although UCLA's Asian American students may have a different relationship with student activism than students from other schools because of UCLA's historical relationship with social justice—the empowering presence of ethnic studies departments and the collective memory of professors who were active in previous Asian American movements inevitably influence the perspectives of new student generations—much has been written about the importance of AAS nationwide and its benefits over the years (especially in the 1990s). A renewed examination of its usefulness for future undergraduates and student activists would be useful for Asian American researchers and higher education practitioners.

However, in today's poor economic climate, maintaining strong ethnic studies programs may be a difficult endeavor. The confluence of an increasingly corporatized higher education and difficult economic times will result in increased pressure to cut ethnic studies programs to save money. Therefore, in the near future, there may be a need to mobilize Asian American communities once again to ensure that these offerings will be available for future generations of Asian American college students.

Asian American Identity Formation

Identity formation continues to be salient when studying Asian American students in college. Our interviewees made constant reference to their activist work, mediated by race and ethnicity, as playing a significant role in who they were as individuals, how they saw themselves, and in their overall personal growth. Their demonstration of Transformational Resistance further showed how their lives have changed to incorporate a social justice agenda. The student testimonies are clear indications that race constitutes a major part of their lives, and they are eager to share these understandings with others.

There is an undeniable symbiotic relationship between activism and Asian American identity made obvious by our interviewees. Participants defined identity as something grounded in responsibility for others, social justice, and membership to broader communities of color. Racial identity theorists have often ignored the plight of the Asian American subject, and there are few useful models available to help explain how this population forms their identity. A better understanding of the range of students' personal growth and vicissitudes is of critical importance in explicating the complexity of the contemporary Asian American experience.

Of course, the recognition of privilege, the alienation of Asian American students, the importance of Asian American studies, and identity formation are all interrelated phenomena that are not mutually exclusive. They are interdependent and feed off each other in myriad ways. However, this study has reemphasized the importance of all of them in understanding Asian American college student experiences so that researchers will consider these elements while conducting their own future studies.

Through this project, we hope to help push scholarly research in new directions that reveal the lives of our newest generations of Asian American activists and community service volunteers. This research begins to provide some insight into the links between past and current activism, as well as earlier and later generations. We hope that these Asian American student activist testimonies will help universities and colleges recognize the value of political and social activist groups on campuses throughout the country and the need to provide space for Asian American student activism today.

References

Cho, M. (1994). Overcoming our legacy as cheap labor, scabs, and model minorities: Asian activists fight for community empowerment. In K. Aguilar-San Juan (Ed.), *The state of Asian America: Activism and resistance in the 1990s* (pp. 253–274). Boston, MA: South End Press.

Chun, C., & Sue, S. (1998). Mental health issues concerning Asian Pacific American children. In V. O. Pang & L. Cheng (Eds.), *Struggling to be heard: The unmet needs of Asian Pacific American children* (pp. 75–87). Ithaca, NY: SUNY Press.

Chun, K.-T. (1995). The myth of Asian American success and its educational ramifications. In D. Nakanishi & T. Nishida (Eds.), *The Asian American educational experience* (pp. 95–112). New York: Routledge.

De Castro, S. (1994). Identity in action: A Filipino American's perspective. In K. Aguilar-San Juan (Ed.), *The state of Asian America: Activism and resistance in the 1990s* (pp. 295–320). Boston, MA: South End Press.

Giroux, H. (1983a). *Theories and resistance in education.* South Hadley, MA: Bergin & Garvey.

Giroux, H. (1983b). Theories of reproduction and resistance in the new sociology of education: A critical analysis. *Harvard Educational Review, 55,* 257–293.

Goodwin, A. L. (2003). Growing up Asian in America: A search for self. In C. Park, A. L. Goodwin, & S. Lee (Eds.), *Asian American identities, families, and schooling* (pp. 3–25). Charlotte, NC: Information Age.

Ho, F. (Ed.). (2000). *Legacy to liberation: Politics and culture of revolutionary Asian Pacific America.* San Francisco, CA: AK Press.

Louie, S., & Omatsu, G. (Eds.). (2001). *Asian Americans: The movement and the moment.* Los Angeles, CA: Asian American Studies Center Press.

Minami, D. (1995). Guerrilla war at UCLA. In D. Nakanishi & T. Nishida (Eds.), *The Asian American educational experience* (pp. 358–372). New York: Routledge.

Pulido, L. (2006). *Black, brown, yellow, & left: Radical activism in Los Angeles.* Berkeley: University of California Press.

Solórzano, D. G., & Delgado Bernal, D. (2001). Examining transformational resistance through a critical race and LatCrit theory framework. *Urban Education, 36*(3), 308–342.

UCLA Office of Analysis and Information Management. (2008). *Quick facts about UCLA.* Retrieved from http://www.admissions.ucla.edu/campusprofile.htm

Umemoto, K. (2007). "On Strike!": San Francisco State College strike, 1968–1969: The role of Asian American students. In M. Zhou & J. V. Gatewood (Eds.), *Contemporary Asian America: A multidisciplinary reader* (2nd ed.). New York: NYU Press.

Wei, W. (1993). *The Asian American movement.* Philadelphia, PA: Temple University Press.

Wei, W. (2004). A commentary on young Asian American activists from the 1960s to the present. In J. Lee & M. Zhou (Eds.), *Asian American youth: Culture, identity, and ethnicity* (pp. 299–312). New York: Routledge.

Yoshikawa, K. (1994). The heat is on Miss Saigon coalition: Organizing across race and sexuality. In K. Aguilar-San Juan (Ed.), *The state of Asian America: Activism and resistance in the 1990s* (pp. 275–294). Boston, MA: South End Press.

Yosso, T. J. (2005). Whose culture has capital? A critical race theory discussion of community cultural wealth. *Race Ethnicity and Education, 8*(1), 69–91.

Young, R. L. (1998). Becoming American: Coping strategies of Asian Pacific American children. In V. O. Pang & L. Cheng (Eds.), *Struggling to be heard: The unmet needs of Asian Pacific American children* (pp. 61–73). Ithaca: State University of New York Press.

12

NEGOTIATING THE COMPLEXITIES OF BEING SELF-IDENTIFIED AS BOTH ASIAN AMERICAN AND LESBIAN, GAY, OR BISEXUAL

Sean C. Pepin and Donna M. Talbot

Over the past decade, a burgeoning number of multiple identity studies have been written in the higher education literature. These studies have greatly assisted student affairs practitioners in understanding the complexity of identity formation for students who are members of more than one social group (Abes & Kasch, 2007; Crawford, Allison, Zamboni, & Soto, 2002; Patton & Simmons, 2008; Stewart, 2008). However, few studies in higher education have focused specifically on the experiences and needs of students who identify as both Asian American and lesbian, gay, or bisexual (LGB) (Chan, 1989). What little research exists on Asian American LGB individuals is often published in the counseling literature. With an increasing number of Asian Americans in higher education and a trend toward students coming out (i.e., disclosing their sexual orientation as gay, lesbian, or bisexual) at earlier ages, increasing knowledge of the experience of this population in higher education is progressively more important.

In this chapter, we share findings from our study of the Asian American LGB population on college campuses, which explore the lived experiences of some of these individuals as they negotiate the complex reality of balancing two seemingly disparate cultures. Traditionally, Asian American culture espouses a more conservative and chaste persona (Kim & Ward, 2007), whereas LGB culture is more politically engaged and inherently outspoken. Although the inquiry discussed here is not an "identity study," issues of identity are integral to understanding the populations we are addressing. In the case of LGB Asian American students, there appear to be several inherent clashes between the respective cultures. For instance, LGB identity development contains more liberal values and actions that are part of the coming out process, which is intrinsically connected with discussing sexuality (Cass, 1979). In contrast, most traditional Asian cultures tend to be conservative and more reserved around issues of sexuality (Okazaki, 2002). These opposing value-laden messages within students' cultural contexts can often result in their feeling as though they are straddling two different worlds, especially in a college atmosphere. This pressure to balance these multiple cultures can cause challenges, or what some student participants in our study described as a bifurcated existence, or living in two worlds.

As with any study that focuses on identity groups, it is important that we, as researchers and authors, share our own issues with using current frameworks that are both helpful in understanding identity and inadequate for fully explaining the diversity within already marginalized populations. Our goal was to dovetail current Asian American research with current LGB research to begin to elucidate the experiences that students voiced throughout our study. Because we are trying to understand the experiences of students with two distinct cultural identities, it was also necessary to review current research on multiple identities.

Asian American Identity

Kim's (1981, 2001) Asian American identity model was the first model to explain the racial identity development process for Asian Americans. She explains that Asian Americans go through the following stages of identity exploration and development:

1. *Ethnic awareness*: In this stage, the child's attitudes toward being Asian American are generally positive or neutral.
2. *White identification*: In this stage, the individual recognizes differences from White people and may internalize White values, which can result in alienation from oneself and other Asian Americans. This stage can be experienced in two different ways:

    a. *Actively*: Asian Americans consider themselves to be very similar to their White counterparts and do not acknowledge any differences between them and their White peers. In other words, they attempt to eliminate their Asian selves.

    b. *Passively*: Asian Americans do not consider themselves to be White or distance themselves from Asians, but they do accept White values, beliefs, and standards.

3. *Awakening to social political consciousness*: Individuals recognize themselves as a minority and their political consciousness and Asian American self-concept become more positive.

4. *Redirection to Asian American consciousness*: Individuals embrace their Asian American identity and heritage.

5. *Incorporation*: The individual learns how to balance his or her own identity and an appreciation for members of other racial groups.

Scholars have highlighted the fact that Kim's model was based on East Asians and other generated alternative models of Asian American identity (e.g., Ibrahim, Ohnishi, & Sandhu, 1997; Nadal, 2004). None of these, however, focuses on the development of multiple identities.

We highlight two contextual factors that have a profound impact on the experiences of Asian American students: societal oppression and Asian cultures. Similar to many people of color in the United States, the identity of Asian Americans is linked to oppression. For example, the media and society perpetuate negative images of Asian Americans that can inhibit development for Asian American students. Two primary negative perceptions with which Asian American students must contend on predominantly White campuses are the model minority stereotype and the image of the perpetual foreigner or alien (Lee, Wong, & Alvarez, 2009).

Additionally, major domains of influence identified for Asian American students are traditional Asian familial and cultural values. These include values such as collectivism, deference to authority, and placing the needs of family above the self (Kim, Atkinson, & Yang, 1999). The extent to which students espouse these traditional cultural values varies substantially and is most commonly influenced by those individuals' generational statuses, levels of acculturation, peer groups, and geographical locations (Kim & Ward, 2007). Thus, it should be kept in mind that, although informative, these summaries of what constitutes "Asian values" do not capture the vast differences that exist within the broad "Asian American" racial label.[1]

Lesbian, Gay, and Bisexual Identity

Before beginning any in-depth discussion of LGB Asian Americans, it is important to define the relevant terms that are used. The following quotation offers useful definitions for the terms *gay*, *lesbian*, and *bisexual*:

> Gay refers to men whose sexual orientation is primarily toward other males. . . . Lesbians are females whose sexual orientation is primarily toward other females. . . . Bisexuals are those who are strongly attracted to both males and females, regardless of whether the attraction is equal to both sexes. (Chung & Singh, 2009, p. 244)

Other more colloquial terms that have evolved regarding sexual orientation are *downe* or *down low, pansexual*, and *queer. Downe* or *down low* is a slang term that originated in the African American community, referring to men who passed as heterosexual while engaging in sexual activities or relationships with other men. This term was popularized in the 1990s and is now more widely used in LGB communities. A pansexual person is one who is sexually interested in another person, regardless of gender or sex; the popular phrase used by pansexual individuals is "loving a person for who they are and not what they are" (*Urban Dictionary*, 2010). The word *queer*, which once was a very negative term for LGB people, is now a term that has been reclaimed by sectors of the LGB community and some academics. Therefore, although the term *queer* is still considered unacceptable in many social circles, some members of the LGB community consider it more positive and associated with politics (Gamson, 1995).

In 1979, Cass developed a fairly comprehensive LGB identity model that incorporated both social and psychological aspects of development. This model defines identity formation as the process by which an individual considers and accepts homosexuality as a relevant aspect of his or her identity (Cass, 1979). The model is composed of six stages:

1. *Identity confusion*: consists of a realization that emotions and behaviors can be considered homosexual, leading to confusion;
2. *Identity comparison*: includes struggle with the social alienation that accompanies the realization of possible homosexuality;
3. *Identity tolerance*: is characterized by a commitment to homosexuality and the seeking of other homosexuals to counter alienation and isolation from others;

4. *Identity acceptance*: consists of increased contact with other homosexuals, which validates the individual's homosexual identity;
5. *Identity pride*: consists of realization of the incongruence between one's identity and cultural acceptance, resulting in the devaluing of heterosexuality and disclosure of the individual's homosexuality;
6. *Identity synthesis*: occurs when an individual synthesizes various identities and discontinues the acknowledgment of a dichotomy between heterosexuality and homosexuality.

There is some question regarding the applicability of this model for Asian American LGB individuals. Chan (1989), for example, found that Asian American gay men had difficulty advancing to the latter stages of Cass's model.

Although more current models of LGB identity development have been published, they consistently indicate that distancing oneself from a heterosexual lifestyle and being outspoken and politically active in the gay community are attributes of individuals who are firmly grounded in their LGB identity. This notion appears to be at odds with traditional Asian values, as we will discuss. Research also highlights the importance of environmental context in understanding LGB identity and experiences (Evans & Broido, 1999; Rhoads, 1994). However, these studies do not focus on the impact of environment on managing multiple identities.

Literature on Lesbian, Gay, and Bisexual Asian Americans

There has been little discussion of Asian American LGB communities within "mainstream" higher education literature, and as Takagi (1996) notes, "What we do know about Asian American gay and lesbians must be gleaned from personal narratives, literature, poetry, short stories and essays" (p. 31). What many essays and personal stories share is that the lives of Asian American gay, lesbian, and bisexual people are filled with negotiating space, living in multiple worlds, and trying to find themselves (Gopinath, 1996; Manalansan, 1996; Mangaoang, 1996). Phellas (1999, as cited in Grov, Bimbi, Nanin, & Parsons, 2006) reported that discussing and disclosing sexual orientation in ethnic minority families, where issues of sexuality are generally not discussed, is challenging for LGB ethnic minorities. Evidence suggests that discussing such issues may be particularly challenging for Asian American LGB individuals (Grov et al., 2006). Grov et al., for example, found that Asian American and Pacific Islander men came out to their parents at significantly lower rates than White or Black men. They also reported that Asian American and Pacific Islander men were significantly older (19.51 years old) than White (18.03 years old) and Black (15.51 years old) men when they had their first same-gender sexual experience, suggesting greater difficulty in coming out as LGB. Similarly, Lippa and Tan (2001) found that Hispanics and Asian Americans were more afraid of social disapproval for being LGB than their White counterparts.

Chung and Katayama (1998) attributed some of the negative associations with an LGB identity in Asian cultures to the notion of LGB being largely a Western concept. Same-sex affection exists in many countries, but it is not considered sexual behavior. Similarly, in many Asian languages, there are no equivalents for the terms *lesbian*, *gay*, and *bisexual*.

As indicated previously, early models of racial or sexual identity development generally addressed only one dimension of identity. Models to explain how individuals belonging to more than one social group integrate their identities were absent from the literature. More recently, those in psychology and counseling fields have published more literature on multiple identities, and the identities of Asian American LGB individuals specifically (Chung & Singh, 2009). However, literature on the effects of identifying as an Asian American and LGB is relatively invisible within higher education—a fact that influenced the development of the current study.

A Mixed-Method Exploration of LGB Asian American College Students' Experiences

In this chapter, we discuss our mixed-method study in which we used a Web-based survey (i.e., Zoomerang) to gather demographic, quantitative, and qualitative data. We also used qualitative methods in the form of interviews, which allowed us to gather students' stories of their experiences negotiating the complexities of identifying with two very different social identities—being Asian American and LGB. This chapter focuses on the findings that emerged from the survey component of the investigation.

For the study, we used two sampling strategies: criterion and modified snowball. To be included in the study, participants had to (1) self-identify as Asian American and LGB, (2) be currently enrolled in a degree program in postsecondary education, (3) be between 18 and 24 years old, and (4) have been born in the United States or moved to the United States by the age of 10. We solicited participants through targeted Asian American and LGB

Listservs in higher education, as well as through professional contacts working in higher education. We asked individuals who received our "call for participants" e-mail to forward it to others who might be interested in the study or who had access to students who met the criteria for participation. We used our contacts in higher education to trigger a snowball technique, using e-mail. In an effort to reach a relatively small population that can be difficult to contact, we used procedures that were not random or systematic. Thus, we must use caution in interpreting the findings of our analysis, because they cannot be generalized to larger populations of LGB Asian Americans.

We intentionally created the parameters of this study. First, the participants needed to identify, at least to themselves, as being LGB. Our goal was to have participants who acknowledged their sexuality as belonging to a larger community of LGB individuals. Transgender individuals were not included in the study, because we believe that transgender students' development and needs may be different from those of LGB students on campus. Second, we only included individuals who self-identified as Asian Americans. Including only self-identified Asian Americans ensured that the participants both identified with their Asian heritage and were raised in the United States, thereby experiencing the sociopolitical realities of growing up in the dominant cultures of the United States. In the e-mail solicitation for participants, we explained that, although the terms *Asian American* and *LGB* are far from inclusive of all the complexities and preferred self-labeling that the community uses, the goal was to cast a wide net to capture the largest group of participants. Finally, we required participants to be between 18 and 24 years old to ensure that they were of a similar generational status.

We asked participants to complete a Web-based survey that consisted of questions about their background, comfort with their identity, and involvement on their campuses. This survey also included questions about what they believed would help them succeed on campus. For almost every forced-choice question asked in the Web-based survey, participants were also given an opportunity to write in comments. At the end of the survey, students could link to another survey to volunteer to be part of the interview process for the qualitative component.

Results of the Survey

The first section of the survey solicited demographic data from participants. Out of 133 respondents, 89 students met the criteria for the study. Thirty-eight participants identified biologically as men and 51 as women. Thirty-four identified as gay, 13 as lesbian, 21 as bisexual, and 21 as other (i.e., downe, pansexual, and queer). The age range for students in the study was 18 to 24, with most participants being 20 or 21 years of age. Ethnically, 23 identified as Chinese, 23 as mixed-race, 13 as Filipino, 9 as Vietnamese, 5 as Japanese, 5 as Korean, and 11 identified with six other ethnic groups. Some participants chose not to disclose their ethnic background. Most of the participants were enrolled at institutions on the West Coast, in the Northeast, or in the Midwest. This skewed geographic distribution could be a function of the Listservs and professional contacts used to access students. All of the participants were enrolled in higher education at the time of the study—72 of the students were undergraduates, and 17 of the students had recently started graduate or professional school. Approximately half of the student respondents (50.6%) attended medium or large public institutions, and 37.1% of the students attended small private institutions. Five students attended faith-based institutions.

Families and Relationships

In the next section of the survey, students discussed their families and relationships. In regard to their family composition, 60 participants were raised by their Asian or Asian American biological parents, 23 participants were raised by their mixed-race biological parents, and 6 participants were adopted (4 by White parents, 1 by mixed-race parents, and 1 by Asian parents). Additionally 66% of the students indicated that they strongly agreed or agreed with the statement that they were raised in families with traditional Asian values and culture. A total of 54 students reported not being in a relationship at the time of completing the survey, 25 were in same-sex relationships, 6 were in a relationship with a person of the opposite sex, and 4 described different patterns of relationships or multiple partners. Of those 35 students who indicated that they were in a relationship, their partners identified in the following ways: 2 Asian, 3 Asian American, 3 mixed-race of partial Asian descent, 3 mixed-race not of Asian descent, 5 persons of color not of Asian descent, 15 White, and 4 stated "other."

We also asked participants about being "out" to their families and on campus. Thirty-two participants indicated they were not "out" to any family members. Those students who were out to family indicated being selective about which family members they informed. Most of them were out to a sibling, 15 indicated that they were out to their father, and 25 to their mother. Many noted that they were out to a "safe" member in their family, such as a sibling, an aunt, or a cousin. Several survey participants wrote that they were only out to their White family members, and they would not come out to their extended Asian family. Lastly, a few students stated that they were out to their entire family or they were unsure which members of their family knew they were LGB, because they were fairly public with their "outness."

On campus, 80 of the participants were out to their friends, 53 were out to faculty, and 49 were out to administrators or staff. Of those who were out on campus, many suggested that their campus activities and involvement meant that they were highly visible as LGB, and, therefore, completely out. In contrast, some students were only out to "safe" staff members, such as multicultural directors, LGBT directors, or openly LGB staff.

On-Campus and Off-Campus Involvement

The last portion of the survey gathered information about participants' level of involvement on and off campus, as well as recommendations for faculty and administrators. Forty-three students indicated involvement with on-campus groups that focus on Asian American issues, whereas only 18 students were involved in off-campus Asian organizations. Similarly, 52 students were involved with on-campus LGB groups, many of which were groups that focused on LGB issues for persons of color, whereas only 23 students were involved with off-campus LGB organizations.

We were interested in relationship involvement and being out to families, friends, and faculty and staff. Chi-square tests revealed that there was a significant (or nearly significant) relationship between students' involvement in LGB groups on campus and being out to their families ($r = .078$), friends on campus ($r = .002$), faculty ($r = .000$), and administrators ($r = .001$). The relationship between involvement and "outness" for students leads us to conclude that if students were not out on campus they were also not involved in LGB groups on their campuses, and if students were out they were more likely to be involved in LGB groups.

When asked if they were currently or would be interested in being involved in groups that focus on both LGB and Asian American issues, 25 students said "no" and gave the following reasons for their negative response: (1) *too narrow of a focus or too small of a group*, (2) *because I'm not out*, (3) *I feel uncomfortable in Asian American–focused groups*, (4) *I am afraid of gays and lesbians*, and (5) *it is Asian male dominated*. The 62 students who said they were currently or would like to be involved in LGB groups wanted to do so because they expressed that these organizations would help them address issues of racism in the queer community, allow them to connect with people who share similar struggles, allow them to connect with much-needed support, allow them to express both their Asian American and LGB identities, and give them an opportunity to explore their identities.

When asked about feeling supported on campus, 77.5% of the students indicated that they agreed or strongly agreed that they felt supported by their peers; 75.3% indicated that they felt supported by faculty and staff. Although data and numbers are important for understanding some of the concrete realities of the Asian American LGB community, hearing the voices of participants through their words helps bring the data alive.

Challenges Associated With Being Asian American and Lesbian, Gay, or Bisexual

At the end of the Web-based survey, we posed a few open-ended questions about the challenges and benefits associated with being Asian American and LGB. We also solicited advice for faculty and staff to help make the experiences of Asian American LGB students more positive. To these four questions alone, students typed in more than 12 single-spaced pages of comments.

Challenges

When asked about the most negative or challenging things that have happened to them that they attribute to being Asian American and LGB, the majority of students wrote just a few succinct words: "being called a fag," "constant stereotyping," "a lot of Asian jokes," "not feeling authentically Asian American or LGB enough." Others wrote lengthy and sometimes emotional paragraphs about their experiences. The longer responses revealed that one of the issues faced by participants was the racial stereotyping of Asian American men:

> Unfortunately, due to my shorter stature, slimmer figure, and Asian genetics, I am often considered quiet, submissive, weak, and only desiring of White men. It's been surprising how many people will turn me down solely because I am Asian. Moreover, it's also apparently surprising to some that I am a vocal and critical gay Asian male. Regardless, because of these gay Asian male stereotypes, I feel like I've been single for a very long time. [Chinese/Filipino gay male]

Some of these lengthier quotations highlighted the discrimination faced by participants as LGB, and others underscored their experienced discrimination as an Asian American on campus:

I am much more "out" in college than I was in high school, so finding a group of friends that were accepting of my sexual orientation was a bit difficult, since many social events are very heteronormative. Also, the stares I would get when walking and holding hands with my girlfriend around campus was definitely something I had to get used to. [Filipina lesbian]

I haven't had any negative LGB-related things happen on campus, but I have had numerous racially motivated events. My first experience with explicit racism happened on campus when some people yelled, "Go back to China—kung-fu," at a friend and me. [Korean adoptee lesbian]

Other written comments related to the challenges of being Asian American within the LGB community or being LGB within the Asian American community specifically. One student, for example, wrote, "Lack of solidarity between Asian American and the LGB students" (Filipino gay male). Another participant wrote the following:

Ongoing issues of inclusion in API [Asian Pacific Islander] and queer organizing spaces, stereotypes, assumptions, and marginalization on both fronts and of the intersection. [Japanese American downe male]

Benefits

When asked what is the best or most positive thing that has happened to them that they attributed to being Asian American and LGB, students focused on finding space, finding community, and finding partners. Although some students stated these responses succinctly and directly, others shared detailed and heartfelt stories about their experiences. One student stated, "The API LGBTQ community is really close, and I am happy to be part of that community" (Chinese/Filipino gay male), and another responded with the comment "finding a good community" (Central Indian bisexual female). Yet another participant wrote, "I met my girlfriend! And, lots of cute Asian American girls!" (Chinese lesbian). As mentioned, other students provided more in-depth answers to this question, such as the following:

Meeting another Asian American who identifies as gay and happens to come from a much more traditional Filipino family was very reassuring for me. We were actually in [an] Asian American studies class, so we were able to openly (and even outside of class) relate some of our experiences. I also joined the women's rugby team, which is very LGB-friendly, since many of the team members identify as either bisexual or lesbian. Having a group that accepted me so willingly was a very positive experience and was one of my first few in college. [Filipina lesbian]

Advice for Educators

Finally, in an effort to give our participants a voice, we asked them to share their advice with faculty and administrators about what the institution needs to do to make the experiences of Asian American LGB students more positive. It was interesting how many students wrote about how administrators are "pretty accepting" and "amazing for the most part." There were some instances of overlap and general suggestions, such as "bring in more speakers," "get to know students individually," "assume less," and "recognize us [the existence of students who are Asian American and LGB]." Students also provided some specific suggestions for faculty and different ideas for administrators. For faculty, students shared the following:

> Overall, faculty who teach issues of diversity must include the complexities of identity issues. Professors must highlight the multiple identities of each student, especially those who are people of color. They must include the queer experience in the Asian American courses along with including the Asian American experience in the queer literature/topics. [Filipino gay male]

> All faculty must undergo a course on privilege: race, class, sexuality, and gender. My campus is predominantly Asian American, but privilege is a concept that is really undertheorized and not deconstructed in actual practice. I don't care that you can theorize about racism. What is more important is how you treat others, especially as an "expert" on culture, society, whatever. [Vietnamese American queer female]

> Use inclusive language when talking about relationships, pronouns, etc., and don't exoticize Asian things. [Chinese/Burmese gay male]

> Most importantly is to watch the language; keep it gender-neutral and be conscious of heterosexist or heteronormative remarks. Also, call out anyone who utters something heterosexist, heteronormative, homophobic, racist, or essentialist. Be active allies to queer, API, and queer API individuals. [Han/Hakka/Manchu queer/downe male]

The recommendations were slightly different for administrators. Students focused on having more inclusion training for staff members who work in multicultural affairs and for gender equity and LGB offices, as well as diversity training in general for all staff. Other specific suggestions included the following:

> The administrators need to stop tokenizing us for this quest of fulfilling diversity and truly provide programs, resources, and support that will develop a safe campus climate for all students. [Taiwanese queer female]

> I think that there should be a promotion of Asian LGBT individuals on campus. There must be a forward effort in showing that being Asian and gay is okay. Right now the Asian cultural values conflict with being LGBT. So, if there is a promotion of both, then we are likely to see more Asians disclose their sexual orientation. [Chinese/Japanese/Hawaiian gay male]

Although there is no unified voice or perspective on making campuses friendlier places for students to negotiate their dual or dueling identities as Asian American and LGB, it is clear that this issue has been on many students' minds. Reading pages of typed comments to open-ended questions made us recognize that students need and want faculty and administrators to invest in efforts to improve the campus environment. It was also clear to us that students are not necessarily bringing their two cultural identities. It was also evident that they did not always want to have them intersect, at least not in all aspects of their lives.

Discussion and Implications

As the Asian American population continues to grow and the LGB students carve out more space on campus, educators must understand the complexity of students who are LGB and Asian American. From classrooms to residence halls, and from cultural centers to student activities, faculty and administrators must create space for the changing needs of students who are attempting to establish identities and build connections with their peers, faculty, and staff. One finding from this research indicates that there is a strong need for more support, which includes space to discuss issues of identity, integrated curriculum that includes LGB Asian Americans, and increased awareness and understanding about students with multiple minority identities.

Many of the participants stated that they wanted physical spaces to talk about their issues and needs. However, finding a space to call home is a constant struggle for LGB Asian Americans (Eng, 2005). In one incident, a participant recalls being told to go back to China, as if her home is not the

United States. Another participant notes the struggle of "being myself in college, but having to repress my identity at home on the weekends." For each of these students, the struggle continues when they feel as though they can only bring one identity into a particular space at a particular time. Fung (1995) explains that LGB Asian Americans have no more of a "multiple identity" than a White straight man. However, he notes that the "burden of 'identity' falls on the socially devalued half of the binaries" and "the binary is only a crude model for conceptualizing the mess of social relations, and the reality of anyone's life is far more complicated and fluid" (p. 128). The burden of identity is addressed by many of the participants, such as by the statement that there are "ongoing issues of inclusion in API and queer organizing spaces, stereotypes, assumptions, and marginalization on both fronts." In order to help these students tackle such issues, practitioners—especially those in cultural, diversity, and LGBTQ centers—must create discussions that value all aspects of students' identity.

There are many things that faculty and staff can do to assist this population, and participants' responses offer some viable options. The most prominent recommendation is the need to integrate LGB issues into Asian American courses and Asian American issues into LGB courses. This need of LGB Asian Americans to find their voice within the literature or course material is critical. Rarely do classes bring together multiple identities, and, when they do, it is cursory. Participants also suggested openly addressing LGB or Asian issues, even in classes that may not focus directly on such identities; for example, recognizing Asian Americans and LGB individuals within history, media, communications, and business courses. One of the most important things, as noted by participants, is to be sensitive to language and address stereotypes and assumptions swiftly and appropriately.

The last recommendation to staff and faculty is a simple, yet difficult, one: Be supportive. As most of the participants demonstrated, negotiating their LGB and Asian American identity is extremely complex and often painful. For these students, college is a challenging place, because they are trying to bring two pieces of themselves together, possibly for the first time. Faculty and staff who recognize students' individual needs and backgrounds seem to be the most influential in these students' lives. Several of the participants stated that faculty allowed them to do independent projects, thereby helping students' voices to be heard. Others noted that some staff went out of their way to find information about LGB or Asian Americans. In either case, students found very few people on campus with whom they could relate, which means it is important for all practitioners to be receptive to hearing the students' stories and supporting them.

Conclusion

This study makes it clear that lesbian, gay, and bisexual Asian American students need the support of their faculty, staff, and peers. Because of inherent cultural differences, these students can often find themselves moving in and out of different worlds. In some cases, they may find themselves in predominantly straight Asian communities that rarely, if ever, discuss issues of sexuality. On the other hand, they may delve into a predominantly White or non-Asian LGB community, which may stress being out and proud. A third space is probably the most obvious: a straight and predominantly White campus that may not even recognize that there is, or could be, significant variation in experiences of individuals within LGB or Asian American communities.

To address the concerns of Asian American LGB students, educators must develop a deeper understanding of their needs, even if this group appears small or invisible. It is critical that educators use inclusive curricula, through which intersecting identities can be explored, and provide a safe space for these students to explore their identity. By cultivating an inclusive environment on campus, in classes, and within programs, educators can encourage Asian American LGB students to carve out a safe space for themselves on campus.

Notes

1. We focus on the most relevant aspects of the Asian American identity literature in this chapter, but researchers can find a more comprehensive discussion of Asian American identity development in Chapter 2 of this volume, by Museus, Vue, Nguyen, and Yeung.

References

Abes, E. S., & Kasch, D. (2007). Using queer theory to explore lesbian college students' multiple dimensions of identity. *Journal of College Student Development, 48*(6), 619–636.

Cass, V. C. (1979). Homosexuality identity formation: A theoretical model. *Journal of Homosexuality, 4*, 219–235.

Chan, C. S. (1989). Issues of identity development among Asian American lesbians and gay men. *Journal of Counseling and Development, 68*(1), 16–20.

Chung, Y. B., & Katayama, M. (1998). Ethnic and sexual identity development of Asian-American lesbian and gay adolescents. *Professional School Counseling, 1*(3), 21–25.

Chung, Y. B., & Singh, A. A. (2009). Lesbian, gay, bisexual, and transgender Asian Americans. In N. Tewari & A. N. Alvarez (Eds.), *Asian American psychology: Current perspectives* (pp. 233–246). New York: Taylor & Francis Group.

Crawford, I., Allison, K. W., Zamboni, B. D., & Soto, T. (2002). The influence of dual-identity development on the psychosocial functioning of African-American gay and bisexual men. *The Journal of Sex Research, 39*(3), 179–189.

Eng, D. L. (2005). Out here and over there: Queerness and diaspora in Asian American studies. In K. A. Ono (Ed.), *A companion to Asian American studies* (pp. 350–369). Malden, MA: Blackwell.

Evans, N. J., & Broido, E. M. (1999). Coming out in college residence halls: Negotiation, meaning making, challenges, supports. *Journal of College Student Development, 40*, 658–668.

Fung, R. (1995). The trouble with "Asians." In M. Dorenkamp & R. Henke (Eds.), *Negotiating lesbian and gay subjects* (pp. 123–129). New York: Routledge.

Gamson, J. (1995). Must identity movements self-destruct? A queer dilemma. *Social Problems, 42*(3), 390–407.

Gopinath, G. (1996). Funny boys and girls: Notes on a queer South Asian planet. In R. Leong (Ed.), *Asian American sexualities: Dimensions of the gay and lesbian experience* (pp. 119–127). New York: Routledge.

Grov, C., Bimbi, D. S., Nanin, J. E., & Parsons, J. T. (2006). Race, ethnicity, gender, and generational factors associated with the coming-out process among gay, lesbian, and bisexual individuals. *Journal of Sex Research, 43*(2), 115–121.

Ibrahim, F., Ohnishi, H., & Sandhu, D. S. (1997). Asian American identity development: A culture specific model for South Asian Americans. *Journal of Multicultural Counseling and Development, 25*(1), 34–50.

Kim, B. S. K., Atkinson, D. R., & Yang, P. H. (1999). The Asian values scale: Development, factor analysis, validation and reliability. *Journal of Counseling Psychology, 46*, 342–352.

Kim, J. (1981). *Processes of Asian American identity development: A study of Japanese American women's perceptions of their struggle to achieve positive identities as Americans of Asian ancestry* (Unpublished doctoral dissertation). University of Massachusetts, Amherst.

Kim, J. (2001). Asian American identity development theory. In M. E. Wilson & L. E. Wolf-Wendel (Eds.), *ASHE reader on college student development theory* (pp. 281–293). Boston, MA: Pearson Custom Publishing.

Kim, J. L., & Ward, L. M. (2007). Silence speaks volumes: Parental sexual communication among Asian American emerging adults. *Journal of Adolescent Research, 22*, 3–31.

Lee, S. J., Wong, N.-W. A., & Alvarez, A. N. (2009). The model minority and perpetual foreigner: Stereotypes of Asian Americans. In N. Tewari & A. N. Alvarez (Eds.), *Asian American psychology: Current perspectives* (pp. 69–84). New York: Taylor & Francis Group.

Lippa, R. A., & Tan, F. D. (2001). Does culture moderate the relationship between sexual orientation and gender-related personality traits? *Cross-Cultural Research, 35,* 65–87.

Manalansan, M. F., VI (1996). Searching for community: Filipino gay men in New York City. In R. Leong (Ed.), *Asian American sexualities: Dimensions of the gay and lesbian experience* (pp. 73–90). New York: Routledge.

Mangaoang, G. (1996). From the 1970s to the 1990s: Perspectives of a gay Filipino American activist. In R. Leong (Ed.), *Asian American sexualities: Dimensions of the gay and lesbian experience* (pp. 101–110). New York: Routledge.

Nadal, K. L. (2004). Pilipino American identity development model. *Journal of Multicultural Counseling and Development, 32*(1), 45–61.

Okazaki, S. (2002). Influences of culture on Asian Americans' sexuality. *Journal of Sex Research, 39*(1), 34–42.

Patton, L. D., & Simmons, S. L. (2008). Exploring complexities of multiple identities of lesbians in a Black college environment. *The Negro Educational Review, 59*(3–4), 197–215.

Rhoads, R. A. (1994). *Coming out in college: The struggle for a queer identity.* Westport, CT: Greenwood Press.

Stewart, D. L. (2008). Being all of me: Black students negotiating multiple identities. *The Journal of Higher Education, 79,* 183–207.

Takagi, D. Y. (1996). Maiden voyage: Excursions into sexuality and identity politics in Asian America. In R. Leong (Ed.), *Asian American sexualities: Dimensions of the gay and lesbian experience* (pp. 21–35). New York: Routledge.

PART THREE

ASIAN AMERICAN AND PACIFIC ISLANDER LEADERS IN HIGHER EDUCATION

Patricia A. Neilson and Peter Nien-chu Kiang

A projected wave of university and college presidential retirements, combined with a national push to diversify leadership in U.S. postsecondary education, affords an unprecedented opportunity for Asian Americans and Pacific Islanders (AAPIs) to fill these executive roles. With this "graying" of predominantly White senior administrators in higher education, it is time for a new generation of leaders who reflect the country's current and future demographics to assume these beckoning leadership positions.

According to a recent report from the American Council on Education (ACE), AAPI undergraduate enrollments at some leading higher education institutions run from 25% to more than 50% (Yamagata-Noji, 2005). ACE reported that 6.4% of all enrolled students in higher education are AAPI (*The Chronicle of Higher Education*, 2004). Yet, AAPIs represent less than 1% (0.9%) of presidents and chancellors (Bridges, Eckel, Cordova, & White, 2008), and less than 2% (1.6%) are full-time administrators (King & Gomez, 2008). The paucity of AAPI senior administrators is glaring and often leads to misperceptions regarding the leadership abilities of AAPIs. What are the obstacles that prevent AAPIs from assuming increasingly prominent executive positions in the academy?

In his analysis of twenty-first-century leadership, Hokoyama (2011) suggests that an effective leader is "comfortable with oneself, takes pride in and [has an] understanding of one's cultural identity and understands how cultural values may influence behavior and how that behavior is perceived by others." For example, according to Funakoshi (2010), a cultural value or quality held in high regard by the Japanese is the concept of *shibumi* (渋み):

> Shibumi is a Japanese word meaning refined simplicity, simple elegance and quiet perfection. In ancient times, warriors (samurai) pursued shibumi in and out of the dojo (training space next to temple). They strove to find that essence of quality, simple and elegant, in everything they did. Warriors are never the life of the party. They do not like to draw attention by talking about themselves or their accomplishments. True warriors never boast, they are humble. They are not interested in small talk and speak only when they have something meaningful to say. When they speak their voices are steady but not loud, confident but not arrogant, bold but not disrespectful. They shake your hand with a nice grip (but not painful). They look at you in the eyes, and you feel an energy you cannot describe. These people keep dignity, sincerity, humility, etiquette, perfection and character alive in the society as well as in the arts. (p. 1)

But, if an AAPI is socialized from childhood to assume these highly regarded qualities of shibumi or their parallel traits in other AAPI cultures, they may be quickly misunderstood and unfairly rendered by others as lacking leadership characteristics that are valued by the dominant society, such as being ambitious, charismatic, and outgoing. Such cultural incongruence may be one of several factors across cultural, racial, linguistic, structural, and other dimensions that complicate how AAPIs aspire and strive toward leadership roles and positions in Western society. How, then, can we use this knowledge of cultural differences to better understand and potentially intervene in the chronic underrepresentation of AAPIs in leadership positions?

The chapters in this part on AAPI leadership begin to provide some of the approaches and answers we seek. By analyzing the issue from distinct perspectives—tenure-stream faculty, female faculty, and students—the following chapters add fresh insight regarding both cultural and structural dynamics related to the underrepresentation of AAPIs in leadership positions in U.S. higher education institutions.

In the domain of faculty, in "Asian American and Pacific Islander Faculty and the Glass Ceiling in the Academy: Findings From the National Study of Postsecondary Faculty" Yan and Museus examine whether a glass ceiling exists for AAPI faculty. Specifically, they conduct an examination of national data to determine whether AAPI faculty are less likely than their racial majority peers to acquire tenured positions in higher education. The authors' analysis sheds light on the fact that, despite myths of AAPIs as the model minority, AAPI faculty face racial inequities in academia. Huang's chapter, "From Revolving Doors and Chilly Climates to Creating Inclusive Environments for Pre-Tenure Asian American Faculty," investigates the factors that affect AAPI progress toward tenure. Huang's findings indicate that mentoring, supportive chairs and colleagues, and departmental climate are especially important influences on faculty retention and progress toward tenure. Complementing Huang's study, Yeung's chapter, "Struggles for Professional and Intellectual Legitimacy: Experiences of Asian and Asian American Female Faculty Members," adds gender and generational lenses to the analysis. Through a mixed-methods design, Yeung illustrates the challenges that Asian and Asian American women face in the academy. In addition, Yeung discusses distinctions in perspective and trajectory between Asian and Asian American female faculty and the value of networks with women of color nationally that should be pursued further in considering Asian American female faculty pathways and pipelines to leadership.

Shifting to the domain of students, in " 'Think About It as Decolonizing Our Minds': Spaces for Critical Race Pedagogy and Transformative Leadership Development," Poon presents a study of the ways in which Asian American students respond to subtle forms of racism, including engaging in acts of resistance as student leaders who engage in efforts to facilitate positive transformational social change. She also describes how academic spaces in which students can engage in critical analysis of issues of racial oppression can contribute to their development as transformative leaders. Balón and Shek, in "Beyond Representation: Confronting the New Frontier for Asian American Leadership," provide an overview of existing conceptual and programmatic models of Asian American leadership. The Social Change Model of Leadership and the Critical Asian Pacific American Leadership Framework, in particular, are two conceptual frameworks that allow for Asian American students to situate themselves as community leaders. Their chapter provides a helpful platform for campuses to develop or enhance their own leadership programs. Finally, in "Selecting and Supporting Asian American and Pacific Islander Students in Higher Education" Sedlacek and Sheu discuss a noncognitive framework that can be used to inform efforts to select and support AAPI college students. They explain how the framework can be used to rethink and improve the way that college educators select AAPIs in admissions and support them once they are admitted, which can ultimately contribute to efforts to develop more AAPI leaders in higher education and society.

AAPIs bring diverse, though underused, approaches to leadership, including commitments to group dynamics and team building over individualism. They bring fresh perspectives, but they can also serve as valuable role models with leadership skills that improve productivity through listening, reflecting, and relationship building. A collective effort is imperative to advocate, educate, and promote AAPIs to leadership positions, based, in part, on insights, data, and recommendations offered by contributors to this part.

References

Bridges, B. K., Eckel, P. D., Cordova, D. I., & White, B. P. (2008). *Broadening the leadership spectrum: Advancing diversity in the American college presidency.* Washington, DC: American Council on Education.

The Chronicle of Higher Education. (2004). *Almanac of Higher Education 2004–5, 51*(1), 3.

Funakoshi, K. (2010). *Practice shibumi every day.* Retrieved May 31, 2012, from www-.newenglandshotokan.com/Documents/Shibumi.pdf

Hokoyama, J. D. (2011, January). *21st Century leader: Surviving and thriving in the 3rd millennium.* Presentation at 2011 Leadership Education for Asian Pacifics Inc. Conference, Los Angeles, CA.

King, J. E., & Gomez, G. G. (2008). *On the pathway to the presidency: Characteristics of higher education's senior leadership.* Washington, DC: American Council on Education.

Yamagata-Noji, A. (2005). Leadership development program in higher education: Asian Pacific American leaders in higher education—An oxymoron? In D. Leon (Ed.), *Lessons in leadership: Executive leadership programs for advancing diversity in higher education* (Vol. 5, pp. 173–206). Bingley, UK: Emerald Group Publishing Limited.

13

ASIAN AMERICAN AND PACIFIC ISLANDER FACULTY AND THE GLASS CEILING IN THE ACADEMY

Findings From the National Study of Postsecondary Faculty

Wenfan Yan and Samuel D. Museus

There is some evidence suggesting that women and people of color face a "glass ceiling" (e.g., Federal Glass Ceiling Commission, 1995; Woo, 2000), which is composed of "artificial barriers based on attitudinal or organizational bias that prevent qualified individuals from advancing upward in their organization into management-level positions" (U.S. Department of Labor, 1991, p. 1). This concept of the glass ceiling suggests that gender and racial bias work against women and people of color as a form of institutional oppression in the workforce. Little is known, however, about whether Asian American and Pacific Islander (AAPI) faculty in higher education face a glass ceiling. It is important to understand whether a glass ceiling does exist, because if AAPI faculty members do face racial barriers to advancement, then institutional leaders must be aware of this problem and understand how to address it (Lee, 2002).

The current study is aimed at understanding whether a glass ceiling does exist for AAPI faculty. In the following sections, we provide the context for the current investigation. First, we introduce Split Labor Market Theory (SLMT) as a framework for understanding the glass ceiling phenomenon.

Then, we briefly discuss research related to whether AAPI faculty might face a glass ceiling, while highlighting the limitations of that literature. The remainder of the chapter focuses on our analysis of AAPI faculty and the glass ceiling.

Split Labor Market Theory and the Glass Ceiling

The concept of meritocracy—the notion that if people work hard enough no barriers can stop them from achieving their dreams—is a value endorsed by the majority of American society today (McNamee & Miller, 2009). Those who believe in meritocracy argue that people are rewarded for hard work regardless of race or ethnicity, which suggests that the nation's meritocracy is color-blind. Thus, according to the notion of meritocracy, AAPI faculty should not face a glass ceiling, because their hard work should determine the extent to which they make professional progress. One limitation of the meritocracy perspective, however, is that racism and other forms of oppression are embedded in the social fabric of society (Haney & Hurtado, 1994).

SLMT offers an alternative to the meritocracy perspective and serves as our conceptual framework. According to SLMT, women and people of color have been historically segregated in the labor market (Bonacich, 1972; Feagin & Feagin, 1986). Moreover, women and people of color have been segregated into the peripheral sector of the split labor market, giving White men more power in the core sector. This gender and racial segregation has disproportionately left women and people of color with jobs in the peripheral sector, which often have lower pay, less job security, and less opportunity for professional advancement (Lee, 2002). In this way, institutionalized gender and racial bias function to oppress women and individuals of color, resulting in an invisible barrier to their advancement—a glass ceiling. Because our study examines whether AAPIs are segregated in nontenured positions and have experienced a decreased probability of acquiring tenured faculty status compared with their White counterparts, SLMT offers a useful framework for this investigation.

Asian American and Pacific Islander Faculty and the Glass Ceiling

On the surface, statistics appear to suggest that AAPIs do well in academia (Nettles, Perna, & Bradburn, 2000). In 2005, AAPI faculty made up more than 7% of full-time faculty and 6.5% of those with full professor status (*The Chronicle of Higher Education Almanac, 2007–8*). These figures are larger than AAPIs' share of the national population, which is 6% (U.S. Census Bureau, 2011). Such cursory statistics might support the notion of meritocracy by confirming that AAPIs, who are racial minorities, are able to achieve their professional goals despite racial oppression. The reality, however, is more complex than these statistics suggest, and there is some indication that AAPI faculty may face a glass ceiling.

Indeed, a growing body of research examines the impact of the glass ceiling. Specifically, these inquiries examine whether being a woman or person of color negatively impacts earnings and promotion, to understand whether these groups face a glass ceiling in the workforce. For example, several studies that focus on gender support the notion that a glass ceiling exists for White women in both nonacademic and academic contexts, because they earn less and are promoted at lower rates than their male counterparts (Bain & Cummings, 2000; Bradburn & Sikora, 2003; David & Woodward, 1997; Hagan, 1990; Kay & Hagan, 1995; Long, Allison, & McGinnis, 1993; Menagh, 1997; Tesch, Wood, Helwig, & Nattinger, 1995; Wood, Corcoran, & Courant, 1993).

Similarly, several inquiries indicate that AAPIs face a glass ceiling, but most of these studies are somewhat dated and focus on nonacademic contexts and professions (Barringer, Takeuchi, & Xenos, 1990; Federal Glass Ceiling Commission, 1995; Fernandez, 1998; Edmonston & Passel, 1994; Hirschman & Wong, 1984; Lee, 2002; Nee & Sanders, 1985; Palepu et al., 1995; Tang, 1993; Woo, 2000). Several scholars, for example, provide evidence that AAPIs experience disparities in earnings and advancement when compared with their White counterparts with similar qualifications in nonacademic arenas (Barringer et al., 1990; Hirschman & Wong, 1984; Nee & Sanders, 1985).

Only a few researchers have explored whether a glass ceiling exists for AAPIs in higher education, and they provide mixed support for the existence of a glass ceiling for AAPI faculty (Lee, 2002; Palepu et al., 1995). In a national study of medical school faculty, for example, Palepu et al. concluded that AAPI, Black, and Hispanic faculty were all less likely than White faculty to be promoted to associate or full professor. Lee, however, conducted a nationally representative study that generated a more complex picture. Using data from the first National Survey of Postsecondary Faculty (NSOPF: 93), she employed multiple regression techniques to explore the impact of several predictors (e.g., academic field, years of experience, productivity, academic rank, and tenure) on faculty salaries. She found no clear evidence of a glass ceiling, but uncovered evidence that AAPI faculty did not benefit from some of the characteristics that translated into higher salaries for White counterparts. For instance, whereas White faculty derived substantial and statistically significant benefits from being male, being native-born, being an associate or full professor, and having at least a low level of publications, the same characteristics exhibited negative or statistically nonsignificant effects for AAPIs. Lee argued that these findings might be consistent with the notion of a glass ceiling, because AAPIs had fewer paths available to increase their earnings than White faculty. Although Lee's study has made a noteworthy contribution to the literature, much remains to be learned about whether a glass ceiling exists for AAPI faculty and how it might influence other outcomes, such as tenure.

Purpose and Significance of the Study

Given the growing presence of AAPIs in the United States, the likelihood that they will continue to compose an increasing share of higher education, and the lack of research on this population, it is imperative that higher education researchers expand current levels of understanding about this group (Museus, 2009; Museus & Chang, 2009; Museus & Kiang, 2009). More specifically, it is critical for institutional leaders to understand whether AAPI faculty members are at a disadvantage, so that they can address the racial inequities that might cause such disadvantages. Yet, much remains to be learned about whether AAPI faculty face a glass ceiling in higher education. Accordingly, one primary question guided this inquiry: When accounting for background and professional factors, is being an AAPI faculty member negatively associated with the probability of acquiring a tenured position in the academy?

The current investigation substantially contributes to existing knowledge in several ways. First, the analysis responds to the exclusion of AAPIs from higher education research, and it calls for more scholarship on this population (Museus, 2009; Museus & Kiang, 2009). Second, this inquiry adds to the knowledge base by offering a nationally representative analysis of AAPI faculty and the glass ceiling that employs tenure as the focal outcome. Third, much existing literature is based on data from or before the early 1990s, and our analysis adds to that research by examining more recent national data on AAPI faculty and the glass ceiling.

Conceptual Framework

Split Labor Market Theory has previously been used to examine the glass ceiling among AAPI faculty (Lee, 2002) and was used as our conceptual framework. SLMT highlights the fact that representation of a particular racial group in the workforce (e.g., the faculty ranks) does not necessarily equate to equity and posits that advancement can be hindered by institutionalized racial segregation and oppression (Feagin & Feagin, 1986). In the context of this investigation, even if AAPIs are represented in the faculty ranks, SLMT suggests that AAPIs could still be racially subordinated as a group within the academy because of institutionalized racial oppression that hinders their professional advancement to tenured ranks. Thus, we use SLMT to hypothesize that endemic institutional inequities contribute to a glass ceiling for AAPI faculty. If this hypothesis is true, and we control for various institutional and professional factors, we would expect to see a negative relationship between being an AAPI and securing a tenured position among postsecondary faculty. Now, we turn to our inquiry into the relationship between being an AAPI faculty member and attaining a tenured position in the academy.

Methods

In the current study, we use the 2004 National Study of Postsecondary Faculty (NSOPF: 04) (Cataldi, Bradburn, Fahimi, & Zimbler, 2005). The NSOPF database is sponsored by the U.S. Department of Education's National Center for Education Statistics and was designed to provide nationally representative data on faculty and staff at two- and four-year degree-granting institutions in the United States. The total sample included 26,100 faculty and instructional staff across the nation. The survey included questions on the activities and instructional duties of postsecondary faculty and instructional staff during the 2003 fall term. For the purposes of the current analysis, we limited our sample to the 8,334 participants who were affiliated with four-year campuses. The survey includes data on background, education, and occupation variables, which we discuss in more detail in what follows.

The NSOPF database has both strengths and weaknesses. On the one hand, it is well suited for our research for several reasons. First, the NSOPF is the most current and comprehensive source of national data on AAPI faculty. Second, the database provides detailed information about faculty characteristics and productivity and has sufficient numbers of AAPI faculty for reliable analysis. Finally, the NSOPF (04) is nationally representative, permitting the generalization of findings to the national population of AAPI faculty.

The NSOPF also has several limitations. First, the database does not permit the disaggregation of the AAPI population by ethnicity. Although there are vast ethnic and socioeconomic differences across AAPI ethnic sub-populations and disaggregated analyses of the glass ceiling for those groups could yield valuable insight into whether some ethnic groups are more hindered by a glass ceiling than others, this was beyond the scope of our investigation because of the limitations of the NSOPF data. Second, the NSOPF includes cross-sectional data that are collected at one point in time, and we are therefore not able to conduct longitudinal analyses of whether faculty members on the tenure track gain promotion and tenure at particular institutions and over a specific period of time. Rather, we are only able to examine whether, holding other factors constant, being AAPI is correlated with having attained a tenured position.

Dependent Variable

In the current study, *tenure attainment*, which is the reward of an indefinite appointment offered to faculty members who have earned tenured status, is the focal outcome. We chose the attainment of tenure as the dependent variable, because having attained tenure is a critical measure of success among faculty for several reasons. For example, it provides faculty with a sense of security and stability, because it protects them from dismissal except for reasons of immoral conduct, financial corruption, or poor performance (Bess, 1998). Related to security and stability is the fact that tenure creates favorable conditions for faculty inside their institutions (Trower, 2009). Clearly, acquiring tenure is an accomplishment for which every tenure-track faculty strives. In this study, the tenure attainment outcome is a dichotomous dependent variable.

Independent Variables

The independent variables that we included in this analysis can be easily grouped into two categories: background characteristics and professional characteristics. Background characteristics include race, gender, age, marital status, and educational attainment. Professional characteristics include research productivity, time on instruction, and job satisfaction.

Background Characteristics

For the *race* variable, we used White as the baseline and included three dummy variables in our analysis, which measured whether respondents were AAPI, Black, or Hispanic. This variable is essential for our ability to determine whether a glass ceiling exists. As mentioned, *gender* has been found to influence faculty salaries, with men earning significantly more than women (e.g., Bellas, 1993; Lee, 2002), and was also coded as a dummy variable, measuring whether the participant identified as male or female. The *age* variable was a continuous measure of respondents' age when they began their current faculty position. We deemed it critical to control for age, because evidence indicates that AAPI faculty are younger than non-AAPI faculty (Lee, 2002). *Marital status* has also been found to be associated with the job performance, but the evidence is mixed, with some studies finding a negative association (Bellas, 1993; Perna, 2001), others finding a statistically insignificant relationship (Conley, 2005), and still others concluding that there is a positive association between the two variables (Bellas & Toutkoushian, 1999). Thus, we included marital status, which was coded as a dummy variable, measuring whether respondents were married or not, in the current analysis. Finally, *educational attainment* is associated with occupational attainment among faculty (Lee, 2002), and it was measured by whether participants held a doctorate, which is the highest degree that one can attain in postsecondary education and a prerequisite for occupying a tenure-track faculty position in most disciplines.

Professional Characteristics

Research is the decisive factor for promotion or tenure in most four-year colleges and universities (Park, 1996), and researchers have found research productivity to be associated with the occupational advancement of both AAPI and non-AAPI faculty (Lee, 2002; Long et al., 1993). *Research productivity* was a continuous measure of the number of published articles in refereed and nonrefereed journals and the number of book chapters produced in the previous two years. We assumed that focusing on the last two years was more reliable than total number of career publications, because respondents might more accurately recall more recent publications and productivity.

Both *time on instruction* and *academic field* are closely related to research productivity (Sax, Hagedorn, Arredondo, & Dicrsi, 2002). In regard to time on instruction, it could be argued that more time on instruction is associated with less time on research (Middaugh, 2001). Moreover, research suggests that there are racial differences in the amount of time that faculty spend on instruction and research, with AAPI and Hispanic faculty spending more time on research and less time on instruction than other groups (Bellas & Toutkoushian, 1999). Thus, time on instruction was included in our analysis and was measured by the percentage of the respondents' time spent on teaching. As for academic field, differences in the resources required for research across fields may lead to disparities in research output (Sax et al., 2002). Moreover, academic field has been associated with the occupational attainment of both AAPI and non-AAPI faculty (Harvey, 2002; Lee, 2002; Xie & Shauman, 2003). Thus, we used "all other fields" as the baseline and coded each other academic field that was included in the NSOPF survey as a separately dummy-coded variable and incorporated them into the analysis.

Job satisfaction can be defined as the positive emotional feeling resulting from attaining what one wants or values from a job (Olsen, 1993). It is important to take job satisfaction into account when studying racial minority faculty (Hagedorn, 2000), because there is evidence that racial minority faculty are significantly less satisfied than their White peers (Lee, 2002; Olson, Maple, & Stage, 1995). For instance, Olson et al. (1995) found that faculty of color except Hispanics were less likely than Whites to feel that they had satisfactory personal interaction with colleagues and a good fit with their departments. The authors also found that AAPIs were significantly less satisfied than Whites in regard to the fairness with which their immediate supervisors evaluate their work, the amount of personal and professional interaction with tenured colleagues, and their sense of "fit" in their departments. In this study, job satisfaction includes satisfaction with employment and teaching in the last two years—both of which are composite index variables. *Satisfaction of employment* is an index created from measures of respondents' satisfaction with (1) workload, (2) salary, (3) benefits, and (4) job overall. The *satisfaction of instructional activity* index was constructed from measures of satisfaction with (1) authority to make decisions on content and methods in instructional activities, (2) institutional support for implementing technology-based instructional activities, (3) quality of equipment and facilities available for classroom instruction, and (4) institutional support for teaching improvement.

Analytic Procedures

The analysis for this study was conducted in two stages. In the first stage, descriptive statistics were used to describe the characteristics of AAPI faculty and non-AAPI faculty. In the second stage, we conducted our logistic regression analysis to examine the relationship between our independent variables and the attainment of tenure. As opposed to ordinary least squares regression (OLS), logistic regression is used when the dependent variable (e.g., attainment of tenure) is a dichotomous outcome. Logistic regression is a useful procedure for predicting the odds of the occurrence of a dichotomous outcome and examining the relationship among multiple independent variables and a dichotomous dependent variable. Accordingly, we use these logistic regression techniques to predict the odds of faculty members' attaining tenure and to understand the impact of several faculty characteristics on the odds of attaining tenured status.

We used a hierarchical procedure to enter the independent variables into the equation in separate blocks and ran three successive models, each containing an additional block of predictor variables. The first, or baseline, model contained the race variables. The second model included other background characteristics, and the final model included all background and professional characteristics. If being AAPI is negatively associated with earning a tenured position when taking these variables into account, we can infer that AAPIs acquire tenure status at lower rates than their non-AAPI peers with similar qualifications and this is evidence of AAPIs facing a glass ceiling. The logit and standardized logit coefficients in logistic regression correspond with the unstandardized coefficients and standardized beta weights in OLS regression, respectively. The pseudo R^2 statistics in logistic regression measure the strength of the relationship, similar to the way R^2 estimates the amount of variation in the dependent explained by the OLS model.

Results of the Analysis

Table 13.1 summarizes the descriptive statistics across racial groups. This table can be used to observe differences in the dependent and each independent variable between AAPI faculty and other racial populations. In regard to background characteristics, White faculty members were more likely to have tenure (71.2%), followed by Black (58.4%), Hispanic (56.0%), and AAPI (55.9%) faculty. A larger proportion of AAPIs are married (82.2%), followed by their White (76.9%), Hispanic (70.7%), and Black (60.6%) counterparts. AAPI faculty are the most likely to be male (74.8%) of all racial groups, followed by White (68.8%), Hispanic (64.2%), and Black (56.8) faculty.

TABLE 13.1
Faculty Characteristics by Race

Variable	AAPI Mean (SD)	n	Black Mean (SD)	n	Hispanic Mean (SD)	n	White Mean (SD)	n
Tenure Status (%)								
Tenure	55.9	462	58.4	262	56.0	130	71.2	4,800
Tenure Track	44.1	365	41.6	187	44.0	102	28.8	1,944
Marital Status (%)								
Married	82.2	680	60.6	272	70.7	164	76.9	6,744
Not Married	17.8	147	39.4	177	29.3	68	23.1	1,559
Gender (%)								
Male	74.8	619	56.8	255	64.2	149	68.8	4,636
Female	25.2	208	43.2	194	35.8	83	31.2	2,107
Age	36.74	827	37.98	449	38.38	232	37.18	6,744
Highest Degree (%)								
Doctoral or Professional	95.2	788	87.5	392	87.6	204	87.9	5,929
Master's	4.3	36	11.6	52	10.3	24	11.4	891
Bachelor's or Less	1.4	13	3.8	23	4.1	15	2.4	201
Research Productivity	8.08 (10.49)	827	4.39 (5.86)	449	6.17 (6.33)	232	5.89 (7.12)	6,744
Time Spent on Instruction (%)	51.76 (25.43)	820	60.28 (24.75)	445	56.21 (25.59)	230	54.47 (26.70)	6,697
Academic Field (%)								
Business	13.4	111	8.7	39	6.4	15	8.2	522
Health	9.1	75	7.8	35	4.7	11	8.0	542
Humanities	7.4	61	10.9	49	17.2	40	12.4	837
Science/Engineering	43.3	358	17.4	78	21.5	50	23.6	1,593
Social Science/Education	9.1	75	22.3	100	24.9	58	17.0	1,143
Satisfaction With Employment	7.29 (2.48)	827	7.74 (2.60)	449	7.49 (2.88)	232	8.01 (2.66)	6,744
Satisfaction With Instructional Activity	8.55 (2.23)	805	8.96 (2.28)	437	8.62 (2.62)	227	8.95 (2.24)	6,530

Note: SD = Standard deviation.

Finally, AAPI faculty (95.2%) are more likely to hold a doctoral degree than their White (87.9%), Hispanic (87.6%), and Black (87.5%) counterparts.

In regard to research productivity, AAPI faculty averaged 8.08 publications over the past two years, which was higher than their Hispanic (6.17), White (5.89), and Black (4.39) counterparts. In contrast, AAPIs (51.76%) exhibited the lowest percentage of time spent on instruction, compared with their Black (60.28%), Hispanic (56.21%), and White (54.47%) counterparts. Almost half of AAPI faculty members were in science and engineering fields (43.3%), whereas non-AAPI faculty were more evenly distributed across fields. Finally, AAPI faculty had the lowest levels of satisfaction with employment and instructional activity. We now turn to the results of the seven steps of our logistic regression analysis.

Logistic regression analysis results are most effectively interpreted by the use of odds ratios rather than logistic coefficients, and table 13.2 displays the odds ratios associated with each independent variable in each step of the analysis. The odds ratios represent the change in the odds of earning a "1" on the dependent variable (i.e., attained tenure) associated with a one-unit change in the independent variable with which the ratio is associated. In this study, the odds ratios represent the change in the odds of holding a tenured position that is associated with a one-unit change in each independent variable. Specifically, an odds ratio greater than one represents an increase in the odds of attaining tenure, whereas an odds ratio of less than one represents a decrease in the odds of attaining a tenured position.

Due to space limitations, we cannot discuss all details of the model, so we highlight the most important findings. Model 1 is a baseline model, which estimates the effects of race variables on tenure attainment. Being AAPI (0.51), Black (0.58), and Hispanic (0.54) were all negatively associated with acquiring a tenured position, and these relationships were statistically significant at the 0.001 level. Thus, AAPI was the race most negatively associated with being in a tenured position. Specifically, compared with being White, being AAPI was associated with a 49% decrease in the likelihood of being in a tenured position. As table 13.2 shows, with each successive model—that is, when controlling for each added block of variables—the relationship between being Asian and holding a tenured position decreased even further.

Model 3 is the final model and included controls for all of the aforementioned background and professional characteristics. In this model, being male (1.47), being married (1.46), having a doctoral or professional degree (1.41), and research productivity (1.03) were all positively associated with

TABLE 13.2
Results of Hierarchical Logistic Regression Model of Tenure Status

Independent Variables	Model 1	Model 2	Model 3
Race			
AAPI	0.51***	0.45***	0.44***
Black	0.58***	0.67***	0.69***
Hispanic	0.54***	0.56***	0.55***
Gender			
Male		1.60***	1.47***
Age		0.98***	0.98***
Marital Status			
Married		1.51***	1.46***
Educational Attainment		1.47***	1.41***
Research Productivity			1.03***
Time on Instruction			0.97***
Academic Field			
Business			0.80*
Health			0.49***
Humanities			0.87
Science/Engineering			0.88
Social Sciences/Education			0.74***
Satisfaction With Employment			1.01
Satisfaction With Instruction			0.98
Model-Fit Statistics			
Cox & Snell R^2	0.01	0.05	0.06
Nagelkerke R^2	0.02	0.07	0.09
χ^2	115.20***	353.40***	515.25***
	(df = 3)	(df = 6)	(df = 16)

Note: *$p < .05$. **$p < .01$. ***$p < .001$.

having acquired a tenured position and statistically significant at the 0.001 level. Age at the point when participants assumed their position (0.98), time on instruction (0.97), being in the health field (0.49), and being in the social sciences or education fields (0.74) were all negatively associated with being in a tenured position, and those relationships were significant at 0.001. Being in business was also negatively associated with tenure, but at the 0.05 level. Being in science and engineering, being in the humanities, and satisfaction variables were all unrelated to the dependent tenure variable. Finally, our focal variable—that is, being AAPI—was negatively associated with the probability of acquiring a tenured position. Even after controlling for a variety of background and professional characteristics, being AAPI was associated with a 56% decrease in the probability of acquiring a tenured position.

Discussion

The current analysis contributes to existing literature in at least two important ways. First, this study contributes to the already existing body of literature that contradicts the model minority myth and provides evidence that AAPIs in higher education *do* face challenges that must be understood (Chang, Park, Lin, Poon, & Nakanishi, 2007; Museus, 2009; Museus & Kiang, 2009). The current inquiry adds to that literature by underscoring that AAPI faculty specifically may face unique barriers to professional advancement in the academy. Specifically, the findings generate evidence of the existence of a glass ceiling for AAPI faculty. Although there is a large body of research that is clear and consistent in its indication that AAPIs face a glass ceiling in the nonacademic workplace, only a couple of researchers have provided evidence of a glass ceiling in the academy, and that evidence is inconclusive (Lee, 2002; Palepu et al., 1995). Through the multivariate analysis of recent nationally representative data, the current inquiry buttresses the notion that a glass ceiling does exist for AAPI faculty. Thus, although the current study has limitations, it does shed significant light on the glass ceiling hypothesis.

Second, this inquiry highlights the misconceptions that researchers can create and perpetuate when they fail to use more critical perspectives and pursue more complex analyses of racial groups and racial issues in higher education. As mentioned, a cursory look at the representation of AAPI faculty suggests high levels of success. Thus, when aggregated descriptive statistics are presented without a more critical explanation of the limitations of such statistics (e.g., Turner, González, & Wood, 2008), it can contribute to the perpetuation of simplistic misconceptions about the experiences of AAPI faculty. The current analysis provides a more holistic and complex picture of the experiences of this population.

Implications for Future Research and Practice

The current inquiry provides several important implications for future research and practice. Because of space limitations, we highlight a few of those implications. First, in regard to research, we echo earlier calls for more scholarship on AAPIs in higher education in general (Museus, 2009; Museus & Chang, 2009; Museus & Kiang, 2009), and we emphasize the need for more research on AAPI faculty in particular. As noted, racial stereotypes and inadequate analyses of data have contributed to the exclusion of AAPIs from higher education research and discourse (Museus, 2009). This manifested in our literature review, which revealed only a few studies that focus on the experiences of AAPI faculty and led us to conclude that little understanding exists about this substantial and growing proportion of the professoriate.

Second, future research on professional advancement among AAPI faculty should take into account intra-race diversity. Our analysis shows that, when a variety of factors are taken into account, AAPI faculty members are 40% less likely to earn tenure than their White counterparts. If future studies analyze a national sample and disaggregate by national identity (e.g., AAPI versus international Asian) and ethnicity (e.g., East Asians versus Southeast Asians), the negative effect of being a member of particular Asian ethnic groups on attaining a tenured position in higher education could be even larger than the negative influences of being AAPI that we found here. Such an investigation would make a substantial contribution to the existing knowledge base.

Third, scholarship that specifically examines *how* the institutionalized racial oppression and the glass ceiling manifest in the experiences of AAPI faculty is needed. There is a substantial and informative body of knowledge regarding the experiences of faculty of color. (For a comprehensive review, see Turner et al., 2008.) That literature underscores several challenges, but few of these studies give specific attention to AAPI faculty. Thus, research that qualitatively analyzes the experiences of AAPI faculty is warranted.

Finally, colleges and universities should conduct institutional assessments of AAPI and other faculty members' experiences, perspectives, and satisfaction. Via such assessments, institutional leaders can also inquire about the kind of support that AAPI faculty desire or feel that they need to advance and be successful in the academy. Such assessments do currently take place at some institutions (see, e.g., The Collaborative on Academic Careers in Higher Education, 2008), but we argue that *all* institutions that care about the success of their faculty should partake in such endeavors and apply them to efforts to improve the experiences and success of AAPI and non-AAPI faculty members alike.

References

Bain, O., & Cummings, W. (2000). Academe's glass ceiling: Societal, professional/ organizational and institutional barriers to the career advancement of academic women. *Comparative Education Review, 44*(4), 493–514.

Barringer, H. R., Takeuchi, D. T., & Xenos, P. (1990). Education, occupational prestige, and income of AAPIs. *Sociology of Education, 63,* 27–43.

Bellas, M. L. (1993). Faculty salaries: Still a cost of being female? *Social Science Quarterly, 74,* 62–75.

Bellas, M. L., & Toutkoushian, R. K. (1999). Faculty time allocations and research productivity: Gender, race and family effects. *The Review of Higher Education, 22,* 367–390.

Bess, J. L. (1998). Contract systems, bureaucracies, and faculty motivation: The probable effects of a no-tenure policy. *The Journal of Higher Education, 69,* 1–22.

Bonacich, E. (1972). A theory of ethnic antagonism: The split labor market. *American Sociological Review, 37,* 547–559.

Bradburn, E. M., & Sikora, A. C. (2003). Gender and racial/ethnic differences in salary and other characteristics of postsecondary faculty: Fall 1998. *Education Statistics Quarterly, 4*(4), 1–7.

Cataldi, E. F., Bradburn, E. M., Fahimi, M., & Zimbler L. (2005). *2004 national study of postsecondary faculty (NSOPF: 04): Report on faculty and institutional staff in fall 2003.* Washington, DC: National Center for Education Statistics.

Chang, M. J., Park, J. J., Lin, M. H., Poon, O. A., & Nakanishi, D. T. (2007). *Beyond myths: The growth and diversity of AAPI college freshmen, 1971–2005.* Los Angeles, CA: Higher Education Research Institute.

The Chronicle of Higher Education Almanac (2007–8). *Number of full-time faculty members by sex, rank, and racial and ethnic group, fall 2005* (Vol. 54, p. 24). Retrieved from http://chronicle.com/weekly/almanac/2007/nation/0102402.htm

The Collaborative on Academic Careers in Higher Education. (2008). *Perspectives on what pre-tenure faculty want and what six research universities provide.* Cambridge, MA: Harvard University.

Conley, V. M. (2005). Career paths for women faculty: Evidence from NSOPF: 99. *New Directions for Higher Education, 130,* 25–39.

David, M., & Woodward, D. (Eds.). (1997). *Negotiating the glass ceiling: Careers of senior women in the academic world.* Washington, DC: Falmer Press.

Edmonston, B., & Passel, J. S. (Eds.). (1994). *Immigration and ethnicity: The integration of America's newest arrivals.* Washington, DC: Urban Institute Press.

Feagin, J., & Feagin, C. (1986). *Discrimination American style: Institutional racism and sexism.* Malabar, FL: R. E. Krieger.

Federal Glass Ceiling Commission. (1995). *Good for business: Making full use of the nation's human capital.* Washington, DC: U.S. Department of Labor.

Fernandez, M. (1998). Asian Indian Americans in the bay area and the glass ceiling. *Sociological Perspectives, 41,* 119–149.

Hagan, J. (1990). The gender stratification of income inequality among lawyers. *Social Forces, 68*, 835–855.

Hagedorn, L. S. (2000). Conceptualizing faculty job satisfaction: Components, theories, and outcomes. *New Directions for Institutional Research, 105*, 5–20.

Haney, C., & Hurtado, A. (1994). The jurisprudence of race and meritocracy: Standardized testing and "race-neutral" racism in the workplace. *Law and Human Behavior, 18*(3), 223–248.

Harvey, W. B. (2002). *Minorities in higher education 2001–2002: Nineteenth annual status report*. Washington, DC: American Council on Education.

Hirschman, H., & Wong, M. G. (1984). Socioeconomic gains of AAPIs, Blacks, and Hispanics, 1960–1976. *American Journal of Sociology, 90*, 584–607.

Kay, F. M., & Hagan, J. (1995). The persistent glass ceiling: Gendered inequalities in the earnings of lawyers. *British Journal of Sociology, 46*, 279–311.

Lee, S. (2002). Do AAPI faculty face a glass ceiling in higher education? *American Educational Research Journal, 39*(3), 695–724.

Long, J., Allison, P. D., & McGinnis, R. (1993). Rank advancement in academic careers: Sex differences and the effects of productivity. *American Sociological Review, 58*, 703–722.

McNamee, S. J., & Miller, R. K., Jr. (2009). *The meritocracy myth*. Lanham, MD: Rowman & Littlefield.

Menagh, M. (1997). The new face of diversity. *Computerworld, 31*, 88–90.

Middaugh, M. F. (2001). *Understanding faculty productivity: Standards and benchmarks for colleges and universities*. San Francisco, CA: Jossey-Bass.

Museus, S. D. (2009). A critical analysis of the exclusion of AAPI from higher education: Research and discourse. In L. Zhan (Ed.), *AAPI voices: Engaging, empowering, enabling* (pp. 59–76). New York: NLN Press.

Museus, S. D., & Chang, M. J. (2009). Rising to the challenge of conducting research on AAPIs in higher education. In S. D. Museus (Ed.), *Conducting research on AAPIs in higher education: New directions for institutional research* (No. 142, pp. 95–105). San Francisco, CA: Jossey-Bass.

Museus, S. D., & Kiang, P. N. (2009). Deconstructing the model minority myth and how it contributes to the invisible minority reality in higher education research. *New Directions for Institutional Research, 142*, 5–15.

Nee, V., & Sanders, J. (1985). The road to parity: Determinants of the socioeconomic achievements of AAPIs. *Ethnic and Racial Studies, 8*, 75–93.

Nettles, M. T., Perna, L. W., & Bradburn, E. M. (2000). Salary, promotion, and tenure status of minority and women faculty in U.S. colleges and universities. *Education Statistics Quarterly, 2*(2), 1–4.

Olsen, D. (1993). Work satisfaction and stress in the first and third year of academic appointment. *The Journal of Higher Education, 64*, 453–471.

Olson, D., Maple, S. A., & Stage, F. K. (1995). Women and minority faculty job satisfaction: Professional role interests, professional satisfactions, and institutional fit. *The Journal of Higher Education, 66*(3), 267–293.

Palepu, A., Carr, P. L., Friedman, R. H., Amos, H., Ash, A. S., & Moskowitz, M. A. (1995). Minority faculty and academic rank in medicine. *Journal of the American Medical Association, 250*, 767–771.

Park, S. M. (1996). Research, teaching, and service: Why shouldn't women's work count? *The Journal of Higher Education, 67*, 46–84.

Perna, L. W. (2001). The relationship between family and employment outcomes among college and university faculty. *The Journal of Higher Education, 72*, 584–611.

Sax, L. J., Hagedorn, L. S., Arredondo, M. A., & Dicrsi, F. A., III. (2002). Faculty research productivity: Exploring the role of gender and family-related factors. *Research in Higher Education, 43*, 423–447.

Tang, J. (1993). The career attainment of Caucasian and Asian engineers. *Sociological Quarterly, 34*, 467–496.

Tesch, B. J., Wood, H. M., Helwig, A. L., & Nattinger, A. B. (1995). Promotion of women physicians in academic medicine: Glass ceiling or sticky floor? *Journal of the American Medical Association, 273*(13), 1022–1026.

Trower, C. A. (2009). Toward a greater understanding of the tenure track for minorities. *Change, 41*(5), 38–46.

Turner, C. S. V., González, J. C., & Wood, J. L. (2008). Faculty of color in academe: What 20 years of literature tells us. *Journal of Diversity in Higher Education, 1*(3), 139–168.

U.S. Census Bureau. (2011). *Overview of race and Hispanic origin: 2010.* Washington, DC: Author.

U.S. Department of Labor. (1991). *A report on the glass ceiling initiative.* Washington, DC: Government Printing Office.

Woo, D. (2000). *Glass ceilings and AAPIs: The new face of workplace barriers.* Walnut Creek, CA: Alta Mira Press.

Wood, R. G., Corcoran, M. E., & Courant, P. N. (1993). Pay differences among the highly paid: Male–female earnings gap in lawyers' salaries. *Journal of Labor Economics, 11*, 417–441.

Xie, Y., & Shauman, K. A. (2003). *Women in science: Career processes and outcomes.* Cambridge, MA: Harvard University Press.

14

FROM REVOLVING DOORS AND CHILLY CLIMATES TO CREATING INCLUSIVE ENVIRONMENTS FOR PRE-TENURE ASIAN AMERICAN FACULTY

Belinda Lee Huang

Today, many colleges and universities are striving for diverse faculty and student bodies. Moreover, many institutions tout the structural diversity that their institutions have already achieved, because it contributes to intellectual development, social engagement, and learning outcomes (Hurtado, Milem, Clayton-Pedersen, & Allen, 1999). However, the growth of faculty of color in colleges and universities has been slow, and they remain a very small percentage of the professoriate (Trower & Chait, 2002). In 2007, faculty of color composed 17.1% of full-time faculty in higher education (Ryu, 2010). Whereas 5.4% were African American and 3.6% consisted of Hispanic faculty, Asian Americans and Pacific Islanders (AAPIs) constituted the largest proportion of this group at more than 7% (Ryu, 2010). However, these statistics can be misleading. For example, when nonresident aliens are removed from the AAPI racial category, their representation decreases significantly (Hune & Chan, 1997; Nakanishi, 1995).

The author would like to acknowledge and thank Sara Cho Kim and Gloria Bouis for assisting with data collection, transcription, and coding of the manuscript. A special thanks to Olan Garrett and Carol Corneilse for editing the manuscript.

Moreover, literature on AAPI faculty suggests that they have lower tenure rates than faculty of other racial groups, confront numerous difficulties and inequities in the academic environment, and encounter subtle and overt forms of racism in academia (Nakanishi, 1995; Nguyen, Huynh, & Lonergan-Garwick, 2007). In this chapter, I explore the factors that may positively and negatively influence Asian American junior faculty members' pre-tenure experiences. I conclude with implications for future research, policy, and practice.

Asian American Faculty in Higher Education

The literature suggests that faculty of color face significant challenges in academia. For example, faculty of color report experiences with prejudice and discrimination, social isolation, and a dearth of mentors in the academy (Gregory, 1995; Moore & Wagstaff, 1974; Trower & Chait, 2002). Moreover, these negative experiences may negatively impact their retention and promotion in the academy (Turner & Myers, 2000). There is also evidence that faculty of color do not receive adequate information and support from majority senior faculty, such as inside information or links to influential leaders in their field (Gainen & Boice, 1993; Turner & Myers, 2000). Faculty of color also experience *cultural taxation*, which Padilla (1994) defined as the obligation to show good citizenship toward the institution by serving its needs for ethnic representation on committees and provide knowledge of minority cultural groups. For instance, in a study conducted by Alexander-Snow and Johnson (1999), an African American faculty member commented, "You are expected to be on committees that require a lot of time commitment when most White faculty, especially males and then entry level . . . first-year or second-year like that . . . they don't have to do that type of service because there are senior people who can do it" (p. 93). Despite the countless hours of service to the university and communities of color, these activities are not often counted toward their tenure requirements.

Research on Asian American faculty, specifically, also highlights less quantifiable forms of discrimination, such as revolving doors, glass ceilings, and a chilly climate. Cho (1996), for example, described prevalent assumptions that Asian Americans are overly successful and, therefore, do not suffer from bias or discrimination in the academic workplace or need support. Research has also shown that Asian American faculty experienced sexual and racial harassment. Asian American faculty experiences might differ by generational status as well, with immigrant Asian American faculty experiencing, for example, discrimination in the form of negative evaluations as a result of their accents (Braine, 1999; Cho, 1996; Hune & Chan, 1997; Kim,

Brenner, Liang, 2003; Lippi-Green, 1997; Nakanishi, 1995; Skachkova, 2007; Vargas & Asay, 2002).

Gender Differences in Asian American Faculty Experiences

Literature on Asian American women faculty revealed that they struggled daily with gender stereotypes that converge with racial stereotypes (Hune, 1998). The images of the exotic or erotic Asian American woman negatively affect their experiences, because they are "orientalized" and seen as quiet, sweet, and obliging to others. This leads to Asian American women encountering sexual harassment in the forms of verbal remarks, unwanted pressures for dates, and deliberate encounters from peers and persons in authoritative positions (Cho, 1996; Hune, 1998). It also leads to assumptions that it is acceptable to discriminate against Asian American women, because they are passive and, if they encounter discrimination, will not fight back (Cho, 1996).

In addition to gender and racial stereotypes, similar to other academic women, a major challenge for Asian American female faculty is balancing work and family in an academic environment (Hu-DeHart, 1983; Hune, 1998). Indeed, in academe, policies and practices are based on males' gender roles that assume faculty have wives at home who ensure their career success, and colleges and universities tend to be more flexible about the work needs of men and less flexible in accommodating the needs of female professors (Hu-Dehart, 1983). In addition, Asian American women and other women in dual career households and female-headed households carry "double shifts," because they have the majority of responsibility for running their households and taking care of their children, on top of succeeding in the workplace. One study revealed that female faculty with children spent 101 hours per week on professional, housework, and caregiving activities, whereas men with children spent 88 hours per week on those activities (Thomas, 2005). Many Asian American female faculty members also have additional pressures of caretaking of parents and relatives (Hune, 1998). These realities are important, because female faculty who experience conflict between roles because of limited time and energy are less likely to be satisfied with their jobs and more likely to leave academia (Daly & Dee, 2006; Ward & Wolf-Wendell, 2004). In response, the American Council on Education (ACE, 2005) recommended that institutions adopt more family friendly policies, such as creating more opportunities to delay tenure, offering spousal or partner employment for new faculty hires, and offering health benefits for dependents.

Methods

The current study was conducted at a research-extensive university with an undergraduate enrollment of 26,000 and graduate enrollment of 10,000. At the time of this study, students of color made up 34% of the undergraduate population: 15% AAPI, 13% Black, 6% Latino/a, and 0.3% American Indian. There were roughly 3,000 full-time faculty members and 1,500 tenured or tenure-track faculty at the institution, including 191 tenured and 72 tenure-track AAPI faculty. Participants were selected using an institutional database of junior faculty, who identified their race as "Asian" when they were initially hired. All 72 Asian American junior faculty members were invited to contact the researcher for a personal interview via letter and e-mail. A total of 12 Asian American junior faculty, who had been at the university between two and six years, agreed to participate in this study.

Six male and six female faculty members participated in the inquiry. Eleven of the participants identified as a member of a specific Asian ethnic group, and one participant identified as biracial. Five participants identified as Chinese, two as Korean, one as Japanese, and four as South Asian. Seven participants identified as first-generation in the United States, one identified as 1.5-generation, and four identified as second-generation. Regarding discipline, to protect participants' identities, they were grouped into three general academic areas, with six in science and technology, two in the arts and humanities, and four in applied fields (e.g., business, hearing and speech sciences, education, communication, and family science).

Data Collection and Analysis Procedures

Data were collected from two sources: data sheets and personal interviews. Each participant was asked to sign a consent form and complete a demographic data sheet, which included birthplace, citizenship, language in which he or she was fluent, and language in which he or she felt most comfortable speaking. Open-ended questions included those that focused on the participants' experiences at the university. Examples of interview questions included (1) What role has your chair played in helping you in these early years of your professional career? and (2) Do you feel being an Asian faculty member has been a factor in the perceptions, actions of, or relationship with your department chair or senior faculty? The data analysis included the identification of themes, which were used to generate categories. The findings were then compared and contrasted with the national literature on Asian American faculty experiences.

Limitations

Before discussing the findings, it is important to note some limitations of the inquiry. First, the findings are context-bound and specific to 12 tenure-track faculty members at a single research-extensive university on the East Coast. Thus, unlike Asian American faculty at other types of institutions (e.g., community colleges), the participants were under pressure to conduct research and publish for promotion and tenure. Nontenure-track faculty at community colleges and teaching institutions have different pressures than tenure-track faculty at research institutions, where the teaching load is much greater and the need to conduct research and publish is considerably less. These two groups of faculty may report very different experiences. Second, there were no Filipinos, South East Asian, or Hawaiian and Pacific Islander faculty, and a study of pre-tenured faculty from these communities could generate different insights than those discussed herein. Third, because the focus of the study was the pre-tenure experiences of Asian American faculty at a research-extensive university, it could not be determined whether the faculty achieved tenure or left the university. Thus, no claims can be made with confidence about whether the factors discussed in this chapter were actually associated with participants' attainment of tenure. Finally, the interview protocol did not query faculty members about their ethnic identity or social class, but these could be salient factors in shaping the experiences of pre-tenured Asian American faculty.

Findings of the Analysis

The findings showed four primary factors affecting participants' experiences and progress toward tenure: (1) critical role of faculty mentoring, (2) importance of supportive department chairs and faculty colleagues, (3) chilly departmental climates, and (4) unique challenges for Asian American women faculty.

Critical Role of Faculty Mentoring

Participants indicated that mentoring was an important factor positively influencing their pre-tenure experiences at the university. Some departments had a formal mentoring program, whereas others established more informal mentoring relationships. Participants who stated that they had a positive experience cited having a mentor whom they felt would advocate for them when it came time for tenure review. They also mentioned that having a formal structured mentoring relationship was also beneficial. This required that the mentor and junior faculty meet every year and have a written formal report by the mentor. One faculty member who had a positive experience stated that some junior faculty are assigned mentors when they are hired:

> The department is very good, outstanding actually, at making or associating each incoming faculty with a mentor. My faculty mentor has been tremendous, he has introduced me to several areas of collaboration, and we have actually collaborated ourselves. We have put proposals together, a very positive experience. —*First-generation South Asian male, science and technology*

Yet, there were many faculty members who did not have positive faculty mentoring experiences. For some, assigned faculty mentors were not helpful, and an informal self-selected mentor who offered to help them was a much better match. One faculty member illustrated this point with the following remarks:

> Mentor assigned was terrible; only talked to me when he wanted me to teach his class. He asked me how things were going. I said I think I'm going to quit, and he didn't respond and asked me to teach his class. "Carol" is my mentor, real mentor. "Carol" helped me—I didn't ask for (it). —*Second-generation South Asian female, science and technology*

Although she did not request assistance, her mentor Carol, a White female senior professor, offered to help her. Her mentor co-taught a class with her, helped her understand how to teach effectively, and helped her learn how to manage her time.

All respondents were asked if their mentors were of the same race. None of them had Asian American mentors, and most said that racial congruence was not necessary to help them with tenure expectations and support. This finding could be partially owing to the fact that, at this university, faculty of color were few in number, and most respondents did not have Asian American senior faculty in their departments. Thus, participants reported that they either did not consider race-related mentoring, or had few interactions with Asian American faculty members.

Importance of Department Chairs and Colleagues

A second theme emerging from the analysis was the importance of having a supportive department chair and senior colleagues. Some participants reported having supportive chairs, and they generally described these chairs as showing care and trust, being open to new ideas, and being a role model. For some participants, chairs also provided proactive support. For example, their chairs provided funding without having to ask for it. One participant described his chair as someone he felt comfortable approaching for support, advice, and feedback:

> [The] chair has been supportive, [and] other junior faculty. Mostly, when I have a problem, I go to [the] chair to get his advice and feedback. He tried to help me with things, sometimes really helpful. —*First-generation Korean male, science and technology*

Some participants, however, also reported having chairs who did not support or encourage them in critical times or in general. One chair demonstrated a lack of responsiveness to a faculty member's severe family illness and did not grant a leave of absence. Another felt his chair alienated him and did not value his research and scholarship in an emerging area. Moreover, other faculty mentioned feeling uncomfortable and pressured, because their chair was consistently pointing out their limited productivity. Lack of support and encouragement, combined with constant reminders that they should be doing better, has a negative impact on participants' morale and experience.

One faculty member who discussed having an unsupportive chair noted that his chair made promises to hire his spouse, give him lab space, and support his teaching assisant for two years. The failure of his chair to follow through on these promises contributed to this faculty member feeling his chair was untrustworthy:

> There was a departure of what was said verbally promise[d] and in each of the cases, the chair tactfully did not put anything in writing and used aggression as his tactic to push his agenda. —*First-generation South Asian male, science and technology*

Related to the theme of support within the department was the support level of senior faculty and colleagues. Participants noted the importance of senior faculty who were supportive and had research interests in common with them. One participant, for example, noted how senior faculty had helped him:

> [I am] really lucky to be in this department. Several senior faculty have been incredibly helpful. . . . Some read grant proposals. When I need to

talk to someone, they listen. Give me good suggestions and advice based on their experience. —*First-generation Korean male, science and technology*

Some junior faculty felt confident that senior faculty had a sense of their progress and would support them when they went up for tenure. This added to their perception of a good departmental climate and one that was supportive of their research.

In contrast, some participants stated that senior faculty in their departments were not collaborative and did not offer to work on projects with them. A few participants also noted that the dearth of senior faculty support in some departments was a problem. A participant in the humanities, for example, commented about the lack of Asian American faculty mentors.

I've never really sought out Asian American faculty because [laughs] there are so few of them. I can think of only one in my field and none in my subfield even. —*Second-generation Korean female, arts and humanities*

Chilly Departmental Climates

A third theme that emerged from the findings was participants' experiences with chilly departmental climates. Specifically, participants reported experiencing isolation and lack of connectedness to their departments, blatant racial discrimination, and discrimination as perceived foreigners. Some participants in the study mentioned that they felt like "outcasts" who were isolated from other faculty and lacked a connection to their academic departments and faculty colleagues. Feeling a sense of isolation was most salient among the five faculty members in the arts and humanities and applied fields, who were the only Asian Americans in their departments. In contrast, faculty in science and engineering were likely to have senior Asian American faculty and multiple Asian American faculty members in their department. Yet, participants in science and technology also felt a lack of connection to their department and colleagues. One participant questioned whether she belonged in the department:

Got here, extremely lonely. People are very critical, environment here, you have to ask for resources, be okay with people disagreeing with you a lot. Hurt my confidence. I talked to other faculty, and they were critical of my ideas. Seemed like what they were doing was so advanced. . . . Left planning to quit. [Chair] talked me into going on leave, good decision in hindsight. —*Second-generation South Asian female, science and technology*

Even though this second-generation faculty member had been an exceptional graduate student, she experienced burnout and was intimidated by people in her department. Her departmental climate and environment contributed to her feelings of doubt and loss of confidence. But because she had a supportive chair, she was able to take a leave of absence and eventually return. Another faculty member stated that his scholarship was not valued in the department, because it was not traditional research.

In addition, first- and second-generation faculty members who asked their chairs to support them during their critical life incidents became the target of blatant racist derogatory comments. For example, one second-generation faculty member commented that, in her annual review, the chair reported, "I don't know if it's because you are an Indian or if it's because of the work that makes you so arrogant." Other faculty reported egregious incidents that are too sensitive in nature to report in this chapter.

Finally, first-generation faculty said that they faced discrimination because of their accents. Specifically, they noted that they received negative evaluations because of their accents, and that students would sometimes walk out of their classes. One participant, for example, recalled how students made disparaging remarks:

> Students were yelling at me. . . . Remember, students complaining about [my] accent. Tell them I am doing my best, [I] cannot control [my accent].
> —*First-generation Korean male faculty, science and technology*

As this quotation illustrates, first-generation Asian American participants who spoke English as a second language and had heavy accents faced criticism and were ridiculed for their speech. This contributed to their experience of a negative departmental climate.

Unique Challenges for Asian American Female Faculty

The salience of gender issues emerged as a fourth theme in the findings. Specifically female participants indicated that cultural values, family ties and responsibilities, and work pressures contributed to their stress. They felt that they should spend more time with family or take care of family responsibilities. Asian American women faculty stated that they felt faculty life was too demanding and wanted to spend more time with their families. Unlike her male faculty colleagues who worked at the university on weekends, a female faculty member noted that she had extended family obligations. All of the

Asian American women stated that their responsibilities to take care of family members came first and felt they had obligations because of cultural roles.

Women faculty members commented that their chair could be insensitive to their need to balance work and family and how they spent their time. One Korean faculty member who had children explained that she had to commute Monday through Thursday, because her partner would not move for her 11-month fellowship. Her chair told her to live closer to the fellowship, but she felt that it would strain her marriage. Another colleague told her she needed to get away from her kids to work. Expressing her work and home conflict, she stated:

> I see myself compared to other male faculty and female faculty [who have] very different arrangements about child care. I have very strong constraints on my time. . . . I thought about it for a long time, and I have now accepted [it], and it does have a direct bearing on my productivity and on my ability to function within the community. I don't go with faculty [to] dinners often or gatherings. For me, I know the most important part of me being there is my research, so that's what I try to focus on. —*Second-generation Korean female, applied fields*

In addition, perceptions of Asian American female faculty as weak were frequently discussed by participants. One female faculty member who spoke up in her department meeting was negatively labeled, and she later decided it was not worth the effort to speak out. As a result, she decided that she would no longer contribute in future meetings. She explained that being quiet did not mean she was submissive, but nevertheless it was perceived in that way. Another female faculty described her experiences with students and how she countered their perceptions:

> I believe [students] have stereotypes, because [they are] of different race, ethnicity. . . . Asian women [are] seen as weak, soft voiced. . . . Have to be aggressive. —*First-generation Chinese female, applied fields*

In addition to stereotypes of Asian American women faculty, marital stress was another factor of concern. Frequently, junior Asian American faculty commented on the constant pressure to publish and to maintain their program. They felt stressed from working constantly. Some stated that this was creating marital stress and spouses complained they were not home enough. One faculty member wondered if she could have a family and keep up the workload.

Gender, generational status, and age also intersected and became an issue for one second-generation participant. She noted that she was expected to be respectful in addressing first-generation Asian American male faculty, who were two generations older than she was. She also did not feel that she could challenge them in public meetings.

> Lots of Asian faculty, from India, all much older . . . I cannot call them by first name. [It is] disrespectful. Honorific in Hindi, Ji, call them. . . . Ji, same age as my parents. I don't feel I can call them my friend. They are so much older than me. I don't feel I can disagree with them. Over time, I have learned to disagree with them. Like a cultural thing. Others are so much older than me, makes it more difficult. . . . I am closer in age to the grad students. —*Second-generation South Asian female, science and technology*

Implications for Research

These findings have important implications for higher education research, policy, and practice. In regard to research, the findings in this study reflect pre-tenure issues for the 12 faculty who were interviewed. To add to the insights generated here, future research might include a follow-up study on post-tenure review. Such an inquiry could provide more insight into the influence of mentoring, supportive chairs and faculty colleagues, and departmental climate on gaining tenure. This future study could also track whether the participants in this study stayed at this research-extensive university, left for another university, or sought other occupations.

Other important areas for future inquiry are nontenure-track Asian American faculty and non-research-intensive institutions. Further studies are needed to examine differences between tenure-track faculty and nontenure-track Asian American faculty at research institutions and Asian American faculty at other types of institutions. How do nontenure-track faculty experience departmental climates? Are the issues that emerged from the current analysis consistent across types of institutions? And, how might race, ethnicity, class, and gender be experienced differently in nontenure-track positions and other types of institutions?

Within institutions, departmental climate may affect retention of faculty. It is important to examine why Asian American faculty members actually leave their institutions. In this study, when faculty members were asked if they had ever considered leaving, 9 out of 12 said that they would consider departing from their institutions—even those who were doing well professionally. Thus, inquiries that examine whether the factors discussed in this chapter are correlated with actual tenure attainment are important to expand our understanding of Asian American faculty. For example, future studies could analyze whether faculty mentoring, supportive department chairs, and support from faculty colleagues and departmental climate played a role in their retention.

Finally, the sample in the current study included first- and second-generation Chinese, South Asian, Japanese, and Korean Americans. However, not represented in this group are Filipinos, South East Asians (Cambodian, Hmong, Laotian, and Vietnamese), and Native Hawaiian and other Pacific Islanders. These populations have unique historical and social contexts, and they face unique challenges. Therefore, future research on these groups is important to understand Asian American faculty experiences in academia.

Implications for Institutional Policy and Practice

In regard to institutional policy, the findings suggest that institutions should be rethinking tenure guidelines. For example, support of emerging research, by extending timelines to include important work that is in the pipeline and soon to be published, could help Asian American and other faculty members succeed. Moreover, tenure review should value research published outside of the traditional journals and recognize that they may be based on smaller data sets.

Institutions should also work to create family-friendly environments. The current rigor of publishing within a specific time frame and requiring faculty to work long hours and weekends is challenging for women who have families or are caregivers for their extended families; in addition it is creating marital stress. Institutions must examine if tenure expectations are achievable in the expected timeline and whether restructuring the tenure and promotion process is necessary to be equitable for Asian American women and other female faculty.

To achieve a pluralistic society in the future, higher education must retain diverse faculty of color. This study affirms the need for universities and colleges to adopt informal and formal mentoring programs for junior Asian American faculty. Mentors should be assigned at the time of the faculty hire. Because some Asian American faculty members are hired into arts and humanities and social science disciplines where they are the sole Asian American in their discipline, strong mentoring is extremely important. The mentor does not necessarily need to be another Asian American, but mentoring by a faculty member of color might be beneficial, because that person might share similar experiences of isolation and discrimination. Effective mentors help junior faculty understand the culture of the department and promotion and tenure expectations. They may help them navigate through the politics of the department and university system as well as help with writing proposals and securing funding for research.

In order to promote the success of Asian American junior faculty, universities must create welcoming departmental climates. Although participants in the study faced many challenges, the findings also indicate that some important factors also positively influenced their experience: Positive faculty mentoring relationships, supportive chairs, supportive senior faculty and colleagues, and positive departmental climates can make a significant difference in the experiences of junior Asian American faculty. These factors could positively influence their satisfaction and increase their likelihood of success. As Chang's (2002) diversity discourse asserts, universities must engage in institutional transformation, rather than preserve existing practices that negatively affect the experiences and outcomes of those from nontraditional populations. Thus, institutional transformation requires an institutional commitment that may challenge cultural norms (Chang, 2002).

References

Alexander-Snow, M., & Johnson, B. (1999). Perspectives from faculty of color. In R. Menges et al. (Eds.), *Faculty in new jobs* (pp. 88–117). San Francisco, CA: Jossey-Bass.

American Council on Education. (2005). Office of Women in Higher Education. *An agenda for excellence: Creating flexibility in tenure-track faculty careers*. Washington, DC: Author.

Braine, G. (Ed.). (1999). *Non-native educators in English language teaching*. Mahwah, NJ: Lawrence Erlbaum.

Chang, M. (2002). Preservation or transformation: Where's the real educational discourse on diversity? *The Review of Higher Education, 25*, 125–140.

Cho, S. (1996). Confronting the myths: Asian Pacific American faculty in higher education. *Ninth annual Asian Pacific American higher education (APAHE) conference proceedings* (pp. 31–56). San Francisco, CA.

Daly, C., & Dee, J. (2006). Greener pastures. *The Journal of Higher Education, 77*(5), 776–803.

Gainen, J., & Boyce, R. (Eds.). (1993). *Building a diverse faculty.* San Francisco, CA: Jossey-Bass.

Gregory, S. (1995). *Black women in the academy.* Lanham, MD: University Press of America.

Hu-DeHart, E. (1983). Women, minorities, and academic freedom. In C. Kaplan & E. Schrecker (Eds.), *Regulating the intellectuals: Perspectives on academic freedom in the 1980s* (pp. 141–159). New York: Praeger.

Hune, S. (1998). *Asian Pacific American women in higher education: Claiming visibility & voice.* Washington, DC: Association of American Colleges and Universities.

Hune, S., & Chan, K. (1997). *Special focus: Asian Pacific American demographics in higher education: Fifteenth annual status report.* Washington, DC: American Council on Education.

Hurtado, S., Milem, J., Clayton-Pedersen, A., & Allen, W. (1999). Enacting diverse learning environments: Improving the climate for racial/ethnic diversity in higher education. *ASHE-ERIC Higher Education Report, 26*(8).

Kim, B. S., Brenner, B., Liang, B., & Asay, P. (2003). A qualitative study of adaptation experiences of 1.5 generation Asian Americans. *Cultural Diversity and Ethnic Minority Psychology, 9,* 156–170.

Lippi-Green, R. (1997). *English with an accent: Language, ideology, and discrimination in the United States.* New York: Routledge.

Moore, W., & Wagstaff, L. (1974). *Black educators in White colleges.* San Francisco, CA: Jossey-Bass.

Nakanishi, D. (1995). Asian Pacific Americans and colleges and universities. In J. A. Banks & C. A. M. Banks (Eds.), *Handbook of research on multicultural education* (pp. 683–695). New York: Macmillan.

Nguyen, A., Huynh, Q., & Lonergan-Garwick, J. (2007). The role of acculturation in the mentoring-career satisfaction model for Asian/Pacific Islander American university faculty. *Cultural Diversity and Ethnic Minority Psychology, 13*(4), 293–303.

Padilla, A. (1994). Ethnic minority scholars, research, and mentoring: Current and future issues. *Educational Researcher, 23*(4), 24–27.

Ryu, M. (2010). *Minorities in higher education 2010: Twenty-fourth status report.* Washington, DC: American Council on Education.

Skachkova, P. (2007). Academic careers of immigrant women professors in the U.S. *Higher Education, 53,* 697–738.

Thomas, G. (2005). *Creating flexibility in tenure-track faculty careers.* Presented at the Hechinger Institute on Education and the Media conference, New York.

Trower, C. A., & Chait, R. P. (2002). Faculty diversity: Too little for too long. *Harvard Magazine, 104*(4), 12.

Turner, C., & Myers, S. (2000). *Faculty of color in academe.* Boston, MA: Allyn & Bacon.

Vargas, L. (2002). My classroom in its context: The struggle for multiculturalism. In L. Vargas (Ed.), *Women faculty of color in the White classroom* (pp. 23–34). New York: Peter Lang.

Ward, K., & Wolf-Wendell, L. (2004). Academic life and motherhood: Variations by institutional type. *The Review of Higher Education, 27*(2), 233–257.

15

STRUGGLES FOR PROFESSIONAL AND INTELLECTUAL LEGITIMACY

Experiences of Asian and Asian
American Female Faculty Members

Fanny PF Yeung

Common misconceptions of Asian and Asian Americans[1] and higher education suggest that they are overrepresented in the academy. This overgeneralization masks the reality that Asian American women are underrepresented in just about every field and among faculty and administrative positions within the academy, which I discuss in more detail in what follows (Hune, 1998). It is likely that the model minority stereotype, or belief that all Asians and Asian Americans achieve universal and unparalleled academic and occupational success (Museus, 2009), contributes to the aforementioned misconception and masks many academic challenges that Asian Americans experience. The current chapter is focused on advancing authentic understandings of Asian and Asian American female faculty, by examining how Asian and Asian American faculty experience institutional climates and how race, gender, and generational status interact to shape those experiences.

Underrepresentation of Asian and Asian American Female Faculty

Data from the National Center for Education Statistics (NCES, 2007) indicate that Asian and Asian American faculty represent approximately 8% of tenure-track faculty members. Asian and Asian American faculty are disproportionately in junior-level positions, with 41% in assistant professor positions, 28% in associate professorships, and 31% holding full professorships. When disaggregated by gender, Asian and Asian American women represent only 2% of faculty nationwide. Moreover, women represent approximately one-third (30%; 10,944 women) of all Asian faculty. And, whereas Asian and Asian American men are more likely to hold full professor status (37%) than associate (28%) or assistant professor (35%) positions, Asian and Asian American women are more likely to be assistant professors (55%) than associate (28%) or full professors (17%) combined. Despite these gender disparities, little is known about Asian and Asian American female faculty.

Importance of Ethnic and Generational Diversity

Researchers have noted that Asians and Asian Americans in higher education are often discussed in a homogeneous manner and without regard to diversity within this population, such as ethnic and generational diversity. For example, the Asian American racial category encompasses a wide range of diverse ethnic groups (see Chapter 1). Unfortunately, existing national data do not permit researchers to disaggregate in ways that they can examine ethnic differences in representation of Asian and Asian American faculty in higher education.

It is also important to note that when data on Asian and Asian American faculty are reported they also often conflate Asian faculty who are foreign nationals, non-U.S. citizens, or international graduate students who remain in the United States to work with Asian American faculty (Turner & Myers, 2000). From 1981 to 1991, the United States Equal Employment Opportunity Commission reported that 40% of Asian and Asian American faculty in higher education were foreign nationals (Carter & O'Brien, 1993). Thus, although researchers have highlighted that Asians and Asian Americans make up 8% of the professoriate overall, when taking into account U.S. citizenship, Asian Americans compose only 3% of all full-time faculty in U.S. higher education (Carter & O'Brien, 1993), which is lower than their representation in the national population (see Chapter 1). Therefore, although this estimate is dated, it does suggest that the conflation of Asian and Asian American faculty in statistics presents a misleading picture, and Asian American women and men might both actually be underrepresented in faculty ranks in academia.

Experiences of Faculty of Color and Women in the Academy

Existing literature on faculty of color and female faculty helps contextualize experiences of marginalization and discrimination that Asian American women may face in the academy. Research has documented that faculty of color often feel excluded from institutional activities and planning and feel disassociated with nonminority faculty members (Aguirre, Martinez, & Hernandez, 1993). Female faculty of color also report chilly campus climates and a general lack of respect for minorities and women in academia (Hune, 1998).

Research on faculty of color has also documented a high degree of job turnover. This "revolving door effect" helps explain the disparity between the number of faculty of color hired and those who remain within their institutions (Carter & O'Brien, 1993; Turner & Myers, 2000). One factor that might contribute to this turnover is the fact that although many institutions report the number of their new minority faculty hires to tout their diversity they pay less attention to the retention of minority faculty. Another factor that contributes to minority faculty attrition is the excessive mentoring responsibilities that contribute to burnout. Indeed, many faculty of color are expected to mentor large numbers of students of color at their institutions, without allowances or compensation for the additional time spent with these students. Given that mentoring responsibilities and service are not given considerable weight compared with publications in promotion and tenure decisions, faculty of color are often negatively affected by their mentoring responsibilities during evaluations (Carter & O'Brien, 1993; Turner & Myers, 2000).

Women faculty are also more likely to encounter challenges between institutional and cultural norms that favor White, middle-class males, particularly career and family responsibilities (Perna, 2005; Turner & Myers, 2000). As a result, significant systemic gender inequities exist, with men continuing to dominate the academic profession (Lee, 2002). Data from NCES (2007), for example, indicate that only 36% of all tenure-track faculty members were women. Furthermore, women are more likely to occupy junior faculty ranks, whereas men occupy tenured positions (Hune & Chan, 1997; Perna, 2005).

Another challenge faced by Asian and Asian American women is commonly referred to as the glass ceiling (Barringer, Takeuchi, & Xenos, 1990; Hune & Chan, 1997). Glass ceilings are defined as attitudinal or organizational barriers that prevent qualified individuals from advancing within their organization (Lee, 2002), and evidence suggests that they hinder career advancement of Asian and Asian American faculty (see chapter 13). In addition, Asian and Asian American female faculty are often perceived as inferior and to be token hires to serve institutional diversity requirements (Carter & O'Brien, 1993).

Conceptual Framework

According to Hurtado, Milem, Clayton-Pedersen, and Allen (1999), the racial climate includes four dimensions: (1) historical legacy of inclusion and exclusion, (2) structural diversity (i.e., numerical diversity), (3) psychological perceptions and attitudes between and among groups, and (4) behavioral climate (e.g., interactions between racial groups). Racial climate has been shown to be a useful framework for understanding how institutional environments shape the experiences of faculty satisfaction and retention in the academy (Jayakumar, Howard, Allen, & Han, 2009). It should be noted that the racial climate interacts with other aspects of the environment, such as the climate toward women faculty or international faculty members. For example, Turner (2002) asserted that "the interlocking effects of gender and race compound the pressure of the workplace environment" (p. 79). Racial climate provided the framework for this inquiry.

A Mixed-Methods Inquiry Into the Experiences of Asian American Female Faculty

This research project incorporated a mixed-methods approach to explore the experiences of Asian and Asian American female faculty. In an effort to offer a more complex analysis of the experiences of Asian and Asian American female faculty, I used information collected from a national data set, the 2001 Faculty Survey administered by the University of California–Los Angeles (UCLA) Higher Education Research Institute (HERI), and in-depth, semi-structured interviews. Independent *t*-tests were conducted to provide a greater understanding of potential differences experienced by Asians and Asian American female faculty members. Finally, I analyzed individual interview and quantitative data jointly.

Semi-structured interviews were formally conducted with six Asian and Asian American female faculty members. Participants were recruited from midsized research institutions within California (total enrollment of 25,000 to 30,000). Faculty members were selected from departments within the social sciences and humanities, where the numbers of Asian American female faculty members are lacking (Hune, 1998). Participants were recruited through e-mail addresses found in institutional faculty directories online. Additionally, institutional websites and faculty members' curriculum vitae were reviewed to acquire a better understanding of the context in which faculty members worked and their productivity.

Combined, interview participants have provided 54 years of service to the academy, produced 132 publications, written 8 books, given 226 presentations (invited and proposed), and were awarded nearly a million dollars of grant funding. Four of the six faculty members have tenure. The sample included one full professor, three associate professors, and two assistant professors. Half of the interview participants were Asian American, and the other three participants were foreign-born. All but one directly mentioned their partners and families during the interview, and four of the six mentioned having young children.

Findings

The analysis of interview and survey data provided insight to better understand how faculty experienced the institutional climate. The results will discuss (1) organizational isolation and the national networks; (2) the struggle for professional and intellectual legitimacy from other faculty, students, and racial stereotypes; and (3) the existence of differential experiences between Asian and Asian American female faculty members.

Organizational Isolation and Importance of National Support Networks

Literature has documented that workplace satisfaction can be influenced by perceptions of intellectual and organizational isolation. Christina, an assistant professor, stated the following:

> I think the university does try to mentor minorities and women in particular, but at the same time, such mentorship can only go so far. . . . If they're not in your field, they don't fully appreciate your field's specific concern. They don't know what the hassle is, say a particular journal that you're harassed by. They're not familiar with the personalities in your field . . . or the important conferences you should be attending. They can't give you advice in the end that really matters.

Contributing to the isolation was the fact that, given the limited number of women of color in any given social science department, participants noted that mentors were not often of the same race, gender, or discipline. Instead, these women sought support from others on a national level in related disciplines and with similar demographics. Although their professional colleagues within their department are not their primary forms of support, all participants acknowledged that their colleagues were mainly congenial and available, if needed. Only one participant reported finding support from another Asian American female colleague in her department.

In lieu of local support, women in this study reported that support came from other women in the same field, scattered across the nation, whom they met at conferences and fellowships. Tracy, for example, spoke about how a fellowship brought her together with women of color in her academic field:

> We just really formed a really tight-knit bond, and we've kept in touch ever since [2004]. We're all kind of on the same trajectory in terms of where we want to publish. We're all working on books; we're all at competitive places. . . . I really benefited from it, and now I see why, kind of how White men do it. I'm a part of a network with women of color, and the thing that's interesting is that these women of color are pretty powerful.

The support, shared experiences, and satisfaction garnered from these relationships were extremely positive. The majority of the women said that they would not know where they would be without this support. Christina described how her support group remained connected:

> We made this thing that we would e-mail each other monthly . . . and even had a format of what we wanted to tell each other: What did you do last, this, next month, what was the nicest and lamest thing that happened to you . . . and it's something you have to work on and nurture. It doesn't just happen. . . . I don't think I would have stayed sane without these women.

Although requiring them to negotiate time commitments, travel long distances, and the fact that such opportunities were infrequent, participants discussed how these interactions had positive influences on their academic careers and provided the support necessary to maintain positive concepts of their faculty role, despite their experienced isolation.

On a related note, interview participants were asked to reflect on the role of generational status in relation to their professional roles and relationships. Asian American women in this study noted that they were more likely to build relationships with other Asian American faculty and other faculty women of color than with Asian faculty members because of generational and cultural gaps. Lisa described her observations of the generational divide:

> I think Asian American faculty feel a lot of solidarity with other ethnic-American faculty groups, and the international people don't necessarily think of that. They don't entirely understand the desire of the Asian American faculty to build up those ties. And I think that basically [it is] the Asian American faculty feeling misunderstood by the Asian international faculty, rather than the other way around.

During the interviews, Asian American female faculty members also discussed their struggles for intellectual legitimacy in the academy.

Struggles for Professional and Intellectual Legitimacy

Participants in this study discussed experiences with racial prejudice and discrimination, as well as challenges to their roles as faculty members from institutional processes, other faculty, and students. For example, the women in this study traced their struggles with racial stereotypes from the start of their academic careers in graduate school to their current situations. Christina provided an example of how racial stereotypes can shape the experiences of and disadvantage Asian and Asian American faculty members:

> The same kinds of things can be said to argue for or against a person. . . . This person who happens to be White male or female has a lot of coauthorships—that means this person must really be well-respected in the area, because lots of people want to coauthor with this person. And then the same kind of coauthorships, the same issues . . . would be used against, say it's an Asian male. . . . The perception is that he's obviously the research assistant on these projects. He's only a coauthor. . . . You may have an objective standard but you can be subjective about the interpretation of the same set of objective standards.

In this comment, Christina discussed the subjective nature of the value prescribed to authorship and research conducted and how race shapes interpretations of those measures of productivity.

Several faculty members discussed how the questionable legitimacy manifested in unequal rewards. Their initial job negotiations, or lack thereof, impacted their overall experience and satisfaction. Tracy explained the following point:

No one had really socialized me or talked with me about how to do it. . . . If you don't get a good deal when you start out, it's hard to negotiate later, unless you have an outside offer. And, I think I had no idea that people could ask for a higher salary, you can ask for more courses off, you can ask for summer salary, you can ask for additional research resources . . . all these things in which I had no idea about. I think coming from graduate school, any job looks great!

As faculty members establish themselves in their professions, they become increasingly aware of unequal merit levels and salaries. However, given the low salaries with which they began, there were obstacles in advocating for equitable pay increases. Tracy provided an example of her difficulties advocating for equitable salary: "[My chair] basically told me that I should be happy with [my salary level], because there were people [in the world] who were poorer than I was." Another participant, Pattie, an associate professor, discussed how she was denied a merit increase, despite her record: "My publication record is way stronger than other people who went up for my level, and I got denied something [merit level] that other people got." These experiences highlight participants' awareness of inequities within their departments and how other factors than merit often influence promotion and tenure cases. Realization of such factors also shaped participants' satisfaction with their workplaces.

Faculty also discussed struggling for the legitimacy of their research and teaching. They discussed how race and gender presented challenges for them as individuals regarding their knowledge and authority in the classroom, at their institutions, and publicly at conferences. For example, early in Tracy's career, she recalls, "Students, usually male students, would kind of take advantage and call me out [for every oversight]. . . . I wasn't confident yet, and I was teaching in really big classrooms." Pattie provided an anecdote from an Asian American female colleague that described how one male student wrote on the evaluation that the professor "thinks she knows more than us." The nonverbal and verbal contexts can also provide telling information. Tracy described how her height and size impacted the encounters she had at conferences: "We were giving a talk together [a non-Asian graduate student and herself], and everyone assumed that she [a non-Asian] was the professor, because she's taller." Other faculty members also discussed how faculty members from other departments on their campuses assumed that they are graduate students because of their height and youthful appearance.

Participants asserted that racial stereotypes shaped these challenges to their legitimacy. They listed several stereotypes that people held about Asian and Asian American women, including the assumptions that they are peace-makers, nonthreatening, nonconfrontational, shy, quiet, nice, compliant, low profile or low visibility, mysterious, and easily mistaken for another Asian or Asian American woman. Christina remarked, "I know being both female and Asian, I'm supposed to be nice. So, you get walked all over. . . . You're taught to be nice, [but] then it's still very cutthroat." Pattie concurred, "The people [Asians] who play by the rules and are nonconfrontational kind of get exploited."

Differential Experiences Between Asian and Asian American Female Faculty Members

In an effort to better understand potential differences between Asian and Asian American faculty members' experiences, independent sample t-tests were conducted. The results of the t-tests are displayed in table 15.1. The variation between Asians (group 1) and Asian Americans (group 2) are noted in the mean differences column. A positive value indicates that Asian survey respondents scored higher on the corresponding variable, whereas a negative value indicates that Asian American female faculty scored higher. For example, on average, Asian respondents were 0.45 years older than Asian American participants, and this difference was significant at the 0.01 level.

In terms of satisfaction with their work environments, on average, Asian American female faculty members are more likely to believe that their teaching is valued by faculty in their department ($t = -.26, p < .01$), are more satisfied with work environment ($t = -.38, p < .01$), are more satisfied with salary ($t = -.28, p < .01$), report more respect among faculty ($t = -.14, p < .05$), and have higher overall job satisfaction ($t = -.20, p < .05$). However, they are also more likely to have dual appointments as a faculty member ($t = -.10, p < .05$) and administrator and have considered leaving academia ($t = -.17, p < .01$). On average, Asian female faculty members have more published articles than Asian American female faculty members ($t = .47, p < .01$). However, this may be more of a function of age and years within profession than a measure of overall productivity.

The qualitative findings suggest that cultural incongruence and resulting isolation might contribute to the less positive experiences of Asian faculty when compared with their Asian American peers. Tracy, an Asian American participant, noted the challenges experienced by another Asian faculty member in their department: "They have accents, so I think students sometimes don't see them as legitimate or authoritative. I know [the Asian faculty members in the department] struggle with that at some point, and I don't face

TABLE 15.1
Significant Differences Between Asian and Asian American Faculty Members

	Mean Differences	Standard Error Difference	
Mother's education	−0.82	0.19	**
Age	0.45	0.21	*
Perception that teaching is valued by faculty in department	−0.26	0.09	**
Number of articles in academic/ professional journals	0.47	0.15	**
Satisfaction with work environment	−0.37	0.10	**
Satisfaction with salary and fringe benefits	−0.28	0.11	**
Consideration of leaving academe	−0.17	0.05	**
Perception that faculty respect each other	−0.14	0.07	*
Dual appointments (faculty and administration)	−0.10	0.04	*
HPW doing other administrative tasks	−0.31	0.14	*
Overall job satisfaction	−0.20	0.08	*

Note: Positive mean differences indicate that Asian female faculty exhibited higher means than Asian American female faculty, and negative mean differences indicate that Asian American faculty exhibited higher means. Data source is the UCLA HERI 2001 Faculty Survey ($n = 428$); $*p \leq .05$, $**p \leq .01$.

that." Christina, an Asian faculty member, commented on her outsider status among colleagues, particularly in social situations:

> I didn't grow up watching certain cartoons . . . and I didn't get all the TV shows. . . . It feels a little like I'm excluded, but it depends on the people you're around. Some people like to dwell on that and enjoy making you feel different, and others don't.

These comments point to some possible causes of the differential experiences, but a systematic qualitative analysis of these differences was beyond the scope of this inquiry and is necessary before conclusions can be drawn about the causes of the differential experiences between Asian and Asian American faculty in the current study.

Implications for Future Research and Practice

This study has several implications for future research and practice. In regard to research, the underrepresentation of faculty of color and women within academia is not a new conversation, but rarely is the attention given to Asian and Asian American faculty. Thus, more research on this population is needed. For example, the intellectual contributions of Asian and Asian American female faculty and other women faculty of color to the academy should be further explored (Yee, 2009). In addition, this study is limited to the perspectives of tenure-track Asian and Asian American faculty members at four-year institutions, and the experiences of faculty members in nontenure-track positions and in different institutional types (e.g., community colleges and vocational institutions) are unique and diverse in their own respects and warrant investigation. Given the limited representation of Asian American female faculty members, it is also crucial to extend research on underrepresented groups in the professoriate to a range of factors beyond generational status (e.g., ethnic groups, parents' educational attainment, or disciplinary field). This study focused specifically on faculty in the humanities and social sciences, where the proportion of Asian and Asian American faculty remains low. Additional research that focuses on the experiences of Asian or Asian American faculty members in the sciences or business fields is critical.

Regarding practice, given the importance of solid support groups for faculty members, participants in this study had to look beyond the boundaries of their academic departments and institution to secure support from women faculty of color nationwide. Relationships with people who shared commonalities based on their disciplines, trajectories, and backgrounds were most productive and supportive to the participants. Financial support that enabled faculty participants to form and maintain national support systems described in this study originated from their institutions in the form of travel support or private foundations that offered fellowships. In a time when academic budgets are tightening, faculty travel grants, release time, and fellowships are often the first to decrease. However, the impact of decreased financial support would contribute to Asian and Asian American faculty members' increased isolation and the diminution of their opportunities to engage in key interactions and relationships with peers nationwide. Institutional efforts to support the retention of women faculty of color would benefit from a broader model of mentorship that encourages the development and collaboration of peers nationwide. Moreover, by acknowledging the need for greater diversity within academic departments and university settings beyond racial identifications alone, we begin to take the steps necessary to identify the landscape and gaps within the professoriate.

Notes

1. For the purposes of this chapter, *Asian* refers to those who are foreign-born and *Asian American* refers to those who are born in the United States.

References

Aguirre, A. J., Martinez, R., & Hernandez, A. (1993). Majority and minority faculty perceptions in academe. *Research in Higher Education, 34*(3), 371–385.

Barringer, H. R., Takeuchi, D. T., & Xenos, P. (1990). Education, occupation prestige, and income of Asian Americans. *Sociology of Education, 63*(1), 27–43.

Carter, D. J., & O'Brien, E. (1993). *Employment and hiring patterns for faculty of color*. Washington, DC: American Council on Education.

Hune, S. (1998). *Asian Pacific American women in higher education: Claiming visibility & voice*. Washington, DC: Association of American Colleges and Universities.

Hune, S., & Chan, K. S. (1997). Special focus: Asian Pacific American demographics and educational trends. In D. Carter & R. Wilson (Eds.), *Fifteenth annual status report on minorities in higher education* (pp. 39–67). Washington, DC: American Council on Education.

Hurtado, S., Milem, J., Clayton-Pedersen, A., & Allen, W. (1999). Enacting diverse learning environments: Improving the climate for racial/ethnic diversity in higher education. *ASHE-ERIC Higher Education Report, 26*(8).

Jayakumar, U. M., Howard, T. C., Allen, W. R., & Han, J. C. (2009). Racial privilege in the professoriate: An exploration of campus climate, retention, and satisfaction. *Journal of Higher Education, 80*(5), 538–563.

Lee, S. M. (2002). Do Asian American faculty face a glass ceiling in higher education? *American Education Research Journal, 39*(3), 695–724.

Museus, S. D. (2009). A critical analysis of the exclusion of Asian American from higher education research and discourse. In L. Zhan (Ed.), *Asian American voices: Engaging, empowering, enabling* (pp. 59–76). New York: NLN Press.

National Center for Education Statistics (NCES). (2007). *Full-time instructional faculty in degree-granting institutions, by race/ethnicity and residency status, sex, and academic rank: Fall 2003 and fall 2005*. Washington, DC: Author.

Perna, L. W. (2005). Sex differences in faculty tenure and promotion: The contribution of family ties. *Research in Higher Education, 46*(3), 277–307.

Turner, C. S. V. (2002). Women of color in academe: Living with multiple marginality. *The Journal of Higher Education, 73*(1), 74–93.

Turner, C. S. V., & Myers, S. L. J. (2000). *Faculty of color in academe: Bittersweet success*. Boston, MA: Allyn & Bacon.

Yee, J. A. (2009). Ways of knowing, feeling, being, and doing: Toward an Asian American and Pacific Islander feminist epistemology. *Amerasia Journal, 35*(2), 49–64.

16

"THINK ABOUT IT AS DECOLONIZING OUR MINDS"

Spaces for Critical Race Pedagogy
and Transformative Leadership Development

OiYan A. Poon

The development of democratic civic engagement has been a long-established and core goal in American education. Within higher education, as early as 1949, the American Council on Education (ACE) clearly articulated that leadership development and civic engagement are central aims in its Student Personnel Point of View statement. More recently, higher education scholars have reiterated the importance of the development of socially responsible leadership (Dugan, 2006; Dugan, Komives, & Segar, 2009) and traits of involved citizenship (Sax, 2004).

However, scholarship on Asian American college students and socially responsible student involvement and leadership is limited, even though they represent the fastest growing undergraduate population in the nation (see Chapter 1). Although some studies show that Asian American undergraduates have the lowest measures of socially responsible leadership (Dugan et al., 2009; Dugan & Komives, 2007), analysis of empirical data from a national survey indicates a 148% increase (13% to 32.3%) in the proportion of Asian American first-year students interested in becoming community leaders between 1971 and 2005 (Chang, Park, Lin, Poon, & Nakanishi, 2007). Yet, little systematic research illuminates how Asian American college students become engaged as leaders committed to positive and transformative social change.

This chapter advances knowledge about how Asian American students become prepared to and actually do engage in transformative leadership behaviors. Specifically, I present an analysis of how Asian American college students, within racialized social settings, resist racial micro-aggressions in various ways. In doing so, I examine how some of these students come to engage in acts of transformative resistance (Solórzano & Delgado Bernal, 2001), which are motivated by values of social justice and a critical analysis of social inequalities. An assumption that underlies this analysis is that students' desires and decisions to engage in transformative resistance behaviors are indicators of their development of social justice–oriented leadership qualities. As I discuss in what follows, the findings of the current inquiry also reveal that these students' engagement in spaces of critical race pedagogy (e.g., ethnic studies classes, diverse and activist-oriented student organizations, and cultural centers) contributed to their increased *conscientization* and commitment to values of social justice. Conscientization refers to a critical consciousness for clearly understanding the ways in which oppressive forces like racism, xenophobia, sexism, and homophobia are institutionalized and operate to produce dehumanizing social inequalities and injustices (Freire, 1993). This conscientization and commitment to social justice can then result in leadership orientations, behaviors, and acts that confront social oppressions with the goal of social transformation.

A Critical Conceptual Framework

In this section, I discuss the conceptual framework for the current inquiry, which was made up of two separate and complementary concepts: Solórzano and Delgado Bernal's (2001) model of resistance and the concept of critical race pedagogy. Regarding the model of resistance, scholars have defined youth resistance as inherently self-destructive and often failed to critique the social conditions that may lead to oppositional behaviors (Solórzano & Delgado Bernal, 2001). However, human agency can be exercised in various ways to resist oppressive structures. Solórzano and Delgado Bernal offer a model to explain a more complex conceptualization of resistance (figure 16.1). The x-axis of figure 16.1 indicates the extent to which one is motivated by social justice ideals. The y-axis evaluates one's ability to critique social oppression.

This typology recognizes that people can engage in various forms of resistance. For example, *conformist* resisters are characterized as students who possess social justice values, but may lack a critique of social structures that

FIGURE 16.1
A Model of Resistance

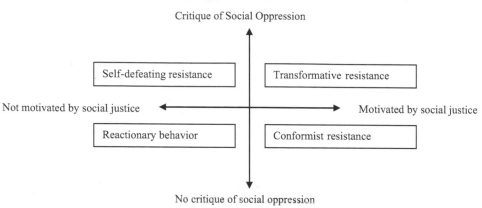

Critique of Social Oppression

Self-defeating resistance | Transformative resistance

Not motivated by social justice ← → Motivated by social justice

Reactionary behavior | Conformist resistance

No critique of social oppression

Source: Solórzano and Delgado Bernal (2001, p. 318).

create inequalities in society, and will often match their behavior to dominant social expectations and values (e.g., blaming themselves or oppressed communities for their conditions). Students who are *self-defeating* resisters are those who have developed a critique of social oppression, but do not necessarily act in ways that can effectively change social structures that lead to oppression. Rather, they may act in self-destructive manners (e.g., choosing to drop out of school). Students who exhibit *reactionary* behavior, which is not characterized as resistance, but rather as oppositional behavior, neither have a critique of social oppression nor exhibit social justice values (e.g., engaging in disruptive or violent behaviors just to agitate others). Finally, *transformative* resistance is characterized by the behavior of students who critique social structures and proactively act against social oppression in either internal or external ways. Individuals who engage in acts of internal resistance possess a critique of social oppression and social justice values. These persons may engage in activities that reflect their analysis, but are less visible. For example, students who pursue a career in public interest law to have a positive social impact exhibit internal resistance. Those who engage in external resistance exhibit behaviors that do not conform to dominant social or institutional norms. An example of external resistance is students who are motivated by social justice to participate in rallies, hunger strikes, or walkouts for a community cause. This resistance model provided one critical component of the conceptual framework for this inquiry.

Regarding the second part of the conceptual framework, I build on Freire's notion of critical literacy and conscientization to offer the concept of critical race pedagogy. Specifically, I argue that the cultivation of strong social justice values and critiques of social oppression require the development of critical literacy through dialogue. The likelihood of students engaging in acts of transformative resistance depends on their opportunities to develop a commitment to social justice and critical literacy, which is a concept drawn from Paulo Freire's (1993) *Pedagogy of the Oppressed*. Critical literacy is the ability to decode and understand socially constructed meanings and relationships of domination in the world embedded in social, economic, and political contexts (Morrell, 2002). Gained through a pedagogical process of community dialogue that encourages people to question social conditions, critical literacy fosters the hope and potential for social transformation. As Freire (1993) states, "The oppressed [learn to] unveil the world of oppression and through the praxis commit themselves to its transformation" (p. 36). In other words, to become an effective agent of social justice change engaged in socially transformative acts, one must first be literate in deciphering structures of injustice and inequalities.

One of the key ways in which social oppression and inequalities in the United States are produced is through racism. Therefore, Critical Race Theory (CRT) offers a useful lens to interrogate the ways in which racism affects the lives of Asian Americans. CRT in education studies allows research to interrogate and identify ways by which racism operates within institutions of education to create inequities (Ladson-Billings & Tate, 1995). Yosso (2006) describes the five tenets of CRT methodology in education as the intercentricity of race and racism, the challenge to dominant ideology, the commitment to social justice, the centrality of experiential knowledge, and the interdisciplinary perspective. Thus, CRT offers a critical lens through which to empower the voices of the oppressed to interrogate structures and cultures of White dominance (Solórzano & Yosso, 2002).

Building on critical literacy theory and CRT, I define critical race pedagogy as moments and opportunities to gain and advance a conscious understanding of the ways in which racism operates to produce and reproduce inequalities. These reflective learning opportunities can be intentionally organized or organically occurring in all types of campus spaces (e.g., residence halls, classrooms, student organizations, on-campus protests) or during off-campus experiences (e.g., internships, study-abroad experiences, family events) where individuals are moved to question and reflect on race relations and inequalities and about their own positions within these social structures and realities. This chapter focuses on the role of critical race pedagogy in the development of critical consciousness and literacy, and ultimately leaders committed to values of social justice, racial equity, and transformative social action. Together, Solórzano and Delgado Bernal's (2001) typology of resistance and the concept of critical race pedagogy provided a useful framework for analyzing (1) how students experienced and resisted racial micro-aggressions and (2) how spaces of critical race pedagogy contributed to their abilities to engage in acts of transformative resistance to promote positive social change.

The study presented in this chapter examined Asian American perspectives on race and racism in the college campus setting, guided by the following questions:

1. How do Asian American college students explain incidents of racial micro-aggressions?
2. When confronted by racial micro-aggression experiences, how do Asian American college students respond, if at all?
3. How does critical race pedagogy shape students' ability and inclination to engage in acts of transformative resistance?

By inquiring about their perspectives on and responses to experiences of racial micro-aggressions, the study was able to shed light on how Asian Americans are making meaning of racism and race relations during their college years. It also allowed interview subjects to share their reflections and resulting responses, which could reveal different forms of resistance in the face of racism.

Study Background

This chapter presents an analysis of data from a larger qualitative study that examined the experiences of 32 Asian American undergraduates at a large public research university on the West Coast, which I refer to as Coastal University. At the time of the study in 2008, around 25,000 undergraduates were enrolled at Coastal. Of these students, 38% were Asian American, 33% White, 15% Chicano or Latino, and 4% African American. The remaining 10% identified as American Indian, identified as international students, or declined to state their race or ethnicity. In all, 14 female and 11 male students participated in individual interviews, and an additional 7 students participated in two group interviews. I recruited students by handing out flyers to

Asian American students in and near the central student union building for a two–week period.

They represented a diversity of ethnic backgrounds, with 14 East Asian Americans, 9 Southeast Asian Americans, 6 Filipino Americans, 2 South Asian Americans, and 1 mixed-race Asian American (Chinese and White). They also came from diverse socioeconomic backgrounds. Specifically, 13 participants indicated that their families had an annual income of less than $60,000, 13 reported family income between $60,000 and $90,000, and the remaining 6 students disclosed annual family income that was more than $90,000. Each individual and group interview lasted between 90 minutes and 2 hours.

Data Collection and Analysis Procedures

During all of the semi-structured interviews, students were asked to share narratives of their experiences with racial micro-aggressions, which are daily experiences of subtle discrimination and racist assaults, insults, and invalidations experienced by people of color that socially maintain their racially subordinated position (Solórzano, 1998). To ease students into sharing experiences that may have been emotionally difficult, each interview started with a general discussion about students' past experiences and observations of race and what it means to be Asian American.[1] After sharing their initial thoughts, students were asked to engage in an academic exercise of reviewing a one-page handout that provided a short definition of *racial micro-aggressions* followed by a summary of eight racial micro-aggression themes identified by Sue, Bucceri, Lin, Nadal, and Torino (2007).[2] Students were then encouraged to describe any experiences they thought fit the definition of racial micro-aggressions.[3]

In the analytical process, I validated the trustworthiness of data and then engaged in a thematic coding process. To establish trustworthiness of data, a process of member checking and extensive documentation of the study was provided for an audit trail and review by committee (Creswell & Miller, 2000). During interviews, I regularly summarized and mirrored subjects' responses and narratives to verify the meanings of answers and to encourage students to provide additional detail. Following the transcription of interviews, subjects were invited to review and validate transcripts. I then manually coded interview data to identify student commitment to social justice, critiques of social oppression, and exemplars of the four types of resistance.

Findings

In this section, I describe the forms of resistance that emerged from the interviews. After presenting exemplar quotes of reactionary behavior, conformist resistance, and transformative resistance, I discuss how students developed critical literacy through their engagement with projects of critical race pedagogy. Finally, I describe the role of critical race pedagogy in facilitating transformative resistance.

All of the interview participants revealed that they believe they had experienced racial micro-aggressions at Coastal University. However, the ways in which they responded to and resisted these incidents varied. None of the students were engaged in self-defeating forms of resistance. Three students shared narratives of responses to micro-aggressions that exemplified reactionary behavior, defined as exhibiting a lack of social critique and social justice values. Twenty participants provided narratives that demonstrated conformist resistance behaviors, characterized by a positive commitment to social justice values without a clear analysis of social oppression. Finally, nine of the students detailed narratives of micro-aggression responses that demonstrated a strong sense of social justice values and critical literacy that exemplifies transformative resisters. The key difference between students who exhibited transformative resistance behaviors and other forms of resistance was their engagement in spaces and opportunities for critical race pedagogy.

Reactionary Behavior

According to Solórzano and Delgado Bernal's resistance typology, students who exhibit reactionary behavior do not possess a critique of social conditions and are not motivated by social justice values. The views presented by Tasanee, Joe, and Claire illustrated this type of resistance behavior in their analyses of race and racial inequalities.

During her interview, Tasanee, a second-generation Thai American student, commented about mainstream ideals of feminine beauty. She stated the following:

> A lot of videos or perhaps women's images of themselves like trying to be . . . but then saying, "Oh, you don't have to be thin." But, generally, I do think that the typical blonde, pretty, skinny, that's the hot image. Maybe I . . . yeah, I probably do this a lot, too. I want to be blond, too.

During the interview, Tasanee first seemed uncomfortable with realizing her subconsciously internalized privileging of Whiteness in standards of feminine beauty, but then seemed to accept her desire to achieve White standards of beauty.

During some interviews, students voluntarily expressed their opinions about affirmative action and university admissions policies, as well as their effects on Asian American students. Both Joe and Claire, for example, shared opinions that demonstrated a lack of critical social analysis and social justice values when it came to this topic. Joe, a second-generation Taiwanese American male, made the following comments:

> I think financially and academically, Asians tend to be the higher groups, pretty close up with White people on academic proficiency and economic proficiency. I know they say polls, studies show that the Asian male is the highest academically proficient person on average. When it comes to affirmative action, kind of giving it to people who may not necessarily work as hard but are from a different race . . . It has to take away from somebody. You can't just let in extra people. It takes away from the top, and a lot of the top just happens to be Asian American.

Joe's comments exhibited an internalization of dominant White ideas that affirmative action policies harm Asian Americans and that Asian Americans have self-sufficiently achieved broad academic and financial successes.

Claire, a second-generation Filipina American student, remained rather quiet through most of her interview, until I asked her, "What do you believe Asian Americans should do in the face of racial micro-aggressions?" At that point, she went on a lengthy diatribe about the college admissions system and minority students who criticized Coastal's admissions policies as discriminatory. She made the following arguments:

> I feel like it's not really right to be like, "Oh, you're discriminating against us. You need to have more here because your [underrepresented minority] numbers are low." But to me, it's like if they worked hard, if they made the grade. . . . I'm not saying they're dumb. I'm just saying that, if they had the same academic level that I guess Asians and others expect out of us . . . then, I truthfully don't see why there should be a problem. . . . I guess in a way, sure, there are a lot of Asians, but it's just because Asians compete. . . . There is that academic level here that you have to be in order to come here. I guess I'm trying to be fair to Coastal. I would hope

[Coastal] would want to maintain that level of intelligence and standards. I prefer not to think that the school I love . . . is racist like that. Yeah, just work hard, because, I mean, if you're going to say they're discriminating against you, then technically . . . *Okay, I got in on appeal but.* . . . I see it as [underrepresented minorities] want to complain so they can get their numbers up so they can get an easier time to get into a university rather than putting in that extra effort and work. (Italics added)

Claire's commentary suggested that she is invested in a dominant color-blind ideology and does not believe in raising concerns about racial inequalities. Her outburst showed that she believes that hard work leads to college access in what she believes to be a fair system. Interestingly, Claire admitted to being accepted by Coastal on appeal (italicized portion of previous quote), which means she was originally rejected by the university but gained entry by submitting an objection to the original admissions decision on her file and a written request for a second review. Yet, Claire still believed that it is wrong to complain or raise concerns about inequalities in admissions. Later in the interview, she discussed how she would respond if she felt that she experienced a racist incident:

I prefer to just be like, "Oh, OK," and if you overlook me, maybe it's because I could do something better, like if it's for a job or something. You overlooked me, not because of my race, but because someone else was more qualified, so I need to step up. That's just how I prefer to look at it. I guess, rather than being angry at someone for discriminating against me, instead of placing the blame on them or like, "Oh, it's not my fault I didn't get this job or I didn't get into this school." It's like saying, "It's your fault because you're being racist." I'd rather not think of something like that.

Claire's comments indicated that she was committed to not implicating racism and discrimination in being passed over for a hypothetical job. Moreover, they suggested that she believed in a color-blind meritocracy. Throughout the interview, Claire seemed agitated by the questions posed, and she confessed that she prefers to believe that racism does not happen in modern everyday society.

Conformist Resistance

Although some participants exhibited reactionary behavior, much more commonly heard during the interviews were perspectives that reflected conformist resistance, whereby students held values for social justice, but lacked a critique of systems of social oppression, which would have provided hope and possibility for acting in socially transformative ways. Students who shared conformist resistance narratives did not feel they could act to change circumstances and, therefore, made meanings of their experiences and acted in ways that conformed to dominant ideologies, but allowed them to persevere within the social system. Mark, Raakhi, and Ruth's narratives provide examples of conformist resistance.

Mark, who was also a second-generation Filipino American, recognized the existence of racism and inequalities in society. However, he did not believe that he could do much to change these conditions. When asked whether and how he responded to racial micro-aggression experiences, he explained the following:

> I don't think I do anything in response to racial micro-aggressions. It's more that I think I've just accepted it. I just accept that it's part of living in America, where there's a bunch of different cultures. Ideally, every culture would be equal and no one would notice culture, but that's not the case. So it's just part of life, I guess.

Mark's comment about how he responds to racial micro-aggressions indicated that he simply accepts that these incidents are part of life as a Filipino American in the United States. He rationalized these experiences as part and parcel of his status as a racially subordinated person. Even though he believed these experiences should not happen, he did not feel empowered to combat them.

Whereas Mark did not feel empowered to consider ways to act against racism, Raakhi, a second-generation Indian American female, expressed that she felt an uncertainty in how to respond to micro-aggressions. Raakhi explained how her roommate's friend, who is a White male, asked her sexually explicit questions about the Kama Sutra:

> After all these questions about the Kama Sutra, he asked, "Where would you say that the women have bigger butts? The north or the south of India?" I didn't even know what to say. When I get nervous, I laugh. So I laughed about it, and was like, "I really can't answer that. I don't know. Probably on average the same." I just laughed at it, because I can't believe he would ask something like that.

To cover her discomfort and avoid engaging in a difficult confrontation, Raakhi chose to laugh, rather than explain to him that his question was inappropriate.

Four students talked about how they used language to establish themselves as native-English speakers. By carefully pronouncing and enunciating their English words, they hoped to avoid stigmas associated with being foreigners. Ruth, a second-generation Chinese American female, discussed a recent experience related to this pressure to avoid stigma:

> I think my doctor asked me that, "Where are you really from?" I wasn't really angry, but it was annoying. Sometimes I find myself doing this, which is really bad, but I find myself wanting to establish really quickly that I speak English, so people won't think, like, "What is this immigrant doing here?" or something. I shouldn't have to do that.

Ruth's quote suggested that she struggled with a conflict between recognizing that people, regardless of immigrant status, should be respected and consciously choosing to assert her English language proficiency to avoid being perceived as having a lower status. As these examples illustrate, several students held social justice values, but did not critique systems of social oppression or act in socially transformative ways.

Transformative Resistance

Motivated by social justice values and a critique of social inequalities, several interviewees also demonstrated an orientation for transformative resistance. Their diverse actions and behaviors included, but were not limited to, the development of a strong sense of identity that enabled them to engage in acts of transformative resistance and engagement in critical race pedagogy projects as either participants or leaders. As one exchange during a group interview demonstrated, developing critical literacy and a commitment to social justice values are part of an important and often difficult personal process. Responding to a fellow group interview participant's expressed embarrassment over a confessed desire for lighter skin, Sheri, a second-generation Vietnamese American female student, stated the following:

> It's okay, because it's always a struggle. Think about it as decolonizing our minds. It's . . . a lifelong process. Because all these thoughts are so socially constructed and you think about it . . . as the moment you become politicized, and you become more aware and start experiencing consciousness, [in college] right? [For] 18 years . . . they were ingrained with all these socially constructed thoughts. It's great that you caught yourself, because it shows that you are in the process . . . that you're committed in that process to undo it.

When asked what they did in response to racial micro-aggressions, some students, who were working toward becoming transformative change agents, explained that the development of a strong sense of identity was important for resiliency. For Kai, a second-generation Hmong American male student, a strong identity cultivated a sense of belonging:

> I guess, just for security, to know that you actually belong somewhere. You could say it's human nature to belong to a group, and if you don't know why you belong to that group, then I think you can feel at a loss. So in order to regain that knowledge, you want to seek to find where your roots are at. It comes to a point where if you don't have that information available to find where your roots are at, then you basically won't. . . . You lose that security you want to have.

Priscilla, a 1.5-generation Chinese American female student, also commented on the importance of developing a strong ethnic identity that enables you to engage in acts of transformative resistance. She shared the following remarks:

> If someone were to say a racial slur about you, you need to be able to respond in an intelligent manner and be like, "No, I'm Asian American, and this is why your comment is racist." People are going to judge you based on the color of your skin, and I think it's good to know your cultural ties because it's like community building. . . . I think there's underlying racism everywhere, but then I think people don't really understand they're being racialized until a particular incident happens. That's why I think everyone should be aware of their culture and identity.

For Priscilla, the task of developing a strong ethnic identity was connected to having an understanding of racial micro-aggressions as unjust and the promotion of critical literacy for transformative action.

Spaces of Critical Race Pedagogy

Participants who exhibited characteristics of being transformative leaders discussed how they had engaged in a variety of social networks and spaces that provided varying levels of support for their critical literacy development. An important key to engaging students in a process to develop their critical consciousness and literacy skills was the opportunity to engage in networks and spaces—such as organizations, classes, and programs—that supported and challenged them to move from a passive position toward a place of growth. Interviewees who were involved in either ethnic-centered or pan–Asian American organizations articulated a common interest in engaging in a safe space or critical race counter-space, where they were able to struggle with questions of belonging and developing strategies of resistance in response to experiences with racial micro-aggressions.

For example, Kyle, a 1.5-generation Taiwanese American male, was able to explore his ethnic identity and gain a better understanding about the world through his participation in a student organization. He got involved with the Asian American Coalition (AAC) through the organization's internship program, which was led by another student, because he was interested in learning more about Asian American issues. Kyle also said that he joined the internship program because he also wanted to become a community leader:

> Through internship, [the peer leader] really challenged me to develop my identity as a person of color. I would never have labeled myself as a person of color, because that to me was beyond my imagination before being involved with AAC. Like, "Asians? People of color? No, no." But I guess that was an important thing, because now that I am a person of color, it says my position with other people is just different because of my skin color, but lets me build coalition for social justice.

Through his AAC internship experience, Kyle was exposed to a curriculum developed by classmates, which challenged him to reconsider what it means to be Asian American within a racialized society. Other students also benefited from AAC community education projects. Gary, a second-generation Thai American male, made the following remarks:

> I joined the community committee of AAC. We got to talk about hate crimes, Islamaphobia, like South Asians and Muslims being targeted. We also talked about homophobia and also discrimination against the undocumented. So, like all those are issues for Asian American communities. So I got to experience that. And then through AAC internship, we did a film project on food justice in south Los Angeles.

Walter, a 1.5-generation Chinese American male, was also exposed to social issues that he was not aware of prior to his involvement in AAC programs. He stated the following:

> AAC is different than engineering classes. You actually learn about real issues that I can relate to. . . . Last year, the deportation of families of

refugees from Southeast Asian countries . . . I wouldn't have known otherwise. They had a rally at [the student union] patio. Had I not known about the issue from AAC, I would have just thought it's just more extremely liberal people trying to sway the rest of campus. Now that I know about the issue, yes it's unfair that the U.S. has these contracts with Southeast Asian countries to send people back for something as little as shoplifting for small crime that was done maybe eight years ago before such contracts were established.

When asked how these issues affected him as a Chinese American, he explained his understanding of the systemic nature of oppression and his connection to that system:

It's something affecting people around me. It doesn't have to be something that directly affects me. If it affects friends and students on campus, if it affects communities in Southern California . . . it's just how unfair. I can relate to it. You feel like you should be part of something like that to make this injustice known to everybody. So we can do something about it. It's all about the people, and having more people know about it, that will pressure the government to do something about it.

Through the community education projects by AAC, Walter and other students gained an awareness of social oppression and developed their commitment to social justice values. In addition to learning, some engaged in projects to counter the injustices they learned about.

Some students offered various explanations for how agents and spaces of critical race pedagogy facilitated their development as socially transformative leaders. Some students discussed the importance of ethnic studies in encouraging them to become involved in politicized Asian American organizations both on and off campus through Asian American studies courses and faculty. Sara, a second-generation Korean American female, shared the following:

I just never considered [getting involved in mainstream campus organizations], because I didn't have ways to network with those people. So, like the groups that I'm already in, for instance, like KIWA (Korean Immigrant Workers Association), I learned about in the Asian American women course. And my professor actually encouraged me to intern with them.

Although Sara is not involved in a pan–Asian American organization on campus, her enrollment in Asian American studies courses and interaction with professors helped her become actively engaged in organizing for economic justice in a low-income Korean American community.

Regarding her success as one of the few Filipina Americans to win student government elections in high school and college, Emmy gave credit to lessons that she learned from her mentors and from ethnic studies classes:

> A lot of my elders would say, "You know we worked so hard to get our children here, and we worked so hard, and it feels so good to see that our work is paying off." . . . [Y]our children could actually be in these positions and make a difference in society. You know? And then I think, like, my parents have always instilled that in me . . . and it's like the ethnic studies classes have been the education, the historical context of where we're at in society today, and why these perceptions came about and, like, how that plays into socioeconomic and the political, and everything, because, I mean, like it's really complex.

Emmy also attributed her orientation toward engaging in socially transformative acts to her involvement with a Filipino American student organization:

> Being involved in the Filipino Student Association and, like, realizing my roots and, like, what my people struggled through to get me where I am, and for us it's called "utang na loob." And so it's, um, like, "They did something for you, so now you owe something back to the community." And I think it's that sense of responsibility back to the community that I'm not taking a stance just for myself, but I'm taking a stance, like, for my brother in the larger movement that needs to happen.

Her recognition of shared community struggle and resistance, as well as her development as a social justice leader, can be attributed to the ways her family, ethnic studies classes, and student involvement reinforced and advanced her social justice values and critiques of oppression. Through these multiple spaces of critical race pedagogy, students like Emmy were able to strengthen their capacities as social justice change agents.

Conclusion and Implications

As the number of Asian American undergraduates on college campuses continues to increase, more research on processes and praxis for social justice leadership development within this population is needed. What are the best practices in cultivating and advancing Asian American leadership that is committed to transformative social justice change? Future research could shed light on how Asian American leadership development goals can specifically respond to the needs of the Asian American community. Specifically, what does it mean to be a transformative community leader for Asian Americans?

Researchers and practitioners should pay more attention to the role of spaces for critical race pedagogy in social justice leadership development. For many students, spaces like AAC, the Filipino Student Association, community-based organizations, ethnic studies courses, and family dialogues served as important spaces of critical race pedagogy in the development of critical literacy. These spaces provide vital counter-spaces for students to create and experiment with strategies of resistance in the face of daily racial micro-aggressions and complex structures of racial and other forms of oppression.

In the interest of developing Asian American and other transformative leadership, policy makers and educators should support the development and expansion of programs that advance critical race pedagogy. As shown through this study, Asian American students face regular experiences of racial micro-aggressions that can undermine their sense of self-worth and normalize racial injustices and inequalities. Students who benefited from spaces of critical race pedagogy exhibited a more advanced understanding of social inequalities, and some became active leaders and social justice change agents. The creation and use of spaces of critical race pedagogy could facilitate the development of more transformative leaders.

Notes

1. Interview question: Did you give much thought to race and being Asian American when you were growing up? Why or why not? What did you think about?

2. Interview question: What are your impressions of Sue and colleagues' theory of eight racial micro-aggression themes?

3. Interview question: Do you believe you have experienced racial micro-aggressions at Coastal University? If so, can you describe the experience? What did you do in response to the micro-aggression?

References

Chang, M. J., Park, J. J., Lin, M. H., Poon, O. A., & Nakanishi, D. T. (2007). *Beyond myths: The growth and diversity of Asian American college freshmen, 1971–2005.* Los Angeles: UCLA Higher Education Research Institute.

Creswell, J. W., & Miller, D. L. (2000). Determining validity in qualitative inquiry. *Theory Into Practice, 39*(3), 124–130.

Dugan, J. P. (2006). Involvement and leadership: A descriptive analysis of socially responsible leadership. *Journal of College Student Development, 47*(3), 335–343.

Dugan, J. P., & Komives, S. R. (2007). *Developing leadership capacity in college students: Findings from a national study.* College Park, MD: National Clearinghouse for Leadership Programs, Multi-Institutional Study of Leadership.

Dugan, J. P., Komives, S. R., & Segar, T. C. (2009). College student capacity for socially responsible leadership: Understanding norms and influences of race, gender, and sexual orientation. *Journal of Student Affairs Research and Practice, 45*(4), 475–500.

Freire, P. (1993). *Pedagogy of the oppressed.* New York: Continuum International Publishing Group.

Ladson-Billings, G., & Tate, W. F., IV. (1995). Toward a critical race theory of education. *Teachers College Record, 97*(1), 47–68.

Morrell, E. (2002). Toward a critical pedagogy of popular culture: Literacy development among urban youth. *Journal of Adolescent & Adult Literacy, 46*(1), 72–77.

Sax, L. J. (2004). Citizenship development and the American college student. *New Directions for Institutional Research, 2004*(122), 65–80.

Solórzano, D. G. (1998). Critical race theory, race and gender microaggressions, and the experience of Chicana and Chicano scholars. *International Journal of Qualitative Studies in Education, 11*(1), 121–136.

Solórzano, D. G., & Delgado Bernal, D. (2001). Examining transformational resistance through a Critical Race and Latcrit Theory Framework. *Urban Education, 36*(3), 308–342.

Solórzano, D. G., & Yosso, T. J. (2002). Critical race methodology: Counterstorytelling as an analytical framework for education research. *Qualitative Inquiry, 8*(1), 23–44.

Sue, D. W., Bucceri, J., Lin, A. I., Nadal, K. L., & Torino, G. C. (2007). Racial microaggressions and the Asian American experience. *Cultural Diversity and Ethnic Minority Psychology, 13*(1), 72–81.

Yosso, T. J. (2006). *Critical race counterstories along the Chicana/Chicano educational pipeline.* New York: Routledge.

17

BEYOND REPRESENTATION

Confronting the New Frontier
for Asian American Leadership

Daniello G. Balón and Yen Ling Shek

The modern civil rights era has seen many barriers overcome in public leadership. Notable advances include the election of Barack Obama as the first African American and biracial president of the United States of America; the first female speaker of the House; the first Latina appointed to the Supreme Court; and numerous leadership positions filled by people from African American, Latino/a, Native American, Asian American, Pacific Islander, and multiracial backgrounds. Unquestionably, our society has progressed in this arena, where leaders in the early twenty-first century increasingly reflect the rich racial and ethnic diversity of our population.

Although we might expect the aforementioned accomplishments to be accompanied by growing discourse on culturally relevant leadership development, discussions of Asian American leadership development, particularly on college campuses, remain relatively nonexistent. In fact, it can be argued that Asian Americans have been deemed irrelevant by many in higher education, owing to their assumed overrepresentation and outperformance of other groups of color, when measured by traditional benchmarks. Yet, statistical data in all sectors of industry, including education, reveal that other communities of color are outpacing Asian Americans in advancement to leadership positions (Committee of 100, 2005; Hyun, 2005).

Given these realities, it is important to develop discourse around Asian American leadership. Accordingly, in this chapter, we provide such a discussion to help understanding of Asian American leadership development. We define Asian American leadership as a conceptual approach that seeks to address the needs of the Asian American college student population. We present theoretical models of leadership development that have particular applicability to Asian Americans, as well as programmatic models that may be implemented on college campuses. We conclude with implications for future research and practice on Asian American leadership.

Asian American Leadership Is Socially Constructed

Researchers have struggled to come to a consensus regarding the definitions of *leadership* (Balón, 2003; Bass & Bass, 2008; Northouse, 2009; Rost, 1991). This is evident in the fact that the foci for contemporary leadership models include organizational change, the development of leadership capacity, and growth in personal awareness (Higher Education Research Institute [HERI], 1996; Northouse, 2009). The expansive body of literature in this area suggests that these frameworks of leadership development create culturally biased and homogeneous conceptualizations of leadership development (Balón, 2004). Even as there are attempts to interrogate the globally diverse approaches to leadership (Derr, Roussillon, & Bournois, 2002; Hampden-Turner & Trompenaars, 1997), there is still little discussion of how social identities, such as racial and ethnic identity, impact leadership development.

Despite the ascension of Asian American leaders in local and national governments, higher education, and other public sectors, leadership is still not often associated with Asian Americans (Balón, 2005; Omi, 2008; Saigo, 1999). The few existing studies on Asian Americans and leadership development suggest that there may not be objective ways to view leadership. In fact, it can be argued that leadership for Asian Americans and for all groups who experience some form of societal oppression should be seen through subjective, socially constructed lenses.

Bordas (2007) highlights the importance of socially constructed conceptualizations of leadership, but his focus on Latino, Black, and American Indian communities on behalf of communities of color reinforces the invisibility of Asian Americans in that discourse. Owing to such omissions of Asian Americans from studies on leadership among communities of color, as well as the absence of studies focused on Asian Americans, the theoretical and empirical foundations for Asian American leadership development have yet to be established.

Asian American Leadership Is Dynamic and Evolving

Extant literature suggests that cultural differences might influence perceptions of and variations in leadership development (Balón, 2004; Hampden-Turner & Trompenaars, 1997). For example, table 17.1 displays a comparison of traditional Asian and White intergroup/"leadership" behaviors. These differences in behaviors can be associated with variations in leadership styles. Moreover, Asian intergroup behaviors might be devalued in Western contexts. Balón (2003) highlights this point in his examination of the leadership attributes of Asian Americans by noting that some perceive Asian approaches to leadership as less valued when compared with those from the dominant White perspective mainstream leadership contexts in the United States.

Clearly, leadership educators should be mindful and critical of the role of culturally and racially biased values and behaviors in defining what constitutes normative leadership behaviors. Indeed, it is relevant to be conscious of such distinctions, because dominant, so-called "race-blind" definitions of *leadership* may not naturally accommodate Asian American perspectives (Asian Pacific American Women's Leadership Institute, 2000; Hune, 1997; Hune & Chan, 1997; Liu & Sedlacek, 1999; Ting, 2001). Thus, Liang, Lee, and Ting (2002) point to the importance of understanding the cultural values that underlie leadership development frameworks. And, leadership educators should be mindful of the fact that dominant leadership frameworks are culturally biased—indeed, White-centric—perspectives of leadership when working with Asian American college students.

TABLE 17.1
Differences Between Perceived Traditionally Asian Intergroup Behaviors and Idealized White "Leadership" Behaviors

Perceived Typically Asian Intergroup Approaches	Idealized (Western/White) "Leadership" Behaviors
Conformity/obedience	Manage/control/organize
Emotion withdrawal	Motivate/influence/persuade
Passive resistance	Strengthen/defend position
Role adherence/formality	Challenge the process/pioneer
Shame/guilt	Confront directly
Silence	Express verbally/take action

Source: Balón, D. G. (2003). *Asian Pacific American leadership development. Leadership insights and applications, Series #14*, p. 9. Copyright by the National Clearinghouse for Leadership Programs. Adapted with permission of the author.

On the other hand, for Asian Americans in contemporary leadership development contexts, the idea of a culturally biased Asian American leadership model is problematic. The dichotomization in table 17.1, for instance, portrays Asian and White behaviors as distinct and mutually exclusive, and such categorizations of Asian and White behavior are misleading and can perpetuate false dichotomies. Moreover, encouraging Asian American college students to be "more Asian" or "more White" in their leadership approaches oversimplifies the emergence and diversity of Asian Americans and complexity of Asian American identity. Asian Americans, as a growing college student population, help complicate simplistic notions of leadership.

The varied experiences of students (e.g., by ethnicity, immigrant generational status, racial composition of their neighborhood, racial composition of their family, transracial adoptee status) suggest a complexity to understanding Asian American identities and a need for new approaches to working on leadership that expand the idea of Asian American culture. For example, Asian American students may grapple with terms like *leader* and *leadership* by using critical race and feminist lenses that include their own personal experiences of culture, power, privilege, and oppression. This approach does not rely on a singular understanding of the cultural backgrounds of Asian Americans, but rather allows leadership to be developed from both intrapersonal and interpersonal experiences and knowledge.

Asian American Leadership Is Situated Within Identity-Based Power Dynamics

Asian American leadership, like all forms of leadership interconnected with social identities, should be viewed within frameworks that are rooted in social justice, identity, and larger dynamics of oppression and power (Bordas, 2007; Ortiz, Benham, Cress, Langdon, & Yamasaki, 1999). Omi (2008) critiqued the perspective that Asian American racial identity may be invisible within mainstream discourse. Rather, Omi contended that Asian Americans are still noticeably minorities and exposed to oppression along racial and ethnic lines, and his argument is emblematic of our leadership discussion herein. Asian American leadership should not be subsumed by mainstream, White paradigms of leadership. Rather, it should be considered within the larger racial and power dynamics among Asian Americans and other racial groups. Various forms of power and privilege must also be taken into account along with other social identities, such as gender, sexual orientation, class, ability, and religion.

Theoretical Models of Leadership

In this section, we present two theoretical models of leadership: (1) the Social Change Model of Leadership and (2) the Critical Asian Pacific American Leadership Framework (CALF). One of the more influential theoretical models for leadership in higher education has been the Social Change Model of Leadership. The Social Change Model addresses leadership dynamics on several contextual levels (HERI, 1996), and it has been useful in facilitating Asian American college students' ability to identify, negotiate, strategize, and act toward social change. Some students and administrators may find an affinity for the Social Change Model because of its interconnected approach to change on three levels: individual, group or team, and community or societal. Developed by 15 leading leadership educators, this model is based on a purposeful approach to leadership for service and change for the common good. Its seven Cs for leadership—consciousness of self, commitment, congruence, collaboration, common purpose, controversy with civility, and citizenship—are central to leadership processes and, ultimately, change toward a better world and society for self and others. The Social Change Model's emphasis on social justice, collaboration, and group-oriented values may provide an effective means for Asian Americans to explore racial identity, address cultural conflicts, and reconstruct their leadership approaches within power-based dynamics.

The Social Change Model of Leadership provides a starting point to explore the phenomenon of Asian American leadership in depth. Tingson-Gatuz, Sakurai, and Centino (2007) offer a fresh perspective in considering Asian American leadership development through the CALF Model. The CALF Model is an adaptation of the Social Change Model of Leadership to the predominant traditionally aged cohort of students (i.e., millennial generation) focusing on Asian Americans and Pacific Islanders (AAPIs).

The model was developed from several years of experience with a college leadership training program that is based on the OCA (formerly the Organization of Chinese Americans) for AAPI students. The emphasis is on core competencies and empowerment through an exploration of AAPI history, community issues, skills development, and advocacy. The three core competencies are identified as (1) understanding self in relation to others, with an emphasis on AAPI identities, issues, and cultural values; (2) understanding interpersonal communication skills; and (3) advocacy through historical and contemporary perspectives, as well as development of concrete community organizing skills.

The CALF Model has not received much attention outside of the college leadership training program offered through OCA, but it reflects similar approaches already undertaken at campuses nationwide. Although the CALF Model is primarily a theoretical model and was applied to onetime, week-end-long trainings administered on college campuses by an outside organization, the following section focuses on existing self-sustaining programmatic models at universities that are cultivating Asian American student leadership. Although there are many such programs across the country, we share a few particularly promising programmatic models along with an example of how the program operates at select campuses.

Programmatic Models for Asian American Leadership

College campuses across the nation have leadership development programs for Asian Americans. Although there is no formal analysis of these programs, we believe the programs have common themes of practical leadership skills development; Asian American community consciousness; and community building among participants in the programs, student leaders across campus, and the broader Asian American community. In this section, we discuss specific programmatic models for Asian American leadership on college campuses.

We present three different programmatic models as options for campuses that wish to create sustainable leadership development programs for Asian American students, using available campus resources (i.e., student organizations, Asian American studies programs or departments, student affairs professionals). The authors have selected some of the most compelling programmatic models based on prior professional experience creating and implementing leadership development programs at seven different universities. Although not exhaustive, the information provided in this section is meant to serve as a launching point for campuses interested in establishing leadership development programs. We discuss the following components of each model: (1) Structure (how the program is organized), (2) Target Group (whom the program aims to serve), and (3) Campus Considerations (characteristics of a campus at which this model would work best). We also present a case study for each model to provide a more in-depth look at each model type, along with testimonies of program participants.

Curricular, Credit-Based Experience Model

Structure

The first model we offer here is the curricular, credit-based experience model, which is a credit-bearing course focused on Asian American leadership development. A central aim of this programmatic model is the reconstruction of Asian American leadership as a culturally based phenomenon to be examined and developed as a skill set. This approach is consistent with best practices of social justice teaching that balance cognitive and emotive development in safe, student-centered learning environments (Hafner, 2006). This credit-bearing model explicitly assists in the exploration of Asian American leadership development, development of knowledge of leadership theory, exploration of Asian American racial and ethnic identity, personal reflection, and skills development to address challenges impacting Asian Americans in the future, such as anti-Asian racism (Liang et al., 2002). When this model is used, the course includes the involvement of instructors, students, and community members. One or more instructors can teach the courses, but they should avoid faculty–student ratios that are too large to be conducive to discussion and participation. The involvement of community resources and presenter panels help personalize the concepts and connect the curriculum to actual, lived-experience examples of leadership in the Asian American community.

Target Group

If educators provide a clear description of the course, it will likely attract a significant cohort of Asian American students looking to develop their leadership knowledge and skills. Whereas more senior students can benefit from this course, there clearly are developmental reasons for introducing the course to students early in their college experience. As research has shown, Asian American students have poor perceptions of themselves as leaders (Balón, 2004, 2005; Sedlacek & Sheu, 2004) or have lower leadership self-efficacy (Dugan, Jacoby, Gasiorski, Jones, & Kim, 2007; Dugan, Komives, & Segar, 2008). Thus, the establishment of positive leadership experiences early in students' college careers might function to counter these beliefs.

Campus Considerations

In this curricular, credit-based model, the ideal leadership course is situated within an academic unit with faculty who can provide credit-based instruction through a variety of disciplines, such as ethnic or Asian American studies; leadership studies; or other academic programs in education, business, or arts and sciences. If applicable, the course could also satisfy a degree or program requirement and possibly fulfill a graduation requisite for non-majors, such as a diversity core or human perspectives requirement.

Campuses with established ethnic studies departments (i.e., Asian American studies), Asian American student organizations, Asian American student affairs functions, leadership development initiatives, and local community resources have a number of advantages in using this curricular, credit-based model. Such campus resources can provide support for (1) recruiting students; (2) identifying instructor teams; and (3) strengthening the depth, creativity, and relevance of the in- and out-of-class Asian American leadership curriculum. Institutions interested in creating such academic courses should be aware that successful courses are usually built upon commitments from full-time faculty and student affairs leaders with part-time academic appointments—thus, faculty support is critical for establishing such a course.

Case Study

The case study that we offer for the credit-based leadership course is the Asian Pacific American leadership development course at the University of Maryland (UMD) in College Park, Maryland. A student from the course at UMD described its impact:

> Taking the Asian American leadership class was instrumental in the development of my social and political consciousness. It provided a safe and critical space to talk about identities, our experiences, and ways of making social change that supported and enhanced a lot of the work I was already doing within student organizations. It also helped me know myself more, not just in terms of how I fit or didn't fit into the world, but in what I valued and how I approached organizing and community building.
> —Jenny Lares, 2004 UMD alumnus

Since 1999, UMD has offered undergraduate and graduate students an Asian Pacific American leadership course as a vehicle for exploring Asian American identity and leadership development, as well as the intersections between them. Housed in the College of Education and cross-listed with the

Asian American studies program, the three-credit course now is a popular elective that counts toward minor certificates in leadership studies and the Asian American studies program. The course is typically taught in instructor teams composed of adjunct faculty members and student affairs professionals with substantial experience in racial identity development, leadership development, student programming, and AAPI advocacy.

The course is constructed as an education course with a focus on developing leadership efficacy. Strong emphasis is placed on individual students developing a personal, historical, and sociological understanding of issues related to AAPI identity in contemporary multicultural leadership environments. Storytelling, family research, role plays, and personal reflection are methods used to reinforce the understanding of concepts such as *model minority,*[1] *perpetual foreigner,*[2] *advocacy,* and *leadership* as social constructs themselves. Rooted in historical frameworks for advocacy and leadership, instructors provide case studies of actual situations from the campus or media involving important AAPI issues to facilitate conversations that illuminate how leadership moments can be found in the context of race, ethnicity, and other relevant identities. Throughout the course, guest speakers from the local community, government agencies, and campus visit with students to share personal applications of leadership in a racialized context to help normalize leadership as something that is accessible for AAPIs who may have been socialized to think that leadership is beyond their reach. As a final project, students work in research teams to tie the course concepts together by identifying a contemporary problem that impacts AAPIs on campus or in the community and offering researched solutions to inform stakeholders' efforts to address that problem.

Cocurricular Experience Model

Structure

The second model that we offer is the cocurricular experience leadership program model. The cocurricular model can be either (1) independently run by students and student organizations or (2) housed within a multicultural or student affairs unit. This model relies heavily on advanced student leaders who can design and facilitate the curriculum, preferably with support from multicultural or student affairs departments. If professional staff support is unavailable, students can create a pipeline to help it be self-sustaining.

According to this model, educators implement the curriculum over the course of several weeks, with a retreat at the beginning and closing ceremony at the end of the term. This model might benefit from creating cohorts, and including a limited number of participants in each cohort can create group sizes for optimal discussion. Therefore, we recommend cohort sizes of approximately 12–15, although more may be accepted to account for attrition.

Under this model, the curriculum focuses primarily on developing AAPI historical, cultural, social, and political awareness, as well as personal leadership skills (e.g., public speaking, consensus building, and listening skills). The model is experiential in nature, allowing participants' experiences to be the focal point for growth, with supplemental information available in readings and other forms of media. Evaluations are conducted at the end of each session, and an overall program evaluation is executed at the culmination of the term.

Target Group

Under this model, the program is marketed to AAPIs from ethnic, cultural, and mainstream student organizations that are looking to build their leadership capacities and lasting networks that will aid their future organizing goals both on and off campus. However, there are potential student leaders who are not currently involved in existing organizations, and targeting this group could increase breadth of the participant pool.

Campus Considerations

A cocurricular model for Asian American and Pacific Islander leadership development may be the best option at certain types of institutions. This model might be ideal for colleges and universities that (1) do not have an Asian American studies program or department, (2) have strong student affairs staff support, and (3) have strong student leadership on their respective campuses.

Case Study

The case study that we offer for the cocurricular programmatic model is the Asian Pacific American Leadership Institute (APALI) at the University of Pennsylvania. An APALI participant illuminated the impact of this program in the following remarks:

> I can honestly say that without my experience with APALI my senior year, I would not be the person I am today. APALI was my foray into exploring Asian American identity and critically approaching issues that affect Asian

Americans and communities of color in the U.S. Having intentionally distanced myself from all things related to being Asian American throughout much of high school and college, I found APALI to be eye-opening, enlightening, and empowering. —Jason Chan, APALI facilitator 2001–2002

A committee in the Pan–Asian American Community House established the APALI program, which included a professional staff member and interested students, during the 2000–2001 academic year. Student involvement was key in crafting the mission statement, quantity and duration of sessions, and curriculum topics. A year was spent planning and promoting APALI.

The initial leadership theory used in the program was Kouzes and Posner's (2008) leadership challenge, which identified five practices for exemplary leadership. However, the program eventually began using the Social Change Model of Leadership, given the inadequacy of the leadership challenge in working with emerging leaders. The initial facilitators were two graduate students who piloted the program. Later, more advanced undergraduate leaders facilitated the program, with APALI graduates eventually serving as the primary pool of applicants for facilitator roles. Facilitators receive one week of training in the summer and are committed for a full year of work, during which they are observed and receive feedback regularly as they facilitate each session.

At the end-of-the-year retreat, APALI volunteers help prepare the meals and session materials. The initial group of volunteers consisted of students involved in organizing the program and, in subsequent years, the volunteers consisted of APALI graduates who wanted to give back to the program. Over the years, the program has evolved along with the changing needs of the students. However, the primary structures for involvement, outreach, and networking have remained critical components of the program.

Partnership Between Student Affairs and Academic Affairs Model

Structure

The final model that we offer is an academic and student affairs partnership model, which is created from input and involvement from both Asian American studies and student affairs units working with AAPI students. In this model, faculty members advise student facilitators, structure the program, and present at workshops. In addition, student affairs educators provide administrative support and expertise in leadership development for the curriculum. Students are also integral to delivery partnership programs, because they help design the mission and curriculum, market, and facilitate. The curriculum provides avenues for participants to be engaged in AAPI leadership development, with an Asian American studies emphasis on linking intellectual energy with community engagement. There is a mix of traditional lecture oriented with experiential activities, as well as field trips to local AAPI communities and events. Student facilitators also receive independent study credit from the Asian American studies program or department through this partnership.

The curriculum includes more purposeful discussion of reading material based on the topic for each session. It can also include action components in which participants organize an educational event for AAPI Heritage Month on campus and promote the event in Asian American studies courses and across the entire campus. Evaluations are conducted at the end of each session, with an overall program evaluation at the end. Facilitators are trained over the summer or a semester to then facilitate the following semester. They also receive regular feedback from a faculty or staff member who observes each of their sessions.

Target Group

Emerging Asian American student leaders and those involved in Asian American studies are the primary target for this model. And, the model serves as a good opportunity to introduce students to Asian American studies. Indeed, Asian American students involved in other campus organizations, such as student government, Greek life, and residence life, can be targeted to connect them with Asian American studies programs or departments.

Campus Considerations

The student affairs and academic affairs partnership works most ideally on campuses that have Asian American studies programs or departments and student affairs staff who will assist with the development and implementation of the program. The Asian American studies program or department would commit to offering course credit for students involved in the program, as either facilitators, staff, or participants. Student affairs staff could provide expertise on leadership development, campus resources, and logistical support.

Case Study

The case study that we present for the partnership model is the Asian American and Pacific Islander Leadership (AAPIL) Institute at the California State

University (CSU)–Fullerton. One AAPIL participant offered the following comments:

> I realized that I want to motivate others and inspire others to become proactive in their communities. . . . I helped our cohort become involved with the establishment of the API resource center at school. . . . I learned from being a facilitator, everyone who participated in the beginning wanted to become a leader but maybe needed that extra push. Having everyone graduated, some I feel strongly that they are now taking their leadership skills into their own hands. —Angelica Keam, AAPIL participant 2008, facilitator 2008–2009

The AAPIL Institute was created in 2006–2007 through the Multicultural Leadership Center (MLC) and Asian American studies program at CSU–Fullerton. The professional staff member of the MLC and Asian American studies program director worked closely with a student who was doing an Asian American studies internship at the MLC. The program took a little more than a semester to create. Two interns working at the MLC as part of their Asian American studies internship facilitated the pilot group with a half-day retreat and six additional sessions. The closing event was combined with an event hosted by the president of the university for the AAPI community, and program participants were recognized there. The following year, one AAPIL graduate served as the program director and provided administrative support and feedback for facilitators, while two other graduates facilitated the next group of participants. Participants were selected via a nomination and application process and had to agree to a high level of commitment and not missing any sessions. The Multicultural Leadership Center provided logistical support for the program and advisement on connecting leadership models with the program, and the Asian American studies program provided resources related to the Asian American community and more direct advisement and feedback for the facilitators.

Conclusion

As the numbers of Asian Americans continue to grow on college campuses, there will be an increased need to develop new leadership theories through ongoing research, as well as pragmatic approaches for developing leadership among Asian American students. The examination of the research base on Asian American leadership reveals an omission of Asian Americans in mainstream leadership research and limited empirical validity of existing models for Asian Americans. Given the complexity of the population along many social identity dimensions, new theories are needed to address the various social influences and intersectionality of identities that shape Asian American college students' identities and the leadership challenges that exist throughout Asian American communities.

Through the presentation of conceptual and programmatic leadership models for Asian American college students, we intend to provide a starting point for campuses to develop new or enhance existing leadership programs. We also emphasize the importance of programs with an emphasis on Asian American racial dynamics and community issues. Moreover, such programs can also serve as a source for potential research projects and theory development.

Balón (2003) suggests that successful leadership development efforts require support from numerous sectors, including the greater neighborhood and local community and dedicated university staff, as well as adequate resources to support sustainable leadership programs for Asian American students. The challenge for college campuses is in directing adequate resources—both human and financial—to provide the infrastructure needed to support Asian American leadership development programs.

Notes

1. The model minority myth is the misconception that all Asian Americans achieve unparalleled and universal academic and occupational success (Museus & Kiang, 2009).
2. The perpetual foreigner stereotype is a racial stereotype that depicts Asian Americans as unable to fully integrate into American society and having questionable loyalty to the nation (Espiritu, 1997).

References

Asian Pacific American Women's Leadership Institute. (2000). *Leadership challenges and opportunities: An Asian American and Pacific Islander woman's lens.* La Mesa, CA: Author.

Balón, D. G. (2003). *Asian Pacific American leadership development. Leadership insights and applications, Series #14.* College Park, MD: National Clearinghouse for Leadership Programs.

Balón, D. G. (2004). *Racial, ethnic, and gender differences among entering college student attitudes toward leadership, culture, and leader self-identification: A focus on*

Asian Pacific Americans (Unpublished doctoral dissertation). University of Maryland, College Park.

Balón, D. G. (2005). *Asian Pacific American college students on leadership: Culturally marginalized from the leader role?* Washington, DC: National Association of Student Personnel Administrators.

Bass, B. M., & Bass, R. (2008). *Bass and Stodgill's handbook of leadership: Theory, research, and managerial applications* (4th ed.). New York: The Free Press.

Bordas, J. (2007). *Salsa, soul, and spirit: Leadership for a multicultural age.* San Francisco, CA: Berrett-Koehler.

Committee of 100. (2005). *Asian Pacific Americans (APAs) in higher education report card.* New York. Retrieved from http://www.committee100.org/publications/edu/C100_Higher_Ed_Report_Card.pdf

Derr, C. B., Roussillon, S., & Bournois, F. (Eds.). (2002). *Cross-cultural approaches to leadership development.* Westport, CT: Quorum Books.

Dugan, J. P., Jacoby, B., Gasiorski, A., Jones, J. R., & Kim, J. C. (2007). Examining race and leadership: Emerging themes. *Concepts and Connections, 15*(2), 13–16.

Dugan, J. P., Komives, S. R., & Segar, T. C. (2008). College student capacity for socially responsible leadership: Understanding norms and influences of race, gender, and sexual orientation. *NASPA Journal, 45*(4), 475–500.

Espiritu, Y. L. (1997). *Asian American women and men: Labor, laws, and love.* Thousand Oaks, CA: Sage.

Hafner, M. M. (2006). Teaching strategies for developing leaders for social justice. In C. Marshall & M. Oliva (Eds.), *Leadership for social justice: Making revolutions in education* (pp. 167–193). Boston, MA: Pearson Education.

Hampden-Turner, C., & Trompenaars, F. (1997). *Mastering the infinite game: How East Asian values are transforming business practices.* Oxford, UK: Capstone.

Higher Education Research Institute. (1996). *A social change model of leadership* (3rd ed.). Los Angeles, CA: Author.

Hune, S. (1997). *Asian Pacific American women in higher education.* Washington, DC: Association of American Colleges and Universities.

Hune, S., & Chan, K. S. (1997). Asian Pacific American demographic and educational trends. In D. J. Carter & R. Wilson (Eds.), *Minorities in higher education, 15th annual status report* (pp. 39–67). Washington, DC: American Council on Education.

Hyun, J. (2005). *Breaking the bamboo ceiling: Career strategies for Asians.* New York: HarperCollins.

Kouzes, J. M., & Posner, B. Z. (2008). *The leadership challenge* (4th ed.). San Francisco, CA: Jossey-Bass.

Liang, C. T. H., Lee, S., & Ting, M. P. (2002). Developing Asian American leaders. In M. K. McEwen, C. M. Kodama, A. N. Alvarez, S. Lee, & C. T. H. Liang (Eds.), *Working with Asian American college students: New directions for student services series* (No. 97, pp. 81–89). San Francisco, CA: Jossey-Bass.

Liu, W. M., & Sedlacek, W. E. (1999). Differences in leadership and cocurricular perception among entering male and female Asian Pacific American college students. *Journal of Freshman Year Experience, 11*(2), 93–114.

Museus, S. D., & Kiang, P. N. (2009). The model minority myth and how it contributes to the invisible minority reality in higher education research. In S. D. Museus (Ed.), *Conducting research on Asian Americans in higher education: New directions for institutional research* (No. 142, pp. 5–15). San Francisco, CA: Jossey-Bass.

Northouse, P. G. (2009). *Leadership: Theory and practice* (5th ed.). Thousand Oaks, CA: Sage.

Omi, M. (2008). Asian-Americans: The unbearable whiteness of being. *The Chronicle of Higher Education, 55*(5), B56.

Ortiz, A., Benham, M., Cress, C. M., Langdon, E., & Yamasaki, E. (1999, November). *Challenging old models, creating new ones: Ethnically relevant leadership studies.* Symposium conducted at the annual conference of the Association for the Study of Higher Education, San Antonio, TX.

Rost, J. C. (1991). *Leadership for the twenty-first century.* New York: Praeger.

Saigo, R. H. (1999, April 23). Academe needs more leaders of Asian Pacific heritage. *The Chronicle of Higher Education.* Retrieved May 31, 2012, from http://roysaigo.com/2011/08/08/academe-needs-more-leaders-of-asian-pacific-heritage-april-1999/

Sedlacek, W. E., & Sheu, H. B. (2004). Correlates of leadership activities of Gates Millennium Scholars. *Readings on Equal Education, 20*, 249–264.

Ting, M. P. (2001). Asian American student leadership. *Concepts and Connections, 10*(1), 3–4, 13.

Tingson-Gatuz, C. R., Sakurai, N., & Centino, N. (2007). *Critical Asian Pacific American leadership framework–CALF model.* Washington, DC: Organization of Chinese American's Asian Pacific Islander American (APIA) U College Leadership Training Program.

18

SELECTING AND SUPPORTING ASIAN AMERICAN AND PACIFIC ISLANDER STUDENTS IN HIGHER EDUCATION

William E. Sedlacek and Hung-Bin Sheu

nfortunately, higher education admissions and student services often are not coordinated. Moreover, both admissions and support are based on inadequate assessment tools, such as standardized tests or descriptive statistics that facilitate overgeneralizations of Asian American and Pacific Islander (AAPI) and other student populations. Thus, the purpose of this chapter is to present and discuss an approach that can be used for both selecting and supporting AAPI students that views AAPI students more holistically and more fully considers variables that are related to their race and culture than more traditional methods based on test scores and grades. However, given that AAPIs continue to be misperceived as universally successful, as college and university budgets tighten, it may be easy for institutions to discount the needs of AAPIs in admissions and student services. The current chapter offers suggestions that may be used to develop cost-effective recruitment and support programs during difficult economic times.

Selecting Asian Americans and Pacific Islanders

Many scholars and researchers have called for alternatives to standardized tests and prior grades as predictors of success. A key issue for measuring the potential of AAPI applicants to colleges and universities is the importance of going beyond their grades and test scores. Although AAPI applicants may be admitted to postsecondary institutions, the model minority stereotype, which can be defined as the misconception that all AAPIs achieve universal and unparalleled academic and occupational success (Museus & Kiang, 2009), is pervasive, and their broader range of possible attributes is never considered in those selection processes (Kodama, McEwen, Liang, & Lee, 2002). Some have called for a more comprehensive definition of college success or have suggested using multiple measures (Camara, 2005; Sackett, Schmitt, Ellingson, & Kabin, 2001). A system of noncognitive variables that measures a wider range of attributes than traditional methods is more equitable for AAPI students, and we discuss the utility of this framework in the current chapter (Sedlacek, 2004). The eight noncognitive variables are positive self-concept, realistic self-appraisal, handling racism and negotiating the system, long-range goals, support person, leadership, community service, and nontraditional knowledge (see table 18.1). These variables correlate with AAPI students' success in higher education. As an example, the Gates Millennium Scholars program has implemented the system of noncognitive variables to select more than 3,000 AAPI college and university students since 2000. Empirical data show that these students are doing well at some of the most selective schools in the country. In addition, after students matriculate, they are using their noncognitive attributes to navigate the higher education system (Sedlacek, 2011; Sedlacek & Sheu, 2008).

Supporting Asian American and Pacific Islander Students

Literature on supporting AAPI students in educational settings is scarce. Researchers have offered possible explanations for the lack of attention in this area, including the model minority myth and culturally incongruent support (e.g., Goto, 1999). The model minority stereotype may perpetuate the impression that AAPIs have encountered few barriers in higher education and that support programs should be targeting other students of color, who do not perform as well (Kodama et al., 2002). Nevertheless, AAPI students do face adjustment challenges and have needs. To address those challenges and fulfill those needs, Liang and Sedlacek (2003b) found that AAPIs use several help-seeking strategies, including avoiding stress, fitting in on the campus, and avoiding student services. Support, such as mentorship, can also help AAPIs, by addressing their challenges; improving their satisfaction

TABLE 18.1
Description of Noncognitive Variables

Variable Name	Variable Description
Positive Self-Concept	Demonstrates confidence, strength of character, determination, and independence.
Realistic Self-Appraisal	Recognizes and accepts any strengths and deficiencies, especially academic, and works hard at self-development. Recognizes need to broaden his or her individuality.
Understands and Knows How to Handle Racism (the System)	Exhibits a realistic view of the system based on personal experience of racism. Committed to improving the existing system. Takes an assertive approach to dealing with existing wrongs, but is not hostile to society, or is a "cop-out." Able to handle racist system.
Prefers Long-Range to Short-Term or Immediate Needs	Able to respond to deferred gratification, plans ahead and sets goals.
Availability of Strong Support Person	Seeks and takes advantage of a strong support network or has someone to turn to in a crisis or for encouragement.
Successful Leadership Experience	Demonstrates strong leadership in any area of his or her background (e.g., church, sports, noneducational groups, gang leader).
Demonstrated Community Service	Participates and is involved in his or her community.
Nontraditional Knowledge Acquired	Acquires knowledge in sustained and/or culturally related ways in any area. May be on any topic, including social, personal, or interpersonal.

with college life and their chosen major; and developing their professional skills, confidence, and personal and professional identity.

Counseling research supports the hypothesis that more acculturated AAPI college students perceive counseling professionals more favorably as sources of help for personal and emotional issues than less acculturated ones. It seems reasonable that non-AAPI professionals could apply this research to their work and should take various cultural aspects, such as acculturation levels and Asian cultural values, into consideration when supporting AAPI students (Sedlacek, Benjamin, Schlosser, & Sheu, 2007). These and related issues will be discussed in this chapter.

Noncognitive Variables

In this section, we discuss each of the eight noncognitive variables in table 18.1 and how student affairs professionals can use them in supporting AAPI college students of varying backgrounds, acculturation levels, and majors. Although we focus on supporting AAPI students in this section, we believe that the noncognitive variables can inform the recruitment and selection, as well as the support, of AAPI students. In addition, we believe that they can provide a starting point for admissions and student affairs to begin coordinating their efforts.

Positive Self-Concept

Having a positive self-concept is a predictor of success for AAPI students (Fuertes, Sedlacek, & Liu, 1994; Sedlacek & Sheu, 2008). Chung and Sedlacek (1999) noted that Asian Americans had lower career and social self-appraisal than students of other races. Wawrzynski and Sedlacek (2003) found that among undergraduate Gates Millennium Scholars, African Americans and Hispanic Americans had more positive self-concepts than AAPIs. Moreover, low levels of academic self-concept led to AAPI students having difficulties deciding what to study and speaking up in class. It is difficult to tell whether cultural differences account for these low self-perceptions, but this requires further exploration (Sheu & Sedlacek, 2004).

As mentioned, AAPIs are often perceived as model minorities who all perform well in educational settings (Liang & Sedlacek, 2003b; Sedlacek, 2004). This stereotype is associated with assumptions that AAPIs encounter very few problems and do not need student services (Kodama et al., 2002). Even more important is what this stereotype does to AAPI students. For example, if they struggle with issues related to their self-concepts, they may be more likely to perceive themselves negatively, because they are not supposed to have problems.

Liang and Sedlacek (2003a) found that student affairs professionals had relatively positive attitudes toward AAPIs. This has important implications for how we engage in student affairs activities. At first glance, attitudes in the positive direction may be construed as harmless or positive. However,

Hune and Chan (1997) suggest that attitudes based on stereotypes that depict Americans of Asian descent as well adjusted, without academic or mental health needs, have hurt many AAPIs, particularly those with Southeast Asian ancestry, because they are overlooked. Sedlacek and Sheu (2008) found that undergraduate Gates Millennium Scholars AAPIs reported more difficulty in finding someone who was interested in their work, could offer support, or provide academic help than did scholars from other racial groups.

The true status of AAPI scholars often yields a different story that contrasts sharply with popular views of their academic success. Many writers have indicated the importance of recognizing the extreme diversity among AAPIs, as reflected by country of origin, language, socioeconomic status, and so forth (e.g., Maki & Kitano, 2002; Uba, 1994). How within-group diversity influences the development of positive self-concept warrants more empirical and practical attention from researchers and student affairs professionals.

Realistic Self-Appraisal

As with any group, AAPIs need to be able to assess their strengths and weaknesses in order to proceed with their development. The issues related to self-concept often have a negative impact on the ability of AAPI students to get a realistic assessment of their situations. For example, the stereotype that AAPIs are only interested in technical fields and are inferior in other areas can interfere with students' ability to adequately appraise their abilities.

As an illustration of possible problems this could cause, the lead author once had to refer an AAPI student for counseling because his peers insisted on seeking computer-related help from him to the point where he had virtually no interpersonal relations on any other basis. Consequently, his self-concept and realistic self-appraisal suffered, and he became depressed. The student wasn't particularly interested in computers, but his peers expected him to be, and they felt they were enhancing his self-concept. Such race-based forcing of expectations on people is a form of racism and can damage their self-concept and ability to do self-assessments, even if that expectation appears to be positive (Sedlacek & Brooks, 1976).

Handling Racism

Expectations that AAPIs are problem-free and should not need support prevent them from using services on campus. As mentioned, the race-based pressure placed on AAPI students to avoid academic and social services is a form of racism, which they must navigate to be successful in higher education (Sedlacek, 2004). Often, seeking student services is seen as the last option for AAPIs, who usually try to deal with problems by themselves, or ask for help from friends, family, or community members (Maki & Kitano, 2002). Indeed, AAPIs' underutilization of available support services has been well documented (Chin, 1998; Leong, 1986; Sue & Sue, 2003).

In general, AAPIs have demonstrated less positive attitudes toward counseling than their White counterparts (Atkinson, Ponterotto, & Sanchez, 1984). However, research concerning within-group AAPI differences in help-seeking attitudes and behaviors is inconclusive. For instance, Atkinson and his colleagues (Atkinson & Gim, 1989; Atkinson, Lowe, & Matthews, 1995) found no gender and interethnic differences among Chinese American, Japanese American, and Korean American college students in their attitudes toward mental health services. In contrast, Sue and Kirk (1975) found an interaction between sex and ethnicity in AAPIs' use of counseling services. Specifically, they found that Chinese American female students used mental health facilities significantly more frequently than did Japanese American female students.

Role of Religion

AAPIs might employ religion to cope with problems in understanding how to work the system. Indeed, the development of religious identity has been theorized to be central to student development among AAPIs (Kodama et al., 2002). Min and Kim (2002), however, noted that limited research has examined the role of religion in AAPI ethnic communities.

The research that does exist suggests that Christian churches are a significant source of support for Korean Americans, in that they were more likely to cope with problems by engaging in religious practices than other AAPI groups (Yeh & Wang, 2000). Hence, college and university departments or programs that seek to facilitate the development of AAPIs may wish to consider the role of religion and spirituality in these students' lives.

Problem Avoidance

AAPIs may tend to avoid problems that arise in their lives. Indeed, Chang (1996) found that AAPIs use problem avoidance and social withdrawal techniques more often than White Americans. Further, cultural nuances may lead educators to misinterpret AAPI students' situations and needs. For example, Kodama et al. (2002) warned against using emotional cues or non-expressiveness to conclude that AAPI students are not experiencing any problems. This is an important consideration because such cues can mean different things to AAPI students and non-AAPI educators. Rather, AAPIs may not express that they are experiencing challenges, in order to avoid social or interpersonal problems. Thus, practitioners working with AAPIs should develop understandings of AAPI cultures and engage in culturally based outreach to provide the most appropriate services to these students.

Academic Focus

Tracey, Leong, and Glidden (1986) found that AAPI students rarely endorsed social-emotional issues as their presenting problems. Instead, they seemed to be more concerned with academic and career issues because these problem areas are more socially acceptable to them. Sedlacek and Sheu's (2008) study of Gates Millennium Scholars provides more evidence of the strong academic focus of AAPIs, as they found that AAPIs studied more and had higher GPAs than African Americans, but also reported experiencing more difficulties with schoolwork than their African American peers. One explanation for these findings could be that AAPIs feel more pressure to get high grades than the other groups.

Sedlacek (2007) underscores how the aforementioned academic focus might be a useful tool for student services professionals. In a forum dealing with the tragedy of the Virginia Tech shootings by a Korean American student, Sedlacek suggested that those wishing to help AAPIs might cast their outreach in terms that focus on students who seek help in getting better grades. By appealing to the academic orientation of AAPIs, one can both acknowledge their cultural traditions and address their needs for coping with other problems at the same time.

Long-Term Goals

The reality that AAPIs tend to be academically focused (Sedlacek & Sheu, 2008; Tracey et al., 1986) may be particularly useful in helping them develop and accomplish long-term goals. More than 90% of undergraduate Gates Millennium Scholars were interested in pursuing a graduate or professional degree. However, AAPIs were more likely than African Americans and Hispanic Americans to talk to their teachers about career plans, although they were less likely to seek career services. By proactively helping AAPI students focus on the various possibilities in achieving long-term career goals, including various funding options, student affairs professionals can demonstrate the value of goal setting in other areas.

Strong Support Person

AAPI students can benefit from having a relationship with student affairs professionals if those relationships are informed by the cultural backgrounds of the students. For example, one-way communication from an authority figure to persons in a group is more the norm in Asian societies than in the United States (Chung, 1992; Sue & Sue, 2003). Silence and avoidance of eye contact often occur when AAPI students listen or speak to someone higher in the hierarchy, such as instructors, advisors, and mentors. AAPI students also may be more likely to await instructions from college faculty and staff. Although these cultural traits should not be assumed to be characteristics of all AAPI students, non-AAPI student personnel should consider how they might influence their interactions with AAPI undergraduates, keeping in mind that they may be expected to play a more active and directive role and should prepare themselves for the possibility of developing a more formal relationship with their AAPI students at the beginning stage of their relationship. A failure to meet AAPI student cultural needs may result in the premature termination of the educator–student relationship.

Leadership

It is important to consider the culture and gender of AAPI students rather than treat them as one homogeneous group. For example, Liu and Sedlacek (1999) reported that Asian American students had unique and culturally related ways of expressing their leadership, such as through family and cultural organizations. Additionally, they found that Asian American men were more likely than Asian American women to feel they lack leadership skills. Such diversity and differences are important considerations in working with AAPI students.

Balón (2005) concluded that AAPIs believe in the importance of culture in leadership as much as other racial groups, but tend not to see themselves as leaders or believe they have leadership skills, and feel less empowered than other racial groups. This could be due to cultural differences in the way AAPI students and the mainstream view leadership. Thus, although leadership development programs have been a basic part of student affairs work, student affairs educators should not base such programs on assumptions of how students may express leadership abilities. By focusing on the culturally relevant ways that AAPIs might demonstrate leadership, and related self-concept issues, progress can be made in developing leadership skills.

Community

Understanding the role of community is critical in working with AAPI students. Identification with a community has been shown to be important for AAPI student success (Fuertes et al., 1994; Sedlacek & Sheu, 2008). In general, AAPI students operate with cultural values that are strongly influenced by their families and cultural heritage (Paniagua, 1994). Students are not encouraged to express their problems to people outside their group, especially strangers. Also, one way to fulfill one's family obligations is to avoid creating problems (Chung, 1992; Uba, 1994). This tendency plays an important role in prohibiting AAPI students from expressing and admitting their problems in settings outside their family and seeking student services. Non-AAPI professionals need to be culturally sensitive and develop their skills in creating a safe relationship in which AAPI students can feel the freedom to seek help and explore their needs.

Although AAPI students may need to find a community within or outside of their racial or ethnic groups, they may feel that doing so takes time away from their studies (Wang, Sedlacek, & Westbrook, 1992). For example, in one analysis of transfer students, AAPIs were more likely than Whites to study in groups and engage in community service (Wawrzynski & Sedlacek, 2003). Providing such opportunities for transfer students may be a way for student affairs professionals to help develop a community for AAPIs.

Nontraditional Learning

AAPI undergraduates may learn many things outside the education system and possess culturally relevant knowledge that is not considered when designing programs or evaluating these students' development (Sedlacek, 2004). For example, AAPI college students may have experience helping family members in different generations communicate by knowing English and another language and serving as an interpreter within the family. AAPI undergraduates may not see this as a valuable or unusual skill. They may also be more likely than other students to have some experience in a family business, which could include such things as learning about accounting, business practices, or customer relations. Student affairs staff can help students explore these and other nonacademic experiences and use this information to develop programs and assessments of these students' learning.

Conclusion

AAPI students have psychosocial needs, face unique adjustment issues, and can benefit from support programs that are compatible with their cultural values. Yet, Goto (1999) suggested that cultural reasons (e.g., incongruence between Asian and U.S. mainstream cultures) might explain why some AAPIs are reluctant to seek guidance and help, especially from those who are White. In Goto's study, AAPI students dropped out of a mentoring program because they worried that the program brought undesired attention to cultural differences and that participation might result in separation and pressure from peers.

Given the importance of culture in supporting AAPI students, college educators should consider the reality that more culturally relevant recruitment and support programs might engage and address the cultural conflict between individualism (seeking support) and collectivism (fitting in with the ethnic group) for AAPI students. Indeed, Kim, Goto, Bai, Kim, and Wong (2001) found that AAPI college students were more likely to participate in peer mentoring programs when these programs were designed to meet their culture-specific needs. By employing noncognitive variables in selecting and developing AAPI students, student affairs professionals can provide coordinated admissions and support programs that focus on AAPI student needs. Noncognitive variables provide a way to plan individual and group programs for AAPI students that reflect the diversity within the group and to work with the differences between AAPIs and other students. The noncognitive variable model also provides a way to evaluate the effects of admissions and post-matriculation efforts (Sedlacek, 2004).

References

Atkinson, D. R., & Gim, R. H. (1989). Asian-American cultural identity and attitudes toward mental health services. *Journal of Counseling Psychology, 36,* 209–212.

Atkinson, D. R., Lowe, S., & Matthews, L. (1995). Asian-American acculturation, gender, and willingness to seek counseling. *Journal of Multicultural Counseling and Development, 23,* 130–138.

Atkinson, D. R., Ponterotto, J. G., & Sanchez, A. R. (1984). Attitudes of Vietnamese and Anglo-American students toward counseling. *Journal of College Student Personnel, 25*(5), 448–452.

Balón, D. G. (2005, April 26). *Asian Pacific American college students on leadership: Culturally marginalized from the leader role?* Washington, DC: National Association of Student Personnel Administrators NetResults.

Camara, W. J. (2005). Broadening criteria of college success and the impact of cognitive predictors. In W. J. Camara (Ed.), *Choosing students: Higher education admission tools for the 21st century* (pp. 53–80). Mahwah, NJ: Lawrence Erlbaum.

Chang, E. C. (1996). Cultural differences in optimism, pessimism, and coping: Predictors of subsequent adjustment in Asian American and Caucasian American college students. *Journal of Counseling Psychology, 43*, 113–123.

Chin, J. L. (1998). Mental health services and treatment. In L. C. Lee & N. W. Zane (Eds.), *Handbook of Asian American psychology* (pp. 485–504). Thousand Oaks, CA: Sage.

Chung, B. Y., & Sedlacek, W. E. (1999). Ethnic differences in career, academic, and social self-appraisals among college freshmen. *Journal of College Counseling, 2*(1), 14–24.

Chung, D. K. (1992). Asian cultural commonalities: A comparison with mainstream American culture. In D. K. Chung, K. Murase, & F. Ross-Sheriff (Eds.), *Social work practice with Asian Americans* (pp. 27–44). Newbury Park, CA: Sage.

Fuertes, J. N., Sedlacek, W. E., & Liu, W. M. (1994). Using the SAT and noncognitive variables to predict the grades and retention of Asian-American university students. *Measurement and Evaluation in Counseling and Development, 27*, 74–84.

Goto, S. (1999). AAPIs and developmental relationships. In A. J. Murrell, F. J. Crosby, & R. J. Ely (Eds.), *Mentoring dilemmas: Developmental relationships within multicultural organizations* (pp. 46–62). Mahwah, NJ: Lawrence Erlbaum.

Hune, S., & Chan, K. S. (1997). Special focus: Asian Pacific American demographic and educational trends. In D. J. Carter & R. Wilson (Eds.), *Fifteenth annual status report on minorities in higher education* (pp. 39–67). Washington, DC: American Council on Education.

Kim, C. Y., Goto, S. G., Bai, M. M., Kim, T. E., & Wong, E. (2001). Culturally congruent mentoring: Predicting Asian American student participation using the theory of reasoned action. *Journal of Applied Social Psychology, 31*, 2417–2437.

Kodama, C. M., McEwen, M. K., Liang, C. T. H., & Lee, S. (2002). An AAPI perspective on psychosocial development theory. In M. K. McEwen, C. M. Kodama, A. N. Alvarez, S. Lee, & C. T. H. Liang (Eds.), *Working with AAPI college students: New directions for student services* (No. 97, pp. 45–60). San Francisco, CA: Jossey-Bass.

Leong, F. L. T. (1986). Counseling and psychotherapy with Asian-Americans: Review of the literature. *Journal of Counseling Psychology, 33*, 196–206.

Liang C. T. H., & Sedlacek W. E. (2003a). Attitudes of White student services practitioners toward AAPIs. *NASPA Journal, 40*(3), 30–42.

Liang, C. T. H., & Sedlacek, W. E. (2003b). Utilizing factor analysis to understand the needs of AAPI students. *Journal of College Student Development, 44*, 260–266.

Liu, W. M., & Sedlacek, W. E. (1999). Differences in leadership and co-curricular perception among male and female Asian Pacific American college students. *Journal of the Freshman Year Experience, 11*, 93–114.

Maki, M. T., & Kitano, H. H. L. (2002). Counseling Asian Americans. In P. B. Pedersen, J. G. Draguns, W. J. Lonner, & J. E. Trimble (Eds.), *Counseling across cultures* (5th ed., pp. 109–131). Thousand Oaks, CA: Sage.

Min, P. G., & Kim, J. H. (2002). *Religions in Asian America: Building faith communities.* New York: Alta Mira Press.

Museus, S. D., & Kiang, P. N. (2009). The model minority myth and how it contributes to the invisible minority reality in higher education research. In S. D. Museus (Ed.), *Conducting research on Asian Americans in higher education: New directions for institutional research* (No. 142, pp. 5–15). San Francisco, CA: Jossey-Bass.

Paniagua, F. A. (1994). *Assessing and treating culturally diverse clients: A practical guide.* Thousand Oaks, CA: Sage.

Sackett, P. R., Schmitt, N., Ellingson, J. E., & Kabin, M. B. (2001). High-stakes testing in employment, credentialing and higher education: Prospects in a post-affirmative-action world. *American Psychologist, 56,* 302–318.

Sedlacek, W. E. (2004). *Beyond the big test: Noncognitive assessment in higher education.* San Francisco, CA: Jossey-Bass.

Sedlacek, W. E. (2007, May 9). *Mental health issues for Asian Americans.* Presentation and panel discussion at the end of the Model Minority Myth: Reflection on the Virginia Tech tragedy from an Asian American perspective. University of Maryland, College Park, MD.

Sedlacek, W. E. (2011). Using noncognitive variables in assessing readiness for higher education. *Readings on Equal Education, 25,* 187–205.

Sedlacek, W. E., Benjamin, E., Schlosser, L. Z., & Sheu, H. (2007). Mentoring in academia: Considerations for diverse populations. In T. D. Allen & L. T. Eby (Eds.), *The Blackwell handbook of mentoring: A multiple perspectives approach* (pp. 259–280). Malden, MA: Blackwell.

Sedlacek, W. E., & Brooks, G. C., Jr. (1976). *Racism in American education: A model for change.* Chicago, IL: Nelson Hall.

Sedlacek, W. E., & Sheu, H. (2008). The academic progress of undergraduate and graduate Gates Millennium Scholars and non-scholars by race and gender. *Readings on Equal Education, 23,* 143–177.

Sheu, H., & Sedlacek, W. E. (2004). An exploratory study of help-seeking attitudes and coping strategies among college students by race and gender. *Measurement and Evaluation in Counseling and Development, 37*(3), 130–143.

Sue, D. W., & Kirk, B. A. (1975). Asian-Americans: Use of counseling and psychiatric services on a college campus. *Journal of Counseling Psychology, 22,* 84–86.

Sue, D. W., & Sue, D. (2003). *Counseling the culturally diverse: Theory and practice* (4th ed.). New York: John Wiley.

Tracey, T. J., Leong, F. T. L., & Glidden, C. (1986). Help-seeking and problem perception among Asian Americans. *Journal of Counseling Psychology, 33,* 331–336.

Uba, L. (1994). *Asian Americans: Personality patterns, identity, and mental health.* New York: The Guilford Press.

Wang, Y. Y., Sedlacek, W. E., & Westbrook, F. D. (1992). Asian-Americans and student organizations: Attitudes and participation. *Journal of College Student Development, 33*, 214–221.

Wawrzynski, M. R., & Sedlacek, W. E. (2003). Race and gender differences in the transfer student experience. *Journal of College Student Development, 44*(4), 489–501.

Yeh, C., & Wang, Y. W. (2000). Asian American coping attitudes, sources, and practices: Implications for indigenous counseling strategies. *Journal of College Student Development, 41*(1), 94–103.

ABOUT THE EDITORS AND CONTRIBUTORS

Editors

Samuel D. Museus is assistant professor of Higher Education at the University of Hawai'i at Mānoa and is a fellow of the Asian American and Pacific Islander Research Coalition.

Dina C. Maramba is associate professor of Student Affairs at Binghamton University.

Robert T. Teranishi is associate professor of Higher Education at New York University.

Contributors

Kamakana Aquino is a graduate student in Higher Education at the University of Hawai'i at Mānoa.

Daniello G. Balón was the director of Diversity Education and Engagement in Burlington School District, Vermont, and president of Barkada Consulting Network, LLC.

Brandi Jean Nālani Balutski is research and evaluation coordinator at the University of Hawai'i at Mānoa.

Tracy Lachina Buenavista is associate professor of Asian American Studies at the California State University, Northridge, and a fellow of the Asian American and Pacific Islander Research Coalition.

Mitchell J. Chang is professor of Higher Education and Organizational Change at the University of California, Los Angeles, and a fellow of the Asian American and Pacific Islander Research Coalition.

Prema Chaudhari is director of Programs and Scholar Relations, Asian and Pacific Islander American Scholarship Fund, and is a doctoral candidate at the University of Pittsburgh.

Warren Chiang is director of the Leland Scholars Program at Stanford University.

Angela Chuan-Ru Chen is a doctoral candidate in Higher Education and Organizational Change, and coordinator of Undocumented Student Programs, at the University of California, Los Angeles.

Rob Ho is a doctoral candidate in Social Science and Comparative Education at the University of California, Los Angeles.

Belinda Lee Huang is a Words of Engagement Intergroup Dialogue facilitator at the University of Maryland–College Park, where she also earned her PhD in Higher Education.

Karen K. Inkelas is associate professor of Higher Education and director of the Center for Advanced Study of Teaching and Learning at the University of Virginia.

Marc P. Johnston is a doctoral candidate in Higher Education and Organizational Change at the University of California, Los Angeles.

Peter Nien-chu Kiang is professor of Curriculum and Instruction and Asian American Studies at the University of Massachusetts Boston, and is a fellow of the Asian American and Pacific Islander Research Coalition.

Jonathan W. Lew is a doctoral candidate in Higher Education at the School of Educational Studies at Claremont Graduate University.

M. Kalehua Mueller is a graduate student in Higher Education at the University of Hawai'i at Mānoa.

Patricia A. Neilson is director of the Asian American Student Success Program at the University of Massachusetts Boston, and is a fellow of the Asian American and Pacific Islander Research Coalition.

Tu-Lien Kim Nguyen is a doctoral candidate in Higher Education and Organizational Change at the University of California, Los Angeles.

Julie J. Park is assistant professor of College Student Personnel at the University of Maryland, College Park.

Sean C. Pepin is a doctoral student in Higher Education, Student Affairs and International Education Policy at the University of Maryland, College Park.

Jane E. Pizzolato is assistant professor of Higher Education and Organizational Change at the University of California, Los Angeles.

OiYan A. Poon is assistant professor of Higher Education at Loyola University Chicago, and is a fellow of the Asian American and Pacific Islander Research Coalition.

Jean J. Ryoo is a doctoral candidate in Urban Schooling at the University of California, Los Angeles.

William E. Sedlacek is professor emeritus of Education at the University of Maryland, College Park.

Yen Ling Shek is a doctoral candidate in Higher Education and Organizational Change at the University of California, Los Angeles.

Hung-Bin Sheu is assistant professor of Counseling Psychology at the University at Albany, State University of New York.

Donna M. Talbot is professor of Educational Leadership at Western Michigan University.

Minh C. Tran is assistant coordinator of the Intergroup Relations Program at the University of California, Los Angeles.

Rican Vue is research associate for the CHOICES Project at the University of California, Los Angeles.

Alina Wong is dean of the Sophomore Class and director of the Intercultural Center at Swarthmore College.

Erin Kahunawaikaʻala Wright is director of Native Hawaiian Student Services at the University of Hawaiʻi at Mānoa, and is a fellow of the Asian American and Pacific Islander Research Coalition.

Wenfan Yan is professor of Leadership in Education at the University of Massachusetts Boston.

Fanny PF Yeung is a postdoctoral researcher at the University of California, Los Angeles.

Also available from Stylus

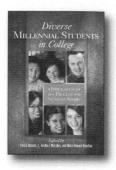

Diverse Millennial Students in College
Implications for Faculty and Student Affairs
Edited by Fred A. Bonner II, Aretha F. Marbley, and Mary F. Howard Hamilton

"This edited volume interrogates the stereotypes ascribed to millennial students in relation to those students' diverse characteristics, primarily their race, ethnicity, and sexual orientation. In revealing how assumptions about millennials may or may not apply across different groups, contributors challenge the view of millennial students as a monolithic group while confirming aspects of millennial identity. The book makes important advances toward complicating assumptions about today's traditionally-aged college students without eschewing a level of generalization necessary to understanding particular groups and subgroups." —*Diversity and Democracy*

"A bountiful resource for the advisor who wants to learn more about millennials as a generational whole and gain deeper insight in to the diverse cultural groups that compromise this generation." —*NACADA Journal* (National Academic Advising Association)

"As students of the so-called 'Millennial' generation make their way into higher education, it's clear to educators that one blanket term does not fit all. In the 15 chapters of this text, 33 American academics, researchers, and administrators explore the diversity of 'Millennial' students in terms of racial and ethnic identity, as well as cultural, sexual orientation, and socioeconomic status differences. The text opens with a discussion about testing assumptions about generational cohorts. Subsequent chapters focus on African American, Asian American, Latina/o, Native American, LGBTQ, and bi- and multiracial students; the college-to-workforce transition of students of color; and curriculum design considerations to address student diversity. The material is intended for faculty, administrators, and student affairs personnel." —*Book News Inc.*

Ethnicity in College
Advancing Theory and Improving Diversity Practices on Campus
Anna M. Ortiz and Silvia J. Santos

"Ortiz and Santos accomplish their goal of discovering how college students make meaning of their ethnicity in a multicultural world . . . The work's key strengths include a comprehensive literature review and multi-method research design. The qualitative data adds exponentially to the findings and conclusions. . . . All involved in higher education need to be aware of students' need to develop and express their ethnic identities. This invaluable resource is a must read. Summing Up: Essential." —*Choice*

"By studying the experiences of 120 Southern California college students, researchers Ortiz and Santos take an in-depth look at the role college plays in ethnic identity development. Their book provides a close look at the divergent developmental paths traversed by students of different ethnicities, and the effect college has on students' understanding of their ethnicity. With smart analysis and helpful suggestions for maximizing the positive effects of campus diversity, the volume is a significant contribution to the literature on identity, diversity, and education." —*Diversity & Democracy* (AAC&U)

"Reading *Ethnicity in College* is like taking a course in ethnicity and its effects on college students. . . . It is useful for not just learning about specific groups but also helpful for gaining perspective into student experiences as garnered from their own words." —*NACADA Journal* (National Academic Advising Association)

22883 Quicksilver Drive
Sterling, VA 20166-2102

Subscribe to our e-mail alerts: www.Styluspub.com